D0082836

50XX

spanish
composition
through
literature

PRENTICE-HALL INTERNATIONAL, INC., *London*
PRENTICE-HALL OF AUSTRALIA, PTY. LTD., *Sydney*
PRENTICE-HALL OF CANADA, LTD., *Toronto*
PRENTICE-HALL OF INDIA PRIVATE LTD., *New Delhi*
PRENTICE-HALL OF JAPAN, INC., *Tokyo*

spanish composition through literature

by Cándido Ayllón and Paul Smith

© 1968 by Prentice-Hall, Inc.
Englewood Cliffs, N. J.

All rights reserved. No part of this book may be
reproduced in any form or by any means without
permission in writing from the publisher.

Library of Congress Catalog Card No.: 68–10168

Current printing (last digit):
20 19 18 17 16 15 14 13

Printed in the United States of America

preface

This text presupposes that the student possesses the skills normally acquired in two years of college Spanish. Each chapter, based on a selection by a modern author, covers vocabulary, comprehension, style, translation, and free composition. Ten of the chapters also discuss important grammar topics that may be profitably reviewed in a composition class. The challenging English selections in the Appendix may be used for translation to complement the text itself. The book is organized to allow considerable flexibility in the use of its materials.

The exercises are designed to develop the student's vocabulary and to assist him in analysis of style, content, and syntax. They thus help to increase those skills necessary for evaluating different types of literature and writing reasonably accurate accounts of such evaluations.

Experience has convinced us that close analysis of literary texts is a very fruitful approach to Spanish composition. As a basis for such analysis, we have selected passages that illustrate a variety of subjects, themes, and literary techniques. Because the most important part of each chapter is the independent composition, the exercises leading up to it are designed to encourage the student to incorporate materials from the entire chapter into this composition. The exercises and notes are intended to help him resist the natural temptation to transpose English patterns into Spanish and to increase his over-all command of the language. We assume that the student has already had experience in organizing ideas and concepts through courses in English composition, but we have included a two-part *cuestionario* in each chapter to guide him in this task. The first part stresses key ideas or content; the second suggests ways of approaching the means of expression or style of the selection.

We have found it practical to present the notes and the grammar discussion in English, but class discussion should be directed in Spanish whenever possible. The grammar and notes are not intended to be prescriptive, but are simply aids to developing sensitivity to literary Spanish and to acquiring competence in writing Spanish. We hope that by using these materials the student will develop his own critical approach to Spanish literature and literary usage (he should, for example, become aware through examination of the literary selections that modern Spanish and Spanish American authors exhibit considerably greater variety grammatically than previous experience has led him to believe). Obviously the greater the student's exposure to Spanish literature and the deeper his awareness of differences in a given passage, the more accurate his own command of the language will be.

We have suggested that these materials are not intended to be prescriptive or complete. They have been chosen, instead, for their interest and practicality. We have included a brief bibliography of useful reference works and articles for the student who may wish to delve into some of the interesting questions of syntax, vocabulary, or grammar.

The literary selections illustrate the marvelous flexibility of the Spanish language to respond to mood, feeling, and personal nuance in the hands of a skilled author. In the notes to these selections we have pointed out a few of the examples that illustrate the numerous differences between spoken and purely literary Spanish. This point, we feel, deserves emphasis, for the student who has had an exclusively audio-lingual preparation in Spanish is sometimes at a distinct disadvantage when he is first confronted with the lexical demands of Spanish literature. The vocabulary exercises will, therefore, help meet this problem by expanding both his active and his passive vocabulary, and by making him aware of different levels of speech.

We have mentioned that this text is adaptable to varying needs and methods of presentation. We should like, nevertheless, to call attention to two procedures that have proved most effective in our own classroom experience. The first involves the student's oral presentation of his theme. Because the class is familiar with the chapter, its vocabulary, etc., a high level of oral comprehension and communication is possible, such that when the student questions his classmates on his presentation and is in turn questioned by them, a spirited class discussion invariably ensues. The second involves a presentation by several students to the class of their own interpretations of the literary selection before the instructor offers any guidance or conclusions. Students have responded enthusiastically to these exercises and have even become adept at correcting their classmates' errors in usage and vocabulary.

Finally, a few words about the passages in the Appendix. Each selection has considerable merit from several points of view. Furthermore, since each is a self-contained unit, each can serve as the basis for profitable discussion in Spanish. Translation of these passages challenges the student to draw on all his resources to render literary selections of intrinsic merit into another language with accuracy and sensitivity. We need not point out how such an exercise also forces the student to rethink much that he has taken for granted in English. We wish to emphasize that the notes accompanying these passages are only suggested renderings of potentially troublesome points. In most cases there are, of course, other equally valid interpretations.

The Vocabulary at the end of the book should suffice for the preparation of the exercises. For the free composition, translations of the Appendix, and analysis of the literary selections themselves, we strongly recommend both a bilingual dictionary and a large Spanish dictionary. The student may also wish to consult his basic Spanish grammar for verb forms or syntactical items not reviewed in this book.

We thank our colleagues Hugo Rodríguez-Alcalá, Joaquín Gimeno Casalduero, Fred Petersen, and Ray Verzasconi for constant help and encouragement. We are also in considerable debt to the following persons who so generously read and criticized parts of the text: Brenton Campbell, Gerard Cox Flynn, Rosalie Gimeno, Julio Rodríguez-Luis, and Donald D. Walsh. Salvador García, Francisco Mena, and Joseph Schraibman made many valuable suggestions, as did our typist, Sherinda Scherer. And to Edmundo García-Girón of Prentice-Hall, Inc., our sincerest appreciation for much sound advice and guidance. We wish also to express our gratitude to the authors, editors, and publishers for graciously granting permission to use the excerpts in this book. Finally, our thanks to the students who used these chapters in mimeographed form. In more ways than one, they wrote the text with us.

ACKNOWLEDGMENTS

We wish to thank the following persons for having generously granted permission to use the selections appearing in this text:

Enrique Anderson-Imbert for "El muerto-vivo" from the Losada edition of his book *El Grimorio*;

José Castillo-Navarro for the short story "Al cabo de los años";

Américo Castro for the selection from the forthcoming revised edition of *Hacia Cervantes*;

Camilo José Cela for the selections from the 1965 Destino edition of his *Viaje a la Alcarria*;

Ediciones Destino and Miguel Delibes for the passages from *La sombra del ciprés es alargada*;

Carmen Laforet for the selections from *Nada* and for *La isla y los demonios* from the 1960 Planeta edition of her *Novelas*;

Olimpia Miró and Editorial Biblioteca Nueva for "Una tarde" from *El libro de Sigüenza*;

Revista de Occidente and José Ortega Spottorno for "Notas: John F. Kennedy 1917–1963" by Julián Marías and "Ensimismamiento y alteración" from the *Obras completas de José Ortega y Gasset* (Tomo VII, 1961);

Augusto Roa Bastos for the passage from the Losada edition of his *Hijo de hombre*;

Luis Romero for the short story "El forastero" from *Esas sombras del trasmundo*.

LEGEND TO ABBREVIATIONS

AT	Arroz y tartana	*Vicente Blasco Ibáñez*
AUT	El automóvil	*Jacinto Benavente*
BA	Blanco en azul	*Azorín (José Martínez Ruiz)*
CA	Crónica del alba	*Ramón Sender*
CBA	Las cartas boca abajo	*Antonio Buero Vallejo*
CP	Camino de perfección	*Pío Baroja*
CPF	Las confesiones de un pequeño filósofo	*Azorín*
DI	Doña Inés	*Azorín*
DP	Don Payasito	*Ana María Matute*
EA	El autobús de las 7'40	*Ignacio Aldecoa*
EBM	El barco de la muerte	*Juan Antonio Zunzunegui*
EC	El circo	*Juan Goytisolo*
EI	España invertebrada	*José Ortega y Gasset*
EJ	El Jarama	*Rafael Sánchez Ferlosio*
EP	Españoles en París	*Azorín*
ER	El regreso	*Carmen Laforet*
ES	España Semanal	
ET	El testamento	*Arturo Barea*
F	Fiestas	*Juan Goytisolo*
FA	Física aplicada	*Arturo Barea*
FM	Flor de Mayo	*Vicente Blasco Ibáñez*
FN	Fiesta al noroeste	*Ana María Matute*
FP	Funcionario público	*Dolores Medio*
FPD	La familia de Pascual Duarte	*Camilo José Cela*
HA	Una historia de amor	*Miguel de Unamuno*
HH	Hijo de hombre	*Augusto Roa Bastos*
HM	Los hijos muertos	*Ana María Matute*
IC	La imposible canción	*Carmen Mieza*
ID	La isla y los demonios	*Carmen Laforet*
IE	Idearium español	*Angel Ganivet*
JM	Juan de Mairena	*Antonio Machado*

JQC	Don Juan, Don Quijote y la Celestina	*Ramiro de Maeztu*
LC	La colmena	*Camilo José Cela*
LE	La enferma	*Elena Quiroga*
LH	La herencia	*Joaquín Calvo Sotelo*
LL	La lección	*Arturo Barea*
LM	Los mercaderes	*Ana María Matute*
LN	La noria	*Luis Romero*
LP	Los pueblos	*Azorín*
M	La marea	*José María Gironella*
MAH	Madrid entre ayer y hoy	*Arturo Barea*
MM	Un millón de muertos	*José María Gironella*
MP	Muerte de perros	*Francisco Ayala*
N	Nada	*Carmen Laforet*
NB	Los niños buenos	*Ana María Matute*
NOC	La nochebuena	*Luis Romero*
PT	Pequeño teatro	*Ana María Matute*
PU	Los pazos de Ulloa	*Emilia Pardo Bazán*
PY	Platero y yo	*Juan Ramón Jiménez*
R	La ronda	*Ana María Matute*
RDQ	La ruta de Don Quijote	*Azorín*
SCA	La sombra del ciprés es alargada	*Miguel Delibes*
SH	La sonrisa y la hormiga	*María Jesús Echevarría*
SMB	San Manuel Bueno, Mártir	*Miguel de Unamuno*
SO	Sonata de otoño	*Ramón del Valle-Inclán*
SRNPG	Simbolismo religioso en las novelas de Pérez Galdós	*Gustavo Correa*
SV	El saltamontes verde	*Ana María Matute*
THI	La ternura del hombre invisible	*Carlos Rojas*
TV	Tormenta de verano	*Juan García Hortelano*
VA	Viaje a la Alcarria	*Camilo José Cela*
VS	Vísperas del silencio	*Ignacio Aldecoa*
ZA	Zalacaín el aventurero	*Pío Baroja*

contents

CHAPTER 13.   193

CHAPTER 14.   205

Pronouns

CHAPTER 15.   223

Relative Pronouns

CHAPTER 16.   241

spanish

composition

through

literature

chapter 1

"TO BE" IN SPANISH

1. BASIC STATEMENT

The most common forms of *to be* in Spanish are **ser** and **estar**. **Ser** establishes or contributes to identity. **Estar** indicates location and state or condition. When used to express state, **estar** implies a degree of perceptible change, or at least an awareness of the possibility of such change. Two sentences differing only in the use of **ser** and **estar** are often both grammatically correct, and at times may even be rendered by the same English equivalent; nevertheless they mean different things in Spanish, for **estar** indicates something that befalls the subject, whereas **ser** reflects what is viewed as a necessary part of it. Noun forms of these verbs also reflect this distinction.

Un **ser** humano es una cosa maravillosa.	A human being is a wonderful thing.
El **estado** del enfermo ha mejorado.	The patient's condition has improved.

2. THE REFERENT WITH SER AND ESTAR

To equate the subject with a predicate noun or pronoun, **ser** is almost always the verb used. When the predicate is an adjective or a past participle, it is necessary to decide if the quality conveyed by the adjective is better viewed as a basic characteristic or as a state or condition. With **ser** the adjective has the quality of a noun, and **ser** functions as an equal sign showing the subject as a member of a class of adjective-nouns.

El marinero **es** un (hombre) borracho.	The sailor is a drunk(ard).
María **es** (una persona) muy sucia.	Mary is (a) very dirty (person).
La tierra aquí **es** (tierra) dura.	The ground here is hard (ground).

With **estar** the adjective refers to the verb and only indirectly to the subject. It thus functions somewhat as an adverb and describes the state of the subject rather than the subject itself.

El marinero **está** borracho.	The sailor is drunk.
María **está** muy sucia.	Mary is very dirty.
La tierra aquí **está** dura.	The ground here is hard.

Estar, then, does not reveal what the speaker feels to be the basic nature of the sailor, Mary, or the ground in question. It indicates instead a condition at a given time, a condition which may be of short, long, or even permanent duration. The sailor may be an alcoholic, an occasional drinker, or a young man who has sampled intoxicants for the first time. Mary may be immaculate, of average neatness, or slovenly (in this case, **estar** might indicate someone's reaction to her state or perhaps that she is dirtier than usual). Similarly, the use of **estar** indicates that the soil, which may be basically of a soft, average, or hard composition, is harder than usual, perhaps from lack of rain. It may also indicate an implied comparison with some other plot of ground that the speaker has in mind.

In short, **estar** refers to a subject's state at a given time and provides little information about the fundamental nature of the subject. **Ser** suggests no temporal limitation and couples the adjective to the subject itself. In Spanish the speaker uses **estar** with an adjective when he feels the adjective indicates some perceptible change in the subject or when he feels the state of the subject is likely to change. **Ser** indicates that he views the quality as a basic, defining characteristic not subject to change, though it may in fact be so.

3. SUBJECTIVITY WITH ESTAR

Estar may indicate a personal reaction to something. It also expresses what is perceived directly through the senses, and is sometimes rendered in English by *seems, looks, tastes, acts, feels.* **Estar** thus contains something of the subjective reaction or experience as opposed to the more objective **ser.**

Estas naranjas **son** muy dulces.	These oranges are (a) very sweet (variety).
Estas naranjas **están** muy dulces.	These oranges are (taste) very sweet.
—¡Qué suavecito **es** el cieno éste!—dijo Carmen; ¿no te da gusto pisarlo, lo mullido que **está**? (EJ)	"How nice and smooth this mud is," said Carmen. "Don't you enjoy stepping in it, because it is (feels) so soft?"

Since **estar** indicates personal reaction, an adjective with **estar** does not reveal what by objective standards we can consider to be an integral part of the subject; instead it reflects a person's response to a change or to a noteworthy circumstance. **Ser** refers to what is considered a necessary part of the subject by relatively objective standards. **Estar** more often indicates the subjective reaction of the perceiver than the objective state of what he perceives.

Tu abuela **está** muy joven.	Your grandmother is (looks, acts) very young.

The preceding sentence with **ser** would refer to age in actual years. **Estar** conveys an impression of the woman's behavior or appearance compared to what the speaker considers normal for people of her age.

—Carlitos, ¡qué alto **estás**!	"Charles, how tall you are!"
—Sí, mañana cumplo cinco años.	"Yes, I'll be five tomorrow."
Carlos **es** muy alto para su edad.	Charles is very tall for his age.

In the first example **estar** may reflect either the speaker's reaction to the boy's increased height since the previous visit or that Charles is tall compared to other children of his age. The example with **ser** is the more objective way of indicating that Charles is tall for a boy of five.

4. POINT OF VIEW AND IMPLIED CONTRAST

It is not always easy to decide whether a given attribute is better viewed as a defining characteristic or as a state which by its very nature is subject to change. It may help to recall that Spanish prefers **estar** with adjectives when contrast is suggested in any degree. The contrast may be between the present and a previous state of a subject or between a subject and other members of the subject's class. When a feeling of such contrast is absent (and when there is no desire to convey an emotional overtone), Spanish prefers **ser**.

El cielo de Arizona **es** (un cielo) azul.	The Arizona sky is (a) blue (sky).
El cielo de Arizona **está** siempre azul.	The Arizona sky is always blue.

Few people would bother to make the first statement. A native of Tucson residing in San Francisco might make the second statement for the affective power of **estar** or to emphasize the contrast in the weather of the two cities. There is little difference in meaning, however, for a defining characteristic in the first sentence is viewed as a permanent state in the second. But it is clear that the connotative force of the adjective is absent in the trite sentence with **ser**. Study the following sentences to see why **estar** and not **ser** is used.

¡Qué verde **está** la pradera después de la lluvia!	How green the meadow is after the rain!
La tierra **está** muy dura. Si hubiera topos, sería fácil cazarlos. (EA)	The ground is very hard. If there were moles, it would be easy to catch them.

Raimundo **estaba** más gordo, más calvo y más sudoroso que el año anterior. (TV)	Raymond was fatter, balder, and more sweaty than the year before.

Since in normal social communication differences, contrasts, and changes in things interest us more than their well-known characteristic features, **estar** is more frequently encountered in conversation than **ser** in pairs like the following:

Carlos **está** casado.	Charles is married (not a bachelor).
Carlos **es** (un hombre) casado.	Charles is (a) married (man).
La película **está** doblada.	The film is dubbed (not in the original).
La película **es** (una película) doblada.	The film is (a) dubbed (film).

There are, then, in most cases two possibilities with adjectives. With **ser** we indicate that we view the subject as a member of a class, whereas with **estar** we offer a personal comment on the subject without relating it to its class. Thus we would normally refer to a friend's sudden loss of weight by saying:

Juan **está** muy delgado.	John is very thin.

One year later we may continue to use **estar**, thereby still comparing John's present and previous conditions. We may, however, cease to regard his thinness as a resultant state and consider it a basic identifying characteristic. **Ser** would indicate that we now see John as one of the class of thin people.

Juan **es** muy delgado.	John is (a) very thin (person).

EXERCISES

1. Love is essential in life. 2. In what state are your affairs? 3. The lawn is wet with the night dew. 4. The lake was very deep. 5. The state of the economy is improving constantly. 6. Our new house is half furnished. 7. It is to the right of the emperor's portrait. 8. The café was jammed with people when we entered. 9. I am sure you will be better tomorrow. 10. I remember that the sand was dirty with (**de**) algae. 11. He is one of those persons who do not know how to be alone for even a moment with their own thoughts. 12. The bedroom was very dark. 13. What is your brother like? Well, he is tall and strong, but recently has been very sick. 14. The saint is buried in this church. 15. How beautiful the sea is tonight. 16. She is somewhat hard of hearing. 17. She must be tired, for she has rings under her eyes. 18. This coal is bad and burns with difficulty. 19. At that time I was very far from knowing the truth. 20. The car she wants is the two-tone convertible. 21. The oven is too large for the kitchen. 22. Engineering

is a popular career. 23. These flowers are all artificial. 24. The Mississippi is the longest river in the United States. 25. This variety of apple is tart. 26. The fruit is rotten. 27. Milk is good for children. 28. Don't drink that milk; it's sour. 29. This homemade ice cream is delicious. 30. The ice cream the dairy sells is not creamy. 31. The cigarettes he left in the sun are dry. 32. The tobacco in this brand is very dry. 33. The chops were somewhat raw, but were very good. 34. In spite of his age, he still looks very young. 35. She was very beautiful in (**con**) her new dress. 36. Don't touch the door, for the paint is still wet. 37. The water wasn't cold but lukewarm. 38. He is tall, bald, and wears glasses. 39. She is [a] divorced [woman]. 40. The glasses are still not empty.

5. SELECCION LITERARIA

Notas: John F. Kennedy 1917-1963

Julián Marías

La selección que sigue es parte de un artículo que apareció en la Revista de Occidente *en febrero de 1964. El autor, Julián Marías, es uno de los más distinguidos filósofos de España y un intérprete perspicaz de la sociedad norteamericana* (léase su Modos de vivir).

El 22 de noviembre de 1963 ha muerto asesinado en Dallas, Texas, el Presidente de los Estados Unidos, John Fitzgerald Kennedy, de 46 años de edad, graduado por Harvard, ganador de un premio Pulitzer. El mundo entero se ha sentido[1] afectado[2] por esta muerte, despojado y disminuído . . . .

5   John Kennedy era muy joven: ésta era la primera característica de su figura,[3] más juvenil aún que su edad. Su mujer[4] era todavía una muchacha; sus hijos eran niños, y todavía estaban llegando; su rostro,[5] su gesto[6] eran[7] la imagen de la juventud; el peso de la responsabilidad proyectaba sobre él una sombra frecuente, pero daba la impresión de que tenía que «ponerse

10   serio» cuando se trataba de las compañías de acero, la segregación o los proyectiles atómicos en Cuba. Kennedy significaba el futuro;[8] cuando en 1960 fue elegido Presidente, nadie pensó en cuatro años, sino en ocho, como si hubiera sido ya reelegido; no ha podido gobernar ni siquiera tres, y conviene no pasarlo por alto.[9] Por ser joven, Kennedy representaba la es-

15   peranza; ni estaba «visto» ni estaba «de vuelta». Se pensara lo que se quisiera de su acierto[10] político, reclamaba[11] la atención de todos. Kennedy era *interesante*, lo que no ha sido ningún otro gobernante desde Churchill y Roosevelt . . . .

Pero, tanto como esto, importa subrayar otro rasgo[12] del hombre que

20   acaba de morir: Kennedy era un universitario. No simplemente[13] un hombre

que «había pasado» por la Universidad, sino alguien en quien la Universidad había quedado;[14] y nada menos que Harvard, que no es, por supuesto, la única gran Universidad americana, ni siquiera la primera sin más distinción, pero, sí una Universidad específicamente intelectual, y esto quiere decir inventiva, innovadora, crítica, alerta. Los usos intelectuales, la sensibilidad[15] por la verdad, la capacidad de rectificación, habían sido llevados por la Nueva Frontera a la política[16] y al ejercicio del Poder[17]. . . . Con Kennedy, la capacidad intelectual de proyectar el futuro había entrado en la Casa Blanca—y a través de ella, *velis nolis,** en el mundo—. Quiera Dios que se haya quedado allí, que no haya salido con la mecedora de John Kennedy, en la cual podía balancearse, ir atrás y adelante, oscilar, vacilar—porque el mundo es complejo e incierto—, antes de ponerse de pie y tomar una decisión.[18]

No sólo era Kennedy un universitario que llevó a otros a compartir[19] con él la carga del mando: era además un escritor, un orador . . . . Kennedy volvió a[20] instalar la retórica en el seno de la vida política; por eso llamó a Robert Frost a su inauguración; por eso requirió[21] la colaboración de hombres de pensamiento, letras y palabras; por eso no le parecía una tontería[22] citar a un poeta o a un filósofo, o invitar a su casa—a su Casa Blanca—al científico Linus Pauling, que acababa de protestar públicamente, una hora antes, con un cartel,[23] en mangas de camisa,[24] contra su política nuclear.

6. NOTES

1. sentirse—to feel
    sentir—to feel; to hear

    Sentirse is followed by an adjective or word used with adjectival force. **Sentir** always requires an object. In written Spanish **sentir** often means *to hear*.

Me sentí muy tímido entre tus amigos.	I felt very timid among your friends.
Yo no voy a engañarte: no **me siento** tu amigo por esto. (R)	I am not going to deceive you: I don't feel myself (to be) your friend on account of this.
Sintió un odio tan acerbo que cerró los puños en signo de rebelión. (MM)	He felt such a bitter hatred that he clenched his fists in a sign of rebellion.
Empecé a **sentir** que estaba enfermo.	I began to feel that I was sick.

Velis nolis (Latin): "whether you want it or not."

Sentía pasos aunque nadie vivía arriba.	I heard steps, although no one was living upstairs.

2. afectado—(emotionally) moved, affected
   afectar—to affect, move, touch; to concern
   el afecto—affection, concern
   el efecto—effect, result

La muerte de Pira le **había afectado** en lo más vivo. (F)	Pira's death had affected him deeply.
Eso **afecta** a nuestros intereses nacionales.	That concerns (affects) our national interests.
Siempre ha mostrado gran **afecto** para con la familia.	He has always shown great affection for the family.
El vino empezó a hacerle **efecto**.	The wine began to have an effect on him.

3. la figura—figure; countenance, face

Cervantes es la **figura** literaria más importante de España.	Cervantes is Spain's most important literary figure.
Don Quijote era el caballero de la triste **figura**.	Don Quixote was the Knight of the Sad Countenance.

4. la mujer—wife

Notice that the word for *woman* also means *wife*. In spoken Spanish it is the standard term to refer to one's own wife. Although **mujer** may be used for someone else's wife, **esposa** is probably more common. The obsequious **señora** (**esposa**), often used by people of little education, is best avoided. **Esposo**, *husband*, a frequent literary synonym for **marido**, is almost never used in ordinary conversation.

Mi **mujer** no podrá venir.	My wife will not be able to come.
¿Cómo está su **esposa** (**mujer**)?	How is your wife?

5. el rostro—face
   la cara—face
   poner una (la) cara—to make a face

Cara is the standard term for *face*. **Rostro** is a common substitute in written Spanish, and often (not always) suggests emotion. *To make a face* is rendered with **poner** and the appropriate adjective.

En su **rostro** veíamos el temor a la muerte.	On his face we saw his fear of death.
Me corté **la cara** al afeitarme.	I cut my face while shaving.

Puso la cara más triste que se puede imaginar.	She made the saddest face one can imagine.

6. el gesto—gesture, expressive movement; facial expression

Me gustaría tener un hijo como él, con su cara, su voz, sus **gestos**. (F)	I would like to have a son like him, with his face, his voice, his gestures.
Puso muy mal **gesto** al saber la noticia.	He made a very unpleasant face when he learned the news.

7. eran—su rostro y su gesto eran

8. el futuro—future
   el porvenir—future

   Lo futuro is also very common. **Porvenir** often has a personal, poetic, or prophetic connotation not always present in **futuro**.

¿Quién sabe lo que nos guarda **el futuro**?	Who knows what the future holds for us?
No pienses en el pasado, sino en tu **porvenir**.	Don't think about the past, but about your future.

9. pasar por alto—to overlook
   hacer caso omiso de—to disregard; to ignore
   (no) hacer caso de—to pay (no) attention to

   Whereas **pasar por alto** sometimes implies that an action is unintentional, **hacer caso omiso** indicates that it is deliberate. The straight negative **no hacer caso de algo** (**a alguien**) is used more than the literary **hacer caso omiso de**.

Su madre **pasó** la observación **por alto** y siguió hablando.	His mother overlooked what he said and went on talking.
Pasaste por alto el capítulo más importante.	You overlooked the most important chapter.
Haciendo caso omiso de los reglamentos, empezó a fumar.	Disregarding the regulations, he began to smoke.

10. el acierto—skill, ability to do just the right thing
    acertado—right, correct
    acertar—to guess right, choose correctly, do what is called for, etc.
    acertar a + infinitive—to succeed in + verb, to manage to + verb; to happen to + verb

Sólo una **acertada** política nuclear salvó al país.	Only the right nuclear policy saved the country.

A veces uno **acierta** y a veces uno yerra.	Sometimes one does the right thing and sometimes the wrong thing.
Acertó cuando dijo que no estaban satisfechos.	He guessed right (hit the nail on the head) when he said they were not satisfied.
Una mujer **acertó a descifrar** unas letras escritas por su marido. (MM)	One woman managed to decipher a few of the letters her husband had written down.
Acertó a ser el día de nuestro aniversario cuando llegaron.	It happened to be the day of our anniversary when they arrived.

11.   reclamar—to demand
      exigir—to demand

Reclamar means *to demand* what one considers his due or his rights. **Exigir** is used in most other cases.

Reclamó justicia ante el tribunal.	He demanded justice before the court.
El maestro ha subido hasta donde se halla Prudencio y **reclama** silencio. (EP)	The professor has gone up to where Prudence is and demands silence.
Exijo que Vd. trabaje más.	I demand that you work harder.

12.   el rasgo—feature
      las facciones—features
      rasgar—to rip, tear
      ojos rasgados—slanted eyes

Rasgo is synonymous with **característica** and refers to any feature or characteristic. **Facciones** are facial features only.

Tu compañero tiene unos **rasgos** (unas características) muy desagradables.	Your companion has some very unpleasant traits.
Sus **facciones** no son feas.	Her features are not ugly.
El chico **se rasgó** los pantalones.	The boy ripped his pants.

13.   simplemente—simply

Simple and **sencillo** are equivalents of the English *simple*. **Simple**, when applied to people, means *foolish* or *simple-minded*. When referring to things, if it precedes the noun it means *merely* or *only*. It also indicates *simple* as opposed to *compound*. **Sencillo** means *unpretentious* or *easy (to understand)*.

El director de la aduana es un **simple** funcionario municipal.	The director of customs is an ordinary (is only a) municipal servant.
El castellano tiene tiempos **simples** y tiempos compuestos.	Spanish has simple tenses and compound tenses.
En él todo parecía **sencillo** y abierto, sin malicias de ninguna clase. (N)	Everything about him seemed simple and candid, without malice of any kind.
El primer paso es muy **sencillo**.	The first step is very simple.

14. quedar—to be left, remain
     quedarse—to remain, stay

Quedar usually indicates that a person or thing is left a certain way because of another's actions. **Quedarse** means *to remain in the same place* as a result of one's own decision or will.

Sólo **quedaban** unas cuantas parejas en el parque.	Only a few couples were left in the park. (Others had departed.)
Será mejor que **nos quedemos** aquí.	It will be better for us to remain here.

15. la sensibilidad—sensitivity
     la sensitividad—sensitivity
     sensible, sensitivo—sensitive
     razonable, sensato—sensible

Sensible is far more common than **sensitivo**. It indicates that which is easily moved to emotion or esthetic appreciation, or is responsive to physical stimuli. **Sensitivo** often replaces **sensible** when the speaker wishes to add a note of greater technical or esthetic sharpness to his use of the word. Consequently, **sensible** is almost always correct, but **sensitivo** may be inappropriate on certain colloquial levels or in some very basic contexts.

Para ser crítico se necesita solamente **sensibilidad**, y yo la tengo. (N)	To be a critic one needs only sensitivity, and I have it.
Parece **insensible** a la belleza del mar.	He seems insensitive to the beauty of the sea.
Los perros son **sensibles** a toda clase de olores.	Dogs are sensitive to all kinds of smells.
Dichoso el árbol, que es apenas **sensitivo**,	Happy is the tree, for it is hardly sensitive, and happier is the hard

y más la piedra dura porque ésa
ya no siente.
(Rubén Darío: «Lo fatal»)

stone, for it cannot feel at all.

16. la política—politics
la política—policy
la póliza de seguro—insurance policy

No nos interesa la **política**.

Politics doesn't interest us.

¿Quién estableció la **Política** de la Buena Vecindad?

Who established the Good Neighbor Policy?

La **póliza de seguro** caduca en agosto.

The insurance policy expires in August.

17. el poder—power
la potencia—power

Poder is generally *power* of a personal, social, or political nature. **Potencia** is employed especially to mean mechanical or electrical *energy*, but it also means *power* when referring to a nation as a world force. **Poder** in the plural often has a legal meaning.

El banco era el símbolo del **poder** del fabricante.

The bank was the symbol of the manufacturer's power.

La **potencia** del motor es enorme.

The power of the motor is enormous.

En aquella época las grandes **potencias** eran tres.

At that time there were three great powers.

Tenía plenos **poderes** para negociar.

He had complete power (authority) to negotiate.

18. tomar una decisión—to make a decision
decidir + infinitive—to decide to do something
decidirse a + infinitive—to decide to do something

Hacer una decisión is much less common than **tomar una decisión**. A slight difference in meaning exists between **decidir** and **decidirse a**. The reflexive form is used to indicate a note of resolve or determination usually absent in **decidir** alone.

Decidió estudiar alemán.

He decided to study German.

Se decidió a hablar con el sargento.

He decided (resolved) to speak to the sergeant.

19. compartir—to share

Notice that **compartir** is **partir**, *to divide*, and **con**, *with*. **Repartir** is *to divide among* or *to distribute*. **Partir** alone indicates dividing something into two approximately equal parts, unless otherwise qualified.

Comparto tu opinión.	I share your opinion.
Repartieron el pan entre los menesterosos.	They distributed (divided, shared) the bread among the poor.
Partió la manzana con un cuchillo.	He cut the apple in half with a knife.
Partió la sandía en varias rajas.	He cut the watermelon into several slices.
En invierno **partía** leña para los pobres. (SMB)	In winter he used to split (chop) firewood for the poor people.

20. volver a instalar—to install again
    volver a + infinitive—to do something again
    volver, regresar—to return
    devolver—to return, give back
    tornar a + infinitive—to do something again (literary usage)

Volver and **regresar** mean the same thing, but **volver** is much more common in spoken Spanish, where **regresar** is used mainly when considerable distance or time is involved. On the literary level this difference tends to disappear, and **regresar** frequently replaces **volver** in all contexts.

No vuelvas a hacerlo.	Don't do it again.
La vieja **regresó** del mostrador con un vaso. (F)	The old lady returned from the counter with a glass.
Ha devuelto todo el dinero.	He has returned all the money.
—¡Cómo pasa el tiempo!—**torna a exclamar** la dama. (BA)	"How time passes!" the lady exclaims again.

21. requerir—to request; to need, require

Requerir is somewhat journalistic in nature; in spoken Spanish, it is often replaced by **pedir, necesitar, exigir**, and other verbs.

Requirió la ayuda de la policía.	He requested the help of the police.
Este asunto **requiere** (**exige**) mucho cuidado.	This matter requires (demands) great care.

22. una tontería—(a) foolish (thing)

La locura, el disparate, la estupidez, and similar words are used to indicate that someone has done or said something *crazy, nonsensical,* *stupid*, etc. Spanish prefers these single words to such little used equivalents as **una cosa estúpida**, *a stupid thing*.

Siempre dices **disparates**.	You are always talking nonsense.
Ha hecho **una locura**.	He has done something crazy.
Estamos cansados de sus **chifladuras**.	We are tired of his crazy ideas.

23.   el cartel—placard, poster
        el letrero—sign
        el rótulo—sign
        el anuncio—announcement, advertisement, sign

A **cartel** is often illustrated. A **letrero** usually contains information or directions, whereas **rótulo** bears a title, name, or similar designation. In literature these differences are observed irregularly.

En el parabrisas hay un **letrero** que dice: «Médico».	On the windshield there is a sign (card) that says: "Doctor."
Había un **rótulo** sobre la puerta del bufete.	There was a sign above the door of the lawyer's office.

24.   en mangas de camisa—in shirt sleeves
        la manga—sleeve
        tener la manga ancha—to be indulgent

Algo se trae entre manos.	He has something up his sleeve.
Tiene la manga tan ancha que ha engreído a su hijo.	He is so over-indulgent that he has made his son very conceited.

EXERCISES ON NOTES

1. The economy is feeling the effect of the strike. 2. What face did she make on learning the news? 3. In June the students return all books to the library. 4. You guessed right when you said it was going to rain. 5. Gold is a simple substance. 6. The children remained alone when their parents went out. 7. Because of the heat, everyone was in shirt sleeves. 8. Every artist is sensitive to color and to form. 9. The brothers shared the bedroom. 10. She finally decided to invest her money in bonds. 11. He disregarded his father's orders and returned after midnight. 12. The holiday happened to be Wednesday. 13. He demanded the money that they owed him. 14. We overlooked their names on the guest list. 15. He felt weak because he had not eaten all day. (Use **en**.) 16. The philosopher loved the simple life. 17. Politics requires much tact. 18. Slanted eyes are very beautiful. 19. The patient's eyes are very sensitive to light. 20. A sign on the elevator door says: "Out of order." 21. When I turned on the light, nothing was left on the tray. 22. His wife asked again what had happened. 23. The occasion seems to demand a radical solution. 24. He was drunk and

didn't say anything but nonsense. 25. His policy affected the entire Spanish society of his time. 26. The injections have had no effect on him. 27. The other party will soon be in power. 28. We heard (*not* **oír**) voices as soon as we reached the garden. 29. We decided to overlook the stupid things he said. 30. I was thinking only of your future. 31. That man has a great deal of power in the government. 32. The world powers have changed in recent years. 33. They were distributing samples among the customers. 34. It will be no simple task to locate him in this city. 35. In spite of everything, I still do not feel old. 36. The walls were covered with (**de**) posters announcing the races. 37. The revolutionary distributed arms to the miners. 38. The policy failed when the king died. 39. The news of her death moved us very much. 40. He was an important figure before he lost his power.

CUESTIONARIO

a. contenido

1. ¿Por qué simbolizaba John Kennedy la juventud?
2. ¿Cómo afectaba la responsabilidad al joven presidente?
3. ¿Por qué cree Vd. que Julián Marías compara Kennedy a Churchill y Roosevelt?
4. ¿En qué sentido de la palabra era el presidente universitario?
5. ¿Qué era la Nueva Frontera?
6. ¿Tenía la mecedora una importancia especial en la vida de John Kennedy?
7. ¿Qué papel desempeñaba el hombre de letras en el gobierno del Presidente Kennedy?
8. ¿Qué episodio muestra la tolerancia intelectual del presidente?

b. estilo

1. ¿Qué efecto le produce a Vd. el orden de los adjetivos **afectado, despojado, disminuído**?
2. ¿Cómo contribuyen las palabras **estaban llegando** a la idea de juventud?
3. Analice Vd. la estructura de la oración que comienza con las palabras «No simplemente un hombre . . . » del tercer párrafo.
4. ¿Por qué ha acertado Julián Marías al destacar la imagen de la mecedora?
5. ¿Qué efecto consigue el autor con la repetición de **por eso** tres veces en el último párrafo?

TEMA—TRADUCCION

The assassination of John Kennedy deprived the American people of a young and vigorous president. For many his youthful face was a symbol of the future. When he was murdered the entire world shared the grief of his wife and his family. From the faces of the people you could see that everyone was deeply moved.

During the time he governed, the President often felt the weight of great responsibility. Although men of the New Frontier advised and helped him, in the last analysis the President alone had to make the decisions that would have a profound effect on the world. Seated in his rocking chair, he decided policy regarding the problem of Russian missiles in Cuba or the increase in prices proposed by the steel companies.

All presidents are sensitive to public opinion, and none can disregard it. Nevertheless, as an intellectual President Kennedy was able to invite to the White House a scientist who only hours before had publicly protested against his nuclear policy by carrying a placard. As a winner of the Pulitzer Prize, the President felt the need of bringing the university world to his New Frontier. He made a good choice when he invited Robert Frost to read his poetry at the inauguration. John Kennedy returned rhetoric to the capital, and his speeches attracted much attention. It was a black day for the nation when this young man was assassinated almost one hundred years after the assassination of another president.

TEMAS A ESCOGER

Escríbanse unas 200 palabras sobre uno de los temas siguientes usando a lo menos 20 de las palabras y expresiones estudiadas en este capítulo.

1. Las responsabilidades de un presidente en el mundo actual
2. La vida particular de un político en los EE.UU.
3. Relaciones entre la universidad y la política

chapter 2

"TO BE" IN SPANISH—Continued

7. LITERAL AND FIGURATIVE USE OF ADJECTIVES

An adjective used with **ser** categorizes the subject as a member of a given class. With **estar** an adjective offers a personal comment (often reflecting an unusual circumstance or change) on the subject. This explains why an adjective's more literal meaning is conveyed by **ser** and its figurative or personal meaning by **estar**. In a very few cases the meaning of the adjective itself changes somewhat according to the verb used.

Adjective	Ser (*Person, Thing*)	Estar (*State*)
aburrido	boring	bored
ciego	blind (loss of sight)	blind (figuratively or momentarily, from bright light, sun, etc.)
cojo	crippled	lame
despierto	clever, sharp	awake (not sleeping)
distraído	absent-minded	distracted
libre	free (unrestrained)	free (not busy; recently freed)
limpio	clean, neat	clean, unsoiled
loco	insane	crazy (act, seem)
nuevo	new (just made, unused)	new (in appearance, in condition)
pálido	pale	pale (from illness, shock)
pobre	poor (needy, indigent)	poor (figuratively)
rico	rich (wealthy); delicious	rich (figuratively); delicious
sordo	deaf (loss of hearing)	deaf (figuratively or momentarily)
vivo	lively, energetic	alive (living)
muerto		dead, deceased

Muerto, unlike **vivo,** is rarely used as an adjective with **ser** except in the passive voice with the meaning of **matado,** the participle of **matar.**

Veinte soldados **fueron muertos.**	Twenty soldiers were killed.

One can, however, use **muerto** as a noun or noun-adjective.

Es un (hombre) **muerto.**	It's a dead man.
Estaba ciego, pero ella me abrió los ojos.	I was blind, but she opened my eyes for me.

—Qué, ¿se ha descansado?	"Well, did you rest?"
—Pues, hombre, sí. **Estoy nuevo.** (VA)	"Yes, indeed. I'm like a new man."
Me han tocado mil pesetas en la lotería. **Estoy rico.**	I have won 1,000 pesetas in the lottery. I'm rich.
Ese profesor **es** muy **distraído.**	That professor is very absent-minded.
Nada ve claro, y hay momentos en los que no sabe si **está vivo** o **muerto.** (LC)	He can't see anything clearly, and there are moments when he doesn't know if he is alive or dead.

8. OTHER USES OF SER

Ser renders *to be* when it indicates:

A. CERTAIN KINDS OF ACCOMPANIMENT

Dios **sea** contigo.	God be with you.
Seré con Vd. en seguida.	I will be with you right away. (said in business establishments)

B. TO TAKE PLACE, TO OCCUR, TO HAPPEN

El concierto **será** en el teatro.	The concert will be in the theatre.
Aquí **es** donde vivió.	Here is where he lived.

Some statements may signal either events (the place an activity happens) or location.

La cena **será** en el comedor.	Dinner will be in the dining room. (seen as an event)
La cena **está** en el comedor.	Dinner is in the dining room. (indicates location of the food)

9. TENER AS AN EQUIVALENT OF TO BE

Tener often means *to be* when referring to people.

Tenga Vd. **cuidado.**	Be careful.
No **tenía miedo** a nadie ni a nada. (LE)	He wasn't afraid of anyone or anything.
El joven **tiene talento** pero es perezoso.	The young man is talented, but he is lazy.
Tenía mucho frío mientras trabajaba en el jardín.	I was very cold while I was working in the garden.

Spanish ordinarily expresses the condition of a part of the body or of an article of clothing with **tener**, although **estar** is also used. **Tener** enables the speaker to associate the condition more closely with the person concerned than **estar**.

El pobre **tiene** el estómago vacío.	The poor man's stomach is empty.
Está tiritando y **tiene** las manos heladas.	He is shivering and his hands are frozen.
Los muchachos **tenían** los zapatos rotos.	The boys' shoes were all worn.

Notice that **tener** renders *to be cold* (*warm*) when it indicates how people feel. However, if we touch someone we express our reaction with **estar**.

Estaba rígido, **frío**, y tocarlo nos dio un miedo vago pero irresistible. (DP)	He was stiff and cold, and touching him gave us a vague but irresistible fright.

10. HACER AND HABER AS TO BE

The equivalent of *to be* in weather expressions is ordinarily **hacer** or **haber** in the third person singular. Some weather phenomena may be rendered with either verb; with others only one of the verbs may be used. **Haber** seems to emphasize visual perception, and (except in rare poetic uses) it alone refers to the moon. Sun and wind take either verb. Although **hacer** is normal and more common, **haber** stresses that the phenomenon or its effects are seen rather than taken for granted or perceived in some other way. Expressions indicative of temperature and the weather in general always require **hacer**. Equivalent expressions with **estar** are literary.

Está ventoso. (literary)	It's windy.
Esta noche **hay luna.**	The moon is out (shining) tonight.
Hoy **hace (hay) sol.**	Today the sun is out (shining).
Hacía (había) mucho **viento.**	It was very windy.
Hace buen tiempo en verano.	The weather is good in summer.
Por la noche siempre **hace frío.**	At night it is always cold.

11. QUEDAR AND QUEDARSE AS TO BE

A very common equivalent of *to be* is **quedar(se)**. **Estar** and **quedar(se)** both indicate resultant state, but **quedar(se)** goes one step further: it shows that the state is the direct result of an action or circumstance that leaves (**deja**) the subject so that it remains [(**se**) **queda**] in this condition.

Me quedé atónito cuando nos lo contó.	I was astonished when he told us.

El café, antes de media hora, **quedará** vacío. (LC)	The café, before half an hour is up, will be empty.
Creo que **quedará** curado para siempre.	I believe he will be cured forever.

EXERCISES

1. In war and in business, man must be cold. 2. I recall a night when the moon was out. 3. The French class is in room (**aula**) number eight. 4. He is a good person, but he is very boring. 5. It was hot and the window was wide open. 6. He saw Mary and immediately was in love with her. 7. Is your wrist broken? No, but my hand is swollen. 8. There is where we had the accident. 9. I am not accustomed to this weather. 10. When she explained the circumstances, she was forgiven. 11. My throat is very dry. 12. They went away because they were tired of waiting. 13. It was not cold yesterday, but the air was humid. 14. He was a little lame after his fall. 15. I touched him and he was [as] cold as ice; I knew then he was dead. 16. We can't use this board, for the wood is wet. 17. Are you deaf? How many times do I have to explain it to you? 18. The dance will be in this wing of the building. 19. The table was already set when we sat down to eat. 20. The soles of his feet were swollen from so much walking. 21. Be careful; the sidewalk is slippery. 22. He is stubborn and always insists that he is right. 23. The curtains were drawn, and the living room was dark. 24. I knew it was windy because the branches were moving. 25. It was so hot that the beach was full of bathers. 26. Come here! Your ears are dirty. 27. You will be surprised when you read (*subjunctive*) the letter. 28. Don't cross now; the light is still red. 29. Where was the last meeting of the Security Council? 30. I believe his son is very talented. 31. You will be hoarse if you continue singing. 32. She is not blind; she knows what we are doing. 33. They wanted to know where we were from. 34. I won't be free until this afternoon. 35. The soup was very hot when they served it. 36. It's useless to talk to him, for he is completely deaf. 37. The clerk will be with you in two minutes. 38. It's warm in this house, but I still feel very cold. 39. She is eighty years old and is very lively. 40. It was cool, and the wind was blowing when we arrived in Florida.

12. SELECCION LITERARIA*

Notas: John F. Kennedy 1917-1963*

Julián Marías

Kennedy era un americano,[1] y no podía ser otra cosa: bastaba ver su rostro en cualquier parte para no poder dudar. Era un bostoniano, un católico irlandés de Massachusetts, uno de los modos en que se realiza[2] pluralmente esa realidad unitaria y múltiple que son los Estados Unidos.

---

*Continuation of the selection in Chap. 1.

Pero había estudiado en Londres, había luchado[3] en el Pacífico, había viajado por la América española; no era un provinciano, sino todo lo contrario: un occidental. Sabía que la serie de sus patrias efectivas[4] se dilataba en círculos concéntricos: Boston, Massachusetts, New England, los Estados
5 Unidos, Occidente. ¿El mundo? No, todavía no; como cristiano, sí, porque todos los hombres somos hijos de Dios: como intelectual, también; como político, no, porque la política es adivinación, anticipación *cum fundamento in re,** no utopía. Sabía que su patria no era todavía el mundo, pero, que *el mundo es ya uno*, que la historia y la política son por primera vez ecumé-
10 nicas . . . .

Por eso, la política de Kennedy significaba el planteamiento[5] de los problemas a escala[6] universal—es decir, a su escala—. El aislamiento[7] de los Estados Unidos está muerto. En rigor, estaba ya muerto antes de Kennedy; pero, ahora se sabe, y no hay disculpa. Y el reverso de la medalla
15 es que los Estados Unidos no son ya ajenos,[8] no son ya otra cosa.[9] La muerte de Kennedy ha servido para ponerlo de manifiesto:[10] todos hemos sentido que lo hemos perdido, que los disparos de Dallas no han sonado «allá», sino «aquí», en este mismo mundo: que los Estados Unidos son nuestros, parte esencial de nuestra circunstancia, con la cual tenemos que habér-
20 noslas,[11] con la que tenemos que contar[12]. . . .

Yo quisiera, para que estas líneas fueran un homenaje adecuado a Kennedy, extraer de ello una consecuencia a la vez intelectual y política. En primer lugar, que cuando el ejercicio del Poder es legítimo, éste es, a pesar de todo, invulnerable. Pocas cosas me han conmovido[13] tanto como
25 esa imagen que todos hemos visto: el nuevo Presidente Lyndon Johnson, hora y media después del asesinato, en un avión, signo de nuestro tiempo,[14] jurando fidelidad a la Constitución, rodeado de tres mujeres: la suya, la bella, desolada, admirable Jacqueline Kennedy, y la juez federal que toma el juramento. Esa imagen mostraba que se puede matar al hombre John
30 Kennedy, pero no se puede matar al Presidente de los Estados Unidos. La otra consecuencia va todavía más lejos, y es la radical inseguridad que nos rodea, a pesar de todo, de todas las previsiones, de todas las técnicas: si la muerte de Kennedy ha sido obra del azar[15] de un dementoide,[16] prueba[17] la inseguridad que acecha[18] al hombre; si ha sido consecuencia del fana-
35 tismo, demuestra la inseguridad de lo humano. En un caso y en otro, vemos claro que sólo se puede vivir humanamente sabiendo que la vida humana es una realidad inestable, amenazada, problemática, que sólo se sostiene[19] a fuerza de aspirar[20] hacia lo alto, como un surtidor.

13. NOTES

1. americano—American

In Spain, **americano** normally means *American* in the sense of *from*

**Cum fundamento in re* (Latin): "with a basis in reality."

or *of the U.S.A.*, as distinguished from **hispanoamericano**. In Spanish America, however, **norteamericano** (or **estadounidense**) is often used instead of **americano**, because Spanish Americans are also **americanos**. When there is no possibility of ambiguity, **americano** may be used to refer to people or things of the U.S.A.

2. realizar—to achieve, accomplish, carry out; to realize
   darse cuenta de—to realize (understand or to become aware of)

   Realizar means *to realize* only in the sense of *to achieve* something, such as an ambition.

La operación es difícil de **realizar**. (JM)	The operation is difficult to carry out.
Casi sin **darse cuenta**, llamó ruidosamente al camarero.	Almost without realizing it, he loudly called the waiter.

3. luchar—to fight, struggle, wrestle (physically or figuratively)
   pelear(se)—to fight, brawl (often reflexive)
   reñir—to fight, quarrel; to scold
   la lucha, la pelea, la riña—fight, quarrel
   la riña de perros (gatos)—dog (cat) fight

   Pelear is a little stronger than **reñir**, although both verbs are commonly employed in everyday speech to indicate quarrels and physical scuffles. **Luchar**, aside from also meaning *to wrestle*, is more literary and usually connotes a more violent struggle or one with more serious and far-reaching consequences.

Luchamos cinco años antes de vencer al enemigo.	We fought (struggled) five years before defeating the enemy.
La lucha por los derechos humanos nunca termina.	The struggle for human rights never ends.
El hombre ha venido al mundo a **pelear**. (JM)	Man has come into the world to fight.
Anoche **se pelearon** otra vez.	Last night they fought again.
Era una locura que las mujeres **riñesen** por un hombre. (FM)	It was insane for the women to quarrel over a man.

4. efectivo—true, real, actual
   eficaz—effective
   actual—present, current
   actualmente, en la actualidad—presently, at the present time

   Efectivo is used much less frequently than its two more common synonyms, **verdadero** and **real**. It usually suggests a contrast with what appears to be true but isn't, or with what is only theoretically or nominally true. **Actual** is not synonymous with any of these three adjectives, but with the adjective **presente**.

El poder **efectivo** estaba en manos del ejército.	The real power was in the hands of the army.
Sus **verdaderos** motivos nunca se sabrán.	His real (true) motives will never be known.
El dueño **actual** piensa alquilar la casa.	The present owner intends to rent the house.

5. el planteamiento—stating, posing, expounding
   plantear—to state, pose, present (a problem or difficulty); to present with (con is not used)

| Durante la república, si usted lo recuerda, el problema ya estaba **planteado**. (F) | If you will recall, the problem had already been posed during the time of the Republic. |
| Tu ausencia nos **plantea** muchas dificultades. | Your absence presents us with many difficulties. |

6. la escala—scale (for measurement); musical scale; (rope) ladder
   hacer escala en—to call at, stop at (said of ships and planes)
   la balanza—(balance) scale
   la báscula—(platform) scale
   la escama—scale (fish, reptile)
   escamar—to scale

El avión **hizo escala en** Lisboa.	The plane stopped in Lisbon.
La sardinera sostenía la **balanza** en la mano.	The sardine vendor was holding up the scale in her hand.
Enardecíales la tardanza de los pescadores en dejar libre la **báscula**. (FM)	The fishermen's slowness in leaving the scale free enraged them.
Ayudé a mi padre a **escamar** todo el pescado.	I helped my father scale all the fish.

7. el aislamiento—isolation; insulation
   aislar—to isolate; to insulate (electrically, thermally)

| Durante la guerra Inglaterra estaba **aislada** del resto de Europa. | During the war England was isolated from the rest of Europe. |
| No hace calor dentro porque la casa está bien **aislada**. | It is not hot inside because the house is well insulated. |

8. ajeno—another's, alien, foreign
   propio—own

| No se debe codiciar los bienes **ajenos**. | One should not covet another's goods. |

*El mundo es ancho y **ajeno***	Novel by Peruvian Ciro Alegría (English title: *Broad and Alien Is the World*)
Es una mujer sin demasiados escrúpulos para la propiedad **ajena**. (N)	She is a woman without too many scruples for the property of others.
Daría mi **propia** vida por ellos.	I would give my own life for them.

9. no son ya otra cosa—they are no longer something else (apart from us)

10. poner de manifiesto—to make clear or evident
poner en ridículo—to make a fool of; to make look ridiculous; to ridicule

Puso de manifiesto la gravedad de la situación.	He made clear the gravity of the situation.
El canónigo don Inocencio **pone en ridículo** sus opiniones acerca de la ciencia . . . . (SR)	The canon priest Don Inocencio ridicules (exposes to ridicule) his ideas about science . . . .

11. habérselas con—to have it out with

No estás preparado para **habértelas** con alguien así.	You are not prepared to have it out with someone like that.

12. contar con—to count on, rely on; to have

Cuento contigo para resolver el problema.	I'm relying on you to solve the problem.
Lima **cuenta con** unos magníficos museos.	Lima has some magnificent museums.

13. conmover—to move (emotionally)
mover—to move (change position) (mover always requires an object in Spanish, even when an object is not expressed in English)
mudarse—to move (mudar means to change something; thus Spanish renders to move, in the sense of changing residence, as reflexive)
trasladar(se)—to transfer; to move

Su actitud humilde me **conmovía** e irritaba a un tiempo. (LM)	His humble attitude moved me and irritated me at the same time.
Movieron el sofá.	They moved the sofa.
Carlos, **no te muevas** de ahí.	Charles, don't move from there.
Todavía no **nos hemos mudado**.	We still haven't moved.

Durante el reinado de Felipe III la corte **se trasladó** a Valladolid.	During the reign of Philip III, the court was transferred (moved) to Valladolid.

14. el tiempo—time (in a general sense; as an historical period, often plural)
    la época—time (synonym of el tiempo in an historical sense)
    la hora—time (hour or moment for doing something)
    la vez—time (series, occasion)

En **tiempos** de Carlos V se leía a Erasmo en España.	During the time of Charles V, people read Erasmus in Spain.
En **época** de la recolección, los campesinos trabajan y se regocijan.	At harvest time, the peasants work and rejoice.
Aquel día no vi a Roberto a **la hora** de la comida.	That day I did not see Robert at mealtime.
A la hora de partir para la otra vida, todos salimos pobres. (EBM)	When it's time to depart for the other life, we all leave poor.

15. el azar—chance, risk, unforeseen disaster
    juegos de azar—games of chance
    la casualidad—chance (without the idea of danger or risk)
    por casualidad—by chance

Uno tiene que estar prevenido contra **los azares** de la vida.	One must be prepared for the hazards of life.
El que tenía que guiar a la patrulla fue escogido **al azar**.	The one who had to guide the patrol was chosen at random.
Es pura **casualidad** que estén aquí.	It's pure chance that they are here.

16. dementoide—demente

17. probar—to test, try; to taste; to prove
    probarse—to try on (clothing)
    la prueba—test; proof, evidence
    comprobar—to confirm, verify, check

Prueba el postre; está muy bueno.	Taste the dessert; it's very good.
Al probarnos los sueters, la abuela observó que habíamos crecido demasiado aquel verano....(LM)	When we tried on the sweaters, our grandmother observed that we had grown too much that summer ....

Hay que someter esto a una **prueba**.	We must subject this to a test.
Está libre por falta de **prueba**.	He's free for lack of evidence.
Comprueba lo que venimos diciendo.	It confirms what we have been saying.
Han comprobado casi todos los ejemplos en el diccionario.	They have checked almost all the examples in the dictionary.

18. acechar—to lie in wait for; to stalk; to spy on

Los bandidos **acecharon** el paso de los viandantes.	The bandits lay in ambush for the passing of the travelers.
Encontramos a la criada, **acechándonos** por la puerta entornada.	We found the servant spying on us through the half-closed door.

19. sostener—to support, maintain; to hold (up)
    mantener—to support, maintain, keep
    aguantar—to endure, put up with, bear
    soportar—not to support, but a synonym of aguantar

Yo **sostengo** que no tendrá éxito.	I maintain that he will not be successful.
El cojo **soportaba** las burlas de los niños con aparente indiferencia.	The crippled man endured the children's taunts with apparent indifference.
Conozco a pocos que **soporten** con más dignidad que Juan la tragedia.	I know few people who bear tragedy with more dignity than John.
El alumno no **aguantaba** los ejercicios que le exigían.	The student could not stand the exercises they demanded of him.
Ha prometido **mantener** a su madre mientras viva.	He has promised to support his mother as long as she lives.

20. aspirar a + infinitive—to aspire to do something
    aspirar—to breathe in, inhale, breathe deeply
    respirar—to breathe (normal process of respiration)

El **aspira a crear** un nuevo movimiento literario.	He aspires to create a new literary movement.
Oí de nuevo el ruido del mar y **aspiré** una ráfaga de aire salino. (TV)	I again heard the noise of the sea and breathed a gust of salt air.
Con el catarro que tengo apenas puedo **respirar**.	With the cold I have I can scarcely breathe.

1. He knows that his friends are moving to Main Street. 2. I have never quarreled with him. 3. Today you are absolutely unbearable. 4. In the morning the air we breathe is purer. 5. Here we can live isolated from the entire world. 6. I breathed in the delicate fragrance that filled the room. 7. She has just bought an American car. 8. The medicine he prescribed was very effective. 9. The woman presented many problems for her son-in-law. 10. They did it on a large scale. 11. At present the school doesn't offer such a program. 12. The fish is scaled and is on the table. 13. I am counting on your support in the election (*plural*). 14. The young man aspires to be a great painter. 15. Don't move from where you are, or they will see you. 16. I don't want to get involved in the affairs of others. 17. These ships call at many Mediterranean ports. 18. Your gossip (*plural*) made me look ridiculous. 19. From time to time he would carry out a careful inspection of the orchard. 20. In a democracy the real power resides in the people. 21. No nation can afford to remain isolated in the twentieth century. 22. The pharmacist is carefully measuring the drugs on a [balance] scale. 23. He has always fought for the working class. 24. He turned on the radio at dinner time. 25. I tried on the jacket several times before deciding to buy it. 26. He never verifies things before announcing them. 27. Our neighbors moved because they couldn't stand the noise our children made. 28. One can't avoid the hazards of life. 29. Here it is not necessary to insulate buildings against the cold. 30. Some day I am going to have it out with him. 31. It is impossible to breathe at such altitudes. 32. Occasionally even the best friends fight. 33. He was so busy with his work that he didn't realize we had left. 34. He has isolated several features that seem very significant. 35. Although it was raining, we did not move from the corner. 36. When did the court move to Rio de Janeiro? 37. I must make clear the importance of this matter. 38. The real reason is that he is supporting a large family. (Use **numerosa**.) 39. I realized my mistake as soon as I finished the test. 40. I will not put up with it even one more time.

CUESTIONARIO

a. contenido

1. ¿En qué sentido era el Presidente Kennedy un occidental?
2. ¿Cuál era su visión del mundo en que vivía?
3. ¿Qué significa «los disparos de Dallas no han sonado "allá," sino "aquí"»?
4. ¿Cómo justifica el autor la idea de que no se puede matar al Presidente de los Estados Unidos?
5. ¿A qué conclusión filosófica sobre la vida le lleva la muerte del joven presidente a Julián Marías? ¿Comparte Vd. esta opinión?

b. estilo

1. ¿Qué técnica emplea el autor para desarrollar la idea central del primer párrafo: Kennedy—de bostoniano a hombre universal?
2. Explique Vd. todos los usos de *ser* y *estar* en el segundo párrafo.
3. ¿Qué nota afectiva añaden a la imagen del juramento del nuevo presidente las palabras *bella, desolada,* y *admirable*?
4. Identifique Vd. y comente el uso del símil de la última oración.

TEMA—TRADUCCION

President Kennedy was an example of the multiple, but unitary, reality that is achieved in the United States. He was from Boston but had studied, traveled, lived, and even fought in other parts of the world. Therefore he realized that the world in these times is one. This point of view, which had been held by few presidents before him, meant stating world problems on a universal scale. His death made this clear when the shots that ended his life sounded throughout the world.

The consequences which one may derive from his untimely death are intellectual and political. The exercise of legitimate power is invulnerable. The picture of the new president swearing allegiance to the Constitution moved the nation and at the same time proved that in a democracy the presidency continues. The role that chance played in the president's death also shows that uncertainty stalks man in this life. But President Kennedy showed us that our unstable existence can be maintained by aspiring to that which is noble and ideal.

TEMAS A ESCOGER

Escríbanse unas 200 palabras sobre uno de los temas siguientes usando a lo menos 20 de las palabras y expresiones estudiadas en este capítulo.

1. El azar en la vida humana
2. Factores en la formación de un presidente
3. Los Estados Unidos y el mundo actual

chapter 3

THE SUBJUNCTIVE MOOD IN SPANISH

14. GENERAL STATEMENT

The subjunctive is a subjective mood, and is used far more often in Spanish than in English. Whereas the indicative mood asserts the independent existence or significance of a statement, the subjunctive mood reveals that a statement is dependent on another expression, often one of attitude. Because of this dependence, the subjunctive is used primarily in subordinate clauses.

The subjunctive often reveals that the speaker has doubts concerning the validity of an assertion or the possibility of accomplishing an action. It reflects the contingency inherent in all future events. It also gives known facts the color of subjectivity or of personal feeling. In short, the subjunctive mood deals with the realms of subjectivity, mental reservation, and uncertainty, in sharp contrast with the reality, independence, and objectivity of the indicative mood.

15. TIME SEQUENCE AND THE FOUR SUBJUNCTIVE TENSES

The subjunctive mood has four frequently used tenses in Spanish, and the appropriate one should always be chosen. The sequence of tenses is a useful, though not an infallible, guide for making the correct choice.

In Spanish the speaker's point of view almost always permits the same action or state to be expressed by an indicative or a subjunctive, with very little difference in the time of the verb in either mood. Thus each of the ten indicative tenses has its approximate temporal equivalent in one of the four subjunctive tenses. Moreover, in most cases the Spanish subjunctive may be translated by the English equivalent of the Spanish indicative form the subjunctive most closely resembles. At times *may* (present) or *might* (past) is also used. The following table is a sample conjugation in the singular of a regular first conjugation verb. There are ten indicative tenses (five simple, five compound), but only four subjunctive tenses (two simple, two compound). The future subjunctive (recognized by its distinctive –**re**) is no longer actively used, but is found in residual forms like proverbs and legal terminology.

Donde **estuvieres**, haz lo que **vieres**.	When in Rome, do as the Romans do.
Sea lo que **fuere**.	Be that as it may.
—De muy buena gana —respondió don Juan— ¡vamos, señor, donde **quisiereis**! (Cervantes: «La señora Cornelia»)	"Very willingly," replied Don Juan, "Let us go, sir, wherever you wish!"

INDICATIVE

	Simple		*Compound*
PRESENT	hablo, –as, –a	PRESENT PERFECT	he, has, ha — hablado
IMPERFECT	hablaba, –as, –a	PLUPERFECT	había, –ías, –ía — ha– blado
PRETERIT	hablé, –aste, –ó	PRETERIT PERFECT	hubo, hubiste, hubo — hablado
FUTURE	hablaré, –ás, –á	FUTURE PERFECT	habré, –ás, –á — hablado
CONDITIONAL	hablaría, –ías, –ía	CONDITIONAL PERFECT	habría, –ías, –ía — hablado

SUBJUNCTIVE

	Simple		*Compound*
PRESENT	hable, –es, –e	PRESENT PERFECT	haya, –as, –a — hablado
IMPERFECT	hablara, –as, –a	PLUPERFECT	hubiera, –as, –a — hablado
	or		or
	hablase, –es, –e		hubiese, –es, –e — hablado

Throughout Spanish America the **–ra** form of the subjunctive is the standard form in the spoken language; it is also the more common form in the literary language. In Spain both forms are common, in both spoken and written Spanish. (It should be pointed out that preference for a given form is often influenced by cultural or regional considerations.) Since the **–ra** form comes from a Latin pluperfect indicative rather than from a Latin subjunctive, it is also occasionally used in this temporal sense in written Spanish, especially among the nineteenth-century Romantic authors in Spain. In more recent times, authors from Galicia and northern Spain have revealed an especial predilection for this use of the **–ra** form.

> Por aquel mismo camino que le **llevara** tierra adentro, Ilé Eroriak volvió a Oiquixa. (PT)
>
> Along that same road that had taken him inland, Ilé Eroriak went back to Oiquixa.

In Spanish all conjugated verbs correspond broadly to past, present, or future time, but the disuse of the future subjunctive has caused the present subjunctive to fill the future gap in that mood. This contributes to making temporal boundaries among subjunctive tenses less sharply defined than those of the indicative. Since each subjunctive tense must embrace a broader temporal range than any indicative tense, it is understandable that there be some variation in the choice of the most appropriate subjunctive in certain circumstances.

The sequence of tenses refers to the general correspondence between the tense of a subjunctive verb and that of the verb on which it depends. Usually, (1) the present subjunctive follows a verb in a present tense; (2) the past subjunctive follows a verb in a past tense. Present here refers to the present, the future, and their compound tenses; past indicates imperfect, preterit, conditional, and their compound tenses.

Let us examine the first case. A present or future should produce a present subjunctive. But the present tense is frequently followed by a verb that clearly refers to a completed action, and in such cases any subjunctive must be in the past. Thus the first part of the sequence of tenses (present ⟶ present subjunctive) is too broad to encompass this one common exception.

No creo que Carlos **venga** hoy.	I don't believe that Charles is coming (will come) today.
No creo que Carlos **viniera** ayer.	I don't believe that Charles came yesterday.

The second part of the statement (past ⟶ past subjunctive) has fewer exceptions than part one. There are few cases in which a past tense does not produce a past subjunctive. Furthermore, the personal nature of the exceptions makes a meaningful description impractical at this level. Previous comments on the nature of the temporal boundaries of the subjunctive suggest why a native speaker of Spanish may feel drawn toward a future event in a given situation and thus use the present subjunctive after a past tense; nevertheless the rule that past ⟶ past will almost always prove right, although the native speaker may modify it from time to time.

SIMPLE TENSE

Le decía		
Le dije	QUE VINIERA	
Le diría		

I was telling him		
I told him	TO COME	
I would tell him		

COMPOUND TENSE

Le había dicho	QUE VINIERA
Le habría dicho	

I had told him	TO COME
I would have told him	

The choice of one tense from the four subjunctive tenses is simplified by the fact that the two compound subjunctives regularly follow the pattern of English compounds. Thus the sequence of tenses may be reserved as an aid in deciding which of the two simple tenses, present or imperfect, is correct in a given situation.

No creo que Vicente **haya venido.**	I don't believe Vincent has come.

| No creía que Vicente **hubiera venido**. | I didn't believe that Vincent had come. |

16. THE SUBJUNCTIVE IN NOUN CLAUSES

Although it may be used for the verb of an independent clause expressing doubt,

| Quizá(s) no **vaya**. | Perhaps he is not going. |

the subjunctive is found mainly in the verbs of three kinds of subordinate clauses: noun, adjective, and adverb. This chapter treats the first of these types.

The verb of a subordinate noun clause is subjunctive when it depends on a verb expressing necessity, (un)desirability, ignorance, doubt, emotion, or (im)possibility. The speaker's attitude about something that may or may not exist outside his mind causes the dependent verb to be subjunctive. It is important to bear in mind that the conjunction **que** introduces the noun clause with the subjunctive verb, and that only rarely is there a subjunctive without both **que** and a change of subject in the subordinate clause. The use of the subjunctive in noun clauses is common after expressions of:

A. Volition or desire
B. Doubt, denial, negation
C. Emotion
D. Certain impersonal expressions

A. VOLITION OR DESIRE

A mere indication that it is one person's will that another person or persons do or not do something, or that something happen or not happen, requires a subjunctive verb in the subordinate clause. In such constructions the subjunctive will follow expressions indicating any degree of volition (command, desire, approval, opposition, preference, advisability, suggestion, etc.).

Tengo ganas de que **sea** domingo otra vez. (CA)	I want it to be Sunday again.
Te ruego que **contestes** a todas mis preguntas.	I beg you to answer all my questions.
Recomendará que la niña **tome** más vitaminas.	He will recommend that the girl take more vitamins.
Ya es hora de que **empieces** a decirnos su nombre.	It's time for you to begin telling us his name.
La madre se opuso a que su hija **se casara** con un artista.	The mother opposed her daughter's marrying an artist.

La Liga de las Naciones quería evitar que la guerra **continuase.**	The League of Nations wanted . to keep (prevent) the war from continuing.
Habían sugerido que Lope **pagara** la cuenta la próxima vez.	They had suggested that Lope (should) pay the bill the next time.

Verbs of communication may also express will or volition, in which cases they require a subjunctive in the subordinate clause.

Le dije (telefoneé) a Carlos que estaríamos en la oficina mañana.	I told (telephoned) Charles that we would be in the office tomorrow.
Le dije (telefoneé) a Carlos que **viniera** aquí pronto.	I told (telephoned) Charles to come here soon.

In certain noun clauses an infinitive construction may be used after an expression of volition instead of the subjunctive. A limited number of verbs that indicate ordering, allowing, prohibiting, and advising are often followed by an infinitive rather than a subjunctive. This is most common when the subject of the subordinate clause is a pronoun, in which case the pronoun is the indirect object of the main verb. The important verbs that may take either the subjunctive or an infinitive construction are **mandar**, **ordenar**, **hacer**, **dejar**, **permitir**, **aconsejar**, **prohibir**, **impedir** (NOT PEDIR), and **proponer**.

Nos impidieron ir a la fiesta.	They prevented us from going to the party.
Me aconsejará ir a Portugal.	He will advise me to go to Portugal.
Te prohibo gastar más dinero.	I prohibit you from spending more money.
Hizo estudiar al muchacho.	He made the boy study.

The preceding sentences may also be rendered with the subjunctive in a subordinate noun clause.

Impidieron que **fuéramos** a la fiesta.
Me aconsejará que **vaya** a Portugal.
Prohibo que **gastes** más dinero.
Hizo que el muchacho **estudiase.**

It would be difficult to estimate accurately the relative frequency of these two widely used constructions. Nevertheless Spanish, like English, usually prefers the more economical means of expression whenever a choice is available.

B.   DOUBT, DENIAL, NEGATION

Nuance and connotation are important when dealing with verbs that indicate uncertainty or doubt. For example, the indicative in the following sentence stresses the speaker's conviction that John has actually eaten; the same example with the subjunctive reveals that a real doubt still exists in the speaker's mind.

Sospecho que Juan ha cenado.	I suspect that John has dined.
Sospecho que Juan **haya cenado.**	I suspect that John has (may have) dined.

In short, a verb's connotative range as well as the nuance intended by the speaker often determines whether the verb in the subordinate clause will be in the subjunctive or in the indicative. Generally verbs of negation, doubt, or uncertainty produce the subjunctive; however, when the element of negation, doubt, or uncertainty is weakened and the verb leans toward affirmation, the indicative is used. The predominant nuance of a particular verb, then, not any fixed meaning, determines the mood of the subordinate clause.

No rule subsumes all possibilities; nevertheless, verbs like **dudar** and **negar** leave little margin for affirmation and are only infrequently followed by the indicative. **No creer**, **sospechar**, and similar verbs usually result in a subjunctive but also have a meaning that permits their use with the indicative for affirmation. Verbs like **creer** and **presumir** ordinarily indicate a greater degree of certainty than do their English equivalents and therefore normally take the indicative. In the most general of terms, any verb used to reveal genuine doubt or absolute denial takes the subjunctive in its subordinate clause; any verb used to indicate affirmation or conviction will take the indicative. Close attention to literary samples will show the considerable variation in mood that results from the personal, connotative use of verbs.

The following sentences illustrate just a few of the many possibilities on a scale ranging from certainty–belief to uncertainty–negation. Some are borderline examples that could also take the verb in the other mood.

Afirmo que viene.	I say that he is coming.
Sé que viene.	I know that he is coming.
Creo que viene.	I believe that he is coming.
Es que viene.	It is that he is coming.
No dudo que viene.	I don't doubt that he is coming.
No es que **venga.**	It isn't that he is coming.
No creo que **venga.**	I don't believe that he is coming.
Dudo que **venga.**	I doubt that he is coming.
Niego que **venga.**	I deny that he is coming.

A question to which the speaker expects an answer confirming his own opinion takes the indicative. A question that indicates real doubt on the part of the speaker requires the subjunctive.

¿No cree Vd. que está enamorado?	Don't you believe he is in love? (I certainly do.)
¿Cree Vd. que **esté** enamorado?	Do you believe he is (may be) in love? (I'm not sure.)

An independent clause after adverbs taking the subjunctive when they indicate uncertainty (**acaso**, **tal vez**, **quizá**[s]) will use the indicative when the sense of futurity is stronger than the sense of uncertainty, or when the latter is weak or absent.

Quizá esperábamos que nos **contara** grandes cosas. (LM)	Maybe we were hoping he would tell us great things.
Tal vez hoy encontraremos a uno de ellos . . . (SV)	Perhaps today we shall find one of them . . .
Tal vez **venga** hoy.	Perhaps he is coming (may come) today.
Tal vez vino ayer.	Perhaps he came yesterday.

Finally, whereas most noun clauses require a change of subject for the subordinate verb to be in the subjunctive, expressions of doubt and uncertainty normally take the subjunctive even without a change of subject.

No creo que **vaya** a verle.	I don't believe that I am going to see him.
Carlos duda que **tenga** bastante dinero.	Charles doubts that he (Charles) has enough money.
Carlos duda tener bastante dinero.	Charles doubts that he (Charles) has enough money. (an infrequent literary equivalent for the preceding sentence)

C. EMOTION

The subjunctive is used in a subordinate clause following expressions that indicate any gradation of emotion or feeling: fear, anger, joy, sadness, shame, surprise, etc.

Siento que **esté** lloviendo.	I am sorry that it is raining.
Lo siento, pero está lloviendo.	I am sorry, but it is raining.

Que subordinates the verb **llover** and makes it dependent on an expression of feeling. **Pero** coordinates two independent statements; hence the indicative.

Me sorprendió que les **hablases** así.	It surprised me that you spoke (should speak) to them that way.

Nos enfada que **hayas usado** el coche sin permiso.	We are angry that you (have) used the car without permission.
Tiene vergüenza (de) que la **vieran** tan mal vestida.	She is ashamed that they saw her so poorly dressed.
A Martín le extraña que el policía no le **reconozca.** (LC)	It seems strange to Martin that the policeman doesn't recognize him.

Temer (to fear) and **esperar** (to hope) may express certainty or future time rather than feeling. The indicative follows these verbs when they are so used. In the following sentence **temer** may indicate, for example, that the speaker is certain Mr. X has returned for yet another handout.

Temo que ha venido a pedirme otro favor.	I am afraid he has come to ask another favor of me.
Pero me temo que te pareces demasiado a tu padre. (LM)	But I fear that you look too much like your father.
Espero que vendrá pronto.	I hope that he will come soon.

When the subject doesn't change after an expression of emotion or feeling, the following verb is normally an infinitive and no clause is used.

Me alegro de estar con Vds.	I am glad to be with you.
Tiene miedo de hablar con el jefe.	He is afraid to speak with the boss.

D.   CERTAIN IMPERSONAL EXPRESSIONS

In an impersonal expression in English there is a meaningless *it* anticipating the true subject which follows. In Spanish *it* is contained in the verb. After an impersonal expression that does not indicate certainty, Spanish uses a subjunctive in the subordinate clause. At this point it is important to distinguish between an impersonal expression followed by the infinitive and one followed by a subordinate clause with a subjunctive verb. When an impersonal expression in English is followed directly by an infinitive, the same construction (impersonal expression + infinitive) is used in Spanish; but whenever the impersonal expression and the infinitive are separated in English by an indirect object, the Spanish equivalent of this construction requires a subordinate clause with a subjunctive verb.

Basta leer el resumen.	It is enough to read the summary.
Basta que **leas** el resumen.	It is enough for you to read (that you read) the summary.
Será necesario terminar en seguida.	It will be necessary to finish immediately.

Será necesario que Vd. **termine** en seguida.	It will be necessary for you to finish (that you finish) immediately.
Convendría ir mañana.	It would be a good idea to go tomorrow.
Convendría que **fuéramos** mañana.	It would be a good idea for us to go (that we go) tomorrow.

The preceding examples illustrate how in Spanish a clause, never a preposition, renders the English *for one to do* after an impersonal expression.

Ha tomado tres cafés y es lógico que **esté** nervioso.	He has had three (cups of) coffee, and it's logical for him to be nervous.
Es (parece) absurdo que un muchacho **necesite** tomar píldoras para dormir.	It is (seems) absurd for a boy to have to take pills in order to sleep.
Más valdría que no **te metieras** en los asuntos de los demás. (N)	It would be better for you not to meddle in other people's affairs.

Compare the mood of the verb in the following sentences.

| Es cierto que la acompañó a su casa. | It is certain that he accompanied her home. |
| No es cierto que la **acompañara** a su casa. | It is not certain that he accompanied her home. |

Notice also that **fácil** and **difícil** do not mean *easy* and *difficult* when used in impersonal expressions followed by a dependent clause.

| Es fácil (difícil) que **venga**. | It is likely (unlikely) that he is coming. |
| Le es fácil (difícil) venir. | It is easy (difficult) for him to come. |

In summary, an impersonal expression is followed by the infinitive (1) when no specified subject follows, and (2) when the logical subject can be expressed as an indirect object pronoun. This second use is an optional substitute for the clause with the subjunctive.

| 1. Importa acabarlo ahora. | It is important to finish it now. |
| 2. Te importa acabarlo ahora.
or
Importa que lo **acabes** ahora. | It is important for you to finish it now. |

EXERCISES

1. Louis insists that you go up to the park with him. 2. Will you allow me to accompany you as far as the corner? 3. The poor criminal can't conceive that they want to hang him. 4. I prevented Charles from seeing

them. 5. It wasn't that he felt like studying. 6. I am glad you have waited for her. 7. Forgive me for having told you not to come. 8. My only desire has been for them to leave me in peace. 9. I asked to see the soldier. 10. I didn't have the slightest idea that you were a musician. 11. He defends me and will not let anyone hurt me. 12. It is a pity that I didn't keep the clipping. 13. John suggested to him that he leave Spain. 14. Someone ordered them to do it. 15. I know it annoys him that we are friends. 16. I have never believed that it is a sin to tell the truth. 17. I wrote the letter in (con) the hope that Mary might read it. 18. It is evident that he hasn't finished the task. 19. It is unlikely that this campus will have more than 10,000 students. 20. I believe they will win the championship. Don't you believe they will win it? 21. His parents were unhappy, but he got a divorce anyway. 22. It will be necessary to pay federal taxes before April 15. 23. I wrote you that we would come in the afternoon. 24. I never suggested that they get married. 25. She is ashamed that her son acted that way. 26. The officer became angry because they disobeyed his orders. 27. She telephoned him to wait for her at the market. 28. The daughter opposed her father's wishes. 29. She would prefer that her husband never mention his first wife. 30. Our enemies deny that we are right. 31. We were surprised that the flight took only six hours. ·32. I am not saying that there is no hope for him. 33. It astonished everyone that the governor pardoned him. 34. The victims were grateful that help arrived so soon. 35. I wish to underline the necessity of everyone's being present. 36. The woman didn't believe her son was lost. 37. It would be preferable for you to study elsewhere. 38. I presume that they will arrive at two o'clock. 39. She suspects they may not be telling the truth. 40. He made me try the wine he brought from Jerez.

17. SELECCION LITERARIA

Viaje a la Alcarria

Camilo José Cela

Camilo José Cela figura entre los grandes estilistas de la literatura española. Es, sin duda, el mejor conocido de los autores de la postguerra, y sus novelas La familia de Pascual Duarte *y* La colmena *gozan de una popularidad internacional. En* Viaje a la Alcarria, *publicada por primera vez en 1952, el autor relata sus viajes a pie por la Alcarria, región de la provincia de Guadalajara. La acción de la selección siguiente tiene lugar la mañana en que el autor-viajero se dirige a la estación para tomar el tren que le llevará a la Alcarria.*

A las verjas del Jardín[1] Botánico, el viajero siente—a veces le pasa—un repentino escalofrío. Enciende un pitillo[2] y procura[3] alejar de su cabeza los malos pensamientos. Dos tranviarios pasan con las manos en los bolsillos,[4] la colilla[5] entre los labios,[6] sin decir ni palabra. Un niño harapiento[7] hoza
5 con un palito[8] en un montón[9] de basura. Al paso del viajero levanta la frente[10] y se echa a un lado, como disimulando. El niño ignora que las apariencias[11] engañan, que debajo de una mala capa puede esconderse un buen bebedor; que en el pecho del viajero, de extraño, quizá temeroso aspecto,[11] encontraría un corazón de par en par[12] abierto, como las puertas
10 del campo. El niño, que mira receloso como un perro castigado, tampoco sabe hasta qué punto[13] el viajero siente una ternura infinita hacia los niños nómadas, que, rompiendo ya el día, hurgan con un palito en los frescos, en los tibios, en los aromáticos montones de basura.

Camino del[14] matadero pasan unas ovejas calvas, mugrientas, que llevan
15 una B pintada en rojo sobre el lomo.[15] Los dos hombres que las conducen les pegan bastonazos,[16] de cuando en cuando, por entretenerse quizá, mientras ellas, con un gesto en la mirada entre ruin y estúpido, se obstinan en lamer, de pasada, el sucio, estéril asfalto . . . .

En la bajada de la Estación, algunas mujeres ofrecen al viajero tabaco,
20 plátanos, bocadillos[17] de tortilla.[18] Se ven soldados con su maleta[19] de madera al hombro y campesinos de sombrero flexible que vuelven a su lugar.[20] En el patio está formada la larga, lenta cola de los billetes.[21] Una familia duerme sobre un banco[22] de hierro, debajo de un letrero que advierte: «Cuidado con los rateros». Desde las paredes[23] saludan al viajero los a-
25 nuncios de los productos de hace treinta y cinco años, de los remedios que ya no existen, de los emplastos porosos, los calzoncillos contra catarros, los inefables, automáticos modos de combatir la calvicie.

18. NOTES

1. el jardín zoológico (botánico)—zoo (botanical garden)
    el jardín—garden
    la huerta—garden
    el huerto—garden, orchard
    el vergel—garden

    Jardín is for flowers and ornamental plants. Vegetables are raised in a **huerta**; in a more particular sense, **huerta** refers to the rich, irrigated farmland of Valencia and Murcia. **Huerto** is a flower garden with or without trees; it is also an orchard. **Vergel** is a literary term suggesting a highly idealized or a perfect garden. (Regional usage may vary a little on **huerto** and **huerta**.)

    Del monte en la ladera   On the slope of the mountain
    por mi mano plantado tengo un   I have a garden planted by my

huerto.
(Fray Luis de León: «Vida retirada»)

own hand.

Tenía además este **jardín**, en el lado que se unía con la **huerta**, un bosquecillo de lilas y saucos. (ZA)

This garden also had, on the side adjoining the vegetable patch, a thicket of lilacs and elderberry bushes.

2. el pitillo—cigarette
   el cigarrillo—cigarette

Cigarrillo is used throughout the Spanish-speaking world; **pitillo** is used in Spain. **Cigarro**, *cigar*, also means *cigarette* in some parts of Spanish America.

3. procurar—to try

Procurar is a synonym of **intentar** and **tratar** (de). *To procure* is usually rendered by **conseguir** or **obtener**.

Yo siempre os aconsejaré que **procuréis** ser mejores de lo que sois . . . (JM)

I shall always advise you to try to be better than you are . . .

Intentó (**trató de**) explicarlo.

He tried to explain it.

Consiguieron lo que querían.

They procured (obtained) what they wanted.

4. el bolsillo—pocket
   el bolso—pocketbook, purse
   la bolsa—bag, sack, pouch; pocketbook, purse
   la bolsa—the stockmarket

Pocketbook is generally **bolsa** when the shape is that of a bag or sack. **Bolso** is usually longer than it is deep.

A doña Monserrate le han robado el **bolso** en la iglesia. (LC)

They stole Doña Monserrate's handbag from her in church.

Ha perdido mucho dinero jugando a la **bolsa**.

He lost a great deal of money (by) playing the market.

5. la colilla—butt of a cigarette or cigar
   la cola—tail
   el rabo—tail
   hacer cola—to stand in line
   con el rabo entre piernas—dejected
   de cabo a rabo—from one end to the other

Cola is the standard term for *tail* and is used much more than **rabo**. It is used for birds, reptiles, and most animals. **Rabo** often replaces

cola on a colloquial level with little change in meaning. It is also used for humorous or ironic effect. For example, an animal's tail, **cola**, might be referred to as **rabo** when crooked, shortened, or in any way changed.

Uno de los pájaros era un pavo real con la **cola** sin desplegar. . . . (CA)

One of the birds was a peacock with its tail unspread. . . .

Le dice «Sultán, ven» y el gato viene moviendo su **rabo** hermoso, que parece un plumero. (LC)

He says, "Sultan, come here," and the cat comes, moving its beautiful tail which resembles a feather duster.

Llevan dos horas **haciendo cola**.

They have been standing in line for two hours.

Atado a la argolla de un portal, moviendo el **rabo** con alegría, está el burro. (VA)

The burro, tied to the iron ring on the door, is happily moving its tail.

6. el labio—lip
   la labia—persuasive speech, fluency

Me corté el **labio** con la navaja.

I cut my lip with the razor.

Buena **labia** ya tienes tú, para lo joven que eres. (NOC)

You are quite a talker for one who is so young.

7. harapiento—ragged, tattered
   hambriento—hungry
   mugriento—greasy, grimy
   sangriento—bloody
   sediento—thirsty

Hambriento and **sediento** are used mainly in literature. **Tener hambre** or **tener sed** is much more common than **estar hambriento** or **estar sediento**; however, **hambriento** and **sediento** are common as adjectives not used in immediate conjunction with a verb.

Las calles de la ciudad estaban llenas de perros **hambrientos**.

The streets of the city were full of hungry dogs.

8. el palito—small stick
   el palo—pole, stick; mast
   el palillo—toothpick
   la paliza—beating, blow with a stick
   de tal palo, tal astilla—a chip off the old block

¿Estarán usados los **palillos**? Aquí son capaces de todo. (LN)

Do you think these toothpicks have been used?
They are capable of anything here.

Su padre le dio una **paliza** por haber roto la ventana.	His father gave him a beating because he broke the window.

9. el montón—pile, heap
   ser del montón—to be ordinary, common

Están allí, delante de aquel **montón** de arena. (BA)	There they are in front of that pile of sand.
Ese hombre **es del montón**.	That man is quite ordinary.

10. la frente—forehead; front
    el frente—(battle) front
    hacer frente a—to face, resist

El ejército estaba en el **frente** ruso.	The army was on the Russian front.
Hicieron frente al ataque con calma.	They faced the attack calmly.

11. la apariencia—appearance
    el aspecto—appearance, look
    tener buen (mal) aspecto—to look well (bad)
    la aparición—appearance; apparition
    juzgar por las apariencias—to judge by appearances

Apariencia refers mainly to the external appearance of a person or thing. **Aspecto** often includes an expression or look. **Aparición** refers to a sudden appearance or coming into sight.

Por su **apariencia** sabíamos que era inglés.	From his appearance we knew that he was English.
Por su **aspecto**, dedujo que había ocurrido algo. (F)	From his appearance, he deduced that something had happened.
El **aspecto** del cielo me da miedo.	The appearance of the sky frightens me.
La **aparición** de Carlos en la fiesta nos sorprendió a todos.	The appearance of Charles at the party surprised us all.

12. de par en par abierto—wide open (often abierto is not expressed)
    par (adj.)—even
    (los números) pares y nones—even and odd (numbers)
    un par de—a few, a couple; a pair (of shoes, gloves, etc.)
    sin par—peerless, without equal
    la pareja—couple; pair of Guardias Civiles
    el matrimonio—(married) couple

Me parece que intenté levantarme **un par de** veces. (LM)	It seems to me that I attempted to get up a couple of times.
Cuando llegamos, varias **parejas** ya estaban bailando.	When we arrived, several couples were already dancing.

No conozco a ningún **matrimonio** que sea más feliz que ellos. | I don't know any couple that is happier than they are.

13. el punto—point
la punta—point
estar a punto de—to be about to, on the point of
en punto—sharp, on the dot
el punto de vista—point of view

Punto means *point* in the sense of *period, dot,* or *point* in an argument or discussion. **Punta** refers to what has a sharp or projecting end or tip, and by extension anything that can be compared with such a point.

Este lápiz no tiene **punta**. | This pencil has no point.

No veo el **punto** de su informe. | I don't see the point of your report.

Vino a las seis **en punto**. | He came at six o'clock sharp.

14. camino de—on the way to, to
rumbo a—on the way to (used especially with reference to the sea)

Camino de Madrid, paramos en Cuenca a almorzar. | On the way to Madrid, we stopped in Cuenca to have lunch.

Rumbo a Cuba, visitaron muchas islas tropicales. | On the way to Cuba, they visited many tropical islands.

15. el lomo—back (of animal or book)
el respaldo—back (of chair)
la espalda—back (of a person); plural, back or shoulders
el dorso—back (of the hand); other side, back (of a piece of paper)
al fondo de—in (at) the back of
los números atrasados de una revista—back issues of a magazine

El pasará su mano por tu **lomo**, te cepillará y peinará tu crin. (SV) | He will rub his hand along your back, brush you, and comb your mane.

Estaban reunidos **al fondo del** café. | They were gathered in the back of the café.

16. pegar bastonazos—to strike blows with a staff, cane, etc.
pegar—to stick, paste (takes an object); to beat, hit
pegarse—to stick, adhere; to catch (a disease)
pegado a—right up next to; stuck to

Pegar, which means *to beat, to strike,* and *to paste,* often replaces **dar** in expressions in which a particular type of blow is specified.

Se pegó un tiro. | He shot himself.

Le **pegué** un bofetón (un puñetazo). | I slapped (punched) him.

Va pegando recortes en un cuaderno que ha sacado del cajón.	He pastes clippings in a notebook he has taken out of the drawer.
Encontraron al chico **pegado** a la pared.	They found the boy right up against the wall.
Yungo sentía como **se le pegaba** la camisa al cuerpo, lleno de sudor. (SV)	Yungo felt how his shirt stuck to his body, covered with sweat.

17. el bocadillo—sandwich
    el emparedado, el sandwich—sandwich

    Bocadillo is made with a roll. **Sandwich,** an Anglicism, has replaced **emparedado** in most parts of the Spanish-speaking world. Both are made with sliced bread.

18. la tortilla—omelette in Spain; thin, baked cornmeal cake in Mexico and other parts of Spanish America

19. la maleta—suitcase
    el maletín—overnight bag; physician's bag
    la valija—valise; mail bag
    el baúl—trunk
    el equipaje—baggage, luggage

Todavía no ha hecho la **maleta**.	He still has not packed his bag.
Dejaron el **baúl** en el garaje.	They left the trunk in the garage.
Pienso mandar nuestro **equipaje** a la estación.	I intend to send our baggage to the station.

20. el lugar—village, hamlet; place
    en lugar de—in place of, instead of
    tener lugar—to take place

En un **lugar** de la Mancha, de cuyo nombre no quiero acordarme . . .	In a village of La Mancha, whose name I have no desire to recall . . . (opening line of Cervantes' *Don Quixote de la Mancha*)
Tuvo lugar mientras estábamos en Italia.	It took place while we were in Italy.

21. el billete—ticket; bank note, bill (currency)
    el boleto—ticket (in Spanish America)

22. el banco—bench; bank; school (of fish)
    la banca—bench; banking, bank

A bench with a back is usually **banco**, whereas **banca** ordinarily has no back. **Banca** sometimes renders *bank* in the technical language of economics or finance. It is also *bank* with reference to gambling.

En este país la **banca** privada está constituida por veinte **bancos** regionales.	In this country, twenty regional banks constitute private banking.
Pasan los **bancos** de sardinas y el agua fosforece. (LE)	Schools of sardines swim by, and the water has a phosphorescent glow.

23. la pared—wall
    el paredón—wall
    el muro, la muralla—wall
    el malecón—sea wall, dike
    la tapia—wall
    el tabique—partition, wall
    más sordo que una tapia—stone deaf

La pared is the standard word for *wall* (inside or outside) in most contexts. **Paredón** normally refers to the part of a wall that remains standing among ruins. **Muro** suggests a thick wall of a building or fortress. **Muralla** is a large defensive wall or rampart. **Malecón** refers to a sea wall, dike, or breakwater, and often has a road on top of it. **Tapia** is an outside masonry wall, usually of adobe or brick, used to enclose a garden, cemetery, orchard, etc. It is frequently used in the plural. **Tabique** suggests a very thin wall or partition.

Un silencio profundo reina en el llano; comienzan a aparecer a los lados del camino **paredones** derruídos. (RDQ)	A deep silence reigns over the plain; ruined walls begin to appear on both sides of the road.
Desde el camino se veían las **murallas** de la vieja ciudad.	From the road the walls of the old city were visible.
Escuchándole, se cree estar, de nuevo, en Veracruz, y, como él, paseando por el **malecón** . . . (IC)	Listening to him, you think you are in Veracruz again, and, like him, walking along the sea wall. . .
A través de un **tabique**, se oye cantar a las niñas de la escuela. (VA)	Through the (thin) wall you can hear the schoolgirls sing.
Volverán las tupidas madreselvas de tu jardín las **tapias** a escalar, (Gustavo Adolfo Bécquer: «Rima LIII»)	The thick honeysuckle will again climb your garden walls,

EXERCISES ON NOTES

1. He moistened the tip of the pencil with his tongue. 2. He played the

market and lost his shirt. 3. To judge by their appearance, that couple must be wealthy. 4. He hit the dog with a stick when it tried to eat the meat. 5. I went to the bank to change a $1,000 bill. 6. They jumped [over] the cemetery wall. 7. The worst thing about traveling is packing and unpacking the suitcase. 8. He was on the point of sending the soldier to the front. 9. On the way to Chicago we stopped in Cleveland. 10. She is always complaining that her back aches. 11. Oregon is famous for its orchards. 12. One of the bloodiest battles of the war took place here. 13. Yesterday afternoon we saw a school of fish near the [sea] wall. 14. He folded the newspaper, and put it in his jacket pocket. 15. The governor called [up] the reserve to resist the insurrectionists. 16. He left the windows wide open, and the rain flooded the room. 17. Lázaro was a ragged and hungry boy. 18. Although she doesn't look well, she is very healthy. 19. His uncle was so depressed that he shot himself. 20. The thirsty soldiers entered the tavern and sat down in the back. 21. Few dishes are as tasty as Spanish omelette. 22. I can't understand the point of his question. 23. The honey on the table stuck to his fingers. 24. Celestina was persuasive, for she had the gift of gab. 25. I miss the cigarettes we used to buy in Rome. 26. The trunk arrived three months after the rest of the baggage. 27. Why don't we spend a couple of days in Málaga? 28. Try to be more punctual the next time. 29. The appearance of the sky worried him. 30. The boy was stroking the dog's back. 31. Sometimes the sheets stick to my body. 32. She doesn't take care of her appearance. 33. He wiped his mouth with the back of his hand. 34. The mirror on the wall was broken. 35. The evening newspapers were in a pile on the sidewalk. 36. The parrot has a long, beautiful tail. 37. He has the appearance and the manners of a gentleman. 38. The student had the answer on the tip of his tongue. 39. Banking is an interesting career. 40. He turned his back on me when I was about to ask him a question.

CUESTIONARIO

a. contenido

1. ¿Por qué cree Vd. que el viajero enciende un pitillo?
2. ¿Qué significa «debajo de una mala capa puede esconderse un buen bebedor»?
3. ¿Cómo sabemos que el viajero es un hombre bondadoso?
4. Describa Vd. la escena de crueldad presenciada por el viajero.
5. ¿Qué clase de personas se ven en la bajada de la estación?

b. estilo

1. ¿Cómo hace Cela que el lector simpatice con el niño?
2. En general, ¿qué connotación tiene la palabra *basura*?
3. ¿Qué fuerzas sugestivas tienen los adjetivos empleados para calificar la basura?
4. ¿En qué consiste el efecto pictórico de la escena de las ovejas?
5. ¿Hay algún ejemplo de ironía en el último párrafo? Coméntelo Vd.

TEMA—TRADUCCION

On reaching the station the traveler learns that he has missed the train. He lights a cigarette and begins to think how he can spend the time he has left until the arrival of the next train. He checks his baggage and then asks the ticket agent to recommend some place that has a great deal of interest for the tourist. The latter suggests that he go to the Botanical Gardens (*singular*).

As he leaves the station, vendors attempt to sell him, among other things, bananas, sandwiches, and tobacco. He sees, along the wall of an old building, soldiers standing in line waiting for a bus. A few minutes later he notices a ragged boy with his hands in his pockets. The lad is calling a dog which is sniffing [at] a pile of trash. A little farther down the street the traveler observes an old man picking up cigarette butts. To judge from the man's appearance, he must be very poor. The traveler turns the corner and on finding an unoccupied bench sits down to rest.

Soon two shepherds pass by leading a flock of sheep to the slaughterhouse. From time to time, perhaps to amuse themselves, they strike the poor animals with their staffs. The traveler is surprised by the indifference of the sheep, which continue to lick the dirty asphalt while the shepherds lead them [along] to their death.

Once rested, the traveler goes (**dirigirse a**) to the Botanical Gardens, which are surrounded by a stone wall. Unfortunately it is Monday, and the Gardens are closed on Mondays. Nevertheless, through the grating of the main entrance he is able to make out an orchard of rare trees. Later, since the city offers few points of interest, the traveler decides to go on to the main square, where he enjoys lunch on the terrace of the city's most popular café. There the hours fly by, and it is soon time for him to return to the station.

TEMAS A ESCOGER

Escríbanse unas 200 palabras sobre uno de los temas siguientes usando a lo menos 20 de las palabras y expresiones estudiadas en este capítulo.

1. Una visita al Jardín Botánico
2. Una descripción de una estación ferroviaria
3. Una experiencia notable de viajero

chapter 4

THE SUBJUNCTIVE MOOD—Continued

19. THE SUBJUNCTIVE IN ADJECTIVE CLAUSES

The verb in an adjective clause is subjunctive when the referent of the adjective clause is (A) negative, (B) indefinite, or (C) hypothetical. An adjective clause modifying a referent that doesn't exist or that is problematical understandably requires a subjunctive verb to reflect the nature of this referent.

A. NEGATIVE REFERENT

Ahora no hay ningún sastre que **corte** una levita como aquéllas. (LP)	Now there is no tailor who cuts a frock coat like those.
No me mostraron ningún sombrero que me **gustase**.	They didn't show me any hat that I liked.
En toda España no hay ciudad que **se parezca** más al infierno que Barcelona. (N)	In all Spain there is no city that is more like hell than Barcelona.

B. INDEFINITE REFERENT

The future or the conditional frequently introduces this construction. Here the subjunctive in the adjective clause indicates something that has not yet happened or is unknown. The adjective clause with a subjunctive verb often modifies the referent so as to give it the force of the English what*ever*, who*ever*, wher*ever*, etc.

Tomaré el tren que Vd. dice.	I shall take the train that you say.
Tomaré el tren que Vd. **diga**.	I shall take the (whatever, any) train that you say.

The antecedent in the first example is known and definite. In the second sentence the train has not yet been identified; the referent is consequently indefinite and requires that the verb of the adjective clause be subjunctive. The adjective **cualquier**, *any*, is sometimes used to strengthen the idea of *any at all, whatever, whoever, wherever* inherent in the subjunctive mood.

Tomaré cualquier tren que Vd. **diga**.	I shall take any train (whatsoever) that you say.
Dijo que haría lo que mandaron.	He said he would do what they ordered.
Dijo que haría lo que (cualquier cosa que) **mandaran**.	He said he would do what(ever) they ordered.

The example with **mandaron** expresses willingness to comply with a known order. **Mandaran** indicates that the nature of the command is still unknown, and strongly suggests that the order will be carried out no matter what it is.

Págale lo que **creas** justo.	Pay him what(ever) you think is fair.
Le pagué lo que creí justo.	I paid him what I thought was fair.
La recibiré lo mejor que **pueda**.	I shall receive her as well as I can.
La recibí lo mejor que pude.	I received her as well as I could.
Hacemos lo que podemos.	We do what we can.
Hicimos lo que pudimos.	We did what we could.
Haremos lo que **podamos**.	We shall do what(ever) we can.
Haríamos lo que **pudiéramos**.	We would do what(ever) we could.
Contaré en mi novela lo que **vea** en París.	I shall tell in my novel what I see in Paris.

C. HYPOTHETICAL REFERENT

The main verb in this construction usually indicates some type of seeking, searching, desiring, or asking. When the object of the search (i.e., the referent of the adjective clause) is hypothetical, the verb of the adjective clause is subjunctive, because the existence of the referent is at most a supposition.

¿Hay alguien que no **esté** conforme?	Is there someone who is not in agreement?
Traiga media docena de huevos que **estén** bien frescos.	Bring half a dozen eggs that are nice and fresh.
Quieren algo viejo que ya no **sirva** para otra cosa.	They want something old that is no longer good for anything else.

Notice, however, that when **un** or **algún** is replaced by the definite article, the referent becomes definite and the indicative is used.

Busco el coche que es barato.	I am looking for the (specific) car that (I know from experience) is cheap.
Busco un coche que **sea** barato.	I am looking for a (any) car that is cheap. (I do not know from experience that it actually exists.)

20. THE SUBJUNCTIVE IN TWO TYPES OF ADVERB CLAUSES

A. In any adverb clause introduced by certain conjunctions (or synonymous conjunctions), the verb must always be subjunctive. The time of this verb is usually future when compared to that of the main verb, and most of these sentences indicate an anticipated event or the dependence of one event on another event. This future contingency (it is possible the action may never be realized) accounts for the subjunctive mood. It will be noticed, however, that unlike most types of noun and adjective clauses, where the use of either the subjunctive or the indicative presents the possibility of sharp contrast, no such contrast is possible in these adverb clauses. Finally, since these conjunctions are very common in Spanish, it is important to be able to recall them without hesitation. Any mnemonic device that proves helpful should be used.

PA CASE AA   **Pennsylvania Case** (for) **Art Appreciation**

1. para que ⎫ in order that, so that
   a fin de que ⎭
2. con tal (de) que—provided that
3. antes (de) que—before
4. sin que—without
5. en caso (de) que—in case
6. a menos que ⎫ unless
   a no ser que ⎭

The subjunctive after the preceding conjunctions presents no special problem. Nevertheless one should keep in mind the contrast between a preposition-infinitive construction and a subordinate adverb clause where there is a change of subject between the main clause and the subordinate clause. Also, the **de** in most conjunctions formed by adding **que** to a compound preposition is normally omitted; **que** is the sign of the conjunction, and the original **de** of the preposition is no longer essential to the meaning of the conjunction.

Trabaja mucho para pagar el coche.	He works hard (in order) to pay for his car. (he—he)
Trabaja mucho **para que** su hijo **tenga** un nuevo coche.	He works hard in order (so) that his son may have a new car. (he—son)
Comimos antes de salir.	We ate before leaving. (we—we)
Comimos **antes (de) que salieran.**	We ate before they left. (we—they)
Entré sin verles.	I entered without seeing them. (I—I)
Entré **sin que** me **vieran.**	I entered without their seeing me. (I—they)

In certain circumstances other conjunctions replace **para que**. **A que** is used after verbs of motion. **Porque** emphasizes the strong purpose behind an action as well as its more uncertain outcome. **De modo (manera) que** may stress both means by which and purpose. It is not, however, always a subordinating conjunction, and is followed by the indicative when used as a locution introducing an independent clause.

Ha venido **a que** el médico le **reconozca**.	He has come so that the doctor will examine him.
Todos los días rezaba **porque volvieras** pronto. (FPD)	Every day I used to pray that you would come back soon.
—Haz todo lo posible **porque** nos **veamos** hoy. (TV)	"Do everything you can so that we can see each other today."
Hágalo Vd. **de modo que** nadie **se entere**.	Do it so (in such a way) that nobody finds out.
¿**De manera que** tú estás dispuesto a encargarte de este asunto? (ZA)	So (that) you are willing to take charge of this matter?
No pasaba un solo día **sin que riñera** con las vecinas.	Not a single day passed without her quarreling (that she didn't quarrel) with the neighbors.
En caso (de) que aún no **hayan llegado**, recíbalos cordialmente.	In case they have not yet arrived, receive them cordially.
Tenga cuidado **de miedo que sospechen** la verdad.	Be careful lest they suspect the truth.
Puedes acompañarnos **con tal (de) que te portes** bien.	You may accompany us provided that you behave well.
Te veremos **antes que salgas** para México.	We shall see you before you leave for Mexico.

B. Conjunctions of a second group introduce adverb clauses that may refer to unattained (future) or attained (past or present) time. When they refer to the future, to something that may never happen, these conjunctions also require the subjunctive. When the verb following the conjunction refers to the past or the present, it is in the indicative mood.

1. en cuanto
   tan pronto como } as soon as
2. cuando—when
3. después (de) que—after
4. hasta que—until
5. mientras—as long as, while
6. una vez que—once

Hablaba de irse a México **cuando obtuviera** el doctorado.	He used to talk of going to Mexico when he received his Ph.D.

No te bañes **hasta que sepas** nadar.

Don't go in the water until you know how to swim.

Una vez que lo **hayas terminado**, avísame.

Once you have finished it, let me know.

Mientras yo **viva**, no existe la muerte. (FM)

As long as I am alive, death does not exist.

La madre murió en un bombardeo **mientras** hacía cola para conseguir alimentos. (LN)

The mother died in the bombing while she was standing in line for food.

Cerraron las puertas **en cuanto** nos vieron.

They closed the doors as soon as they saw us.

Cerrarán las puertas **en cuanto** nos **vean**.

They will close the doors as soon as they see us.

Después que termina, siempre viene a verme.

After he finishes, he always comes to see me.

Después que terminó, vino a verme.

After he finished, he came to see me.

Después que termine, vendrá a verme.

After he finishes, he will come to see me.

Aguardó **hasta que** devolvieron el libro.

He waited until they returned the book.

Aguardará **hasta que devuelvan** el libro.

He will wait until they return the book.

A que is used not only for **para que** (20 A), but also for **hasta que**. It means *for*, with a nuance of *until*, and is used regularly after *to wait*. **Hasta que** is used to stress the idea of *until* or *up to the moment when*. Since **a que** indicates purpose, it always takes the subjunctive.

Sin aguardar **a que** me **contestara**, eché a correr hacia la puerta.

Without waiting for him to answer me, I began to run toward the door.

Fernando se tendió a esperar **a que** el sol **se ocultase** para seguir su marcha y se durmió. (CP)

Fernando stretched out to wait for the sun to set before continuing his journey and fell asleep.

Aunque, *although*, and **a pesar de que**, *in spite of the fact that*, take the subjunctive to express doubt, to indicate that something is not conceded to be a fact, and to give an emotional stress to any fact.

Aunque lo han hecho, lo negarán.

Although they have done it, they will deny it.

Aunque lo **hayan hecho**, lo negarán.

Although they (may) have done it, they will deny it.

The first example indicates knowledge or belief that they have done it.

The second may indicate the speaker's uncertainty or may stress emotionally what he knows to be a fact.

A pesar de que Juan **es** listo, no logrará su propósito.	In spite of the fact that John is clever, he will not achieve his goal.
A pesar de que Juan **sea** listo, no logrará su propósito.	In spite of the fact that John may be (is) clever, he will not achieve his goal.

The example with **es** underlines the speaker's conviction that John is, indeed, clever. **Sea** indicates that his cleverness is only conceded to be a possibility or, if conceded to be a fact, is stressed emotionally by the speaker.

21. THE SUBJUNCTIVE IN CONDITIONAL SENTENCES

A.   GENERAL STATEMENT

Si llueve, nos mojamos (mojaremos).	If it rains, we get wet.
Si **lloviera**, nos mojaríamos.	If it were to rain (rained), we would get wet.
Si **hubiera llovido**, nos habríamos mojado.	If it had rained, we would have gotten wet.

There is little difference in meaning in the three preceding sentences: each expresses a conditional relationship between rain and our getting wet. Nevertheless, the way of looking at the condition expressed in the subordinate clause is different in each case. The first sentence neither affirms nor denies that the event will take place, but simply indicates a causal relationship between the subordinate and the independent clauses should the event take place. This neutral type of condition requires an indicative verb in the clause after **si**. The second sentence views the rain as unlikely, or at the most as a possibility. The uncertainty involved in this type of conditional sentence requires that the verb after **si** be in the subjunctive. The third sentence illustrates a contrary-to-fact condition, since the clause following **si** indicates it did *not* happen. Contrary-to-fact conditions require a subjunctive verb in the subordinate clause.

Si vino ayer, no lo sabíamos.	If he came yesterday, we didn't know it.
Si nos **ayudara**, podríamos ir.	If he were to help (helped) us, we would be able to go. (not probable, or merely a possibility)
Si yo **fuera** Vd., no iría.	If I were you, I would not go. (contrary to fact)

Si Galdós **hubiera escrito** en inglés, sería (habría sido) tan famoso como Dickens.	If Galdós had written in English, he would be (have been) as famous as Dickens. (contrary to fact)

The following rule of thumb may be useful: In Spanish, when the verb in the independent clause is in the conditional or in the conditional perfect tense, the verb in the clause introduced by **si** must be in the subjunctive. When the verb in the independent clause is in any other tense, the verb in the clause introduced by **si** is in the indicative. The sequence of tenses [conditional (perfect) —→ imperfect (pluperfect) subjunctive] precludes the use of a present subjunctive after **si**. Instead, the indicative or an infinitive regularly follows **si**. (The present subjunctive is occasionally used after **si** in cases where **si** means *whether*. This, however, is a very rare usage; it is mentioned here only to permit the reader to recognize it should he encounter it. Normally an infinitive or the present indicative is used.

«No sé si ir, Gloria . . . ¿Qué te parece?» (N)	"I don't know whether to go, Gloria . . . What do you think?"

B. THE SUBJUNCTIVE SUBSTITUTE FOR THE CONDITIONAL TENSE

Instead of the usual conditional—past subjunctive sequence in sentences with **si**, Spanish often replaces the conditional tense with a past subjunctive. The result is a sentence with two verbs in the past subjunctive. The second verb, however, retains the quality of the original conditional.

Si le **escribieras**, te **contestara** (**contestaría**) en seguida.	If you were to write (wrote) to him, he would answer you immediately.
Si no lo **hubiera sospechado**, no **hubiera** (**habría**) venido.	If he had not suspected it, he would not have come.

C. SUBSTITUTES FOR THE SUBJUNCTIVE IN CONDITIONAL SENTENCES

1. The preposition **de** + infinitive often replaces the subjunctive (or the indicative) in conditional sentences.

Sabía con certeza que **de olvidarlo**, todo estaría perdido.	He knew for sure that if he were to forget it, everything would be lost.
De haber sido más inteligente, no habría depositado el dinero en aquel banco.	If he had been more intelligent, he would not have deposited his money in that bank.
De no producirse descensos de temperatura, la cosecha de almendras promete ser magnífica. (ES)	If there is no drop in temperature, the almond crop promises to be excellent.

2. **Que** may replace the verb *to be* in the subjunctive.

Yo **que** Vd., no iría.	If I were you, I would not go.

In colloquial Spanish the imperfect indicative often replaces the conditional tense in conditional contrary-to-fact sentences.

Yo, ahora mismo, si **tuviera** quinientos hombres, **tomaba** Estella por asalto y le **pegaba** fuego. (ZA)	Right now, if I had five hundred men, I would storm Estella and set fire to it.

E.   COMO SI

Como si, *as if*, and its literary equivalent **cual si** may be considered separately. They are always followed by a past (imperfect or pluperfect) subjunctive, no matter what the tense of the verb in the other clause may be.

El profesor movía la cabeza **como si se negara a** dar crédito a lo que oía. (F)	The professor shook his head as if he refused to believe what he heard.
Trata a su mujer **como si fuera** una esclava.	He treats his wife as if she were a slave.

22. OTHER USES OF THE SUBJUNCTIVE IN SPANISH

A.   Clauses introduced by **el que**, *the fact that*, or **de ahí que**, *hence, this is the reason that*, regularly take the subjunctive.

El que yo no le **haya pagado** no es motivo para que se enfríe nuestra amistad. (AUT)	That I haven't paid you is no reason for our friendship to cool.
De ahí que llamara españolas a las Cuevas de Altamira.	This is the reason why he called the Caves of Altamira Spanish.

B.   Verbs expressing a stimulus to action (**alentar**, **animar**, **incitar**, **persuadir**) and verbs of invitation (**invitar**, **convidar**) are normally followed by the preposition **a** + infinitive, but there is a much less common alternative construction employing **a que** or **para que** that takes the subjunctive.

Invito al lector **a meditar** (**a que medite**) sobre este problema.	I invite the reader to think about this problem.
Doña Rosita animó a su hija **a cantar** (**a que cantara**).	Doña Rosita encouraged her daughter to sing.

EXERCISES

1. There is nothing that tastes better than fresh fruit.   2. He said they would come when they finished.   3. Buy a [piece of] liver that is nice and tender.   4. The generous Mr. Moreno invited us to dine with his family. 5. I shall do for them all that I can.   6. He waited for the envelope to dry.

7. It is natural for him to be sleepy; he spent the entire night at the wheel. 8. He said he would do whatever you wished. 9. They are looking for a servant who knows three languages. 10. If (**de**) I had known it, I would not have come. 11. I am sending him to Burgos so that he may learn to speak Spanish. 12. She waited patiently for her husband to return home. 13. While the traveler reads his newspaper, his companion has breakfast. 14. If it were not for her glasses, that girl would be attractive. 15. When you finish reading *Werther*, I am going to lend you another short novel. 16. So long as there is no good library here, the students will not be able to progress. 17. I don't believe there is anyone in the class who knows how to write. 18. He will accept the [any] position they offer him. 19. The day he disappears I don't know what will become of us. 20. As soon as he got up, he came to my room. 21. When you are older, you will understand why a woman can't go out alone. 22. There is no other person whom she loves more. 23. If you have a problem, let me know. 24. When you finish, he would like you to read it to him. 25. It was as if he were looking for a hidden meaning in my words. 26. If he didn't have children, perhaps he would do it. 27. I shall do the best I know how. 28. She took him to the park to play with the other children. 29. Today you are going to eat whatever you want. 30. Even though he wasn't old, he decided to retire. 31. They planted the tree so that it could be seen from the balcony window. 32. If you wake up frightened, call me. 33. If I had had more money, I would have remained in Torremolinos all summer. 34. I address my words to everyone who needs help. 35. I did everything possible so that (*strong purpose*) he would go away. 36. I put out the light, although I knew I wasn't going to fall asleep. 37. In spite of the fact that he has promised to change, I want him to go away. 38. Unless you finish tomorrow, he will not accept the report. 39. I was looking for something that was a little cheaper. 40. I wanted to talk to him before he made his decision.

23. SELECCION LITERARIA

Nada

Carmen Laforet

Carmen Laforet nace en Barcelona en 1921. Pasa su juventud en las Canarias y al terminar la guerra civil regresa a su ciudad natal. Tiene sólo veintidós años al acabar Nada, *novela que le gana el premio Nadal y revela la fluidez narrativa que caracterizará a toda su obra.*

Andrea, la protagonista, llega a Barcelona a estudiar en la Universidad. Se aloja con unos parientes y desde el primer momento tiene que luchar para no dejarse vencer por la atmósfera anormal en que vive. Encuentra momentos de alivio entre los amigos univer-

sitarios y al fin garantiza su independencia apartándose de su triste
y neurótica familia. La escena siguiente revela su creciente resis-
tencia a Angustias, su tía frustrada y amargada.

No sé a que fueron debidas aquellas fiebres[1] que pasaron como una
ventolera dolorosa, removiendo los rincones de mi espíritu, pero barriendo
también sus nubes negras. El caso es que desaparecieron antes de que
nadie hubiera pensado en llamar al médico y que al cesar me dejaron una
extraña y débil sensación de bienestar.[2] El primer día que pude levantarme   5
tuve la impresión de que al tirar la manta hacia los pies quitaba también
de sobre mí aquel ambiente[3] opresivo que me anulaba desde mi llegada
a la casa.

Angustias, examinando mis zapatos, cuyo cuero[4] arrugado como una cara
expresiva delataba[5] su vejez, señaló las suelas[6] rotas que rezumaban[7]   10
humedad y dijo que yo había cogido un enfriamiento[8] por llevar los pies
mojados.

—Además, hija mía, cuando se es pobre y se tiene que vivir a costa de[9]
la caridad de los parientes, es necesario cuidar más las prendas personales.
Tienes que andar menos y pisar con más cuidado . . . No me mires así,   15
porque te advierto[10] que sé perfectamente lo que haces cuando yo estoy
en mi oficina.[11] Sé que te vas a la calle y vuelves antes de que yo llegue
para que no pueda pillarte.[12] ¿Se puede saber adónde vas?

—Pues a ningún sitio concreto. Me gusta ver las calles. Ver la ciudad . . .

—Pero te gusta ir sola, hija mía, como si fueras un golfo. Expuesta a las   20
impertinencias de los hombres. ¿Es que eres una criada, acaso? . . . A tu
edad, a mí no me dejaban salir sola ni a la puerta de la calle. Te advierto
que comprendo que es necesario que vayas y vengas de la Universidad
. . . pero de eso a andar por ahí suelta[13] como un perro vagabundo . . .
Cuando estés sola en el mundo haz lo que quieras. Pero ahora tienes una   25
familia, un hogar y un nombre. Ya sabía yo que tu prima del pueblo no
podía haberte inculcado buenos hábitos. Tu padre era un hombre extraño
. . . No es que tu prima no sea una excelente persona, pero le falta[14] refi-
namiento. A pesar de todo, espero que no irías a corretear por las calles
del pueblo.   30

—No.

—Pues aquí mucho menos. ¿Me has oído?

Yo no insistí, ¿qué podía decirle?

De pronto se volvió, espeluznada, cuando ya se iba.

—Espero que no habrás bajado hacia el puerto por las Ramblas.[15]   35

—¿Por qué no?

—Hija mía, hay unas calles, en las que si una señorita se metiera alguna
vez, perdería para siempre su reputación. Me refiero al barrio Chino[16] . . .
Tú no sabes dónde comienza . . .

—Sí, sé perfectamente. En el barrio Chino no he entrado . . . pero ¿qué hay allí?

Angustias me miró furiosa.

—Perdidas, ladrones y el brillo del demonio, eso hay.

5   (Y yo, en aquel momento, me imaginé el barrio Chino iluminado por una chispa de belleza.)

El momento de mi lucha contra Angustias se acercaba cada vez más, como una tempestad[17] inevitable. A la primera conversación que tuve con ella supe que nunca íbamos a entendernos. Luego, la sorpresa y la tristeza
10   de mis primeras impresiones, habían dado una gran ventaja a mi tía. Pero—pensé yo, excitada después de esta conversación—este período se acaba. Me vi entrar en una vida nueva, en la que dispondría libremente de[18] mis horas y sonreí a Angustias con sorna.

Cuando volví a reanudar las clases en la Universidad me parecía fermentar
15   interiormente de impresiones acumuladas. Por primera vez en mi vida me encontré siendo expansiva y anudando amistades. Sin mucho esfuerzo conseguí relacionarme con un grupo de muchachas y muchachos compañeros de clase. La verdad es que me llevaba a ellos un afán indefinible que ahora puedo concretar como un instinto de defensa: sólo aquellos seres
20   de mi misma generación y de mis mismos gustos podían respaldarme y ampararme[19] contra el mundo un poco fantasmal de las personas maduras. Y verdaderamente, creo que yo en aquel tiempo necesitaba este apoyo.

24. NOTES

1. la fiebre—fever
    la calentura—fever
    tener (estar con) fiebre—to have a fever

    Fiebre is more common than **calentura**, which often indicates a sudden or especially high temperature. **Fiebre** should be used to refer to a specific disease: **fiebre amarilla**, *yellow fever*; **fiebre tifoidea**, *typhoid fever*; etc.

Hace dos semanas **tenía fiebre** y ahora está más sano que nunca.	Two weeks ago he had a fever, and now he is healthier than ever.

2. el bienestar—well-being, welfare; comfort
    el malestar—malaise, indisposition

El **bienestar** económico del país depende del precio del café.	The economic well-being of the country depends on the price of coffee.
Un raro **malestar** me invadió . . . (NB)	A strange malaise (discomfort) invaded me . . .

3. el ambiente—environment, atmosphere
   la atmósfera—atmosphere

Esta novela de Galdós describe un determinado **ambiente** social.	This novel by Galdós describes a particular social environment.
No se sabe cómo es la **atmósfera** del planeta.	We don't know what the atmosphere of the planet is like.
La **atmósfera**, sofocante y húmeda, parecía empequeñecerle. (IC)	The stifling and humid atmosphere seemed to diminish him.

4. el cuero—leather, rawhide
   la piel—skin; leather
   el cutis—skin
   estar en cueros—to be stark naked
   salvar el pellejo—to save one's skin (hide)

   Cuero is standard for leather or hide. When leather refers to a very supple material, it is usually rendered by **piel: guantes de piel**, *leather gloves*. **Piel** may refer to the skin of a person, animal, or fruit, but **cutis** is used almost exclusively for the skin of the human face. Although **pellejo** is a synonym of **piel**, it replaces it regularly only in idioms and on a very colloquial or familiar level of speech.

Le regaló una cartera de **piel de foca**.	He made him a gift of a seal-skin wallet.
—Toma. Tápate. Te enfriarás yendo **en cueros** por la casa. (IC)	"Here! Cover yourself up. You'll catch cold going around the house with nothing on."
En el momento de mayor peligro sólo pensaba en **salvar el pellejo**.	At the moment of greatest danger, he thought only of saving his own skin (hide).

5. delatar—to give away; to betray (something); to inform on (a person)
   denunciar—to denounce
   traicionar—to betray

   Delatar, with things, means simply *to reveal* or *to give away*; with people it suggests something clandestine or criminal. **Denunciar**, like its English equivalent, refers to an overt action. **Traicionar** implies treachery.

Su aire inquieto, extraño en ella, la **delataba**. (IC)	A restless manner, which was strange for her, gave her away.
El inquilino **denunció** al propietario por no cumplir con el reglamento municipal.	The tenant denounced the owner for not complying with the municipal regulation.
Benedict Arnold **traicionó** a su patria.	Benedict Arnold betrayed his country.

6. la suela—sole (of a shoe)
   la planta—sole (of the foot)

Borja y yo sustituimos las sandalias por gruesos zapatos con **suela** de crepé . . . (LM)	Borja and I replaced our sandals with stout shoes with rubber crepe soles . . .
Me duelen las **plantas** de los pies de tanto andar.	The soles of my feet hurt from so much walking.

7. rezumar—to ooze, seep (sometimes used reflexively)
   el zumo—juice (synonym of el jugo, although not used with the same
   frequency everywhere in the Spanish-speaking world; most often
   used with reference to grapes and the making of wine)

Las paredes de la vieja taberna **rezumaban** humedad.	The walls of the old tavern oozed dampness (were sweating).
Los bacalaos secos en el escaparate **rezuman** sal.	The dry codfish in the window are exuding salt.
Mi desayuno es siempre **zumo** de naranja y tostadas.	My breakfast is always orange juice and toast.
Sus dientes y sus labios estaban manchados de vino y de **zumo** de uvas negras. (LM)	His teeth and his lips were stained with wine and the juice of black grapes.

8. coger un enfriamiento—to catch a cold
   constiparse—to catch a (head)cold
   resfriarse, acatarrarse—to catch a cold

The various nouns (**enfriamiento**, **catarro**, **resfriado**) indicating a cold
are often used with one of the verbs *to catch* (**coger**, **pillar**, **atrapar**) to
mean what is more frequently rendered with a reflexive verb. Notice
also that **estar constipado** (**constiparse**) rarely translates *to be(come)*
constipated, for which **estreñirse** is used, but rather *to have* (*to catch*)
a cold.

Por haberse sentado en una corriente de aire frío, el muchacho **se resfrió** (atrapó, pilló, cogió un resfriado).	Because he sat down in a draft, the boy caught cold.

9. a costa de—at the expense of
   la costa—cost
   el coste—cost, price
   el costo—cost
   a toda costa—at any cost
   costear—to pay the cost of; to pay for

Costa refers to something very inexpensive or anything to which a
specific value is not ordinarily assigned. **Coste** is standard for *cost*
or *price* in monetary terms; it is close to **precio** in meaning. **Costo** is

for large-scale projects, often corporate or governmental in nature; it is also *cost* in the language of economics. At times, however, these distinctions disappear in actual usage.

Pero el año siguiente se presentó en Mass con unos prismáticos de **coste** equivalente. (M)	But the following year he showed up in Mass* with some binoculars that cost the same amount (of the same price).
El **costo** de las obras se cifra en casi 300 millones de pesetas. (ES)	The cost of the work (project) is calculated at almost 300 million pesetas.
Las huelgas van dirigidas contra un alza del **coste** de la vida.	The strikes are directed against an increase in the cost of living.
Cuando niño, don Julio le **había costeado** la escuela. (EC)	Don Julio had paid the cost of his schooling when he was a boy.

10. advertir—to warn; to advise
    aconsejar—to counsel, advise
    avisar—to inform, let know, advise
    asesorar—to advise (usually in technical matters)
    el consejero, el asesor—adviser

Cuidado. Ya estás **advertido**.	Be careful. You have been warned.
Hay que **avisar** a la policía.	We must advise (inform) the police.
Reside en Washington, donde es **asesor** económico del Presidente.	He lives in Washington, where he is the President's economic adviser.

11. la oficina—office (usually several persons work in an oficina)
    el despacho—private office, study (oficina is sometimes used for despacho)
    la dirección—office (from which an institution is administered)
    el consultorio—doctor's office
    la redacción—newspaper office
    la administración—office (especially of officials in a public or governmental bureau)

Desde la ventana de su **despacho** el profesor ve la cordillera.	From his office window the professor can see the mountains.
El maestro le mandó a la **dirección**.	The teacher sent him to the (principal's) office.
El periódico tenía su **redacción** en la Plaza de Armas.	The newspaper used to have its office on the Plaza de Armas.
El médico reconoció al enfermo en su **consultorio**.	The doctor examined the patient in his office.

---

*Mass: a town in Germany.

12.   pillar—to catch
       coger, atrapar—to catch

Coger means *to catch* in all contexts. **Pillar** is similarly used, but most often indicates catching someone in a lie or doing something he shouldn't do. **Atrapar** is *to catch* or *to trap*, often through cunning. It suggests **la trampa**, *a physical or figurative trap.*

¿Dónde **cogieron** al asesino?	Where did they catch the murderer?
Pilló al niño en una mentira.	He caught the child in a lie.
El cazador **atrapó** al zorro cerca del gallinero.	The hunter caught (trapped) the fox near the chicken coop.
Extiende la mano blandamente sobre la hoja de una planta y hace ademán de **atrapar** la mariposa. (BA)	He gently reaches his hand over the leaf of the plant and makes a move to catch the butterfly.

13.   suelto—loose, free (not confined)
       soltar—to let loose, let go of
       flojo—loose, slack (not tight); weak (in some subject)
       aflojar—to loosen, slacken

Notice that **soltar** has two past participles: **soltado** is the active form used in compound verbs; **suelto** is used as an adjective.

Soltaron algunos ratones en el comedor.	They let some mice loose in the dining room.
No **soltaba** la cesta ni al sentarse.	He didn't let go of the basket even when he sat down.
El comilón tuvo que **aflojarse** el cinturón.	The glutton had to loosen his belt.
¿Por qué está tan **flojo** el cable?	Why is the cable so loose?
Estoy muy **flojo** en latín.	I'm very weak in Latin.

14.   faltar—to lack, be lacking; not to have
       hacer falta—to need; to be necessary

The above expressions, used with the indirect object pronouns (**me, te, le, nos, os, les**), have different meanings. **Faltar** equals **no tener**; **hacer falta** is **necesitar**. In **hacer falta** only **hacer** changes; **falta** is an invariable noun. Both expressions follow the pattern of **gustar**, *to please.*

Te hace falta dormir más.	You need to sleep more.
Necesitas dormir más.	You need to sleep more.
Para trabajar lo único que **hacen falta** son ganas. (LC)	(In order) to work the only thing that is needed (necessary) is the desire.

| **Me falta** tiempo para terminar. | I lack (don't have) time to finish. |
| **Nos faltan** los recursos económicos para ayudarle. | We lack (don't have) the economic resources to help him. |

15. las Ramblas—a broad, tree-lined thoroughfare, popular with strollers, that traverses much of Barcelona (the word rambla is now used to designate any such street in Catalonia)

16. el barrio Chino—the red-light district in Barcelona
    el barrio—district, quarter, section (of a city)

By analogy with Barcelona, the designation **barrio chino** is used in a limited number of Spanish and Spanish-American cities. Obviously when a city has a concentrated Chinese population, the term refers to this particular district or section.

| Este es el **barrio** obrero. | This is the working-class district. |
| Siempre que vamos a San Francisco, visitamos el **barrio chino**. | Whenever we go to San Francisco, we visit Chinatown. |

17. la tempestad—storm, tempest (often at sea)
    la tormenta—storm
    el temporal—storm
    el chubasco—rainstorm, squall
    el aguacero, el chaparrón—shower, rainstorm

Tempestad suggests a violent storm, often accompanied by lightning and thunder. **Tormenta**, a close synonym, is more common in spoken Spanish than **tempestad**. Both words may be used figuratively, although **tempestad** (as used in the selection here) is more common. **Temporal**, usually long in duration, is like a storm front and is especially associated with the sea. **Chubasco** ordinarily is accompanied by considerable wind and is short in duration. **Aguacero** and **chaparrón** often refer to very heavy rains of short duration.

Toda Europa está de **temporal**. (TV)	All Europe is having this stormy weather.
El **temporal** durará dos días por lo menos. (FM)	The storm will last at least two days.
Llegaron corriendo bajo un **aguacero** furioso . . . (FM)	They came running under a violent rainstorm . . .

18. disponer de—to have free; to have at one's disposal
    deshacerse de—to get rid of, dispose of
    librarse de—to get rid of, free oneself of

| ¿**Dispone de** media hora? (IC) | Do you have thirty minutes free (at your disposal)? |

(Ella) intrigó con los jueces para **deshacerse de** un hombre que no le servía para nada. (JM)	She conspired with the judges to get rid of a man who was no longer of any use to her.
No puedo **librarme de** su influjo pernicioso.	I can't get free from his pernicious influence.

19. amparar—to shelter, help
    ayudar—to help, assist
    socorrer—to help, succor
    apoyar—to help, support
    no poder menos de + infinitive—can't help but + verb
    el amparo, la ayuda, el socorro, el apoyo, el auxilio—help

Ayudar, the basic term for *to help*, implies assistance in the accomplishment of a goal or end. **Amparar** suggests assistance or protection of someone weaker. **Socorrer** suggests urgency or immediate aid to someone in danger or assistance to someone in great distress. **Apoyar** is to help by backing or standing behind someone. **Auxiliar** is a general term with a meaning broad enough to encompass those of the preceding verbs.

Durante la tormenta, los monjes **ampararon** al peregrino.	During the storm the monks sheltered the pilgrim.
Don Orlando se enterneció, se creyó en el deber de **socorrer** a aquella familia. (VS)	Don Orlando was moved to pity; he believed it was his duty to succor (help) that family.
Sin **el apoyo** de mi padre, no habría conseguido el puesto.	Without my father's help (support) I would not have obtained the position.
No puedo menos de agradecerlo.	I can't help but be grateful for it.
¿Quieres que vaya a la ciudad a buscar **auxilio**?	Do you want me to go to the city to get help?

EXERCISES ON NOTES

1. The shoemaker put soles on (**a**) the old shoes. 2. Without the help of the army, the rebellion would have failed. 3. Miraflores is one of the most elegant residential districts in Lima. 4. On Thursday the secretaries worked in the office until 6 P.M. 5. I couldn't help telling the truth. 6. Advise me when you are ready to go out. 7. The doctor's office is near the city hall. 8. He would do anything to save his skin. 9. The industrial age has polluted the earth's atmosphere. 10. Spain produces some of the best leather gloves in the world. 11. The employee informed on his boss for not having paid all his taxes. 12. Leather boots are not so fashionable now as before. 13. Antonio Pérez, who betrayed Philip II, died in Paris. 14. Every year the cost of furniture goes up. 15. He has to stay in bed (**guardar cama**) until his fever goes down. 16. He did it all at our expense. 17. The guard caught the employee opening the safe. 18. If you don't rest more, you

will never get rid of your cold. 19. This rope is too (**muy**) loose to hang clothes. 20. Help came when we needed it most. 21. He will advise you to accept the position. 22. They never caught the wolf that had been attacking their sheep. 23. I think he has a [head] cold because he never wears [a] hat. 24. As we grow older, we need less money. 25. I warned her not to do it again. 26. The doctor didn't know (**ignorar**) the cause of his indisposition. 27. The fishermen remained in port, for a great storm was approaching the coast. 28. If I had more time at my disposal, I could finish the reading. 29. In Central America the afternoon storm always cools the air. 30. The handle became so hot that he let go of the frying pan. 31. When they found the shipwrecked man, he was stark naked. 32. For the tourist, the cost of traveling in Portugal is relatively low. 33. It was very hot, and Anthony decided to loosen his tie. 34. The oil was oozing out of the small cracks in (**de**) the barrel. 35. The parents put their children in the institute to get rid of them. 36. The child wouldn't let go of his mother's hand. 37. A feeling of well-being seized us as we returned home. 38. Wisconsin has frequent downpours in the summer. 39. His adviser's words betrayed great anger. 40. He had paid the cost of the orphan's education in a modest school.

CUESTIONARIO

a. contenido

1. ¿Qué efectos tuvieron las fiebres sobre Andrea?
2. ¿A qué achacaba Angustias el enfriamiento de Andrea?
3. ¿Por qué insiste Angustias en que Andrea cuide más las prendas personales?
4. ¿Por qué le disgusta a Angustias que Andrea ande sola por las calles?
5. ¿Por qué se imaginaba Andrea el barrio Chino iluminado por una chispa de belleza?
6. ¿En qué pensába Andrea al sonreírle a Angustias con sorna?
7. ¿Qué atraía a Andrea al grupo joven de compañeros de clase?

b. estilo

1. ¿Cuántos subjuntivos aparecen en esta selección? Explique Vd. el uso del subjuntivo en cada caso.
2. ¿Por qué no se usa el subjuntivo en las dos frases que empiezan con «A pesar de todo, espero que . . . » y «Espero que no habrás bajado . . . »?
3. ¿Cómo nos revela la autora el mal genio de Angustias?
4. ¿Cómo establece la autora una situación dramática entre Angustias y Andrea?
5. ¿Del punto de vista de quién se narra este episodio? ¿Qué efecto produce?

TEMA—TRADUCCION

The fever, which had disappeared before anyone had thought of calling the doctor, had swept the black clouds from my mind and left me with a strange feeling of well-being. When I threw off the blanket, it was as if

I were removing the oppressive atmosphere in which I had been living (*use imperfect*) since my arrival.

Angustias' face betrayed her displeasure as she pointed to my old shoes, whose soles oozed dampness.

"When you live at the expense of others, you should take better care of your personal belongings. Perhaps if you were to walk a little less, your shoes would be in better condition. Besides, I know very well that you go walking alone through the streets when I am at the office. May I ask where you go?"

"No place in particular. I just like to see the city."

"At your age, no girl should walk alone through the streets like a stray dog. Even though they didn't teach you good habits in your village, I am sure that you didn't go wandering through the streets there. Here you should do it even less because now you have a family and you should think of the family's reputation."

Angustias was leaving the room when suddenly she turned around. It had just occurred to her that if I had gone down to the port, I would have passed through the red-light district. When she explained the kind of people that were found there, the district seemed more fascinating than ever.

I realized that my aunt and I would never get along, and that the moment of our confrontation was approaching like an inevitable storm. Because I had changed since the day I arrived at this gloomy house, I now smiled cunningly at my aunt. I knew that I would be entering a new life. Soon I would attend classes at the University, would make new friends, and would be able to do with my life whatever I wished.

TEMAS A ESCOGER

Escríbanse unas 200 palabras sobre uno de los temas siguientes usando a lo menos 20 de las palabras y expresiones estudiadas en este capítulo.

1. La falta de comprensión entre personas de diferentes generaciones
2. La reputación de una familia
3. Un diálogo dramático entre un hijo y uno de sus padres o parientes

chapter 5

25. SELECCION LITERARIA

Idearium español

Angel Ganivet

Ganivet, precursor de la Generación del 98, acabó el Idearium* *español en 1896, dos años antes de su trágica muerte a los treinta y tres años. Los ensayos de esta obra seminal son brillantes pero a veces muy discutibles. Intentan explicar la psicología y la historia del pueblo español para ofrecer una solución a la abulia que paralizaba a la España finisecular. Como «la fe en sí mismo es el germen de todas las grandezas humanas», llega el autor a la conclusión de que es necesario restaurar el espíritu de los españoles para restaurar a la patria. En la selección abreviada que sigue, Ganivet exalta este espíritu al narrar un episodio de gran valor humano, ocurrido mientras servía de cónsul español en Amberes, Bélgica.*

Voy a referir[1] un suceso[2] vulgarísimo[3] en que intervine por «razón de mi cargo», cuando residía en Amberes... Me avisaron que en el Hospital Stuyvenberg se hallaba en gravísimo[4] estado un español, que deseaba hablar con la autoridad de su país; fui allá, y uno de los empleados del establecimiento me condujo a donde se hallaba el moribundo, diciéndome de paso[5] que éste acababa de llegar del Estado del Congo, y que no había esperanzas de salvarle, pues se hallaba en el período final de un violento ataque de fiebre amarilla o africana. Ahora mismo estoy viendo a aquel hombre infelicísimo,[6] que más que un ser humano parecía un esqueleto pintado de ocre, incorporado[7] trabajosamente sobre su pobre lecho[8] y librando su último combate contra la muerte. Y recuerdo que sus primeras palabras fueron para disculparse por la molestia[9] que me proporcionaba,[10] sin título suficiente para ello. «Yo no soy español— me dijo—; pero aquí no me entienden[11] y al oírme hablar español han creído que era a usted a quien yo deseaba hablar.» «Pues si usted no es español—le contesté— lo parece, y no tiene por qué apurarse.»[12]

«Yo soy de Centro-América, señor, de Managua, mi familia era portuguesa; me llamo Agatón Tinoco.» «Entonces— interrumpí yo— es usted español por tres veces.[13] Voy a sentarme con usted un rato y vamos a fumarnos[14] un cigarro como buenos amigos. Y, mientras tanto, usted me

---

*Idearium (Latin): body or total of ideas on a particular subject

dirá qué es lo que desea.» «Yo, nada, señor; no me falta nada para lo poco que
me queda que vivir; sólo quería hablar con quien me entendiera; porque
hace ya tiempo que no tengo ni con quien[15] hablar . . . Yo soy muy desgraciado, señor: como no hay otro hombre en el mundo. Si yo le contara
a usted mi vida vería usted que no le engaño.» «Me basta verle a usted,   5
amigo Tinoco, para quedar convencido[16] de que no dice más que la verdad;
pero cuénteme usted con entera confianza todos sus infortunios, como si
me conociera de toda su vida.»

Y aquí el pobre Agatón Tinoco me refirió largamente sus aventuras y sus
desventuras; su infortunio conyugal que le obligó a huir de su casa porque   10
«aunque pobre, era hombre de honor»; sus trabajos en el canal de Panamá,
hasta que sobrevino la paralización de las obras, y, por último,[17] su venida
en calidad de[18] colono al Estado libre congolés, donde había rematado[19]
su azarosa existencia con el desenlace vulgar y trágico que se aproximaba[20]
y que llegó aquella misma noche. «Amigo Tinoco— le dije yo después de   15
escuchar su relación; —es usted el hombre más grande que he conocido
hasta el día; posee usted un mérito que sólo está al alcance de[21] los hombres
verdaderamente grandes: el de haber trabajado en silencio; el de poder
abandonar la vida con la satisfacción de no haber recibido el premio que
merecían sus trabajos . . . Su obra ha sido nobilísima, puesto que no sólo   20
ha trabajado para vivir, sino que ha acudido como soldado de fila[22] a prestar
su concurso a empresas[23] gigantescas, en las que otro había de recoger el
provecho y la gloria. Y eso que usted ha hecho revela que el temple de su
alma es fortísimo, que lleva[24] usted en sus venas sangre de una raza de
luchadores y de triunfadores, postrada hoy y humillada por propias culpas,   25
entre las cuales no es la menor la falta de espíritu fraternal, la desunión,
que nos lleva a ser juguete de poderes extraños y a que muchos como usted
anden rodando[25] por el mundo, trabajando como oscuros peones cuando
pudieran ser amos con holgura . . . .

Cuando abandoné[26] el hospital pensaba: Si alguna persona de «buen   30
sentido» hubiera presenciado[27] esta escena, de seguro que me tomaría por
hombre desequilibrado e iluso y me censuraría por haber expuesto seme-
jantes razones ante[28] un pobre agonizante, que acaso no se hallaba en disposición de comprenderlas. Yo creo que Agatón Tinoco me comprendió y
que recibió un placer que quizá no había gustado[29] en su vida, el de ser   35
tratado como hombre y juzgado con entera y absoluta rectitud.

26. NOTES

1.   referir—to tell, relate
     referirse a—to refer to

     Referir is mainly a literary synonym of **contar** and the less common
     relatar. **Referir** alone does not mean *to refer to*.

Mi objeto es simplemente **referir** lo que pasó.	My object is simply to relate (tell) what happened.
En honor de don Lucas, no se **referirá** esta tarde ningún cuento verde. (EBM)	In honor of Don Lucas, no off-color stories will be told this afternoon.
El conferenciante **se refirió a** dos críticos con quienes no estaba de acuerdo.	The lecturer referred to two critics with whom he disagreed.

2. el suceso—event
    el acontecimiento—event, happening
    el acaecimiento—happening, occurrence
    el evento—(unforeseen) happening or event
    suceder, acontecer, acaecer—to happen
    el éxito—success
    tener éxito—to be successful

Suceso, the most common word for *event*, may refer to something of little or of great significance. It is also preferred when referring to something unfortunate. **Acontecimiento** is synonymous, but usually indicates something especially important or unforgettable in history or in the life of a person. **Acaecimiento** has a decided literary flavor and is uncommon in spoken Spanish. **Evento**, a sudden or unexpected event, is an Anglicism which, although frowned on by most people, seems to be gaining some acceptance in Spain. As is so often true, literary usage frequently disregards these distinctions.

Las elecciones constituyeron el **suceso** más importante del año.	The elections were the most important event of the year.
El trágico **suceso** trastornó los planes de la familia.	The tragic event upset the family's plans.
El primer viaje a Marte será un **acontecimiento** de importancia mundial.	The first trip to Mars will be an event of world-wide importance.
Advirtamos, por ejemplo, lo que **acontece** en las conversaciones españolas. (EI)	Let us notice, as an example, what happens during a Spanish conversation.
Siempre **ha tenido éxito** en su carrera.	He has always been successful in his career.

3. vulgar—common, ordinary, popular, vulgar
    grosero, basto—vulgar, coarse

In Spanish, **vulgar** usually means *common* or *popular* in the sense of unexceptional or in reference to the common people, their tastes, etc. The English use of *vulgar* as *crude*, *ostentatious*, etc., is **grosero** or **basto** in Spanish.

He aquí un hombre perfectamente **vulgar**;... tal vez un empleado de Ministerio; acaso un pequeño industrial. (LP)	Here is a perfectly common (ordinary) man;... perhaps a government employee; perhaps a small industrialist.
Era tan **grosero** que el anfitrión decidió no volverle a invitar a su casa.	He was so vulgar that the host decided not to invite him to his home again.

4. grave—serious, grave; seriously ill
    serio—serious

These words are synonyms mainly in written Spanish. In spoken Spanish **serio** is *serious* in the sense of *earnest, thoughtful,* or *important.* **Grave** generally means *serious* in the sense of *dangerous, somber, seriously ill.* **En serio**, not **seriamente**, renders *seriously* in the first sense.

Es una persona muy **seria**.	He's a very serious person.
Nosotros no hemos de incurrir nunca en el error de tomarnos demasiado **en serio**. (JM)	We should never make the mistake of taking ourselves too seriously.
La enferma estaba tan **grave** que tuvieron que llamar al cura.	The patient was so seriously ill that they had to call the priest.
Adolfo Stolberg, con expresión un tanto **grave**, declaró que amaba mucho a su mujer. (M)	Adolph Stolberg, with a rather serious (grave) expression, stated that he loved his wife very much.

5. de paso—in passing
    estar de paso—to stop over

Mencionó **de paso** que ya había pedido los billetes.	He mentioned in passing that he had already ordered the tickets.
Ya que voy a **estar de paso** en Nueva York, pienso llamar a mi antiguo profesor.	Since I am going to stop over in New York, I intend to call my former professor.

6. infeliz—unhappy, wretched
    feliz—happy
    alegre—happy, gay, merry
    contento—satisfied, content, happy

Feliz and **alegre** are both widely used for *happy.* **Alegre** suggests a happiness evident in some external sign or behavior, or a happiness easily subject to change. **Feliz** usually implies a deeper or more permanent type of satisfaction or well-being. Until the twentieth century **feliz** was used exclusively with **ser**. Although still much more common with that verb, it is now also used with **estar**. **Alegre** may, of course, take either verb; contento requires **estar**.

Hoy debería estar **alegre** como ningún otro día de mi vida. (SCA)	Today I should be happy as on no other day of my life.
Esto inquietaba bastante al abuelo, pero no lo suficiente para que no se permitiera estar **alegre, feliz** y orgulloso . . . (VS)	This worried the grandfather considerably, but not enough that he didn't allow himself to be gay, happy, and proud . . .

7. incorporarse—to sit up (from a reclining position)
   incorporar—to incorporate

Cuando entramos, estaba **incorporada** en la cama.	When we entered, she was sitting up in bed.
Incorporaron sus investigaciones al proyecto.	They incorporated his research into the project.

8. el lecho—bed
   la cama—bed
   el cauce—river bed

Cama is a piece of furniture. **Lecho** has more figurative uses and is most commonly employed for the bed of a sick or dying person.

Don Quijote estaba en su **lecho** de muerte cuando Sancho quería que salieran a nuevas aventuras.	Don Quixote was on his deathbed when Sancho wanted them to go out on new adventures.
No te olvides de hacer la **cama.**	Don't forget to make the bed.

9. la molestia—bother, trouble
   la molestia que me proporcionaba—the trouble he caused me
   molestar—to bother, trouble
   molestarse en + infinitive—to trouble oneself + infinitive
   tomarse la molestia de + infinitive—to take the trouble + infinitive
   molesto—bothersome (adjective)

Muy amable, pero **no se moleste.** (LL)	(That's) very kind (of you), but don't bother (trouble yourself).
No hay duda de que a Juan le **molesta** el tema.	There is no doubt that the subject annoys John.
Es tan desconsiderado que no **se tomó la molestia** de avisarnos que no venía.	He is so inconsiderate that he didn't take the trouble to let us know he wasn't coming.

10. proporcionar—to provide (with) (con is not used)

Tenía enchufe y me **proporcionó** un empleo en la fábrica.	He had pull and provided me with a job in the factory.

11. entender—to understand
comprender—to understand, comprehend; to comprise

In most cases one cannot distinguish clearly between these two verbs.
Entender is much more common, in both spoken and written Spanish.
Entender alone means *to understand* in the sense of being intelligible
with regard to the means of communication. **Comprender** sometimes
indicates a deeper or more complete understanding. In most other
cases no attempt is made to differentiate between the two.

No es cosa de no **entender** su español, es que no le **comprendo**.	It's not a matter of not understanding his Spanish, it's that I don't understand him.
Yungo no **entendía** por qué razón se entristecía tanto. (SV)	Yungo couldn't understand why he became so sad.
Claro que el astrólogo no **entendía** a las mujeres . . . (M)	Of course the astrologer didn't understand women. . .
Esta nación **comprende** cincuenta estados.	This nation comprises fifty states.

12. apurarse—to worry, fret
preocuparse—to worry, fret
apurarse—to hurry (Spanish America)
apurar—to finish; to drain
el apuro—trouble, difficulty
sacar de un apuro a una persona—to get someone out of trouble

Se apuró mucho cuando la hija estuvo enferma.	He worried a great deal when his daughter was sick.
Juan **apuró** su vino de un sorbo. (EJ)	John finished his wine in one gulp.
Es tan rico que con una palabra nos podría **sacar de** este **apuro**.	He is so rich that with a single word he could get us out of this difficulty.

13. por tres veces—best rendered here by the English three times over

14. fumarse—to smoke (the reflexive pronoun is used both as an intensifier
and to add a note of familiarity, concern, or human interest)
fumarse la clase—to cut (literally to smoke away) class
hacer novillos—to play hooky (literally to play torero using novillos,
young bulls)

15. con quien hablar—ni una persona con quien hablar

Spanish frequently employs an elliptical expression with **quien**,
omitting the noun or pronoun antecedent.

16.   quedar convencido—to be (left) convinced*

17.   por último—finally
      por fin—finally, at last
      al fin—finally, at last
      en fin—in short

      Por fin often implies a note of relief; it is also appropriate to communicate one's impatience to somebody arriving late. **Al fin** may imply a long series of steps or difficulties to be overcome before an end may be achieved, but it usually does not carry the note of impatience associated with **por fin**.

Por fin consiguieron un piso.	They finally got an apartment.
En fin, ya se ha dicho todo.	In short, everything has been said.

18.   en calidad de—as, in the capacity of
      la cualidad—characteristic, quality
      la calidad—quality

      Cualidad and **característica** are virtually synonymous: in neither noun is there any implication of judgment. **Calidad** is distinguished from them in that it carries an implicit judgment of the excellence or superiority of that which is under consideration.

Pero rara vez llegan a ser de primera **calidad** los versos de Cervantes. (JQC)	But rarely is Cervantes' poetry of high quality.
Para proteger el motor conviene comprar gasolina de buena **calidad**.	To protect the engine it's a good idea to buy high-quality gasoline.
La **cualidad** que me desagrada en Carlos es su orgullo.	The characteristic that I don't like in Charles is his pride.

19.   rematar—to finish off, kill (a dying animal, etc.); to knock down (at an auction); to finish, put finishing touches on; to adorn, top off
      de remate, rematado—completely, entirely (i.e., hopelessly)

El jinete **remató** el caballo herido.	The rider finished off the wounded horse.
La bandera francesa **remata** la embajada.	The French flag adorns the top of the embassy.
Hoy vamos a **rematar** un buen negocio.	Today we are going to conclude (polish off) a good business deal.
Tenía por tonto **rematado** a su profesor.	He considered his professor to be a complete fool.

---

*See Chap. 2-11, pp. 20-21, for use of **quedar(se)** rather than **estar** to indicate resultant state.

20. aproximarse—to approach, draw near

Acercar, its synonym aproximar, and its antonym alejar are used reflexively with a preposition to indicate that the subject moves toward or away from something. They are also used as transitive verbs to indicate that someone is moving something (or someone) toward or away from a particular place.

Se acercaban a Vera Cruz, capital del estado de Jalapa.	They were approaching Vera Cruz, capital of the state of Jalapa.
¿Quieres acercar (aproximar) la lámpara un poco más?	Will you please move the lamp a little closer?
Ya el tren había empezado a alejarse cuando llegamos.	The train had already begun to pull away when we arrived.
Ella me había alejado por completo de su vida. (N)	She had put me completely out of her life.

21. al alcance de—within reach of
el alcance—reach, range
alcanzar—to reach; to catch up with; to overtake
alcanzar—to obtain (synonyms: lograr, obtener)

Esta escopeta tiene un alcance muy limitado.	This shotgun has a very limited range.
Los árboles de La Alameda son tan altos que parecen alcanzar las estrellas. (IC)	The trees of the Alameda are so tall that they seem to reach (touch) the stars.
Alcanzó lo que quería.	He obtained what he wanted.

22. soldado de fila—ordinary soldier (soldier of the ranks)
la fila—row, rank, line
la cola—line (waiting turn)
la línea—line (most common term)
el renglón—(written) line
la hilera—string, line, row
el verso—line of poetry

La distancia más corta entre dos puntos es una línea recta.	The shortest distance between two points is a straight line.
Como colecciono autógrafos, me puso unas líneas (renglones) en el álbum.	Since I collect autographs, he wrote a few lines in my album.
Detrás de su casa se veía una fila de altos chopos.	Behind his house one could see a row of tall poplars.
Una hilera de luces iluminaba el jardín.	A row (string) of lights lit up the garden.

23. la empresa—undertaking, enterprise
     la tarea—task, work; homework
     el trabajo—work (los trabajos—hardships)
     la labor—work, labor; needlework
     la obra—work (la obra maestra—masterpiece, masterwork)
     el quehacer—chore, task
     la faena—job, task, work

Trabajo, the general word for *work*, may indicate either physical or mental effort. (Note the special meaning of the plural.) **Labor**, though less common, is generally synonymous with **trabajo**. It has, however, two special meanings: *agricultural work* and *needlework* or *sewing*. **Quehacer**, as the word suggests, is something *to be done*: **quehaceres domésticos**—*housework*. **Faena** is most commonly physical labor, often strenuous in nature. **Obra** has many meanings: It refers to construction and undertakings requiring the efforts of a large group. It also refers to the works of an author or artist, and to charitable or religious work. Each of these words has other meanings, many of which overlap. In literary usage the above distinctions do not always hold.

La Feria Mundial fue una **empresa** en que participaron muchas naciones.	The World's Fair was an undertaking in which many nations took part.
Plácida levanta la cabeza de su **labor** y sonríe. (DI)	Placida raises her head from her sewing (needlework) and smiles.
Su **labor** arquitectónica, directamente inspirada en lo clásico, influía en forma decisiva en Dinamarca y Escandinavia. (M)	His architectural work, largely inspired by the classics, had a decisive influence in Denmark and Scandinavia.
El estudiante no ha terminado la **tarea**.	The student hasn't finished his homework.
. . . a pesar de lo ruda que era esta **faena** y del mal tiempo, mostráronse alegres. (FM)	. . . in spite of how hard this work was and the bad weather, they were happy.
La santa era conocida por sus buenas **obras**.	The saint was known for her good works.

24. llevar—to have

Llevar often replaces **tener** when the latter means *to contain, to bear*, or *to carry within*. **Traer** is similarly used.

La paella valenciana **lleva** muchos mariscos.	Valencian paella contains (has) a lot of seafood (in it).
Yo leo siempre este periódico; **trae** muchas noticias de por aquí. (VS)	I always read this newspaper; it has much local news in it.

25. rodar—to wander, roam; to roll

En el siglo XIX los poetas románticos **rodaban** por el mundo buscando lo ideal.

In the nineteenth century the Romantic poets roamed the world seeking the ideal.

La diligencia **rodaba** por la región triste y desolada.

The stagecoach rolled on through the sad, desolate region.

Piedra que **rueda** no cría musgo.

A rolling stone gathers no moss.

26. abandonar—to leave, abandon, foresake
dejar—to leave

Dejar is *to leave* (*behind*). **Abandonar** is a common literary synonym. Each verb may have people or things as its direct object. *To leave* is **salir** when it means *to exit* or *to go out of*. When *to leave* means *to depart* and a destination is neither mentioned nor implied, **irse** is commonly used.

La madre **abandonó** al niño en el portal de la iglesia.

The mother abandoned (left) her child at the church door.

Abandonó (**Dejó**) el hotel la semana pasada.

He left the hotel last week.

Acaban de **salir**.

They have just left (gone out).

Se fue hace tres semanas.

He left (went away) three weeks ago.

27. presenciar—to witness
atestiguar—to bear witness, testify
el testigo—witness
testigo presencial—eyewitness

El **testigo** se negó a declarar ante el juez.

The witness refused to testify before the judge.

Una vez, en Oñate, pude **presenciar** una cosa sumamente interesante. (ZA)

Once, in Oñate, I witnessed something extremely interesting.

28. ante—before, in the presence of, in front of
delante de—in front of

Ante nuestros ojos surgen cosas inauditas.

Astonishing (unheard of) things appear before our eyes.

Dime, ¿hay aún **delante de** la casa aquellos olmos grandes? (LP)

Tell me, are those large elm trees still in front of the house?

29. no había gustado—he had never experienced (savored)

1. The Cariocas have the reputation of being very happy. 2. He planted a long row of rosebushes. 3. From the harbor we saw the weather vane that tops the cathedral. 4. I shall leave you to your task. 5. Move the chair closer to the table. 6. The temptation to cut class is always great before holidays. 7. The publication of his correspondence provided me with many useful facts. 8. I called my brother in Spain, but I couldn't understand him because the connection was bad. 9. The tragic events of recent months have made (**poner**) me more pessimistic than ever. 10. The only witness left the scene of the crime before the police arrived. 11. I wouldn't take the trouble to help such an ungrateful person. 12. The biography is dull, for it relates too many daily events in (**de**) the general's life. 13. He never writes anything that doesn't refer to the war. 14. The nurse helped her to sit up in bed. 15. Before lighting a cigarette, I asked if the smoke would bother him. 16. It surprised me that such an attractive woman would marry such an ordinary man. 17. I am familiar with your good qualities, and that is why we are friends. 18. The dying man's wife spent the night at his bedside. 19. What you tell me is very serious. 20. His trip to Madrid was an event that he will never forget. 21. His vulgar comments reveal his true character. 22. We saw the boat moving away from the coast. 23. The discovery of penicillin was an important event in the history of medicine. 24. When you read the letter, you will be pleasantly surprised. 25. We witnessed the game from seats in the first row. 26. That disease is never serious. 27. He is prolific, but the quality of his work leaves much to be desired. 28. The stagecoach rolled down the street, splashing mud along the narrow sidewalk. 29. I can't understand his handwriting. 30. After months of waiting, they finally obtained (**sacar**) a visa. 31. In passing, he asked me if I wanted to give a public lecture. 32. The line of ants ended at the sugar bowl. 33. A real artist is more interested in quality than in quantity. 34. Each new reading of *Don Quixote* enables the reader to understand more profoundly the creative genius of Cervantes. 35. If you work hard, everything is within your reach. 36. She has become ill from fretting so much. 37. I have never known a happier couple. 38. They are going to publish his complete works. 39. What does this soup have in it, that it (**para**) tastes so good? 40. No one understands why he has dedicated himself to works of charity.

CUESTIONARIO

a. contenido

1. ¿Por qué querían que Ganivet interviniera en un suceso tan vulgar?
2. Según el empleado, ¿en qué estado se encontraba el enfermo?
3. ¿Cuáles fueron las primeras palabras del moribundo?
4. ¿Por qué era Agatón Tinoco español «por tres veces»?
5. ¿Qué era lo único que quería Agatón Tinoco antes de morir?

6. ¿Por qué había ido a trabajar en el canal de Panamá?
7. ¿Dónde se había contagiado de la fiebre amarilla?
8. ¿Por qué razones le dice Ganivet a Agatón Tinoco que es el hombre más grande que ha conocido?
9. ¿Cuál era el placer que tal vez había gustado por primera vez en su vida?

b. estilo

1. ¿Cómo nos hace Ganivet visualizar y compadecer a Agatón Tinoco en la frase: «Ahora mismo estoy viendo . . .»?
2. ¿Qué tono y lenguaje emplea el cónsul para inspirarle confianza al moribundo?
3. ¿Cómo logra Ganivet resumir todas las desgracias de su vida en una sola frase?
4. ¿Cómo convierte poéticamente Ganivet la vida trabajosa de Agatón Tinoco en una noble existencia?
5. Describa Vd. en términos generales las características del estilo de Ganivet tales como se manifiestan en esta selección. Refiérase a: (1) la estructura de las frases, (2) el tono del lenguaje, (3) la elección de palabras, y (4) las imágenes.

TEMA—TRADUCCION

I would like to relate an unforgettable event that occurred while I was Spanish consul in Antwerp. One day they took me to the local hospital to see a dying Spaniard who had asked to speak with his country's representative. I can still recall that unhappy man struggling to (**por**) sit up in bed and begging my pardon for having troubled me. The only thing (use **lo**) he wanted was to speak to someone who understood his language, and so I sat down to chat and smoke a cigarette with him.

Agatón Tinoco then began to tell the story of his wretched existence. After leaving his wife over a question of honor, and after working in Panama, he had finally gone as a colonist to the Congo. There he contracted yellow fever, which had reduced him to his wretched state and which was to finish him off that very night. I saw that this ordinary man possessed certain qualities which are within the reach of only truly great men. For example, he had worked silently in important undertakings for which others reaped the rewards and the glory. I told him that the events of his life revealed that he had in his veins blood of a race which, although today prostrated through its own faults, was nevertheless great.

On leaving the hospital I thought that if anyone had witnessed this scene, he would have taken me for a completely unbalanced man. He probably would have censured me for having said such things to a dying man. Nevertheless, I feel that Agatón Tinoco understood my words and received pleasure from being judged honestly and being treated as a human being.

TEMAS A ESCOGER

Escríbanse unas 200 palabras sobre uno de los temas siguientes usando a lo menos 20 de las palabras y expresiones estudiadas en este capítulo.

1. El problema de caer enfermo en un país extranjero
2. La verdadera grandeza de un hombre
3. El hombre ante la muerte

chapter 6

27. SELECCION LITERARIA

La isla y los demonios

Carmen Laforet

Los demonios que según la superstición habitan las Canarias resultan ser en esta novela los neuróticos miembros de la familia de Marta. Al mismo tiempo que compadecemos a la muchacha notamos que ha sido afectada por la atmósfera anormal en que vive, pues además de egoísta es insensible a la suerte de su madre, una loca que los otros guardan encerrada. En el pasaje siguiente percibimos su odio a Pino, la celosa e histérica esposa de su hermanastro, José.

Todos fueron entrando; Marta quedó detrás, sin decidirse a seguirles. Se fijó[1] por primera vez en la casa donde había nacido. La miró críticamente como pudiera hacerlo una desconocida. En el jardín crecían ya los crisántemos y seguían florecidas las dalias. Por las paredes del edificio
5 trepaban[2] heliotropos, madreselvas, buganvillas. Todos estaban en flor. Sus olores se mezclaban ardorosamente.

«En otros países, ya en esta época[3] del año hace frío. Se caen las hojas de todos los árboles, nieva quizá . . .»

Trató de imaginarse que ella venía de un país muy frío lleno de nieblas,[4]
10 y llegaba a esta casa . . . Se sentó en el escalón[5] de la entrada y puso la palma de su mano en el cálido picón que jamás había recibido la caricia de la nieve.

· El sol le daba en los ojos y tuvo que guiñarlos. Enfrente de ella las montañas ponían su oleaje de colores; la alta y lejana cumbre[6] central
15 lucía[7] en azul pálido,[8] parecía navegar hacia la niña, como horas antes había navegado el gran buque[9] en la mañana.

Marta pensó en las tres personas que acababan de desembarcar. Por el ventanal[10] abierto oía sus voces.

*   *   *   *   *

Todo esto era suficientemente plácido y encantador, como ella quería
20 que lo fuese para los refugiados de guerra que habían llegado. Pero Marta no estaba tranquila. Dentro de los muros de la casa esta placidez y tranquilidad desaparecían. Allí dentro no había felicidad, ni comprensión, ni dulzura.

Marta frunció el ceño.[11] Por el ventanal llegaba la voz de su cuñada contestando a una insinuación de Hones:

—¡No, qué va![12] La niña no es ninguna compañía[13] para mí. Está siempre con sus estudios. Y además ... ¡si vieran cómo es! ¿Quieren creer que[14] esta mañana la encontraron durmiendo en el comedor con una botella de vino en la mano?   5

El corazón de Marta latió[15] desagradablemente, porque lo que decía Pino era verdad. No había medio de defenderse[16] de ello .... La voz de Pino la hería.[17] Pero algún día estas gentes[18] recién llegadas sabrían que ella, Marta, había sufrido entre los recelos y la vulgaridad que escondían[19] aquellos   10
muros, y este pensamiento la consolaba infantilmente.

«He sufrido.»

Murmuró esto y sintió que se le llenaban de lágrimas los ojos. Entonces supo que alguien la estaba mirando.

Volvió la cabeza y vio, separada de ella por varios macizos de flores,   15
la figura de una mujer, vestida con un traje de faldas largas, como las campesinas viejas. Llevaba un pañuelo negro a la cabeza y sobre él se había colocado[20] un gran sombrero de paja, como siempre que salía algún momento al jardín o al huerto. Era Vicenta, la cocinera de la casa. Comúnmente la llamaban allí la majorera, porque majoreros y majoreras se les   20
llama a los habitantes de Fuerteventura, y ella era oriunda[21] de esta isla.

Marta no sabía que Vicenta había estado acechando en el comedor a los recién llegados, que en la reunión[22] familiar la había echado de menos[23] a ella y que salió al jardín con la intención de averiguar dónde estaba.

No le dijo nada. Marta a ella tampoco. Pero se levantó poseída de una   25
gran vergüenza de que la criada la hubiera cogido en un momento de debilidad. Sintió que enrojecía lentamente al impulso de sus pensamientos. Abrió con cuidado la puerta de la casa, con cierta torpeza salvaje y conmovedora, y desapareció allí dentro.

La mujer, que estaba en la esquina[24] de la casa, se marchó también.   30
El jardín quedó solitario, lleno de luz de mediodía.

28. NOTES

1. fijarse (en)—to notice
   fijar—to fix, make fast; to set (a date, a price, etc.)
   reparar en—to notice, observe
   notar—to notice, observe

   Fijarse (en) is more common than **reparar en** for *to notice*. **Fijar**, *to make fast*, is patent in its meaning. **Reparar (en)**, used mainly in written Spanish, most often means *to notice* in the sense of *merely to become aware of*, but it may also indicate close attention and thus be synonymous with **fijarse** (**en**). **Notar** may be used in either of these senses.

¿**Te has fijado en** cómo me miraba aquel soldado?	Did you notice the way that soldier was looking at me?
Han fijado el precio muy alto.	They have set the price very high.
Doña Cecilia fingió no **reparar en** el tono colérico de su hijo. (F)	Doña Cecilia pretended not to notice her son's angry tone of voice.
Jamás **reparó en** lo que decía. (R)	He never noticed (was aware of) what I was saying.
Después tapamos el agujero con una maderita y nadie lo va a **notar**. (FA)	Later we will plug up the hole with a tiny piece of wood and no one will notice it.

2. trepar—to climb
   trepador(a)—climbing (adjective)
   subir—to go up, climb; to rise; to take (bring) up

   Trepar usually indicates *to climb* with the aid of all the limbs or legs. **Subir** gives no indication of means; its broader meaning subsumes that of **trepar**.

Miraba inmóvil un escorpión negro, que **trepaba** por el muro encalado . . . (THI)	Motionless, I watched a black scorpion climbing up the white-washed wall. . .
La trepadora es una novela de Rómulo Gallegos.	*The Social Climber* is a novel by Rómulo Gallegos.
Subieron a la azotea a ver el panorama de la ciudad.	They climbed (went) up to the roof (terrace) to see the view of the city.

3. la época—season, time (when something customarily happens)
   la estación—season (one of the four seasons)
   la temporada—season (in which a cultural, religious, or sporting event, etc., is held)

El otoño es la **época** de la cosecha.	Autumn is the harvest season.
Está ahora en su quinta **temporada** como director.	He is now in his fifth season as director.

4. la niebla—fog
   la neblina—fog, mist
   la bruma—mist

   Niebla is the most widely used of these three terms. In standard usage it refers to *fog* or *heavy fog*. **Neblina** is ordinarily *lighter fog* or *mist*, but, as attested by the literary example below, at times no distinction is made. **Bruma** generally has poetic overtones; sometimes, however, it is used in a meteorological sense as *haze*.

La **neblina** avanza sobre la ría, densa, lenta. (LE)	The fog moves forward over the estuary, thick and slow.

5. el escalón—step; rank (figurative)
   el peldaño—step
   la escalinata—steps
   la escalera—stairway, staircase (frequently plural); ladder
   el rellano—landing (of a staircase)

Escalón and **peldaño** are virtually synonymous. **Escalinata**, used in the singular, refers to a series of broad masonry or concrete steps located outside a building and serving as its entrance. **Escalera** is most often plural when the reference is to a number of individual steps rather than to a single stairway.

Sarrió va bajando lentamente, apoyado en la barandilla, los **peldaños** de la **escalera**. (LP)	Leaning on the banister, Sarrió comes slowly down the steps of the staircase.
Se llega a la pequeña plaza subiendo tres **peldaños** de piedra.	One reaches the little square by going up three stone steps.
Te espero en la **escalinata** del Museo del Prado.	I'll wait for you on the steps of the Prado.
Sus discípulos pertenecían al último **escalón** de la escala social. (MAH)	His pupils belonged to the bottom rung of the social scale.
El **rellano** está obscuro; a tientas busca el picaporte. (LN)	The landing (of the stairs) is dark; he gropes for the latch.

6. la cumbre—summit, top; height
   el pico—mountain with a pointed summit; the summit itself
   la cima—top, highest part of a mountain
   encima de—on top of
   dar cima a—to carry out; to finish (successfully)
   andar a picos pardos—to loaf around

En Austerlitz llegó Napoleón a la **cumbre** de su fortuna.	At Austerlitz Napoleon reached the high point of his good fortune.
El sol empezaba a dorar las **cumbres** de los montes. (SO)	The sun was beginning to turn the mountain tops to gold.
Dieron cima a una empresa importante.	They carried out successfully an important undertaking.

7. lucir—to shine; to wear
   lucirse—to show off
   el lucero—(an especially bright) star

En las ferias **luce** sus altas botas de cuero. (SV)

At the fairs he wears his high leather boots.

8. azul pálido—pale-blue
   azul claro—light-blue
   azul oscuro—dark-blue

9. el buque—ship, large boat
   el barco—ship, boat
   la barca—(small) boat
   el bote—rowboat
   el vapor—steamship, steamboat

Whereas **buque** refers to a large, oceangoing vessel, **barco**, the most common word for *boat*, ranges in size from very large to small. **Barca**, a smaller boat, is usually a fishing vessel limited to coastal or river navigation.

Los **buques** resultaban enormes con sus altísimos costados. (N)

The ships turned out to be enormous with their very high sides.

Mi padre era amigo de un importador, que me proporcionó empleo en un **barco** de carga.

My father was the friend of an importer, who provided me with a job aboard a freighter.

*La **barca** sin pescador*

The Boat without a Fisherman (a play by Alejandro Casona)

10. el ventanal—(large) window
    la ventanilla—(small) window of a vehicle, for the sale of tickets, etc.
    el balcón—balcony window; balcony

11. fruncir el ceño—to frown

Fruncir, *to wrinkle* or *contract*, is also used with **el entrecejo**, *the brow*, to render *to frown*. **Arrugar** is employed in most other contexts to translate *to wrinkle*, because **fruncir** suggests *to wrinkle in a pattern*.

Es imposible **arrugar** esta corbata.

It is impossible to wrinkle this tie.

12. ¡No, qué va!—Come on! What do you mean?

13. no es ninguna compañía para mí—isn't any company for me
    hacerle compañía a alguien—to keep someone company
    acompañar—to accompany; to escort
    escoltar—to escort

Escoltar implies that the person escorted or accompanied is being honored, protected, or prevented from escaping.

Acompañé a Carlos hasta la puerta.

I accompanied Charles to the door.

Escoltaron al general a su coche. | They escorted the general to his car.

14. ¿Quieren creer que . . . ?—Would you believe that . . . ?

When **querer** is encountered in an interrogative sentence in combination with an infinitive, especially in a request, it is often translated *will you* or *would you*.

¿**Quiere** Vd. **hacerme** un favor? | Will you do me a favor?

15. latir—to beat (said of the heart), throb;
batir—to beat; to whip (food)
batir palmas—to clap
batirse—to fight

Latir is the standard term to refer to the beating of the heart. When **batir** is used in conjunction with the heart, there is a definite implication of greater physical or emotional intensity or stress.

La música de la corrida hace **batir** todos los corazones. | The music at the bullfight makes everyone's heart beat fast.

El patrón **batió palmas** para que se apurasen. (LE) | The boss clapped so that they would hurry up.

Los soldados españoles **se batieron** con valor en aquella campaña. | The Spanish soldiers fought bravely in that campaign.

16. defenderse—to defend oneself; to get along
defender—to defend; to protect
proteger—to protect

En primavera los agricultores colocan toldos sobre las plantas para **defenderlas** de los vendavales. | In the spring the farmers place cloth coverings over the plants to protect them from the strong winds.

Ya **me defenderé** como sea yo solo. | I'll get along by myself somehow.

Siempre nos **ha protegido**. | He has always protected us.

17. herir—to wound; to injure
la herida—wound
el chichón—bump (on the head)
la lesión—injury, wound
lesionar—to injure
lisiar—to injure; to maim
salir ileso—to be unhurt; to come out unhurt
la cortadura—cut
cortarse—to cut oneself
la contusión—bruise

Herir generally implies a laceration or breaking of the skin. **Chichón** is found over bone. **Lesión** is a very general term for *injury* or *wound*, more general than, and subsuming, **herida**. **Lisiar** (**lisiadura**) tends to replace **lesionar** (**lesión**) when the injury is very serious or permanent.

Sus días en el fútbol están contados, porque tiene varias **lesiones** que le impiden correr bien.	His days in soccer are numbered, because he has several injuries that keep him from running well.
El domador quedó gravemente **herido** cuando el león le atacó.	The trainer was seriously injured when the lion attacked him.
Cervantes acabó por perder el movimiento de la mano **lisiada**.	Cervantes ended up losing the movement of his injured hand.

18. la gente, las gentes—people

Like many other words in Spanish, **gente** is used in both the singular and plural with no appreciable difference in meaning.

19. esconder, ocultar—to hide, conceal
    encubrir—to conceal, hide

Esconder is used more in spoken Spanish than **ocultar** and is preferred for tangible things; **ocultar** tends to be used for what is more abstract. In literature, however, there is often no distinction. **Encubrir** is most often used instead of **ocultar** when the meaning is *not to reveal something unpleasant or distasteful in nature*.

Nunca averiguaron donde **escondió** las joyas robadas.	They never found out where he hid the stolen jewelry.
De pronto, la luna **se ocultó** tras una nube. (R)	The moon was suddenly hidden behind a cloud.
Pero en la casa . . . las sonrisas de satisfacción **encubrían** algo que Pablo no veía. (BA)	But in the house . . . the smiles of satisfaction concealed something that Paul couldn't see.
Siempre **oculta** sus verdaderos motivos.	He always conceals his true motives.

20. colocar—to place, put; to place in a position or job
    la colocación—job, position
    meter—to insert; to put
    poner—to put

Poner, the basic word for *to put*, has a meaning that includes those of both **colocar** and **meter**. Often, but not always, **colocar** replaces **poner** when exact location is specified or when special care is used in placing an object. **Meter** is used instead of **poner** when something is being put within or inside something else or when a person is being confined.

Le **colocaron** en un banco.	They placed him in a bank.
El artista **colocó** un manojo de pinceles en el vaso.	The artist placed a handful of brushes in the glass.
Traía una bandeja y fue **colocando** las tazas. (LM)	She brought a tray and went about placing the cups.
Metieron al niño en una caja de madera y le clavaron la tapa. (FN)	They put the child in a wooden box and nailed the top closed.
Doblé el papel, lo **metí** en la cartera . . . ¡Estaba libre! (FPD)	I folded the paper, and put it in my wallet . . . I was free!
Le **metieron** en la cárcel.	They put him in jail.

21. ser oriundo de—to come from, hail from

Pereda **era oriundo de** Santander.	Pereda came from Santander.

22. la reunión—gathering, meeting (formal or informal)
    reunirse—to gather; to meet
    la junta—meeting (usually a small group with the power to take action)
    el mitin—(public) meeting (often to debate political or social questions)

Vamos a **reunirnos** para discutir el problema.	We are going to meet to discuss the problem.
Dirigía la palabra al público en un **mitin** político.	He was addressing the public at a political meeting.
Se celebra esta **junta** para elegir a nuestro nuevo director.	This meeting is being held to elect our new director.

23. echar de menos—to miss (feel the absence of something)
    extrañar—to banish; to miss (in parts of Spain and most of Spanish America)
    perder—to miss (not to arrive on time, to fail to understand, etc.)
    añorar—to long for
    la añoranza—longing

Echo de menos (**extraño**) a mi familia.	I miss my family.
Los refugiados siempre **añoran** a su tierra.	Refugees always miss (long for) their native land.
Perdí lo que dijo.	I missed what he said.

24. la esquina—corner (outside corner of anything)
    el rincón—corner (inner angle); hidden or out-of-the-way place
    el ángulo—corner (mainly literary, may replace either esquina or rincón)
    la(s) comisura(s) (de los labios)—corner(s) (of the mouth, lips)

Esta me saludó fríamente sin dejar de agarrar las **esquinas** de su delantal. (SCA)	She greeted me coldly without letting go of the corners of her apron.
Le llamaron a Carlos cuando doblaba la **esquina** de la casa.	They called Charles as he was going around the corner of the house.
Están pasando las vacaciones en un pintoresco **rincón** de Irlanda.	They are spending their vacation in a picturesque corner of Ireland.
Pepa se sentó en un **ángulo** de la sala.	Pepa sat down in a corner of the living room.
Siempre tenía un cigarrillo en la **comisura** de los labios.	He always had a cigarette in the corner of his mouth.

EXERCISES ON NOTES

1. From the balcony he saw that a military guard was accompanying the ambassador. 2. The soldiers had to climb a very steep rock in order to reach the fortress. 3. They banished him to a remote island. 4. Only then did I notice that it had stopped raining. 5. The writings of Galdós and Cervantes rank (**figurar**) among the highest achievements (*one word*) of world literature. 6. They put the orphan in a school without consulting me first. 7. The bump on his forehead was the result of a fall. 8. My heart never beat more violently. 9. He couldn't work after he was (**quedar**) injured in the factory. 10. Today we meet for the last time during the opera season. 11. The squirrel got into the house by climbing up the ivy. 12. I'm sorry I missed the lecture last night. 13. After putting the letter in the envelope, he handed it to the mailman. 14. To make a good omelette, it is necessary to beat the eggs well. 15. The child always wants someone to keep him company. 16. Why have you concealed so many details of your life [from] me? 17. He frowned when he saw the demonstrators gathering on the steps of City Hall. 18. Whom are you escorting to the dance? 19. Man invented the umbrella to protect himself from the rain. 20. In the next (**vecina**) boat fishermen were unloading baskets of sardines. 21. They removed the tablecloths and placed the chairs on top of the tables. 22. He is still looking for hidden treasure. 23. When I saw her, she was (**ir**) accompanied by (**de**) a tall gentleman. 24. The family wanted to put her in a convent. 25. Because of the fog, the plane will have to land at another airport. 26. She went up on foot, for the elevator wasn't working (**funcionar**). 27. It was a miracle that she was unhurt. 28. The little girl fixed her gaze on the waiter's enormous mustache (*plural*). 29. The doctor came slowly down the stairs. 30. He hid the toy under his pillow. 31. She placed the bottle on the corner of the table. 32. I saw the top of the mountain shining in the sun, but its base remained concealed by a layer (**capa**) of mist. 33. He's a good person, but he's always showing off. 34. He didn't obtain the position he wanted. 35. It's natural that you feel a longing for (**de**) your old home. 36. The lieutenant was wearing (*not* **llevar**) an elegant dark-blue

uniform. 37. I miss the excitement of the baseball season. 38. Have you noticed that they put the light-green chair in the corner? 39. The child didn't wipe (**limpiar**) the corners of his mouth after drinking the milk. 40. He is irresponsible and has probably gone on a spree again.

CUESTIONARIO

a. contenido

1. ¿Qué hizo Marta al quedar detrás?
2. ¿Por qué pensaba Marta en un país muy frío?
3. ¿Por qué no estaba tranquila?
4. ¿Qué le hizo fruncir el ceño?
5. ¿Qué pensamiento la consolaba?
6. ¿Por qué llamaban a Vicenta la majorera?
7. ¿Por qué se avergonzó Marta al notar que Vicenta la estaba mirando?

b. estilo

1. ¿Qué ambiente crea la autora con sus alusiones a la naturaleza en el primer párrafo?
2. ¿Cómo nos hace entrar la autora en la imaginación de Marta?
3. ¿Cómo se contrastan el mundo de la naturaleza y el de las personas?
4. Comente Vd. el retrato de Vicenta.
5. ¿Cómo logra la autora convencernos de la gran sensibilidad de Marta?

TEMA—TRADUCCION

Martha didn't know why she had never noticed this beautiful garden before. Now, for the first time, she really saw the bougainvillaea and honeysuckle that climbed the walls of the house where she had spent most of her life.

She thought of the refugees and wondered what impressions she would have if she had just arrived from a cold climate. Then she sat down on a stone step and soon was gazing at the horizon, where the Canary Islands' highest peak stood out like a giant steamer sailing through a dark-blue sea.

Suddenly Pino's voice brought Martha back to reality, for through an open window she heard her talking with the new guests. It reminded her that tranquility and understanding disappeared within the walls of that house. No one had noticed the open window, for Martha heard the sharp voice of her sister-in-law complaining about her. Pino was also telling them that Martha preferred her studies to their company.

What hurt Martha most was that she could not defend herself, for there was some truth (**algo de verdad**) in what Pino had said. Nevertheless she promised herself that one day she would reveal the secrets concealed by the walls of that house. It consoled her to think that in (**con**) time others would know how much she had suffered.

Suddenly Martha sensed that someone was watching her. On turning her head she saw Vicenta, the cook. On noticing the girl's absence, Vicenta had gone out to the garden to look for her. Despite her sadness, Martha couldn't help smiling when she saw the cook's strange appearance, for she (**ésta**) had placed a large straw hat over her black kerchief. Nevertheless Martha blushed, for she was ashamed that the cook had caught her in a moment of weakness and had seen her crying. Without a word Martha went into the house, and Vicenta followed her. Under the midday sun the fragrance of the honeysuckle soon filled the silent garden.

TEMAS A ESCOGER

Escríbanse unas 200 palabras sobre uno de los temas siguientes usando a lo menos 20 de las palabras y expresiones estudiadas en este capítulo.

1. Una visita a una isla tropical en pleno invierno
2. Impresiones de un refugiado al llegar a su asilo
3. El efecto de la falta de cariño en la formación de una persona

chapter 7

29. TO BECOME

There are many ways of translating the English verb *to become* (and its variants, *to get, to turn, to grow,* etc.) into Spanish. Sometimes only one Spanish verb or verb phrase is appropriate to render *to become*; sometimes it is possible (or necessary) to choose between two or more Spanish locutions, depending upon circumstances, shades of meaning, etc.

A. Ponerse refers especially to changes in appearance or in physical or emotional state. It applies to people or things and is used with adjectives.

Andrea le vio **ponerse** pálido, luego cenizoso, después verde. (EBM)	Andrea saw him become (turn) pale, then ash-gray, and then green.
¿Por qué **te has puesto** tan triste?	Why have you become so sad?

B. Hacerse is employed with both nouns and adjectives. With people, it indicates what is the result of a voluntary effort or the standard and natural transition from one state to another.

Tiene mi edad y ya **se ha hecho** rico.	He is my age and he has become rich already.
Los dos hermanos quieren **hacerse abogados**.	Both brothers want to become lawyers.

With things, **hacerse** is sometimes interchangeable with **ponerse**. The latter, however, stresses the suddenness of a change or gives it greater emotional force.

Se ha hecho casi imposible obtener entradas para la función.	It has become almost impossible to obtain tickets for the show.
La situación **se puso** (**se hizo**) muy tirante.	The situation became very tense.

C. Volverse has two principal uses. It is used primarily to stress that the change from one state to another is violent, sudden, or comprehensive in nature. It is also used with approximately the same value as **ponerse** and **hacerse**.

El viejo **se volvió** loco.	The old man went (became) insane.
Se volvió rico de la noche a la mañana.	He became rich overnight.
Cada día **se vuelve** usted más listo. (F)	You become more clever every day.

| La gente **se vuelve** mucho más conformista cuando puede pasear por parques como éste . . . (SH) | People become much more conformist when they can stroll through parks like this one . . . |

D. Llegar a ser indicates a gradual process or outlines the steps leading to an end result.

| Después de muchos años **llegó a ser** director general del banco. | After many years he became president of the bank. |

E. Meterse indicates *to become* in the sense of *to take religious orders*. **Meterse a** is used for a sudden change of occupation and sometimes suggests that the subject is poorly prepared for, or unlikely to persevere in, his new endeavor. **Meterse a** differs from **volverse** in that it is used only to refer to occupations, vocations, professions, etc.

Y usted, ¿qué piensa hacer? ¿Salir del colegio para casarse o **meterse** monja? (CP)	And what do you intend to do? Leave school in order to get married or to become a nun?
Ahora **se ha metido a** poeta.	Now he has become a poet.
Cuando Don Juan se arrepiente, **se mete a** fraile . . . muy rara vez a padre de familia. (JM)	When Don Juan repents, he becomes a friar . . . only rarely the father of a family.

F. Convertirse en refers to a change in the basic nature of a person or thing.

| **Me he convertido en** una mujer triste, cansada y temerosa. (CBA) | I have become (changed into) a sad, tired, and fearful woman. |

G. Tornarse is largely a literary synonym for **ponerse** and **volverse**.

| Pero al beber otra vez, **tornáronse** melancólicos. (AT) | But when they drank again, they became melancholy. |

H. In certain cases a reflexive or an intransitive verb without an adjective can replace an adjective used in combination with one of the preceding equivalents of *to become*. The idea conveyed by the verbs listed below may also be expressed by **ponerse triste, hacerse viejo, volverse loco,** etc.

Reflexive	To Become	Intransitive	To Become
cansarse	tired	empeorar	worse
empobrecerse	poor	enloquecer	crazy
enfriarse	cold	envejecer	old
enrojecerse	red (to blush)	enviudar	a widow(er)
enriquecerse	rich	mejorar	better
entristecerse	sad		
obscurecerse	dark		

Isabel **se endureció, envejeció** extrañamente. (HM)	Isabel became hard, and she aged strangely.
Tu abuela **ha enloquecido.**	Your grandmother has gone crazy (become insane).
De repente **se calló.**	He suddenly became quiet.
El cielo **se oscureció** más en el momento de expresarse así Nucha. (PU)	The sky became darker at the moment when Nucha expressed herself that way.

I. Quedar(se), used with an adjective or a noun, is the equivalent of *to become* when deprivation or loss is involved. **Quedar**(se) is sometimes also rendered by the English *to be left*.

Sabe que **se va quedando** ciego.	He knows that he is becoming (going) blind.
Quedó huérfano a los seis años.	He became (was left) an orphan when he was six years old.
Es probable que **me quede** calvo—decía—; pero tuberculoso, no. (M)	"I will probably become bald," he said, "but not tubercular."

30. SOME PREPOSITIONS

Prepositions express various relationships between two or more words. Here we review only a few uses of several common prepositions.

A. a—*to, at, in*

1. **A** expresses direction or motion toward some place or goal and consequently follows verbs of motion whenever the object is expressed. **En** sometimes renders *at* following verbs of motion, but **a** is more common.

Llegamos tarde **a** casa.	We arrived home late. (direction or destination)
Estoy enseñándole **a** escribir.	I am teaching him to write. (implied motion in progress toward a goal)
Voy **a** Madrid a estudiar **a** la Universidad. Voy **a** Madrid a estudiar **en** la Universidad.	I am going to study at the University of Madrid.

2. **A** regularly follows a verb of motion, but before an infinitive **para** may replace **a** to stress the idea of purpose or to intensify the idea of uncertainty as to the outcome.

Corrí **a** alcanzarlos. ⎫ Corrí **para** alcanzarlos. ⎭	I ran to catch up with them.
Ha venido **a** hablarte.	He has come to talk to you.
Ha venido **para** hablarte.	He has come to talk (for the specific purpose of, in the hope of, talking) to you.

3. **A** is used before a direct object when the direct object is a specific person; it is also used when the speaker personifies an animal or thing that is a direct object. When the direct object is an indefinite person, however, **a** is omitted. Finally, despite their indefinite nature, indefinite personal pronouns always take the personal **a** as a sign of the accusative when used as direct objects.

Esta mañana vi **a** su tío.	I saw your uncle this morning.
No todos temen la muerte. ⎫ No todos temen **a** la muerte. ⎭	Not everyone fears death.
El caballero necesitaba un escudero.	The knight needed a squire.
Buscamos una nueva criada.	We are looking for a new maid.
No vi **a** nadie ayer.	I didn't see anyone yesterday.

When the direct object is a single person, the use or omission of the personal **a** depends upon the explicitness of the noun employed as direct object. The use of **a** with collective nouns, for example, reflects the action more directly in its effect on the individuals composing the group than on the group as a whole.

Conozco la familia de que estás hablando.	I know the family you are talking about.
El orador pudo conmover **a** toda la familia.	The speaker was able to move the entire family.
. . . unos dirán que eres caritativo, otros que sostienes borrachos. (ET)	. . . some people will (probably) say you are charitable, others that you support drunkards.
Daniel no ha tenido que trabajar, ni mantener un hijo.	Daniel has neither had to work, nor support a child.

B. **de**—*of, from*

1. Certain verbs (**robar**, **quitar**, **comprar**, etc.) require that a preposition separate the direct and the indirect objects. The preposition to use in such cases is not **de** (which would indicate possession) but **a**.

| Le pedí prestado un dólar **a** Juan. | I borrowed a dollar from John. |
| Le quitaron el juguete **al** niño. | They took the child's toy away from him. |

2. Sometimes **de** is used to translate *with*. This use indicates final state or result as opposed to the means or agent leading to the result. **De** is also used to identify a person or thing accomplished in English by means of a prepositional phrase introduced by *with*.

Las montañas estaban cubiertas **de** nieve.	The mountains were covered with snow.
Cubrieron el cadáver **con** nieve.	They covered the body with snow.
El perro **de** la pata rota es del vecino.	The dog with the broken paw is the neighbor's.
Vive en la casa **del** tejado rojo.	He lives in the house with the red roof.

3. The correlatives *from . . . to* are rendered by **de . . . en**

| Van **de** casa **en** casa buscando a su hijo. | They go from house to house looking for their son. |

C. en—*at, in, on, upon*

Since **en** has many uses, other prepositions sometimes replace it in order to express a given relationship more exactly. When **en** means *on* (*top of*), for example, it is ordinarily replaced by **sobre** or **encima de**.

1. **Sobre** means *over*, *above*, and *on*, and is used to avoid ambiguity when **en** could mean either *on* or *in*.

| Dejé el dinero **en** el escritorio. | I left the money in (on) the desk. |
| Dejé el dinero **sobre** el escritorio. | I left the money on the desk. |

2. **Encima de**, *on top of*, indicates location even more precisely than **sobre**. Thus it may translate *on top of* and *on* when specific location is being emphasized.

| Te he dicho que lo dejé **encima de** la mesa. | I told you that I left it on top of the table. |
| El lápiz está **encima de** aquel libro. | The pencil is on top of that book. |

D. por, para—*for*

Por and **para** are the two common equivalents of the English *for*.

The basic meaning of **por** is *movement through*; **para** is *movement toward* or *destination*. Many other meanings of these words are largely extensions of this basic distinction.

1. **Para** implies motion toward something and thus is used for (a) destination, (b) purpose, (c) future time.

   a. Salieron **para** Caracas.

   They left for Caracas.

   b. Mi hijo estudia **para** (ser) médico.

   My son is studying to be a doctor.

   c. Termínelo Vd. **para** el viernes.

   Finish it by Friday.

2. **Para** indicates an implied comparison and has the value of the English *considering the fact that*.

   Es alto **para** un muchacho de trece años.

   He is tall for a boy of thirteen.

3. **Por** is used to indicate (a) motion through, (b) exchange, (c) cause, (d) time during which, (e) motivation, (f) manner or means.

   a. Colocó las flores **por** la sala.

   She placed flowers around the living room.

   b. Te doy las gracias **por** el regalo.

   I thank you for the gift.

   c. **Por** la lluvia las calles están resbaladizas.

   Because of the rain the streets are slippery.

   d. **Por** noviembre suele llover mucho.

   Around November it usually rains a great deal.

   Habló (**por**) veinte minutos.

   He spoke (for) twenty minutes.

   e. Sacrificó la vida **por** su patria.

   He sacrificed his life for his country.

   Ha trabajado mucho **por** su familia.

   He has worked hard for the sake of his family.

   f. Oímos la música **por** radio.

   We heard the music on the radio.

The distinction between **por** and **para** is often quite subtle. **Para** indicates purpose or the goal of an effort or quest. **Por** is preferred to stress personal motivation and to convey a feeling of urgency or greater uncertainty as to the success of the undertaking. In many cases purpose (**para**) and motivation (**por**) are not clearly separable; in such cases either preposition is proper.

Siempre he trabajado **para** (**por**) mi familia.

I have always worked for my family.

En el mundo no se debe des- truir nada, porque todo existe **por** algo y **para** algo. (IE)	Nothing in the world should be destroyed, for everything exists for the sake of something and for some end.

E. Other prepositions

It is often necessary to choose between two related prepositions to express a certain relationship. Usually the longer of the two indicates more precisely a purely physical or spatial relationship, whereas the shorter is preferred for figurative or personal situations. Nevertheless in actual usage there is in a few cases no clear distinction between the long and the short form.

1. **ante—delante de. Delante de** indicates location *in front of*, whereas **ante** often adds the idea of criticism or judgment and thus is preferred in figurative uses.

Le dejé **delante de** la casa.	I left him in front of the house.
Apareció **ante** el tribunal.	He appeared before (in front of) the court.

2. **bajo—debajo de.** To translate *under* or *beneath* in a figurative sense, **bajo** is better. Contamination between the two forms has resulted in **bajo de**, not grammatically correct but frequently used in spoken and written Spanish.

Trabajó dos años **bajo** el gran científico. (incorrect with **debajo de**)	He worked two years under the great scientist.
Murió sobre mi manta, **bajo** un cielo lluvioso. (CA)	He died on my blanket, under a rainy sky.
Debajo de un cielo cada vez más amenazador, aparecía el panorama de las azoteas. (N)	Under an increasingly threatening sky, the panorama of roofs appeared.

3. **Detrás de—tras.** The longer form means *in back of* or *behind*. **Tras** is best rendered by *after* or *just behind*. In a figurative sense, **tras** conveys the idea of following, pursuing, or seeking expressed in English by *after*.

Le encontraron **detrás de** la tienda.	They found him behind the store.
Corrió **tras** el coche.	He ran after the car.

F. Combinations of prepositions

Spanish juxtaposes two or three prepositions to express a relationship for which a single preposition is inadequate. **Por** and **de** are the most common initial elements of such compounds, but other prepositions also occupy this position. Although each preposition retains much of its original meaning in Spanish, often a single English preposition must suffice to render these prepositional compounds.

Le vi al pasar **por delante de** la biblioteca.

I saw him when I passed in front of the library.

Lo saca **de debajo de** la mesa.

He takes it out from under the table.

Desde por entre los árboles, el enemigo nos observaba.

From among the trees, the enemy was observing us.

EXERCISES

1. Our group is fighting for the well-being of the workers. 2. The night of the party he became drunk. 3. There is a new bridge over the river. 4. I can't believe she has become so beautiful. 5. Every day things get more expensive, and it becomes more and more difficult to feed four mouths. 6. He suddenly became (*two ways*) very sad. 7. We were strolling under the warm (**tibio**) December sun. 8. Only by stealing hours from his (**el**) sleep was he able to finish the report on time. 9. This lecture is becoming very boring. 10. Everyone laughed when Don Quixote decided to become a knight-errant. 11. Mary turned red when I mentioned her rival. 12. They are asking for money to help the needy. 13. When I became a widow, I went to ask him for advice. 14. You forget that I have a family to support. 15. They put it [right] under the stage. 16. The boys ran after the dog. 17. The news went (**correr**) from mouth to mouth through the entire town. 18. At the critical moment the brave soldiers became cowards. 19. She went (**acudir**) toward where the voice was coming from. 20. The laundress deposited the basket of clothes on the table. 21. It is difficult to know what is under the surface. 22. He went crazy when he learned the news. 23. Nobody wants to lodge the strangers in his house. 24. The farmer's wife has put some tomatoes to ripen on the window sill. 25. The rain became stronger in the afternoon. 26. His brother has not become accustomed to life in Madrid. 27. The eyes behind the glasses were gentle, almost timid. 28. He came running out from under the bridge. 29. The couple has to pay twenty duros a month for the attic in which they live. 30. The poor clerk slept under the counter. 31. He was so impatient to know the news that he ran to open the door. 32. Why did such a cruel man become humble? 33. I would give two years of my life to see her again. 34. The doctor warned her she would become blind if she didn't take better care of her eyes. 35. In (**con**) time he will become chief clerk of the store. 36. After living two years in this town he has become another person. 37. He was called before the court. 38. He was making a great effort to remember. 39. On top of the table there was a small dish of strawberries. 40. The doctor buys a paper from the small boy and forgets that his coffee is getting cold.

31. SELECCION LITERARIA

Viaje a la Alcarria*

Camilo José Cela

En la selección que sigue, Cela presenta al viajero, mochila al hombro, ya andando por el campo. Aquí le vemos, al poco de salir de Guadalajara, hablando con Armando Mondéjar López, un muchacho de trece años.

—¿Cuántos hermanos tienes?

—Somos cinco: cuatro niños y una niña. Yo soy el mayor.[1]

—¿Sois todos rubios?

—Sí, señor. Todos tenemos el pelo[2] rojo; mi papá también lo tiene.

5 En la voz del niño hay como una vaga cadencia de tristeza. El viajero no hubiera querido preguntar tanto. Piensa[3] un instante, mientras guarda la toalla y el jabón y saca de la mochila los tomates, el pan[4] y una lata[5] de *foie-gras*, que se ha pasado de rosca[6] preguntando.

—¿Comemos un poco?

10 —Bueno; como usted guste.

El viajero trata de hacerse amable, y el niño, poco a poco, vuelve a la alegría de antes de decir: Sí, todos tenemos el pelo rojo; mi papá también lo tiene. El viajero le cuenta al niño que no va a Zaragoza, que va a darse una vueltecita[7] por la Alcarria; le cuenta también de dónde es, cómo se 15 llama, cuántos hermanos tiene. Cuando le habla de un primo suyo, bizco,[8] que vive en Málaga y que se llama Jenaro, el niño va ya muerto de risa. Después le cuenta cosas de la guerra, y el niño escucha atento, emocionado, con los ojos muy abiertos.

—¿Le han dado algún tiro?

20 El viajero y el niño se han hecho muy amigos y, hablando, hablando, llegan hasta el camino de Iriépal. El niño se despide.[9]

—Tengo que volver; mi mamá quiere que esté en casa a la hora de merendar.[10] Además, no le gusta que venga hasta aquí; siempre me lo tiene dicho.[11]

25 El viajero le alarga la mano, y el niño la rehuye.

—Es que la tengo sucia, ¿sabe usted?

—¡Anda, no seas tonto! ¿Qué más da?[12]

El niño mira para el suelo.

---

*Continuation of the selection in Chap. 3.

—Es que me ando siempre con el dedo en la nariz.

—¿Y eso qué importa? Ya te he visto. Yo también me hurgo, algunas veces, con el dedo en la nariz. Da mucho gusto, ¿verdad?

—Sí, señor; mucho gusto.

El viajero echa a andar[13] y el niño se queda mirándole, al borde[14] de la carretera. Desde muy lejos, el viajero se vuelve. El niño le dice adiós con la mano. A pleno sol,[15] el pelo le brilla como si fuera de fuego. El niño tiene un pelo hermoso, luminoso, lleno de encanto. El cree lo contrario.

*　*　*　*　*

Poco más adelante, el viajero se sienta a comer en una vaguada, al pie de un olivar.[16] Bebe después un trago[17] de vino, desdobla[18] su manta y se tumba a dormir la siesta bajo un árbol. Por la carretera pasa, de vez en cuando, alguna bicicleta o algún coche oficial. A lo lejos, sentado a la sombra de un olivo, un pastor canta. Las ovejas están apiñadas, inmóviles, muertas de calor. Echado sobre la manta, el viajero ve de cerca la vida de los insectos, que corren veloces de un lado para otro y se detienen[19] de golpe, mientras mueven acompasadamente sus largos cuernos, delgaditos como un pelo. El campo está verde, bien cuidado, y las florecitas silvestres[20]—las rojas amapolas, las margaritas blancas, los cardos de flor azul, los dorados botones del botón de oro—crecen[21] a los bordes de la carretera, fuera de los sembrados.[22]

32. NOTES

1.　**Mayor** and **menor**, equivalents of **más grande** and **más pequeño**, are also used to indicate age.

Mi hermano **mayor** está en la marina.	My older (or oldest) brother is in the Navy.

2.　el pelo—hair
　　el cabello—hair
　　las canas—gray hair
　　rubio—blond
　　rubia oxigenada—peroxide blonde
　　moreno—brown
　　pelirrojo—redhead
　　calvo—bald
　　la calvicie—baldness
　　tomarle el pelo a alguien—to pull someone's leg

Pelo means *hair* in all contexts, human or animal. **Cabello** (often plural) is more elevated in tone, for it refers only to human hair, almost always on the head. This rather poetic synonym of **pelo** is used frequently in advertising and in literary Spanish.

César se quitó la gorra. Tenía el **pelo cano**, ralo. (VS)	Caesar took off his cap. He had thin, gray hair.
Su mujer estaba muy preocupada porque había encontrado algunas **canas**.	His wife was very concerned, for she had found a few gray hairs.
Siempre **están tomándole el pelo**.	They are always pulling his leg.
El muchacho tenía largos **cabellos** dorados . . . (SV)	The boy had long golden hair . . .

3. pensar—to think
    pensar + infinitive—to intend + infinitive
    pensar de—to think of
    pensar en—to think about
    ¿Qué le parece(n) esta(s) silla(s)?—What do you think of this (these) chair(s)?

    ¿Qué piensa(s) de . . . ? and **¿Qué le (te) parece** . . . ? both render *What do you think of*. . . ? The first, however, means *to have a definite opinion* about something, whereas the second usually indicates an initial impression close in meaning to the English *How do you like* . . . ? **Pensar en** indicates *to direct one's thoughts* to someone or something.

Casi nunca **piensa en** su familia.	He almost never thinks of (about) his family.
¿Qué **piensas del** nuevo senador?	What do you think of the new senator?

4. el pan—bread, loaf of bread
    dos panes—two loaves of bread
    una lechuga—a head of lettuce
    un mueble—a piece of furniture
    un rayo—a bolt of lightning

    Although Spanish has words for *loaf* and *head* (**hogaza** and **mata**), they are little used. In general, the English counter is best left untranslated. (In many cases, like **mueble** and **rayo**, no counter exists.)

5. la lata—(tin) can; annoyance
    el bote—can
    dar la lata—to pester, annoy
    latoso—annoying

    While **lata** may have any shape, **bote** is usually cylindrical.

Es una **lata** tener que hacer tanto papeleo.	It's a bother to have to do so much paper work.
Abrió otro **bote** de guisantes.	He opened another can of peas.

6. pasarse de rosca—to go too far

The colloquial expression **pasarse de rosca** is an extension of the expression that a screw will no longer fit in a threaded hole (**rosca**) because it has been forced too much.

Te pasaste de rosca cuando revelaste la edad de María.	You went too far when you revealed Mary's age.

7. darse una vueltecita—to take a walk, stroll, turn (usually the reflexive pronoun is omitted)
   dar un paseo—to take a walk, stroll, ride (in a vehicle)
   pasear(se)—to walk, stroll (commonly without the reflexive pronoun)

Daremos una vuelta (un paseo) por el parque después de la cena.	After dinner we shall take a walk in the park.
Dio un paseo en coche hasta la presa.	He took a ride in the car as far as the dam.
Estaban paseando por la Gran Vía.	They were walking along the Gran Vía.

8. bizco—cross-eyed
   miope—myopic; nearsighted
   présbita—farsighted
   tuerto—one-eyed

9. despedirse (de)—to say good-by (to), take leave (of)
   decir adiós—to say good-by
   despedir a—to dismiss; to fire (someone from a position)

Antes, debo **despedirme de** ellos.	First, I must say good-by to them.
Le **despidieron** sin motivo alguno.	They fired him without any reason at all.

10. merendar—to have a snack
    la merienda—snack
    almorzar—to have (a light) lunch
    el almuerzo—lunch
    la comida—meal, food
    cenar—to have dinner, supper
    la cena—dinner, supper
    desayunar(se)—to have breakfast

La comida, usually the main meal of the day, is served about 2 P.M. or after. **Merienda** may be a snack at any time, but most often it refers to a light repast taken late in the afternoon to stay the appetite until dinner, which is generally served at an hour that is quite late by American standards. **Desayunarse**, by analogy with **almorzar** and

cenar, is now ordinarily used without the reflexive pronoun. Finally, **tomar** with the name of the meal frequently replaces the verb conveying this idea.

¿Qué quieres **almorzar**?	What do you want to have for lunch?
Mañana vendrán a **tomar el desayuno** con nosotros.	Tomorrow they are coming to have breakfast with us.

11. me lo tiene dicho—she has told me so

Tener may replace **haber** in a compound to stress the result rather than the action. English does not always have a good translation equivalent for this construction.

Tiene escritas tres cartas.	He has three letters written.
Ha escrito tres cartas.	He has written three letters.
Tengo entendido que nos dejas.	I understand that you are leaving us.

12. ¿Qué más da?—What difference does it make? What does it matter?
¿Qué importa?—What difference does it make? What does it matter?

The verb of a subordinate clause following either of these expressions must be in the subjunctive.

¿**Qué más da que no tengamos** dinero?	What difference does it make that we don't have money?

13. echar a andar—to start to walk, begin to walk
echarse a reír—to start to laugh; to burst out laughing

Notice that the reflexive pronoun is used with **echar a** when emotion is involved. When motion alone is indicated, the reflexive pronoun is not included.

14. el borde—edge; border; shore
la frontera—border, frontier

Nos miraban desde el **borde** del jardín.	They were watching us from the edge of the garden.
Era imposible cruzar la **frontera** en invierno.	It was impossible to cross the border in winter.

15. pleno—full
a pleno sol—in the full sun
lleno—full
en pleno invierno—in the heart of winter
en pleno día—in broad daylight

Lleno means *full* in a more material sense than **pleno**, which is more literary or figurative in its uses. **Pleno** is standard, however, in spoken

and written Spanish to indicate the idea of *in the very middle of.*
Its many translation equivalents in English include: *in the middle of,
in the midst of, in the heart of, at the height of, in broad (full),* etc.

Me dio **plenos** poderes para decidir el asunto.	He gave me full power to decide the question.
Parece mentira que haya guerra, que España esté en **plena** guerra civil. (ID)	It seems incredible that there is war, that Spain is in the midst of a civil war.
En **plenas** vacaciones estalló la guerra. (LM)	The war broke out in the middle of vacation.
El tranvía va **lleno**; tendremos que esperar otro.	The streetcar is full; we shall have to wait for another.
El vaso está **lleno** hasta los bordes.	The glass is full to the top.

16. el olivar—olive grove
    el olivo—olive tree
    la oliva—olive*

Spanish regularly forms the words for a particular type of grove or
orchard, tree, and fruit through the use of a stem and the endings
-**ar** (**al**), -**o**, and -**a**, respectively. **Huerto**, *orchard*, and **árbol**, *tree*, are
not used to perform these functions. (There are a few exceptions to
the pattern: *pear*, for example, is **pera**, but *pear tree* (*orchard*) are **peral**
and **peraleda**). Also, when the word for the fruit does not end in -**a**,
the noun for the tree often bears a different ending: **limón**, **limonero**,
limonar.

Fueron al **naranjal** a coger **naranjas**.	They went to the grove to pick oranges.
Este **melocotonero** es muy viejo.	This peach tree is very old.
El nuevo **manzanar** da muchas manzanas.	The new apple orchard produces many apples.

17. el trago—swallow, drink; shot
    tragar—to swallow
    echar un trago—to have a drink

Hace demasiados años que lo oigo repetir para que pueda **tragármelo**. (NOC)	I have been hearing it repeated too many years to be able to swallow it.
Terminó todo el café de un solo **trago**.	He finished all his coffee in one swallow.

18. desdoblar—to unfold

Des- regularly renders the English verbal prefix *un-*.

---

*Oliva is used for **aceite de oliva**, *olive oil;* the standard word for *olive* is **aceituna**.

Cruzó una pierna sobre la otra y luego las **descruzó**.	She crossed one leg over the other and then uncrossed them.
Castilla ha hecho a España y Castilla la **ha deshecho**. (EI)	Castile created Spain and Castile undid her.

19. detenerse—to stop
parar(se)—to stop
cesar de + infinitive—to stop
dejar de + infinitive—to stop

Detener is *to stop* or *to arrest someone* for something. When a person stops himself, **detener** must be reflexive. **Parar(se)**, unlike **detener**, frequently omits the reflexive pronoun to indicate a halting of one's own motion; it is more widely used than **detener(se)**. There is no clear distinction in meaning except that **detenerse** is sometimes preferred to stress that the stopping is temporary and that motion will be resumed. **Parar** alone should be used for *to stop over* or *to stop at the end of one's destination*. **Dejar de** and the less common **cesar de** are used with infinitives to indicate the suspension of an activity, whereas forms of **detener** and **parar** are used mainly to indicate the temporary or permanent cessation of some type of motion.

Si los hombres se desalentaran, el mundo **se detendría** en el camino del progreso. (LN)	If men were to become discouraged, the world would stop on its road to progress.
Nos **detuvieron** en la frontera, pero pronto nos dejaron pasar.	They stopped us at the border, but soon let us pass.
Nos **detuvimos** ante mi casa. Pagué y el taxi arrancó en seguida, calle abajo. (THI)	We stopped in front of my house. I paid, and the taxi started immediately down the street.
Intimidados, **nos detuvimos** en la puerta. (LM)	Intimidated, we stopped at the door.
Me detuve a hablar un momento con Carlos.	I stopped a moment to talk to Charles.
El reloj de la torre **se había parado** a las cinco y cinco. (F)	The tower clock had stopped at 5:05.
Paró cuando me oyó llamarle.	He stopped when he heard me call him.
. . . el tiempo que en él **paré** lo dediqué a divertirme lo más barato que podía. (FPD)	. . . I dedicated the time I spent there enjoying myself as cheaply as I could.
Esta noche vamos a **parar** en aquel motel.	Tonight we are going to stop at that motel.
Si acaricias al perro, **dejará de** ladrar.	If you pet the dog, he will stop barking.

20. silvestre—wild
    salvaje—wild (not domesticated); savage, uncivilized
    fiero—fierce, ferocious, wild
    la fiera—wild beast

Silvestre, said of plants, means *uncultivated* or *growing in a natural state*. **Salvaje** may be applied to land, animals, plants, and people. **Fiero** is used mainly for animals. Notice the meaning of **la fiera**.

Comían fresas **silvestres**.	They were eating wild strawberries.
La selva está llena de animales **salvajes**.	The jungle is full of wild animals.
Las **fieras** del circo iban en grandes jaulas.	The wild animals at the circus were in large cages.
La isla está habitada por una tribu de indios **salvajes**.	The island is inhabited by a tribe of wild Indians.

21. crecer—to grow
    cultivar—to grow, raise
    criar—to bring up; to rear (children); to raise (animals)

Crecer is intransitive and refers to the normal increase in size of any animal or plant. **Cultivar** means *to grow plants*. **Criar** is used for people and animals.

Parece que la planta ha dejado de **crecer**.	It seems that the plant has stopped growing.
Está cultivando fresas detrás de la casa.	He is growing strawberries behind the house.
Cría gallinas en el corral.	He raises chickens in the back yard.

22. el sembrado—field
    el campo—field
    el trigal, el maizal, el cañaveral—wheat field, corn field, cane field

Campo, the standard word for **field**, is often replaced by **sembrado** (**sembrar**—*to sow*) to indicate a planted field. Spanish regularly indicates a field of a particular grain or crop by adding -**al** or -**ar** to the name of that grain or crop.

Estos **campos** están todavía sin arar.	These fields are still unplowed.
Encontraron al niño en el **melonar**.	They found the child in the melon patch.
Trabajó toda su vida en los **arrozales**.	He worked all his life in the rice paddies.

1. As soon as she collected her pay, she thought about buying another hat.
2. In the spring, wild flowers bloom in the desert. 3. You have purchased a very elegant piece of furniture. 4. A near-sighted person can disguise his weakness with contact lenses. 5. Italy embraces an area greater than that of Greece. 6. He stopped a moment to light a cigarette. 7. Often it is difficult to tell the difference between a real blonde and a peroxide blonde. 8. After the operation, she was unable to swallow for two days. 9. There is no cure for baldness. 10. Many professors have gray hair by the time (a) they are thirty. 11. What do you think of this picture? 12. We used to stroll near the lake after dinner. 13. When they fired the man, he broke down and cried. 14. He grew up in the hunger and misery of the war. 15. The wheat fields of Kansas stretch for hundreds of miles. 16. He untied the mules and we set out. 17. The Romans threw many Christians to the wild beasts. 18. I woke up in the middle of the night. 19. She bought a head of lettuce for the salad. 20. In the market, the old lady sold the pigs she had raised in the country. 21. Gloria was sitting on the edge of the bed. 22. I like the wild bushes that grow near the laboratory. 23. The oldest son was always pulling someone's leg. 24. What difference does it make that we go now or later? 25. The apples on (de) this apple tree ripen later than those. 26. She wrote under the name of Fernán Caballero. 27. The ship goes to Genoa, but our friends disembark in Barcelona. 28. You will never become bald if you use our tonic, nor will you have gray hair. 29. The edge of the dirty plate was covered with flies. 30. The country is enjoying a period of full economic development. 31. He was far-sighted and never read without his glasses. 32. We wanted to stop at that cafe, but it was full of people. 33. He went out to buy a loaf of bread and a can of sardines. 34. We shall have all the rooms painted by noon. 35. After a snack, we took leave of our friends. 36. They intended to take a trip to the Caribbean, but the hurricane prevented it. 37. The immense city swallowed [up] the immigrants. 38. In the heart of winter, the days become very short. 39. We raise many kinds of trees in our nursery. 40. In Spain the afternoon meal is heavier than the one in (la de) the evening.

CUESTIONARIO

a. contenido

1. ¿De qué color tienen el pelo los cinco hermanos?
2. ¿Por qué piensa el viajero que se ha pasado de rosca?
3. ¿Qué cosas le cuenta el viajero al niño?
4. ¿Por qué tiene que despedirse el niño?
5. ¿Por qué rehuye el niño la mano cuando el viajero se la alarga?
6. ¿Qué hace el viajero después de decirle adiós al niño?
7. ¿Qué observa el viajero mientras está echado sobre la manta?

b. estilo

1. ¿Cómo retrata Cela al niño?
2. ¿Cómo se revela la penetración psicológica del viajero?
3. ¿Cómo destaca el autor el pelo del niño?
4. ¿Cómo crea el autor cierto sentido de actividad en el último párrafo?
5. ¿Cómo emplea el autor la naturaleza en el último párrafo?

TEMA—TRADUCCION

When the traveler asks him how many brothers and sisters he has, Armando replies that he is the oldest of five. He also asks if they all have blond hair, and the boy answers yes. On noticing a sadness in Armando's voice, the traveler fears that he has gone too far in asking so much. He takes tomatoes, bread, and a can of *foie-gras* from his knapsack and invites him to share them with him. The boy listens as the traveler explains why he has come to the Alcarria and laughs on hearing of the traveler's cross-eyed cousin from Málaga. He listens, thrilled, to his new friend's adventures in the war.

When they reach the road to Iriépal, Armando explains that he must return home because his mother has forbidden him to come so far. The boy says good-by, and the traveler tries to shake hands. He refuses because his hand is dirty. From the edge of the road the boy watches sadly as the traveler walks away. When the traveler turns around, the boy waves good-by. His hair shines in the full sun as if it were fire.

Farther on, the traveler sits down at the foot of an olive grove. After a drink of wine, he takes a nap under an olive tree. In the distance a shepherd is singing while his sheep stand motionless because of the heat. Lying on his blanket, the traveler watches closely the insects running in the grass around him. It fascinates him to see their antennae, which resemble long, thin hairs. He feels an immense joy on seeing the green fields and the wild flowers that grow everywhere along the road.

TEMAS A ESCOGER

Escríbanse unas 200 palabras sobre uno de los temas siguientes usando a lo menos 20 de las palabras y expresiones estudiadas en este capítulo.

1. Una conversación entre un niño y una persona mayor
2. Una experiencia personal con insectos
3. El campo o el desierto en la primavera

chapter 8

TENSES OF THE INDICATIVE MOOD

33. PRESENT

The simple present tense in Spanish is approximately equivalent to three forms of the present tense in English.

Habla francés.	{ He speaks French.
	He is speaking French.
	He does speak French.

In Spanish a progressive form may replace the present tense (or any other simple tense) to emphasize the immediacy of an action or to present it more vividly.

Está hablando con ellos ahora mismo.	He is speaking with them right now.

In English certain auxiliary words are employed with the verb to give it emphasis: *does* in the present, *did* in the past, *will* or *shall* in the future. In Spanish such emphasis is imparted to the verb by the presence of the particle **sí** before it.

La materia no desaparece, pero **sí** cambia de forma.	Matter doesn't disappear, but it *does* change its form.
"Aquello **sí** que era bonito," decía Borja, suspirando. (LM)	"That *was* pretty," Borja used to say, sighing.

34. IMPERFECT AND PRETERIT

English has one simple past tense, whereas Spanish has two, the imperfect and the preterit. In Spanish it is always necessary to distinguish *verbal aspect*, that dimension of the verb that signals perfective (completed) or imperfective (not completed) action. (Perfective aspect can be initiative or terminative action.) In English verbal aspect is usually ignored, though sometimes imperfective aspect is conveyed through a progressive form.

"Imperfect" means, among other things, "incomplete." The imperfect tense in Spanish is used to describe an action not completed in the past within a given, fixed, or determinate period of time. The Spanish preterit tense is used when an action in the past has been completed or accomplished within a given, fixed, or determinate period of time.

The preterit shows that an action was completed within a particular past period. The imperfect shows the continuity of an action going on during a certain period in the past. It does not indicate that the action began or ended during this time, either because the beginning or ending or both are outside the temporal framework or because the speaker has no desire to emphasize the aspect of completion. The imperfect is thus the tense that enables us to relive an event by transferring us to the past to witness it as if it were taking place before our eyes. It is as if we were permitted to witness the past impinging upon the present. The preterit, however, views a past situation (or even a series of events) objectively and as a completed entity that is part of the past. Obviously, in many cases it is not the nature of a past situation itself that determines whether the verb is in the preterit or the imperfect, but the way the speaker wishes to view it. The alternation of these two past tenses can be an important literary tool. In the works of authors like Gabriel Miró* it constitutes a recognizable stylistic feature of the author's prose.

It may be helpful to draw an analogy to a film. To describe the events that advanced the plot, those that were completed *within the film itself*, we use the preterit. Scenery, music, unresolved actions, etc., require the imperfect.

Comían (**estaban comiendo**) cuando **llamó** a la puerta un policía.	They were eating when a policeman knocked on the door.
Llevaba un traje gris el día que **cumplió** los veinte años.	He was wearing a gray suit the day he turned twenty.

The English simple past tense does not indicate aspect, but some translations of the Spanish imperfect do.

La **veía** todos los días.	I saw (used to see, would see) her every day.
Me **hablaba** cuando **estaba** en mi despacho.	He spoke (was speaking) to me when I was in my office.

We have seen that the imperfect indicates continuity and process, whereas the preterit shows end or completion. In Spanish the aspect will always be clear. A small number of very common Spanish verbs seem at first glance to acquire somewhat different meanings depending upon the tense employed. The difference, however, is in aspect rather than in meaning, and the apparent difference derives mainly from the inability of English to do justice to this distinction. The imperfect tense in Spanish shows a state or process already in force, whereas the preterit indicates that something has actually happened *and achieved completion* during the past time in question.

Infinitive	*Imperfect*	*Preterit*
conocer (yo)	I knew, was acquainted with	I met, made the acquaintance of
haber (third person singular only)	there was, there were (there existed)	there was, there were (there took place, occurred)

---

*See the selections in Chaps. 12 and 13, pp. 183-185 and 194-195.

Infinitive	Imperfect	Preterit
poder (yo)	I could, was able to (I was in a position to)	I was able to (and I did)
no poder	I was not able to, could not	(I tried but) I couldn't, wasn't able to
querer (yo)	I wanted to, desired to	I went to, started to, tried to
no querer (yo)	I didn't want to	I refused, would not
saber (yo)	I knew (I was aware that, had knowledge that)	I learned, found out
tener (yo)	I had (in my possession)	I had, received
tener que (yo)	I had to (but did not necessarily do it)	I had to (and did do it)

A pesar de sus muchas preocupaciones, **pudo** conciliar el sueño y descansar profundamente.

In spite of his many worries he managed to fall asleep (was able to fall asleep) and rest well.

Una vez **hubo** un accidente aquí mismo.

Once an accident occurred (there was an accident) right here.

Aquí tienes un libro sobre la guerra. Es el mejor que **pude** encontrar.

Here is a book on the war. It's the best one I found (I could find).

Quise abrir la puerta pero estaba cerrada con llave.

I tried to open the door, but it was locked.

35. FUTURE

Spanish often uses the present tense to indicate an event that is in the near future. This substitution of present for future is especially common with adverbs of time.

Lo **hago** en seguida.

I'll do it immediately.

Si usted me lo pide, yo lo **escondo** aquí unos días. (LC)

If you ask me to, I'll hide you here for a few days.

¿Le **sirvo** el café ya? (TV)

Shall I serve your coffee now?

The future tense in Spanish is also employed by a speaker to indicate a conjecture or a statement he feels to be probable. Brevity is the main reason this future of probability is much more common in Spanish than other closely equivalent constructions.

| ¿Quién **será** aquella señora tan atractiva? | Who can that attractive woman possibly be? (I wonder who that attractive woman is.) |

Tendrá mucho dinero.	
Probablemente tiene mucho dinero.	He probably has (he must have) a great deal of money.
Debe (de) tener mucho dinero.	

The present tense, not the future, of **querer** + infinitive is equivalent to *will you* + infinitive in a request or to express willingness.

| ¿**Quieres ayudarle** con su tarea? | Will you help him with his homework? |

36. CONDITIONAL

The English *would* (infrequently *should*) renders the Spanish conditional. The imperfect, however, must be used to translate into Spanish the English *would* when the reference is to a past habitual action.

| Le dije que **iría.** | I told him I would go. |
| Siempre que la **veía,** la **saludaba.** | Whenever I saw (would see) her, I greeted (would greet) her. |

The conditional in Spanish also indicates probability or conjecture in the past. This use parallels that of the future of probability, and is also preferred to closely equivalent constructions because of its brevity.

Probablemente eran las cinco cuando llegué.	
Debían (de) ser las cinco cuando llegué.	It was probably (it must have been) five o'clock when I arrived.
Serían las cinco cuando llegué.	

37. PRESENT PERFECT

In Spanish one often expresses *I saw him two hours ago* as: *I have seen him two hours ago.* The present perfect, not the preterit, is normally used to refer to a recently completed past event, though in some parts of the Spanish-speaking world the preterit is preferred in this case. Sometimes the present perfect is also used to refer to an event that is not so recent, one normally alluded to in the preterit. In such cases, the action is seen as still impinging upon and affecting the speaker at the present moment.

| ¿**Ha escrito** la carta? | Did he write (has he written) the letter? |
| ¿Le **ha gustado** la película esta tarde? | Did you like the picture this afternoon? |

Mi amigo **se ha ahogado** (**se ahogó**) hace dos meses.	My friend drowned two months ago.

38. PRESENT FOR PRESENT PERFECT

In discussing the imperfect and preterit tenses we emphasized the importance of aspect and the need to view a past event either as completed or as going on in a given period in the past. We have also pointed out that the present perfect indicates an event initiated and completed in the recent past. It is important here to realize that the present perfect cannot be used for an action begun in the past and continuing into the present moment. In such cases Spanish uses a present tense (simple or progressive form) in a number of related constructions.

Hace dos horas que estudiamos la lección.	We have been studying the lesson for two hours (so far).
Hemos estudiado la lección dos horas y ahora volvemos a casa.	We (have) studied the lesson for two hours, and now we are going home.

The first example gives no indication that the period of study has ended, and it is reasonable to assume that the subject will continue studying. The perfective aspect of the tense in the second example implies that the two hours is viewed as a period of time that was completed within the recent past. This distinction is one that is regularly made, but there are some borderline cases in which either tense may be used.

There are four main patterns into which the substitution of the present or present progressive for the present perfect construction is made.

1. hace + time unit + que + present

Hace + **media hora** + **que** + **espero** (**estoy esperando**).	I have been waiting for half an hour.

2. present + desde hace + time unit

Espero (**estoy esperando**) + **desde hace** + **media hora.**	I have been waiting for half an hour.

3. present + desde + date (day, month, etc.)

Espero (**estoy esperando**) + **desde** + **ayer** (**lunes**).	I have been waiting since yesterday (Monday).

4. llevar (present) + time unit + adverb

Lleva + **tres meses** + **aquí.**	He has been here for three months.

or

llevar (present) + time unit + gerund

Llevo + media hora + espe- **rando.**	I have been waiting for half an hour.

Notice that **llevar** without the gerund usually implies *to be*. When the **hace . . . que** construction is negative, it may take either the present perfect or the present; the former, however, is more common.

Hace cinco días **que no le he** **visto.**	I haven't seen him for five days.
Hace cinco días **que no le veo.**	

39. PLUPERFECT; IMPERFECT FOR PLUPERFECT

In most cases the pluperfect is used in Spanish as in English. As its name (more than perfect or complete) suggests, the pluperfect shows that one event preceded another in the past.

Cuando llegué, ya **habían sa-** **lido.**	When I arrived, they had al- ready gone out.
Les había dicho que no **íbamos.**	He had told them that we were not going.

In a series of patterns that parallels the substitution of the present for the present perfect (38), the imperfect is used for the pluperfect to show an action still in progress at a given moment in the past.

1.   hacía + time unit + que + imperfect

Hacía muchos años que no iba nadie de mi familia allí. (CA)	No one from my family had gone there for many years.

2.   imperfect + desde hacía + time unit

Tropezó con una silla que **permanecía desde hacía seis** **años** en el mismo sitio.	He bumped into a chair which had remained in the same place for six years.

3.   imperfect + desde + date (day, month, etc.)

Vivía allí **desde enero.**	He had been living there since January.

4.   llevar (imperfect) + time unit + adverb

Llevábamos dos años allí cuan- do estalló la guerra.	We had been (living) there for two years when the war broke out.

or

llevar (imperfect) + time unit + gerund

El joven poeta **llevaba** ya **varios meses trabajando** en su poema. (LC)	The young poet had been working for several months on his poem.

40. PRETERIT PERFECT

The preterit perfect tense is little used in spoken Spanish; the simple preterit is used instead. In literature, however, the preterit perfect follows certain conjunctions to indicate that one past event immediately followed another. The conjunctions include **apenas**, **después que**, **cuando**, and **luego que** (*as soon as*).

Apenas **hubo salido** (**salió**) cuando empezó a llover.	Hardly had he left when it began to rain.

41. FUTURE PERFECT AND CONDITIONAL PERFECT

These tenses are used in Spanish as in English. Like the future of probability, the future perfect of probability expresses conjecture or probability.

Habrá salido ya.	He has probably (must have) gone already.
¡Cómo **habría reído** de él la gente! (FM)	How people must have laughed at him!

EXERCISES

1. Did you know that he is thinking about getting married? 2. She must have been very beautiful when she was young. 3. Right now the speaker is discussing a new novel. 4. The book has been out of print for a long time. 5. We shall have finished the book before you leave for Spain. 6. I don't believe he waited twenty minutes for us. 7. During the Civil War there was a bloody battle near the river. 8. I'll see you tomorrow. 9. The teacher had been preparing her lecture for two hours when the phone rang. 10. It was snowing when we reached the house. 11. Although there were many patients in the waiting room, the doctor had to go to the hospital. 12. The next time you come to see us, we shall be living in our new house. 13. If the weather had been better, we would have gone to Mexico. 14. The children were playing when their father called them to dinner. 15. He hadn't gotten up so early (**madrugar tanto**) in many years. 16. She will probably come back as soon as she has spent all her money. 17. Did you know Mary before? 18. The old man no longer comes to see us; he must be very sick. 19. The soldier rejoiced when he received the letter. 20.

He's a friend of mine but I haven't seen him for a while. 21. It was probably midnight when they found the body. 22. I had been (*use* **llevar**) there five months when the war broke out. 23. The doctor had hardly graduated from medical school when he died in an accident. 24. He wouldn't admit that she deserved the prize. 25. We explained to her that it would be necessary to send more letters of recommendation. 26. If you finished your homework, we would be able to go to the movies. 27. They found out yesterday that he couldn't come. 28. Although he promised to wash the windows, now he will not do it. 29. When we were children, we went to the beach every summer. 30. She doesn't earn much money, but she does know how to spend it. 31. The husband waxed the car while his wife prepared lunch. 32. What shall I do now? Everything is lost. 33. Will you be quiet? 34. The taxi that took us to the airport was (*use* **ir**) full. 35. You have not come around here (**por aquí**) for a long time. 36. The neighbors gave a party last night, and I couldn't sleep. 37. Did you like the game this afternoon? 38. When we moved here, the Blancos had already been living in this neighborhood for eight years. 39. I had to do it, or he would have failed me in French. 40. Good heavens! What shall we say?

42. SELECCION LITERARIA

La sombra del ciprés es alargada

Miguel Delibes

Miguel Delibes ha pasado gran parte de su vida en Valladolid, ciudad en que nació en 1920. Doctor en Derecho por la Universidad de Madrid, Delibes se ha dedicado a la enseñanza, al periodismo, y a la literatura. En 1948 ganó el Premio Nadal con su primera novela, La sombra del ciprés es alargada. *Desde aquella fecha ha venido publicando cuentos y novelas, entre las cuales se destacan* El camino (*1950*) *y* La hoja roja (*1958*).

En La sombra del ciprés es alargada, *el huérfano Pedro quiere evitar los dolores y desengaños que son parte de toda existencia humana. Durante cierto tiempo logra su fin huyendo todo lazo íntimo, pero con Jane el amor entra en su vida y la felicidad vence al estoicismo. La siguiente selección relata las circunstancias de la muerte de Jane, tragedia que destruye la ilusión de Pedro.*

Me lavé apresuradamente y ascendí a la cubierta.[1] El día ya estaba hecho y las costas de Providencia se divisaban[2] muy próximas. Rememoré[3] mi sueño: «Todo es muy raro, torné a pensar; cuando el hombre evoca con todos los detalles[4] su pasado es que le amenaza algún cambio transcendental en su existencia.» 5

Notaba un cosquilleo[5] insistente por la columna vertebral. «Bah, todo son nervios.» Me calmé un poco. De repente me di cuenta de que me faltaba paciencia para contemplar como nos arrimábamos[6] metro a metro a la costa. Descendí de nuevo a mi camarote e intenté distraerme[7] con un libro. Pero mi imaginación estaba fuera de allí. «Jane seguramente estará ya esperándome en el muelle. A pesar de ser sólo las siete de la mañana . . . »

* * * * *

Me dejé caer en la litera y pensé en nuestra casa, en la casa que nos aguardaba acogedora[8] a la otra orilla del mar. «Feli, tendrá usted buen cuidado de tenerlo todo dispuesto para cuando la señora llegue.» «Lo que más y lo que menos[9] todo está ya en orden, señor», me había respondido.

Oí inopinadamente un aullido[10] de la sirena. Me levanté de un salto:

—¡Diablo, esto significa que ya estamos entrando en el puerto![11]

Abrí la puerta de mi cabina y me encaramé[12] por la primera escotilla. Efectivamente, la proa del «Antracita» enfilaba ya la ostial del puerto de Providencia. Ascendí en un vuelo hasta el puente. Me entró por los ojos la agitada convulsión del muelle; el ir y venir de los ligeros barquitos para distancias reducidas, el alarido[10] aturdidor de los remolcadores,[13] la labor chirriante[10] de las grúas ocupándose en la carga y la descarga de los buques atracados . . . «Por entre esta baraúnda se encontrará Jane. ¿Cómo podré localizarla?»[14] Cada vez se acercaban más las casas de Providencia . . . .

De improviso divisé su automóvil atravesando[15] la conmoción de la plaza. Sentí una impresión tan violenta que hube de clavar[16] las uñas en la barandilla del puente para no caer. ¿Era posible todo? Ahora sacaba Jane su mano por la ventanilla abierta y la agitaba de arriba a abajo saludándome. El práctico me dijo algo en aquel momento que no entendí. Seguía los movimientos del coche con el menor detalle. En ese instante se apartaba[17] de la cadena de automóviles, entre la que venía emparedado y se dirigía a uno de los costados[18] del muelle. Continuaba Jane agitando su mano por fuera de la ventanilla. Me dio la impresión de que todo, por dentro y fuera de mí, se perdía en la penumbra de un plano[19] lejano, y que sólo ella, su figura, adquiría consistencia relevante, perfiles fundamentales y macizos.

Súbitamente todo varió en un segundo. Un obrero impulsando una vagoneta cargada se interpuso en el camino que seguía Jane. Se oyó el chirrido del frenazo[20] y se elevó en el aire una vaharada de goma quemada.[21] Coleó el automóvil y sin que nadie pudiera preverlo cayó dando tumbos[22] sobre las sucias aguas del muelle. Aún se le vio un instante sobre la superficie, pero inmediatamente desapareció entre una serie de círculos concéntricos que iban haciéndose cada vez mayores.

Cuando extrajeron su cadáver una hora más tarde estaba nevando. Y al ver su cuerpo por última vez logré percibir sobre su rígida esbeltez la leve ondulación del hijo iniciado.

43. NOTES

1. la cubierta—deck; jacket of a book
   el cubierto—(overhead) cover; place (setting)
   cubrirse—to put on a hat or kerchief
   descubrirse—to take off one's hat; to discover

Los pasajeros pasaban por la **cubierta** principal del vapor.	The passengers were walking on the main deck of the liner.
No se mojaron porque estaban bajo **cubierto**.	They didn't get wet because they were under cover.
A la puerta del templo varios hombres **se descubrieron**.	At the door of the temple several men removed their hats.

2. divisar—to see or perceive something distant or only partially visible

   Divisar is common in both spoken and written Spanish; its synonyms are **vislumbrar**, *to glimpse*, and **columbrar**, a literary term. **Distinguir**, *to distinguish* or *make out*, is common on both levels and is used to indicate that which is clearly or barely perceptible.

Las tapias de un cementerio **se vislumbraban** por entre el follaje.	The walls of a cemetery were just visible through the foliage.
Desde el Paseo de los Fueros en San Sebastián, **se columbra**, en lo alto de la colina verde, la casa verde y blanca. (BA)	From the Paseo de los Fueros in San Sebastián, you can distinguish (just make out) the green and white house on top of the green hill.
Distinguía ahora con claridad la muchedumbre pululante sobre la escollera. (FM)	Now he could make out clearly the crowd of people swarming about the breakwater.

3. rememorar—to remember
   recordar—to remember, recall; to remind
   acordarse de—to remember

   Rememorar is purely literary. **Recordar** and **acordarse** (**de**) are common on all levels. **Acordarse** always requires the preposition **de** when used with an object. Notice that **recordar** means *to remind* (*of*) and takes no preposition, except the customary **a** when a person is the object of the verb.

Rememoraba sus conversaciones de la noche anterior . . . (TV)	He remembered his conversation of the previous night . . .
Permítame que le **recuerde** que ya no hay monarquía en Francia.	Allow me to remind you that there is no longer a monarchy in France.

| Tú me **recuerdas** al joven que estuvo aquí el mes pasado. (CA) | You remind me of the young man who was here last month. |
| Nunca **se acuerda del** dinero que sus amigos le prestan. | He never remembers the money his friends lend him. |

4. el detalle, el pormenor—detail

| Voy a prescindir de los **detalles** e ir al grano. | I am going to dispense with the details and come right to the point. |
| Espero que me perdonarás que entre en tantos **pormenores**. | I hope you will forgive my going into so many details. |

5. el cosquilleo—tickling sensation
hacer cosquillas—to tickle
tener cosquillas—to be ticklish
tener malas cosquillas—to be touchy

| El niño se reía porque sus compañeros le **hacían cosquillas**. | The boy was laughing because his pals were tickling him. |
| No me toques, que **tengo cosquillas**. | Don't touch me, for I'm ticklish. |

6. arrimarse a—to draw (pull) up to
arrimar—to put (push) next to (against)

| El chófer **se arrimó al** borde de la acera para que no le multaran. | The driver pulled up next to the curb so they wouldn't fine him. |
| Si **arrimas** la mesa contra la pared, tendremos más espacio aquí en el centro. | If you move the table up against the wall, we shall have more room here in the center. |

7. distraerse—to distract (amuse) oneself
entretenerse—to occupy oneself; to entertain, amuse oneself
divertirse—to have a good time; to enjoy oneself
pasarlo bien, pasar un buen rato—to have a good time

Entretenerse normally does not suggest pleasure, but merely *to entertain* or *busy oneself* in some activity. **Divertirse** indicates full pleasure or enjoyment. **Pasarlo bien** and **pasar un buen rato** usually refer to a specific moment or occasion.

| Nunca **se divierte** uno en estas fiestas. | A person never has a good time at these parties. |
| En el quiosco, **me entretuve** hojeando el periódico, sin decidirme a comprarlo. (THI) | At the newspaper stand I busied myself (whiled away some time) leafing through the paper, without making up my mind to buy it. |

Verás **lo bien** que **lo pasamos**. (EJ)	You will see what a good time we have.

8. acogedor(a)—welcomingly (common use of an adjective as an adverb)
   acoger—to receive; to welcome
   la acogida—reception, welcome
   acogerse a—to take refuge in; to come (be included) under
   dar la bienvenida a—to welcome

Acoger means *to welcome* and often conveys the idea of shelter. It is close in meaning to **dar la bienvenida a**, although the latter is preferred for any type of official welcome.

Cuando echaron a Paco, nosotros le **acogimos** aquí.	When they threw Paco out, we welcomed him here.
Evitó la detención **acogiéndose a** la inmunidad diplomática.	He avoided arrest by seeking refuge in diplomatic immunity.
Un alumno nuevo **es** siempre **acogido** con recelo. (NB)	A new pupil is always received with distrust.
Dieron una calurosa **bienvenida a** nuestro presidente.	They gave our president a warm welcome.

9. lo que más y lo que menos—the important and unimportant details

10. el aullido—howl; here, the wailing noise of the siren
    el alarido—shout, yell; here (line 17), the deafening noise of the tugs
    el chirrido—creak, squeak
    chirriar—to creak; to sizzle
    chirriante—creaky, squeaky

Notice Delibes' use of sounds to describe the activity of the harbor. **Aullido** is usually used to refer to the sound made by a dog, and **alarido** most often refers to a sound indicating pain or fear.

Los **aullidos** del perro no nos dejaron dormir en toda la noche.	The howls (howling) of the dog didn't let us sleep all night.
Si la abuela hubiera sabido que subíamos a allí, habría lanzado un **alarido**. (LM)	If Grandmother had known that we were going up there, she would have yelled.

11. el puerto—harbor, port; mountain pass
    el aeropuerto—airport

Los **puertos** de los Pirineos están cerrados en el invierno.	The passes in the Pyrenees are closed in the winter.

12. encaramarse—to climb up; to go up; to get up

Encaramarse, a purely literary term, is used with reference to persons

or animals as a synonym for **trepar**. It differs from **trepar** in that it places greater stress upon the effort involved.

Daban gritos, desenrollaban cuerdas, **se encaramaban** sobre la proa. (LM)	They were shouting, unrolling ropes, and climbing (scrambling) up the prow.
Se encaramaba en las techumbres para colocar tejas.	He would get (climb) up on the roofs to replace shingles.
Los muchachos **se encaramaron** al árbol.	The boys went (climbed) up the tree.

13. el remolcador—tug(boat)
    remolcar—to tow, pull (on either land or water)

14. localizar—to locate (to find)
    situar—to locate (to place)
    estar situado—to be located

Durante nuestra estancia en Madrid, no pude **localizar** a su hermano.	During our stay in Madrid, I couldn't locate your brother.
¿Dónde **está situado** nuestro hotel?	Where is our hotel located?

15. atravesar—to cross
    cruzar—to cross

These two words are often close synonyms. **Atravesar** does have one meaning not found in **cruzar**, *to go across and through*, thus *to penetrate*.

Distinguí claramente una silueta **atravesando** (**cruzando**) la plaza.	I clearly made out a silhouette (shadow) going across the square.
La flecha **atravesó** la puerta.	The arrow went through the door.

16. clavar—to nail; to fix (synonym of fijar)
    el clavo—nail
    la clave—key (to a riddle, problem, etc.)
    la llave—key (to [un]lock some physical object)
    echar la llave—to lock

María **clavó** los ojos en su rival.	Mary fixed her eyes on her rival.
Esta es **la clave** de mi felicidad. (LM)	This is the key to my happiness.
No te olvides de **echar la llave** a la puerta.	Don't forget to lock the door.

17. apartarse de—to move away from
    apartar—to move or push away or aside; to separate

La barca **se apartó** suavemente y entró mar adentro. (LM)	The boat moved gently away and headed out to sea.
El hombre se abrió camino **apartando** a la gente a codazos.	The man made his way by pushing people aside with his elbows.

18. el costado—side (of a person, boat)
    el lado—side
    la cara—side (of a phonograph record)
    tomar partido—to take sides
    desternillarse de risa—to split one's sides laughing

Se oía el ruido del agua contra los **costados** de la «Leontina». (LM)	You could hear the sound of the water against the sides of the "Leontina."
Algunas mujeres lavaban ropa al otro **lado** del arroyo.	Some women were washing clothes on the other side of the stream.
Me desternillé de risa anoche al ver la representación de una obra de Molière.	I split my sides laughing last night on seeing the performance of a play by Molière.

19. el plano—plane
    plano—flat, level
    llano—flat, level; simple, unassuming

Plano often has a connotation of smooth (**liso**) that is absent in **llano**. A table would be **plana**; a field (**campo**), **llano**. Most topographical features are rendered by words with **llano** as the base (**llanuras**, **llanos**—*plains*). Nevertheless the somewhat more learned **planicie**, *plain* or *level ground*, is also used on occasion.

Había unas rocas **planas** cubiertas de musgo cerca del río.	There were some flat, moss-covered rocks near the river.
Será fácil construir la casa porque este terreno es muy **llano**.	It will be easy to build the house because this lot is very flat.
Es un hombre muy **llano**.	He is a very plain (simple) man.

20. el frenazo—slamming on the brakes
    el codazo—blow with the elbow
    el puñetazo—punch or blow with the fist (**puño**)

The augmentative ending **-azo** ordinarily indicates crudeness or ugliness. In the words listed here, however, **-azo** indicates a blow with the brakes, elbow, fist, etc., and as such is common with verbs like **dar**.

Dio un **puñetazo** en la mesa.	He struck the table with his fist.
La mujer le dio un **codazo** al entrar en el metro.	The woman elbowed him as she got into the subway.

21. quemar—to burn (something)
    quemarse—to burn
    arder—to burn; to be on fire
    incendiar—to burn down; to set on fire
    fundirse—to burn out; to blow out

The words for *to burn* are usually clearly distinguished, although sometimes **quemarse** and **arder** are used with little distinction between them. **Quemar** normally means *to burn something no longer wanted* in order to destroy it. It is used reflexively to indicate *to burn oneself accidentally*. The reflexive use can also refer to the accidental burning of other things like food or to the actual combustion of something that is on fire. **Arder** is not used transitively but shows that the subject itself is burning or on fire. It stresses the visible aspect of the combustion rather than the destruction of the subject. **Incendiar** suggests the destructive burning down of something that is not normally burned. **Fundir(se)**, *to melt* (said of metals), is used for fuses, light bulbs, etc.

Quemó todos los papeles antes de dejar la embajada.	He burned all the papers before he left the embassy.
Quemábase el pescado en la sartén si ella cuidaba el fogón . . . (FM)	The fish would burn in the pan if she watched the stove . . .
Esta madera **se quema** muy bien.	This wood burns very well.
Nerón tocaba el violín mientras Roma **ardía**.	Nero played his fiddle while Rome burned.
Se acaba de **fundir** la bombilla.	The bulb has just burned out.

22. dar tumbos—to turn
    tumbar—to knock down, knock over
    tumbarse a la cama—to get into bed

Tumbarse a la cama is colloquial. In this expression **tumbar**, like **echarse a la cama**, *to lie down,* does not have the idea of violent motion found in **tumbar** alone.

Le gustaba **tumbarse** en la cubierta de la barca, boca arriba.	He liked to lie face up on the deck of the boat.

EXERCISES ON NOTES

1. We shall have to set one more place at the table. 2. The president welcomed the king at the airport. 3. Last year she had to remind him of the date of their anniversary. 4. I had another key made for the back door. 5. Put on the other side of the record. 6. From the cathedral tower I clearly made out the main square of the city. 7. They had a good time in the mountains last week. 8. The large dog knocked over the postman

as he tried to deliver the mail. 9. You remind me of someone I met last summer in Burgos. 10. The mother was afraid her son would burn himself with the matches. 11. The foreman asked the worker to put the box way up on top of the shelf. 12. He finally hit upon the key to the problem. 13. Arthur spent two months in the archives without locating the manuscript he was looking for. 14. He is a fool, and his ideas are never well received by his colleagues. 15. He never enjoys himself if he doesn't win money from (*which preposition?*) Charles. 16. He put the ladder closer to the wall in order to climb up on the roof. 17. She crossed the street without waiting for the light to change. 18. As soon as he would catch sight of his cottage roof he would begin to sing. 19. He nailed the picture to the wall. 20. Our new house has a flat roof. 21. After she broke with her fiancé, she burned all his letters. 22. Do you know where the post office is located? 23. If you keep yourself busy with (**en**) something, you won't think about your misfortune. 24. There are so many Smiths in this town that it will be impossible to locate him in the phone book. 25. She left the roast in the oven for five hours, and it burned. 26. The wild goats climbed to the top of (*one verb*) the rock. 27. The pebbles (**chinas**) on (**de**) the beach tickled the soles of his feet. 28. After the mayor welcomed the refugees warmly, the inhabitants of the town received them poorly. 29. Children do not want to be separated from their mothers on the first day of school. 30. In the darkness, the squeaking door frightened the old lady. 31. I split my sides laughing when they played the other side of the record. 32. He liked to recall his student days at the University of Salamanca. 33. At the moment of greatest suspense, the tube of the television set burned out. 34. Only twenty-five nobles could speak to the king without removing their hats. 35. At the end of a long row of apple trees we could just make out the shore of the lake. 36. My wife busied herself looking at the shop windows while I was in the barber shop. 37. You are still too young to be included under the new insurance plan. 38. It is Sunday, and nobody will tow our car. 39. After driving through miles of flat land, it was a relief suddenly to make out mountains in the distance. 40. After the bombing the entire port was burning.

CUESTIONARIO

a. contenido

1. ¿Qué vio Pedro al ascender a la cubierta?
2. ¿Por qué estaba preocupado?
3. ¿Por qué bajó de nuevo Pedro a su camarote?
4. ¿En qué pensó al echarse en la litera?
5. ¿Por qué se levantó de un salto y subió al puente?
6. Describa Vd. brevemente la agitada convulsión del muelle.
7. ¿Qué hacía Jane que le facilitaba a Pedro reconocerla en la conmoción de la plaza?
8. ¿A qué se debió el accidente fatal?

b. estilo

1. Explique Vd. el uso del imperfecto y del pretérito en el primer párrafo.
2. ¿Bajo qué condiciones y con qué fin emplea el autor otros tiempos en los tres primeros párrafos?
3. ¿Desde qué punto de vista se narra este episodio? ¿Qué efecto produce?
4. ¿Cómo logra el autor una atmósfera de agitada convulsión? ¿Cómo se relaciona ésta con el estado anímico de Pedro?
5. ¿Cómo consigue el autor individualizar a Jane dentro de tanta conmoción?
6. ¿Cuáles son las imágenes visuales del penúltimo párrafo?

TEMA—TRADUCCION

It was early in the morning, and the sky was still gray. I had been waiting on deck for (*which tense?*) I don't know how long before I was able to make out the coast. I am not superstitious, but on remembering the details of the dream I had had the night before I couldn't help wondering if it were not a forewarning of an important change in my life.

I felt uneasy and went down to my cabin to busy myself with a book. But I couldn't read, for my thoughts went back to Jane, who was probably waiting for me on the pier. When I heard the cry of the siren, which meant that we were entering the harbor, I climbed up the hatchway and went up to the bridge. At once the many activities of the port filled my eyes. The noise of the tugs merged with the screeching of the cranes that were unloading the ships moored to the pier.

I was wondering how I could locate Jane when I made out her car crossing the square. She had already seen me and was waving to me though the window as the car advanced slowly toward the end of the pier. Suddenly I couldn't believe (**dar crédito a**) my eyes. Jane, to avoid hitting a worker, had applied the brakes (**frenar**) violently. The car skidded and fell into the dark waters, remaining just a moment on the surface before disappearing from sight. It was snowing when I saw Jane for the last time, and I realized that my dream had (*emphatic*) been prophetic.

TEMAS A ESCOGER

Escríbanse unas 200 palabras sobre uno de los temas siguientes usando a lo menos 20 de las palabras y expresiones estudiadas en este capítulo.

1. Los accidentes en la vida moderna
2. Un sueño que se ha realizado
3. La llegada de un barco desde el punto de vista de un pasajero o del que espera al pasajero

chapter 9

44. SELECCION LITERARIA

La sombra del ciprés es alargada*

Miguel Delibes

El autor narra la conclusión de su novela con el mismo estilo rítmico, lento, y a veces arcaizante que hemos visto antes. En una escena de extraordinaria sensibilidad, Delibes introduce la nota de resignación esperanzada con que acaba la novela.

Inopinadamente me vi frente a la verja[1] cerrada del camposanto. La vegetación circundante conservaba el tenso y helado agarrotamiento del invierno. No se veía a nadie a mi alrededor. Sobre la puerta de una casita contigua[2] decía: «Conserje». Llamé con los nudillos,[3] embargado de un
5 opaco sentimiento de temor. Era algo monstruoso ponerse uno frente por frente del[4] dueño[5] de los muertos. Me le imaginé enteco,[6] alcoholizado,[7] ansioso de olvidar su helada vecindad. Transcurrió[8] bastante tiempo sin que nadie respondiera[9] a mi llamada. Al fin escuché una voz que iba haciéndose perceptible a medida que[10] la puerta, después de un ruidoso correr
10 de cerrojos,[11] iba abriéndose sin prisas.[12]
—¿Qué desea usted?
No era un tono demasiado áspero el de la voz teniendo en cuenta el aspecto soñoliento de mi interlocutora. Respeté su indiscreto y repentino bostezo con una pausa que ella empleó, además, en restregarse[13] concien-
15 zudamente los ojos con el dorso de sus manos.[14]
—Querría entrar en el cementerio . . .
Alargué mi mano hacia la suya en una ingenua tentativa de soborno.[15]
—No hace falta . . . —aulló dolorida y digna retirando su mano—; dentro de media hora abriremos para todos.
20 Cuando me contemplé desfilando entre dos hileras de muertos sentí abalanzarse sobre mí una oleada[16] de infinita paz; me hizo el efecto de que dejaba en la puerta una insoportable carga de sinsabores y pesadumbres. «Mi sitio está aquí, me dije; entre los vivos y mis muertos, actuando[17] de intercesor.» Sentí agitarse mi sangre al aproximarme a la tumba de Alfredo.
25 La lápida estaba borrada por la nieve, pero nuestros nombres—Alfredo y Pedro—fosforecían sobre la costra[18] obscura del pino. Me abalancé sobre él y palpé[19] su cuerpo con mis dos manos, anhelando captar[20] el estremecimiento de su savia. Así permanecí un rato absorto, renovando en mi mente los primeros años de mi vida, el latente sabor de mi primera amistad.

---

*Continuation of the selection in Chap. 8.

Luego, casi inconscientemente, extraje de un bolsillo el aro[21] de Jane circundado por la inscripción de Zoroastro y me aproximé a la tumba de mi amigo. Por un resquicio[22] de la losa introduje[23] el anillo y lo dejé caer. Experimenté[24] una extraña reacción al sentir el tintineo del anillo al chocar contra los restos del fondo. Ahora ya estaban eslabonados, atados, mis afectos; las dos corrientes que vitalizaran[25] mi espíritu habían alcanzado su punto de confluencia.

Cuando una hora más tarde abandonaba el cementerio me invadió una sensación desusada de relajada[26] placidez. Se me hacía que ya había encontrado la razón suprema de mi pervivencia en el mundo. Ya no me encontraba solo. Detrás dejaba a buen recaudo mis afectos. Por delante se abría un día transparente, fúlgido, y la muralla de Avila se recortaba, dentada y sobria, sobre el azul del firmamento. No sé por qué pensé en aquel instante en la madre de Alfredo y en «el hombre». Y fue casualmente en el momento en que tropecé con un obstáculo oculto por la nieve. Al mirar hacia el suelo comprobé que a la nieve la hace barro el contacto del pie . . . Me sonreía el contorno de Avila allá, a lo lejos. Del otro lado de la muralla permanecían[27] Martina, doña Gregoria y el señor Lesmes. Y por encima aún me quedaba Dios.

45. NOTES

1. la verja—grating
   la reja—grate, grating
   rallar—to grate

   Verja is a *grating* used as a door, fence, or gate, and frequently replaces these words. **Reja** is a *grating* put on windows.

Una **verja** alta rodea la embajada.	A high fence surrounds the embassy.
Hablaba todas las noches con su novio por la **reja**.	She would talk to her fiancé every evening through the bars (grating) of the window.
Este plato se sirve con queso **rallado**.	This dish is served with grated cheese.

2. contiguo—contiguous, touching
   inmediato—next, adjoining
   de al lado—next door

Mi despacho está en el ala **inmediata**.	My office is in the next wing.
La familia en la casa **de al lado** es muy numerosa.	The family in the house next door is very large.

3. los nudillos—knuckles
   el nudo—knot
   desnudo—bare, nude
   anudar—to knot
   hacérsele a uno un nudo en la garganta—to get a knot in one's throat

Notice that **desnudo**, *bare*, follows the pattern of **descalzo**, *barefoot*. The adjective **nudo** for *bare* is a rare literary use.

Se ajustó el **nudo** de la corbata y se puso a silbar. (EA)	He adjusted the knot in his necktie and began to whistle.
Al hablar en público por primera vez, **se me hizo un nudo en la garganta**.	When I spoke in public for the first time, I got a knot in my throat.

4. frente por frente de—directly opposite
   en frente de, frente a—opposite; in front of
   delante de—in front of, before

Nuestro piso está **frente del** banco.	Our apartment is opposite the bank.
Estaba sentado **frente a** Carlos.	He was sitting across from Charles.
Hay muchos jardines **delante del** palacio.	There are many gardens in front of the palace.

5. el dueño—owner
   el propietario—owner, proprietor

Dueño is the more frequently used of these two synonyms. **Propietario** is preferred in legal parlance and in reference to real property, though in this latter sense **dueño** is also used.

¿Quién es el **dueño** de este coche?	Who is the owner of this car?
Una compañía de seguros es **propietaria** de la emisora.	An insurance company is owner of the radio station.

6. enteco—sickly, weak
   enfermizo—sickly
   el achaque—(habitual) illness, ailment (often used in the plural)
   achacoso—chronically sick or indisposed
   enclenque—feeble, weak, sickly

Era tan **enfermizo** que no le dejaban participar en los deportes.	He was so sickly that they didn't allow him to take part in sports.
Mi abuelo lleva años quejándose de sus **achaques**.	My grandfather has been complaining about his illness for years.

7. alcoholizado—alcoholic
borracho—drunk(ard), intoxicated
estar bebido—to be tipsy, somewhat drunk
ebrio, embriagado, beodo—literary synonyms of borracho
dormir la borrachera (la mona)—to sleep off a drunk
ir de juerga—to go on a spree (colloquial)

Siempre se queda callado cuando **está bebido**.	He always becomes quiet when he is a little drunk.
La próxima vez que te **vayas de juerga**, no te emborraches tanto.	The next time you go off on a spree, don't get so drunk.

8. transcurrir—to pass; to elapse
el transcurso—passing (of time)
mediar—to elapse; to pass; to intervene

Transcurrir is very close to **pasar** in its meaning and its uses. **Mediar** is also synonymous with **pasar** but is used mainly to indicate the passage or lapse of time between two or more events, as suggested by another meaning of **mediar**, *to intervene*.

Todavía han de **transcurrir** un par de horas antes de que penetremos en sus calles. (RDQ)	A couple of hours will have to pass yet before we enter its streets.
Entre los *Lusiadas* y el *Quijote* **media** el curso de una generación. (JQC)	Between the *Lusiadas** and the *Quixote* the course of a generation passes (elapses).

9. responder—to answer, respond
acudir—to respond; to go (come)

Acudir is a verb which has many translation equivalents in English. It conveys the basic idea of *to rush in response to*, or *to go* where one is called or needed or where some advantage is to be found. In other words, **acudir** most often indicates reaction or response.

A la primera señal de sangre, **acudieron** tiburones a bandadas.	At the first sign of blood, sharks came (appeared) in swarms.
Llamó con prisa a la puerta, y el párroco **acudió**. (NB)	He knocked hurriedly at the door, and the priest went to answer.
Los policías **acudieron** a la llamada.	The policemen immediately answered (responded to) the call.

10. a medida que—as
como—as

Lusiadas: Portuguese epic poem based on the exploits of Vasco da Gama, written by Luís de Camoens, the great sixteenth-century Portuguese poet.

Como means *as* at the beginning of a clause in the sense of *since* or *because*, whereas **a medida que** means *in proportion as* or *progressively*.

Como no has terminado, no podemos ir.	As (since) you haven't finished, we can't go.
Hace más calor **a medida que** nos acercamos al desierto.	It gets warmer as we approach the desert.

11. el cerrojo—bolt
    la cerradura—lock
    cerrar con llave—to lock
    bajo llave—under lock and key
    el bucle—lock (of hair)
    la esclusa—lock (of a canal, river, etc.)

Se levantó y descorrió el **cerrojo**. (FN)	He got up and slid back the bolt.
Introduje la llave en la **cerradura** sin hacer ruido.	I put the key in the lock without making any noise.
El canal de Suez no tiene **esclusas**.	The Suez Canal doesn't have locks.

12. sin prisas—unhurriedly

This particular example is a purely literary use. It is, however, common practice in Spanish to pluralize words without causing any significant change in meaning. Some words frequently pluralized include: **gente**(s), **bigote**(s), **palacio**(s), **paraje**(s), and **condición**(es).

El coche está en magníficas **condiciones**.	The car is in wonderful condition.
La condesa nos invitó a visitar sus **palacios**.	The countess invited us to visit her palace.

13. restregar—to rub
    rozar con—to rub against; to brush against
    frotar—to rub
    friccionar—to rub down; to massage

Restregar means *to rub hard* or *to scrub*; its use here is figurative. Were the example in standard colloquial Spanish, the verb would have been **frotar**.

Se **había restregado** contra las rocas para romper la cuerda con que estaba atado.	He had rubbed (hard) against the rocks to break the rope with which he was bound.
Se **frotaba** las manos porque hacía mucho frío.	He rubbed his hands together because it was very cold.
Ten cuidado de no **rozar con** la pared, porque está recién pintada.	Be careful not to rub against the wall, because it is freshly painted.

14. sus manos—her hands

This use of the possessive adjective with a part of the body is largely literary. Normally, the definite article is used instead. The native speaker of English should avoid the natural temptation to use the possessive adjective with articles of clothing and parts of the body when the ownership relation is clear.

15. el soborno—bribe(ry)
el cohecho—bribe(ry)
sobornar, cohechar—to bribe

Sobornar is used in all contexts, although in a literary or technical context **cohechar** may be substituted when the reference is to a public official.

Despidieron al empleado por haber aceptado un **soborno**.	They dismissed the employee for having accepted a bribe.
No lograron **sobornar** (**cohechar**) al juez.	They didn't succeed in bribing the judge.

16. la oleada—wave
la ola—wave
la onda—wave

Oleada is *a large wave*, and the word suggests force. It very often refers to *a wave of people* or to that which is not tangible in nature. **Ola** is standard for *a wave in the ocean or sea*, and also renders *wave* in the context of heat or cold wave. **Onda** most often refers to *a sound* or *light wave*; it is also used for *waves* or *curls* in the hair as well as *waves* in bodies of water smaller than the ocean or sea.

El norte del país está paralizado por una **ola** de frío.	The northern part of the country is paralyzed by a cold wave.
Hay emisoras españolas que transmiten todas las noches por **onda** corta.	There are Spanish stations that broadcast every night on short wave.

17. actuar—to act
obrar—to act
(com)portarse—to act; to behave
hacer zalamerías a—to act up to

Actuar is *to act* in the sense of *to exert an influence on* or *to work in the capacity of*. **Obrar** is similar in meaning but is somewhat less common in Spanish than **actuar**. **(Com)portarse** is *to behave* or *to conduct oneself* in a particular way. **Portarse** is used mostly to refer to young children, whereas **comportarse** is preferred in other contexts.

El desaliento que el *Quijote* imparte **actúa** sobre todo en las naturalezas sensitivas. (JQC)	The discouragement that the *Quixote* conveys acts especially on the sensitive temperament.

Había obrado como un criminal . . . (FM)	He had acted like a criminal . . .
Hoy los niños **se han portado** horriblemente, y anteayer, peor.	Today the children acted horribly, and the day before yesterday, worse.

18. la costra—scab; crust
    la corteza—bark (of a tree); crust (of bread)

Cuando se enfrió nuestro planeta, la **costra** de la tierra se endureció.	When our planet cooled, the crust of the earth became hard.
La **corteza** del pan español es muy sabrosa.	The crust of Spanish bread is very tasty.

19. palpar—to touch; to feel
    tocar—to touch

Tocar is the basic word for *to touch*. **Palpar** suggests *to touch* (in order) *to examine or inspect* something. By extension, it means *to grope one's way through* darkness, a difficult situation, etc.

Se puede **palpar (tocar)** la fruta para ver si está madura.	You can feel the fruit to see if it's ripe.
Iba **palpando** por el pasillo oscuro para no tropezar.	He was feeling his way down the dark hall in order not to stumble.

20. captar—to catch; to capture
    cautivar—to captivate; to charm
    capturar—to capture

Captar means *to capture* or *to win someone's affection, attention, or confidence*. It also means *to get* or *to tune in* a radio station. **Cautivar** was once commonly used in literature to mean *to take prisoner*, now it is used only in the sense of *to captivate* or *to capture through charm*. The primary sense of **capturar** is *to seize*, often a fugitive.

El orador pudo **captar** la confianza del público.	The speaker succeeded in capturing the audience's confidence.
Es un tema que logra por sí mismo **captar** nuestra atención.	It is a subject that by itself manages to capture our attention.
Al regresar de Italia, Cervantes fue **capturado** por los moros.	While he was returning from Italy, Cervantes was captured (taken prisoner) by the Moors.
Con la ayuda inesperada de algunos campesinos, el policía **capturó** al ladrón.	With the unexpected help of a few farmers, the policeman captured the thief.

21. el aro—hoop, large ring
    la sortija—ring
    el anillo—ring
    la anilla—ring
    la arena—ring, arena (literally, sand)

Delibes here uses **aro** to mean *a ring on the finger*. **Sortija** and **anillo** are synonyms, except that **sortija** usually contains a stone. **Anillo** often has a symbolic or ceremonial significance. It is generally more modest in nature than **sortija**, but may also have precious *stones:* **anillo de compromiso**, *engagement ring*. **Anilla** means *a large ring*, such as the ring on a door or curtain rod. In Spanish when the same noun can end in either -**o** or -**a**, the form ending in -**a** usually refers to a larger entity than the one ending in -**o**.

El perro saltó por el **aro**.	The dog jumped through the hoop.
No quitó la **sortija** de papel al cigarro antes de encenderlo.	He didn't remove the paper band from the cigar before lighting it.
Su **anillo** de boda es de platino.	Her wedding ring is made of platinum.
El piso de la iglesia tenía una losa con **anilla** de hierro.	The church floor has a slab of stone with an iron ring in it.

22. el resquicio—crack
    la grieta—crack
    la rendija, la resquebra(ja)dura—crack

Grieta is the standard word for *crack* and is applicable to almost any situation. **Resquicio** refers in most cases to the crack under a door or around a window frame. **Rendija** and **resquebra(ja)dura** are often used for **grieta**, but they frequently suggest splitting. In literary usage the words are often used interchangeably.

La pared está llena de **grietas**.	The wall is full of cracks.
Aún es de noche; todavía la luz del alba no clarea en las **rendijas** de la puerta y de la ventana. (LP)	It is still dark; the light of dawn does not yet appear in the cracks of the door and window.

23. introducir—to insert, put in(to); to introduce
    presentar—to introduce, present

Notice that **introducir** is mainly a synonym of **meter**. It does not mean *to introduce* in the sense of *to present one person to another person*, for which **presentar** is used, but it does mean *to introduce* in most other contexts.

Introduje mis pies en las zapatillas . . . (SCA)	I put my feet into the slippers . . .

Dobló el mensaje y lo **introdujo (metió)** en el bolsillo de su pantalón.

He folded the message and put it in the pocket of his trousers.

Pira la **había introducido** en un mundo fantástico . . . (F)

Pira had brought (introduced) her into a fantastic world . . .

Quisiera **presentarle** a mi hermano.

I should like to introduce (present) you to my brother.

24. experimentar—to experience, undergo; to experiment

Ossorio **experimentó** una gran tristeza, mezcla de celos y de dolor. (CP)

Ossorio experienced a deep sadness, a mixture of jealousy and grief.

Vamos a **experimentar** y ver lo que pasa.

We are going to experiment and see what happens.

25. vitalizaran—not the imperfect subjunctive, but the pluperfect indicative in meaning

26. relajar—to relax
descansar—to relax; to rest
esparcirse, esparcir el ánimo—to relax

Relajar is *to relax* something by loosening or slackening it. **Descansar** (which, unlike its opposite, **cansarse**, *to get tired*, is not reflexive) is by far the most common translation of *to relax*. **Esparcirse** and **esparcir el ánimo** are more literary.

Después de media hora en la piscina, tenía todos los músculos **relajados.**

After half an hour in the pool all his muscles were relaxed.

Quiero **descansar** un momento antes de continuar.

I want to relax a moment before going on.

Los domingos se hicieron para **esparcirse** un hombre. (EJ)

Sundays were made for a man to relax.

27. permanecer—to remain; to stay
quedarse—to remain; to stay

In literature the words **permanecer** and **quedarse** are used the same way. In spoken Spanish **permanecer** is less common than **quedarse** and sometimes conveys a note of permanence not present in **quedarse**.

Juan Medinao **permanece** indeciso. (FN)

Juan Medinao remains undecided.

Hasta las diez de la mañana esta calle **permanece** casi desierta.

Until 10 A.M. this street remains almost deserted.

Pensaba **quedarse** ocho días en Nueva York, pero **permaneció** allí toda la vida.

He intended to remain in New York for one week, but he stayed all his life.

1. People rushed to see the body. 2. Alexander the Great cut the Gordian knot. 3. That man is our next-door neighbor. 4. He offered to act as mediator between the two men. 5. The new library will be built directly opposite the museum. 6. Don't forget to grate the cabbage for the salad. 7. Do you know the owner of the barber shop? 8. The child had a large scab where he hurt his knee. 9. Of course it's dangerous to drive a car when you are intoxicated. 10. Don't touch the plate; it's still hot. 11. The lights grew brighter as the ship approached the harbor. 12. I felt very proud when I was introduced to the president. 13. After his illness, the couple went to the Caribbean to relax. 14. They captured him as he was preparing to leave the hotel. 15. After the final examination, the students went on a spree. 16. She is still (*use* **seguir**) weak after her operation. 17. Seattle is one of the few cities in this country that has locks. 18. The firemen responded to the call without wasting a moment. 19. The students always behaved well when the principal entered the room. 20. The customs official indignantly rejected the bribe. 21. In the course of ten years this city has experienced many improvements. 22. He rubbed the fender with sandpaper to remove the paint. 23. A wave of tourists forced the government to relax many laws. 24. Ten years elapsed between the publication of the first part of the *Quixote* and that of the second part. 25. The mother kept a lock of her child's hair in a large book. 26. The gentle waves of the Mediterranean bathe the Valencian coast. 27. The earthquake left the walls full of cracks. 28. He prefers his toast without the crust. 29. The child untied the knot. 30. It was difficult for the girl to slide (**correr**) the bolt. 31. Water seeped through the cracks of the wooden bucket. 32. The guide pointed out a beautiful grating that dated from the sixteenth century. 33. He carefully put (*not* **meter**) the receipts in the envelope. 34. When they opened the spa, tourists came immediately from all over to enjoy the mountains. 35. We shall remain here as long as the weather is good. 36. His parents gave him a class ring when he graduated. 37. Keep those documents under lock and key. 38. The mother told her son not to rub his eyes. 39. When the weather becomes warm, the children go around barefoot. 40. I can't get the short-wave station you mentioned.

CUESTIONARIO

a. contenido

1. ¿Por qué va Pedro al camposanto?
2. ¿Cómo le ha afectado el tiempo al cementerio?
3. Describa Vd. brevemente al dueño de los muertos.
4. Relate Vd. el encuentro entre la mujer del conserje y Pedro.
5. ¿Cómo se explica la paz que sintió Pedro al estar entre los muertos?
6. ¿Qué le hizo recordar a Pedro su vida pasada?
7. ¿De qué manera une Pedro a los dos afectos de su vida?

8.   ¿Qué cambio profundo había experimentado Pedro en el cementerio?
9.   ¿Cómo logra Delibes introducir una nota de esperanza para terminar la novela?

b. estilo

1.   Explique Vd. el uso del imperfecto y del pretérito en los primeros cinco verbos.
2.   ¿Ha logrado Delibes una caracterización acertada de la mujer? ¿Cuáles son las tres características que le han impresionado más?
3.   ¿A qué se debe la atmósfera de paz del segundo párrafo?
4.   ¿Cómo emplea el autor la personificación?
5.   Señale Vd. ocho palabras de uso literario.
6.   ¿Qué efecto le produce a Vd. el contraste entre luz y oscuridad en el último párrafo?

TEMA—TRADUCCION

One frozen winter day I found myself alone in front of a cemetery gate. On the door of a cottage next to the gate there was a small sign which said: "Caretaker." A strange fear invaded me as I knocked on the door. As I waited for the custodian to answer, I tried to imagine what he must be like. He was probably a feeble old man who had recourse to alcohol in order to forget the cold, sad world in which he lived. It seemed to me as if a great deal of time had elapsed before I finally perceived a voice and suddenly noticed that the door was opening unhurriedly. A sleepy woman appeared and asked me somewhat harshly what I wanted. Respecting her yawn and waiting until she finished rubbing her eyes with the back of her hand, I finally replied that I would like to visit the cemetery. Then I extended my hand toward hers to compensate the woman for her trouble with a small bribe. With indignation she withdrew her hand and replied: "That's not necessary. Within half an hour the cemetery opens for everyone."

A wave of immense peace, as if I had left behind at the gate an intolerable burden of sorrows, overwhelmed me as I walked between the rows of the dead. My heart beat faster as I approached the grave of Alfred, who had been my only close friend. A crust of snow covered his gravestone, but our names, carved years ago, were still legible on the bark of a nearby pine. I embraced the tree, longing to capture the quiver of life which ran through its sap. My thoughts returned to my boyhood and my first friendship. Then, almost without realizing what I was doing, I took Jane's ring from my pocket and let it drop through a crack in the stone that covered Alfred's grave. When I heard the ring strike the bottom, I knew that the two vital currents that had nourished my spirit were finally united forever. I left the cemetery an hour later and I knew that I was no longer alone, for I had found a reason to live [on]. As I walked toward Avila, the clouds above the city wall were giving way to (**ceder a**) a resplendent new day.

TEMAS A ESCOGER

Escríbanse unas 200 palabras sobre uno de los temas siguientes usando a lo menos 20 de las palabras y expresiones estudiadas en este capítulo.

1. Impresiones de una visita solitaria a un cementerio
2. Una comparación entre un cementerio tradicional y otro moderno
3. La esperanza como factor esencial en la vida humana

chapter 10

46. SELECCION LITERARIA

El muerto-vivo

Enrique Anderson Imbert

*El argentino Enrique Anderson Imbert (nacido en 1910) ha sido
redactor de* La Vanguardia *de Buenos Aires y catedrático en su
país y en los Estados Unidos. Es conocido por su importante*
Historia de la literatura hispanoamericana *y por penetrantes estudios sobre la crítica literaria. Además, ha escrito novelas y cuentos.
«El muerto-vivo», tomado de* El Grimorio (*Buenos Aires, 1961*),
muestra su originalidad en este género.

Fuimos al cementerio[1] a despedir los restos[2] de León. Era una cruda[3]
mañana de invierno. Ya desde muy temprano el cielo negro, redondo,
tirante nos avisó así, con su forma de paraguas, que iba a llover. Ahora
llovía a cántaros.[4] El viento agitaba los paraguas. El padre y el hermano
5   de León, abrazados, lloraban. Tiritando,[5] empapado[6] hasta los huesos,
con laringitis, estornudos[7] y fiebre cumplí mi deber: empecé a leer un
discurso[8] fúnebre, en nombre de la redacción de *La Lira.* De pronto lo vi
en las últimas filas del cortejo. ¡A él, al muerto, a León! Estaba gozándome,
con la cara oculta entre las solapas levantadas del impermeable y el gran
10   sombrero. Fue tanta la sorpresa que solté la pata[9] del paraguas,[10] y el
paraguas se fue volando[11] con su ala negra. Alguien me lo devolvió, res-
petuosamente. Continué mi discurso, pero sin gana.[12] Comprendí que León
nos había hecho la broma[13] de fingirse[14] muerto para asistir a su propio
entierro[15] y obligarnos a elogiarlo. Entre frase y frase lo espié, y siempre
15   estaba allí, con las manos en los bolsillos, regocijado. Al terminar el discurso
me precipité hacia él, pero se escurrió[16] entre la multitud.[17] Caminaba
rápidamente y a pasos[18] cortos para no resbalar sobre el empedrado. Lo vi
perderse por las callejuelas de la necrópolis.
    Han pasado varios años. El mundo sigue[19] creyéndolo muerto. No me
20   atreví a contar a nadie su broma pesada. ¡Para qué! No me hubieran creído.
León figura[20] ahora en la historia de nuestra poesía: «eximio poeta, muerto
prematuramente». Patatín patatán. Bla, bla, bla. De mí nadie recuerda
sino aquel discurso, que luego publicaron como prólogo a sus poesías[21]
«póstumas». No le perdonaré jamás. Cada vez que oigo hablar de las poesías
25   de León me viene un ahogo de ira. Espero verlo, el día menos pensado,[22]
al doblar una esquina. Me da miedo andar por la ciudad porque sé que
cuando lo vea tendré que matarlo.

47. NOTES

1. el cementerio—cemetery
   el camposanto—graveyard, cemetery

   Cementerio is the standard word for *cemetery*. Literary usage often employs **camposanto** to avoid repetition of **cementerio**. In spoken Spanish **camposanto** often has regional (southern Spain) or popular overtones.

Enterraron los muertos en el **camposanto** del lugar.	They buried the dead in the village cemetery.

2. los restos—remains
   las sobras—leftovers
   el resto de—the rest of, the remainder of
   restar—to remain (literary); to subtract, take away
   quedar—to remain; to be left; to have left (with an indefinite objective pronoun)
   sobrar—to be more than enough; to be left over
   el (la, los, las) demás—the other(s), the rest of

   Restos is especially common as *mortal remains*, although in literary usage it often has a broader range of meaning. **Sobras** is mainly *leftover food*. **El resto de** is used mostly to indicate a period of time or something measurable as a quantity. **Demás** is used with the definite article as a noun or adjective in approximately the same way as its synonym **otro** (**-a, -os, -as**).

Comía alguna cosa que le daban, **restos** del rancho de algún barco, que recogía en una lata vacía. (PT)	He used to eat something they gave him, scraps (leftovers) from some ship's mess, which he collected in an empty can.
El **resto** del trabajo es difícil.	The rest of the work is difficult.
Valentín sabía **restar** con una facilidad increíble.	Valentine could subtract with unbelievable ease.
Poesía pura es lo que **resta** después de quitar a la poesía todas sus impurezas. (JM)	Pure poetry is what remains after removing all the impurities from poetry.
Eso no **resta** valor a sus obras.	That doesn't detract from the value of his works.
¿Cuántos días nos **quedan** antes de las vacaciones?	How many days do we have left before vacation?
Talento te **sobra** (tienes talento de sobra) para ser gran poeta.	You have more than enough talent to be a great poet.
Las demás chicas no van.	The other girls aren't going.

3. crudo—raw
   tosco—crude, rough

Crudo means *raw* referring to weather and *uncooked* or *insufficiently cooked* when referring to food. **Tosco** ordinarily means *crude* in the sense of primitive or unpolished and may refer to either people or things.

Este invierno ha sido muy **crudo**.	This winter has been very raw.
En el altar había una figura **tosca** de la virgen.	On the altar there was a crude figure of the Virgin.

4. llover a cántaros—to rain pitchforks, cats and dogs (literally, to rain jugs)
   llover a torrentes—to pour (rain)

5. tiritar—to shiver; to shake
   temblar—to tremble; to shake
   estremecer(se)—to shake; to shudder
   sacudir—to shake
   el temblor—earthquake

Tiritar ordinarily means *to shake with cold*, although **de frío** may be added. **Temblar** has the widest range of meanings of any of the above words. It may indicate *to shake from cold, from an emotion*, or *because of some physical force*. **Estremecer** is most often *to shake* or *quiver from horror*. **Sacudir** requires an object and means *to make move back and forth*, etc. **Temblor** is often used in the plural.

Yo comprendía que Borja, mientras sonreía con dulzura, **temblaba** de odio, de envidia y de rabia. (LM)	I knew that Borja, all the while he was smiling so sweetly, was shaking with hatred, jealousy, and anger.
La sangre hizo **estremecer** de horror a todos allí reunidos.	The blood made everyone gathered there shudder with horror.
. . . sólo me aplico a **sacudir** la inercia de vuestras almas. (JM)	. . . I apply myself only to shaking loose the inertia of your souls.

6. empapar—to soak, drench
   calar—to soak
   remojar, poner en (de) remojo—to soak
   calado hasta los huesos; hecho una sopa—soaked to the skin

Empapar is the word of widest use for *to soak*. **Estoy empapado** is even more common than **estoy calado** for *I am soaked*. **Remojar** and its equivalents suggest *to soak something* (usually in water) for a specific purpose.

Nos sirvieron un bizcocho **empapado** en ron, que llaman panetela borracha.	They served us cake soaked in rum which they call *panetela borracha.*
Caía una fina lluvia que poco a poco iba **empapando** sus cabellos y su ropa. (PT)	A fine rain was falling, and little by little it was soaking her hair and her clothes.
La lluvia, pocas veces tan uniforme, le **calaba** la ropa. (IC)	The rain, which was rarely so steady, was soaking his clothes.
Para preparar la sopa, primero es necesario **remojar** (**poner de remojo**) los garbanzos.	To prepare the soup, first it is necessary to soak the chickpeas.

7. el estornudo—sneeze, sneezing
   estornudar—to sneeze
   sonarse (las narices)—to blow one's nose (literally, to sound one's nose)
   no menospreciar—not to sneeze at (literally, not to underrate)

Su alergia le hizo **estornudar** toda la noche.	His allergy made him sneeze all night long.
El hombre **se sonó** largamente en el blanco pañuelo . . . (EA)	The man blew his nose for a long time in the white handkerchief . . .
No hay que **menospreciar** su contribución.	You must not sneeze at his contribution.

8. el discurso—speech
   pronunciar un discurso—to give a speech
   la conferencia—lecture; conference; long-distance telephone call
   echar un párrafo—to have a chat (colloquial)
   pegar la hebra—to gab
   charlar—to chat
   la charla—chat

—Julián . . . Hay una **conferencia** para usted. ¿Quiere venir al teléfono? (ER)	"Julian . . . There is a long-distance call for you. Will you come to the phone?"
Tuvimos una **charla** muy animada en el café.	We had a very lively chat in the café.
A los viejos siempre les gusta **pegar la hebra**.	Old people always like to gab.

9. la pata del paraguas—umbrella handle
   el asa (feminine)—handle
   el mango—handle
   el puño—handle
   la pata—leg
   meter la pata—to blunder; to put one's foot in it

estirar la pata—to up and die, kick the bucket

Notice the Americanism for *umbrella handle*. **Asa** refers to (small) handles on vases, trunks, baskets, etc. **Mango** refers to the long, narrow handle of certain tools, cooking utensils, etc. **Puño**, which also means *fist*, is used for umbrellas, canes, etc. **Pata** is the leg of a piece of furniture or of an animal. It is also used in idioms to refer to people.

Cogen el baúl, cada uno por un **asa**.	They grab the trunk, each one by a handle.
La pala tiene un **mango** de madera.	The shovel has a wooden handle.
Ese bastón tiene **puño** de plata.	That cane has a silver handle.
Siempre **está metiendo la pata**.	He is always putting his foot in it.

10. el paraguas—umbrella

Notice that **paraguas** is formed with the third person singular of **parar**, *to stop*, and a noun. Such verb-noun compounds are masculine; in form they are invariable in singular and plural: **el paraguas, los paraguas**. Explain **pararrayos, paracaídas, parabrisas, parachoques**. Analyze **abrecartas, cortaplumas, pisapapeles, saltamontes**.

11. volar—to fly; to blow up or to explode
el vuelo—flight
en (de) un vuelo—in a flash

Aviones enemigos **volaron** sobre nuestro pueblo.	Enemy planes flew over our town.
Para hacer la presa tuvieron que **volar** el cerro.	They had to blow up the hill in order to make the dam.

12. sin gana—unwillingly, unenthusiastically

Gana(s), which conveys the idea of desire or will, is common in colloquial expressions meaning *to feel like* or *to desire*. It is employed mainly with the verbs **dar, entrar**, and **tener**. Although normal in everyday speech, expressions with **ganas** often convey a directness or intensity of desire that causes them to be avoided in formal or polite conversation. **Real** is an intensifier that adds a note of coarseness to such expressions.

No tengo **ganas** de verle.	I don't feel like seeing (I have no desire to see) him.
Le entraron (dieron) unas **ganas** enormes de irse a España.	He got a tremendous urge to go to Spain.
No me **da la real gana** de ir.	I couldn't care less about going.
Contestó de (mala) **buena gana**.	He answered (un)willingly.

13. la broma—joke, trick (usually good-natured)
la broma pesada—practical joke
gastar una broma—to play a joke
el chiste—joke (verbal witticism)
embromar—to tease; to joke with

Hoy no está para **bromas**.	Today he is in no mood for jokes.
El forastero dijo que no sabía contar **chistes**.	The stranger said that he didn't know how to tell jokes.

14. fingir—to pretend, feign
aparentar—to pretend (often followed by a noun)
hacerse + definite article + past participle—to pretend to be
hacerse el sueco—to play dumb; to pretend not to understand
pretender + infinitive—to try to + verb
pretender + clause — to claim

Pasó sin contestar a mi saludo, **fingiendo** no advertirlo.	He passed by without returning my greeting, pretending not to notice it.
No abre los ojos; **se hace el dormido**.	He won't open his eyes; he's pretending he is asleep.
Hasta **pretende** no pensar en sus problemas.	He even tries not to think about his problems.
Pretende que la idea es suya.	He claims that the idea is his.
Eso es lo que el poeta **pretende** eternizar . . . (JM)	That is what the poet tries (strives) to make eternal . . .

15. el entierro—burial
enterrar—to bury, inter
enterar—to inform
enterarse de—to find out, learn about

En el cementerio había cadáveres de soldados todavía sin **enterrar**.	In the cemetery there were bodies of still-unburied soldiers.
No dejes de **enterarme** sobre lo que pase.	Don't fail to inform me about what happens.
Me he enterado de quien ha escrito la carta.	I have found out who wrote the letter.

16. escurrirse—to slip (out, through, from, away)
escurridizo—slippery
resbalar(se)—to slip; to slide
deslizar—to let slip; to slide
el desliz—slip

To slip is almost always **resbalar(se)** when it refers to people and means *to slip or slide on a smooth surface*. **Escurrir** is mainly for things that slide or slip out of the hands or away from someone. **Deslizar** is less common than the other verbs. In literature these distinctions are frequently disregarded.

Se le **escurrió** el hielo de las manos.

The ice slipped from his hands.

El viejo **se resbaló** en la acera.

The old man slipped on the sidewalk.

Había **deslizado** varias palabras latinas en nuestra conversación.

He had slipped a few Latin words into our conversation.

17. la multitud, la muchedumbre, el gentío—crowd
¡Cuánta gente!—What a crowd!

Tres policías iban abriéndose paso a través de la **muchedumbre**.

Three policemen were forcing their way through the crowd.

18. el paso—step, pace
a ese paso—at that rate, at that pace
dar un paso—to take a step
abrirse paso—to force one's way

Aquí nadie **da un paso** sin su permiso.

Nobody takes a step here without his permission.

No he sentido un ruido, ni un **paso** en la casa. (LE)

I haven't heard a noise, not even a footstep in the house.

¿Quién camina a **ese paso**? (JM)

Who walks at that pace (speed)?

A este **paso** nunca llegaremos.

At this rate we shall never arrive.

19. seguir creyéndolo—to still believe that he is

Seguir with a present participle or adjective frequently replaces the adverbs **todavía** and **aún** to indicate *still*.

¿**Sigue enferma** la chica?
¿Está **todavía** (**aún**) enferma la chica?

Is the girl still sick?

Viven **todavía** en la misma casa.
Siguen viviendo en la misma casa.

They are still living in the same house.

20. figurar—to appear in; to be included in
figurarse—to imagine, figure

¿Por qué no **figura** Petrarca en esta antología?

Why isn't Petrarch (why doesn't Petrarch appear) in this anthology?

¡**Figúrate**! Ahora no quiere casarse con mi hija.

Imagine! Now he refuses to marry my daughter.

21. la poesía—poem; poetry
    el poema—poem
    el verso—verse, line (of poetry)
    versos—poetry, verses (of poetry)

Notice that the word for *poetry* is commonly used for any type of poem. Only **poema**, however, should be used for long works such as *epic poetry*. In most other cases **poesía** and **poema** are interchangeable. **Versos** is also frequently used for *poetry*, especially when recited or presented orally.

Esta **poesía** (este **poema**) es excelente.	This poem is excellent.
El Cid es un gran **poema** épico.	*The Cid* is a great epic poem.
Recitaba **versos** hasta quedarse ronco.	He recited poetry until he became hoarse.

22. menos pensado—least expected

EXERCISES ON NOTES

1. They buried the soldier with honors in the National Cemetery. 2. Soak the sponge in hot water before cleaning the table. 3. Imagine! He left her without a cent. 4. The soldiers felt the earth tremble beneath their feet. 5. The idea of flying frightens my grandmother. 6. This wicker basket has two strong handles. 7. Because he followed orders, they promoted him quickly. 8. He was soaked to the skin and had to change all his clothes. 9. I found out yesterday that the burial is on Friday. 10. I couldn't hear because the person behind us blew his nose continually. 11. The teacher asked the child to recite a poem. 12. He slipped on the wet sidewalk. 13. I feel like going to the beach this afternoon. 14. The handle of the shovel broke as he was digging a hole. 15. A large crowd awaited the return of the hero. 16. The child took his first step when he was eleven months old. 17. The old miser has kicked the bucket. 18. He pretends that he doesn't understand. 19. There was so much pepper in the salad that everyone sneezed. 20. Don't forget to soak the dried fruit before making the dessert. 21. They entered the town at night and blew up the ammunition dump. 22. At six o'clock one has to force his way through the crowd to get into the subway. 23. Many years after the poet died they returned his mortal remains to his native city. 24. He slipped a peseta into the beggar's hand. 25. Since only fifteen students took the class, there were five books left over. 26. It was raining pitchforks and the poor woman couldn't open her umbrella. 27. He was quiet although he had more than good reason to protest. 28. He always pretends to listen, but he is thinking about what he is going to say. 29. Earthquakes are frequent in the Andes. 30. A good cook can prepare a tasty dish with leftovers. 31. There is a cemetery behind this small church. 32. They shuddered on passing an accident on the freeway. 33. While filling the basket the fisherman let

a few sardines slip through his fingers.   34. Last summer flew by and we were unable to finish our project.   35. Whenever he plays a joke on his friends, it costs him dearly.   36. We can fire him when we feel like it. 37. Sometimes it comes out raw, sometimes burnt.   38. Do you have enough money left to pay the bill?   39. We suddenly got an urge to reveal everything.   40. He likes to slip jokes into his lectures.

CUESTIONARIO

a. contenido

1. ¿Por qué fuimos al cementerio?
2. ¿Quién es el narrador del cuento?
3. ¿Por qué se sorprendió el narrador?
4. ¿Qué clase de persona debió de ser Léon?
5. ¿Cómo contribuyó el narrador a la fama de León como poeta?
6. Según el narrador, ¿qué ocurriría algún día si él viera a León?

b. estilo

1. ¿Qué tiempos emplea el autor en el primer párrafo?
2. Explíquese cada uso del imperfecto y del pretérito en las primeras cinco oraciones.
3. Comente Vd. el uso de adjetivos descriptivos.
4. En general, ¿hay economía de palabras en este cuento?
5. ¿Le parece natural la transición del pasado al presente en el segundo párrafo? ¿Por qué?

TEMA—TRADUCCION

It had been threatening (*what tense?*) rain since dawn. But it didn't begin to rain until we left for the cemetery to pay our last respects to Leon. It was a raw winter day, and a strong wind shook the umbrellas. As I shivered with cold and prepared to deliver my eulogy, I noticed Leon's father and brother weeping. Soaked to the skin and sneezing, I began to read my speech on behalf of the newspaper.

Suddenly, I looked up and thought that my eyes were deceiving me, for there in the crowd I saw Leon. The shock was so great that the umbrella slipped out of my hand and the wind carried it away. Furious over Leon's trick, I nevertheless had to go on reading. Yes, Leon, by pretending to be dead, was able to witness his own burial and to force us to praise him. Between sentences I looked up and saw Leon, who was standing there with his hands in his pockets and a smile on his face. As soon as I finished, I rushed toward him, but he slipped away into the crowd. The pavement was wet and I was afraid I would slip. It would be impossible to overtake him.

Since that day many years have passed. I alone know that Leon is still alive. While he is included in the history of our poetry as a distinguished poet who suffered an untimely death, I am remembered only for the speech

I delivered at his funeral. I shall never forgive him. When I hear his poems mentioned, I choke with rage. It frightens me to think that he is in this city, for if by chance I encounter Leon on some street, I shall have to kill him.

TEMAS A ESCOGER

Escríbanse unas 200 palabras sobre uno de los temas siguientes usando a lo menos 20 de las palabras y expresiones estudiadas en este capítulo.

1. Una broma pesada
2. El funeral en la sociedad actual
3. Impresiones de un entierro en un día lluvioso

chapter 11

SOME OTHER VERBAL FORMS

48. THE INFINITIVE

A. The infinitive sometimes functions as a verbal noun, and as such may be (1) the subject of a clause, (2) the object of a verb, or (3) the object of a preposition. Notice that although any infinitive may be used as a noun, a number of common Spanish nouns are infinitives preceded by an article.

el amanecer—the dawn
un deber—a duty
el parecer—the opinion
un poder—a power

1. Although Spanish often omits the article before an infinitive used as a subject, its inclusion is always correct.

(El) viajar por el interior del país es todavía muy peligroso.	Traveling (to travel) through the interior of the country is still very dangerous.
(El) tener que callarlo me parece muy injusto.	Having (to have) to be quiet about it seems very unjust to me.

2. An infinitive dependent on another verb may be thought of as the object of that verb, even though both obviously share the same subject. This is true even when the infinitive itself is followed by some type of object.

No quiero **salir.**	I don't want to go out.
Esperaba **ver** aparecer a María de un momento a otro.	He expected to see Mary appear from one moment to another.

3. The infinitive after a preposition in Spanish is rendered in English as *preposition + infinitive* or *gerund*.

Para tener éxito, hay que trabajar.	(In order) to be successful, one must work.
Se empeñaba **en ver** al paciente.	He insisted on seeing the patient.
Al terminar, se sentó.	Upon finishing, he sat down.

B. Notice that **por** + *infinitive* equals *because of, on account of,* etc., + *gerund* or *conjugated verb* in English. It is NOT the equivalent of *by* + *gerund*, because in Spanish this construction is rendered by the gerund alone.

Por correr (**haber corrido**) tanto, llegó muy cansado.	Because he ran (had run) so much, he arrived very tired.
Corriendo hasta la esquina, logró coger el último autobús.	By running to the corner, he managed to catch the last bus.

C. Sin + *infinitive*, in addition to its standard use as *without* + *gerund*, also renders *un-* + *participle*.

Pasó **sin hablar**.	He passed without speaking.
Muchas calles de esta ciudad están todavía **sin pavimentar**.	Many streets of this city are still unpaved.
Dejó la casa **sin barrer**.	She left the house unswept.

49. THE PAST PARTICIPLE

A. GENERAL STATEMENT

The past participle (which participates or shares in the qualities of both verb and adjective) is used in two ways. When its auxiliary is **haber**, it functions as a verb (always retaining the **-o** ending) to form compound tenses. When its main auxiliary is **ser**, **estar**, or any other verb except **haber**, it is adjectival and must agree in number and gender with the word it modifies.

El **ha escrito** dos libros.	He has written two books.
Dos libros **fueron escritos** por él.	Two books were written by him.
Dos libros **están escritos**.	Two books are written.
Tengo dos libros **escritos**.	I have two books written.
Dos libros **han sido escritos** por él.	Two books have been written by him.

In the last example above the main auxiliary of **escritos** is **ser**, so agreement is required. **Haber** itself is an auxiliary of the main auxiliary, **ser**.

B. FORMS

Many frequently used Spanish verbs have irregular past participles: **decir**—**dicho**, **poner**—**puesto**, **volver**—**vuelto**, etc. There is also a small number of verbs with two past participles. The regular form (**-ado**, **-ido**) has the active or verbal meaning and forms compound tenses. The irregular form is used principally as an adjective to describe a resultant state.

bendecir	to bless	bendecido	bendito
convertir	to convert	convertido	converso

despertar	to awaken	despertado	despierto
maldecir	to curse	maldecido	maldito
soltar	to let loose	soltado	suelto

No me has **despertado** porque estoy **despierto** desde las seis.

You didn't wake me up, for I have been awake since six o'clock.

C. ABSOLUTE CONSTRUCTIONS

1. The past participle without a verb is used in the absolute construction (absolutely apart from the rest of the sentence) to indicate an action or state previous in time to the time of the main clause. This use is mainly literary.

Concluída mi tarea, me senté a mirar la televisión.

My homework finished, I sat down to look at television.

Hechos los preparativos, salimos para Roma.

The preparations made, we left for Rome.

Después de **echada** la carta al correo, recordé que no la había firmado.

After the letter had been mailed, I remembered that I had not signed it.

2. Some adjectives which are not participles, but which have a verbal meaning, are also used in this absolute construction.

Limpias las armas, salió don Quijote a nuevas aventuras.

His arms polished (cleaned), Don Quixote went out on new adventures.

50. THE GERUND

A. GENERAL STATEMENT

The Spanish gerund (which corresponds to *both* the gerund *and* the present participle in English) ends in **-ando** or **-iendo** and has simple and compound forms. The simple form indicates time corresponding closely to that of the main verb, past or present. The compound form refers to time previous to the main verb and is used exclusively to refer to past events.

Viajando por México, siempre se ven pueblos pintorescos.

While (when, by) traveling in Mexico, one always sees picturesque towns. (contemporaneous events)

Habiendo dimitido el director, se declaró una huelga general.

After the director resigned, a general strike was declared. (the resignation preceded the strike)

B. USES

1. As an adverb:

El año pasó **volando**.	The year flew by (passed flying).
Carlos entró **corriendo**.	Charles ran in (entered running).
Cruzamos **nadando** el río.	We swam across (crossed by swimming) the river.

2. To relate an action or a state to the subject of a clause and thus to show how the action or state is associated with it:

Estando yo en Europa, estalló la guerra.	While I was in Europe, war broke out.
Estudiando un poco más, podrás aprobar inglés.	By studying a little more, you will be able to pass English.

3. As the equivalent of a relative clause used as an adjective:

Mirábamos a dos niños **jugando** (que jugaban) en la playa.	We watched two children (who were) playing on the beach.
Mirábamos jugar a dos niños en la playa.	We watched two children play on the beach.

The Spanish gerund may replace a relative clause that functions as an adjective after verbs of sense perception (**mirar**, **observar**, **oír**) or representation (**pintar**, **describir**, **representar**). Such verbs convey the impression of something in progress, which is the essence of the gerund. The infinitive is probably used more often than the gerund in spoken Spanish with verbs such as these, but as a result there is a considerable loss in the sense of immediacy conveyed by the gerund.

Since the gerund never loses its aspect of verbal continuity, it may not be used in Spanish as an adjective to modify a contiguous noun directly. (In English the gerund always takes the place of a noun. It is the present participle that modifies a noun.) Even the two common exceptions, **hirviendo**, *boiling*, and **ardiendo**, *burning*, are invariable in form although they follow the noun they modify. An adjective or circumlocution with a clause, therefore, must often be used in Spanish to render an English present participle.

un lechero madrugador—an early-rising milkman
un pueblo pescador—a fishing village
unas palabras lisonjeras—some flattering words

51. THE PRESENT PARTICIPLE

Words ending in **-ante** or **-(i)ente** serve as adjectives, nouns, or prepositions in Spanish. Unlike the past participle, which is both verb and adjective, the present participle is in effect an adjective only, for it is not used to form compound tenses. Furthermore, unlike **-ado** or **-ido**, its suffixes may not be appended to all verbs, but are found only in forms sanctioned by actual use. Listed below are several common present participles used as (A) adjectives, (B) nouns, and (C) prepositions.

A. ADJECTIVES

ausente—absent
conveniente—proper
corriente—running
creciente—growing
chispeante—sparkling
durmiente—sleeping
interesante—interesting
obediente—obedient
pendiente—hanging; dependent
sonriente—smiling
sorprendente—surprising
tocante—touching

La mirada de Francisco Olano era abierta, profunda y **carente** por completo de expresión **interrogante.** (IC)	Francisco Olano's gaze was open, intense, and completely lacking in any questioning expression.

B. NOUNS

el (la) asistente—assistant
la corriente—current
el (la) creyente—believer
el (la) dependiente—clerk
el (la) estudiante—student
el (la) pariente—relative
el presidente—president
el sirviente—servant

A few of the above words also admit a purely feminine form in modern Spanish.

la estudianta
la parienta
la presidenta
la sirvienta

PREPOSITIONS

durante—during
mediante—by means of
no obstante—in spite of

52. REFLEXIVE VERBS

A verb is used reflexively in Spanish when the subject does something to itself, i.e., when its direct or indirect object is a reflexive pronoun (**me, te, se, nos, os, se**).

A. In Spanish a few verbs always require the reflexive pronoun.

arrepentirse (de)—to repent (of)
atreverse (a)—to dare (to)
jactarse (de)—to boast (of)
quejarse (de)—to complain (of)

B. Although English regularly omits the reflexive pronoun with many transitive verbs where a reflexive object pronoun is clearly understood, this reflexive pronoun may not be omitted in Spanish.

Se escondieron.	They hid (themselves).
El niño no quiere **lavarse.**	The child refuses to wash (himself).
Con tanto ruido no puedo **concentrarme.**	I cannot concentrate with so much noise.
Hay que concentrar más atención sobre este punto.	We must concentrate more attention on this point.

C. Although the following examples are not pure reflexives (the action does not reflect back directly on the subject itself, but on some part of the subject), they are rendered in Spanish with the reflexive pronoun, not the possessive adjective. This construction is sometimes referred to as one of the uses of the dative of interest.

Me lavé las manos.	I washed my hands.
Víctor **se rascaba** la cabeza.	Victor scratched his head.

When, however, the subject does something *with* but not *to* a part of his body, the reflexive pronoun is usually omitted in Spanish. It may, nevertheless, be included to make the situation more graphic or emphatic.

Metió las manos en los bolsillos.	He put his hands in his pockets.
Se metió las manos en los bolsillos.	He stuck his hands in his pockets.

53. THE PASSIVE VOICE

A. GENERAL STATEMENT

The passive voice changes the subject (normally the performer of an action) into the object of an action. In Spanish the true passive is rendered with **ser** and the past participle, with an agent either expressed or implied. The essence of the passive voice is that it stresses the action itself as it affects what in English is normally the subject. When, however, the state resulting from an action, but not the action itself, is referred to, **estar** (or a verb like **quedar**) is used with the past participle rather than **ser**.

Esta ventana **fue rota** ayer.   }   This window was broken
Esta ventana **estaba rota** ayer. }   yesterday.

Only the first example above is passive in Spanish, for it refers to the actual breaking of the window and is roughly equivalent to **rompieron**. The second example indicates that the window was *already* broken yesterday, a condition which was the result of a previous action.

B. THE AGENT IN THE PASSIVE VOICE

Whenever the agent is expressed in a sentence with a verb in the passive voice, it must be introduced by the preposition **por**. (**De** may replace **por** when the verb in a passive construction stresses a mental or an emotional attitude—**temer**, **odiar**, **aborrecer**, **amar**, etc.—but even in this context **por** is found more than **de**.)

Fue pintado **por** Andrés.

It was painted by Andrew.

Fernando VII fue odiado **de** (**por**) toda la nación.

Ferdinand VII was hated by the entire nation. (**por** connotes a more direct hatred)

54. REFLEXIVE VERBS WITH CAUSATIVE MEANING

Certain reflexive verbal expressions like **cortarse el pelo**, **retratarse**, **hacerse una fotografía**, etc. clearly cannot have a true reflexive meaning. They are used, instead, with the causative meaning of *to have something done*.

Mañana tengo que **cortarme** el pelo.

Tomorrow I must have my hair cut.

Yo me hago dos trajes al año.

I have two suits made each year.

Yo estuve en Madrid el año que acabó la guerra, fui a **operarme** unas cataratas. (VA)

I was in Madrid the year the war ended; I went there to have my cataracts operated on.

1. This continual living in doubt is killing me. 2. Striking the table with his fist, he declared that he would never speak to them again. 3. He seemed to want to know what we were doing. 4. The two companions separated at the door. 5. He is a young man completely lacking in common sense. 6. Eating seemed to be his sole pleasure. 7. She ran upstairs to look for her son. 8. The bearing of an English gentleman was evident in his walk and in his way of speaking. 9. He spent his leisure moments leafing through magazines. 10. They locked him up for having falsified some documents. 11. He went out dragging his feet. 12. The revolutionary concentrated all his hatred on the nobility. 13. He ran across the beach and threw himself into the water. 14. He washed and dressed and then went to school. 15. The temperature went down so much that the water froze. 16. I saw her slipping away into the crowd. 17. The boy stuck his finger in his mouth. 18. The strike in Bilbao is still unsettled. 19. Sleeping well is necessary for good health. 20. Biting his lip, he answered no. 21. The war ended, the soldiers returned home. 22. My head is a continuous shuffling of ideas. 23. He raised his hand to ask a question. 24. Mary is very hard-working. 25. The purpose of his visit fulfilled, he got up and went toward the door. 26. The prince will be crowned in May. 27. You are deserving of these honors. 28. We watched him dry the sweat from his forehead with a handkerchief. 29. She continued pulling on the door. 30. Our secrets can't be revealed in the presence of new members. 31. He put on his glasses in order to concentrate better. 32. I had my photograph taken yesterday. 33. The tyrant dead, the country enjoyed liberty again. 34. You can save fifty dollars by working two weeks. 35. He wiped his mouth with a napkin. 36. My report is still unfinished. 37. The bleating of the sheep is pleasing to the poet's ears. 38. England is admired by many nations. 39. The plan is very promising. 40. He noticed a smiling face in the first row.

55. SELECCIÓN LITERARIA

Ensimismamiento y alteración

José Ortega y Gasset

José Ortega y Gasset (1883–1955) es el máximo pensador español de este siglo. Sus ensayos abarcan casi todas las actividades del horizonte humano desde el arte hasta la política. La deshumanización del arte *y* La rebelión de las masas, *para mencionar sólo dos obras, han tenido una influencia importante sobre las ideas de nuestro siglo. La popularidad de la obra de Ortega se debe en gran parte a la belleza y claridad de su estilo. Se echará de ver en el*

siguiente pasaje tomado de «Ensimismamiento y alteración»
(que puede consultarse en el tomo VII de sus Obras completas,
Revista de Occidente, Madrid, 1961) la característica habilidad
orteguiana para desarrollar un concepto mediante una serie de
imágenes, metáforas y símiles.

En ninguna parte advertimos mejor que es, en efecto, la posibilidad de
meditar el atributo esencial del hombre, como en el Jardín Zoológico,
delante de la jaula de nuestros primos, los monos.[1] El pájaro y el crustáceo
son formas de vida demasiado[2] distantes de la nuestra para que, al con-
5 frontarnos con ellos, percibamos otra cosa que diferencias gruesas,[3] abstrac-
tas, vagas de puro excesivas.[4] Pero el simio se parece tanto a[5] nosotros,
que nos invita a afinar el parangón, a descubrir diferencias más concretas
y más fértiles.[6]

Si sabemos permanecer un rato quietos[7] contemplando pasivamente la
10 escena simiesca, pronto destacará[8] de ella, como espontáneamente, un rasgo
que llega a nosotros como un rayo de luz. Y es aquel estar las diablescas
bestezuelas constantemente alerta, en perpetua inquietud, mirando, oyendo
todas las señales[9] que les llegan de su derredor, atentas sin descanso al
contorno, como temiendo que de él llegue siempre un peligro al que es for-
15 zoso[10] responder automáticamente con la fuga o con el mordisco, en mecánico
disparo de un reflejo muscular. La bestia, en efecto, vive en perpetuo miedo
del mundo, y, a la vez, en perpetuo apetito de las cosas que en él hay y
que en él aparecen, un apetito indomable[11] que se dispara también sin
freno ni inhibición posibles, lo mismo que el pavor. En uno y otro caso
20 son los objetos y acaecimientos del contorno quienes[12] gobiernan la vida
del animal, le traen y le llevan[13] como una marioneta. El no rige su existencia, no vive desde *sí mismo*, sino que está siempre atento a lo que pasa
fuera de él, a *lo otro* que él. Nuestro vocablo[14] *otro* no es sino el latino *alter*.
Decir, pues, que el animal no vive desde *sí mismo*, sino desde *lo otro*, traído
25 y llevado y tiranizado por *lo otro*, equivale a decir que el animal vive siempre
alterado, enajenado, que su vida es constitutiva *alteración*.

Contemplando este destino de inquietud sin descanso, llega un momento
en que, con una expresión muy argentina, nos decimos: «¡Qué trabajo!»
Con la cual enunciamos con plena ingenuidad, sin darnos formalmente
30 cuenta de ello, la diferencia más sustantiva entre el hombre y el animal.
Porque esa expresión dice que sentimos una extraña fatiga,[15] una fatiga
gratuita, suscitada[16] por el simple anticipo imaginario de que tuviésemos
que vivir como ellos, perpetuamente acosados[17] por el contorno y en tensa
atención hacia él. Pues, qué, ¿por ventura el hombre no se halla lo mismo
35 que el animal, prisionero del mundo, cercado[18] de cosas que le espantan,
de cosas que le encantan, y obligado de por vida, inexorablemente, quiera
o no, a ocuparse de ellas? Sin duda. Pero con esta diferencia esencial: que

el hombre puede, de cuando en cuando, suspender[19] su ocupación directa con las cosas, desasirse de su derredor, desentenderse de él, y, sometiendo su facultad de atender a una torsión radical—incomprensible zoológicamente —, volverse, por decirlo así, de espaldas al mundo y meterse dentro de sí, atender a su propia intimidad o, lo que es igual, ocuparse de *sí mismo* y no de *lo otro*, de las cosas.

Con palabras que, de puro haber sido usadas, como viejas monedas, no logran ya decirnos con vigor lo que pretenden, solemos llamar a esa operación: pensar, meditar. Pero estas expresiones ocultan lo que hay de más sorprendente en ese hecho: el poder que el hombre tiene de retirarse[20] virtual y privisoriamente del mundo, y meterse dentro de sí, o dicho con un espléndido vocablo, que sólo existe en nuestro idioma: que el hombre puede *ensimismarse.*[21]

56. NOTES

1. el mono—monkey, ape
    el mico—(long-tailed) monkey
    mono (adjective)—cute, pretty; una monada (noun) is used in a similar way
    estar de monos—to be on the outs, at odds

¡Qué vestido más **mono** lleva la niña!	What a cute dress the girl is wearing!
Es muy **mona** (**una monada**).	She's very cute.
Las peleas en voz baja y el **estar de monos** días enteros eran hechos frecuentes en estos amores . . . (AT)	Whispered quarrels and being at odds for days were common events in this love affair . . .

2. demasiado—too; too much, too many; excessively; excessive

    Demasiado is usually an adverb. It is often omitted or replaced by **muy** when the idea of *excessively* is implicit in a sentence. When used as an adjective, *too much, too many,* **demasiado** must agree with the word it modifies. **Estar de más** renders *to be amiss* or *to be useless or unwanted.* Since **estar** may indicate personal reaction and comparison with what one considers normal in a given class, **estar** used with certain adjectives may also convey the idea of **demasiado.**

Es **temprano** para ir a ningún lado. (LC)	It's too early to go anywhere.
Es muy **trade** para ir.	It's too late to go.
Tenemos **demasiadas** cosas que hacer.	We have too many things to do.

No **estaría de más** agradecerle el regalo.	It wouldn't be amiss to thank him for the gift.
Estos zapatos **me están grandes**.	These shoes are too big for me.
Es que **estoy viejo**.	It's that I am too old.

3. grueso—thick (in depth or diameter), used here by Ortega to mean large or evident differences
   espeso—thick (especially liquids)
   de espesor—thick (in measurements)
   denso—dense, thick, compact
   torpe—thick-headed
   por las buenas y por las malas—through thick and thin

El único plato consiste en una sopa **espesa** y nutritiva.	The only course consists of a thick, nutritious soup.
Sacó el tomo más **grueso** del estante.	He removed the thickest volume from the shelf.
Para su piso de lujo compraron una alfombra de dos pulgadas **de espesor**.	They purchased a carpet two inches thick for their luxurious apartment.

4. vagas de puro excessivas—vague because they are purely excessive

   De puro followed by an adjective renders *from sheer (pure)* + noun or *because* + conjugated verb + *completely* + adjective.

De puro enfadadas, se fueron sin despedirse de nosotros.	Out of sheer anger they went away without saying good-by.
Lo hizo **de puro enojo**.	He did it out of sheer anger.
De puro enamorado, renunció a su puesto.	Out of pure love he gave up his position.

5. parecerse a—to look like; to resemble (a specific person or thing)
   parecer—to appear; to look like; to seem; to have the appearance of
   el parecer—opinion
   cambiar de parecer—to change one's mind
   el parecido—similarity; likeness

Ahora, de repente, al verla, comprendió **a quién se parecía**. (ER)	Now, on suddenly seeing her, he knew whom she looked like.
El hombre que parecía un caballo.	*The Man Who Looked Like a Horse.* (title of a novelette by the Guatemalan Rafael Arévalo Martínez)
Parecen franceses, no italianos.	They look like Frenchmen, not Italians.

Hemos sido siempre **del parecer** que los niños deben ser educados con disciplina.	We have always been of the opinion that children should be reared with discipline.
El parecido entre sobrina y tío era sorprendente.	The resemblance between niece and uncle was surprising.

6. fértil—fertile (applicable in almost all cases)
   fecundo—fertile, fecund (somewhat literary)
   feraz—fertile (said only of earth)
   ubérrimo—very fertile and abundant (literary)

La tierra de las pampas es de las más **fértiles** del mundo.	The earth of the pampas is among the richest in the world.
Inclitas razas **ubérrimas**, sangre de Hispania **fecunda**, (Rubén Darío: «Salutación del optimista»)	Most fertile and illustrious races, blood of fecund Spain.

7. quieto—still, quiet (not moving)
   estarse quieto—to hold or be still
   callado—still, silent

¡Estáte **quieto**!	Be still (quiet)!
Cuando está preocupado siempre está **callado**.	When he is worried he is always quiet.

8. destacar—to emphasize; to (make something) stand out
   destacarse—to stand out
   destacado—outstanding
   sobresalir—to excel; to stand out
   sobresaliente—excellent, outstanding

Ahora me interesa sólo **destacar** un par de rasgos. (EI)	Now I am interested only in emphasizing (making) a couple of features (stand out).
Sobresale (**se destaca**) por la calidad de su poesía.	He stands out because of the quality of his poetry.
Felicitaron al muchacho por su **sobresaliente** en química.	They congratulated the boy for his A in chemistry.

9. la señal—signal, sign
   el signo—sign, mark
   huella—track, trace, sign
   hacer a uno señas para (de) que + subjunctive—to make a sign for
      someone to do something
   las señas—address (Spain)

la dirección—address (mainly Spanish America)
señalar—to point out

El trompetazo será la **señal** para empezar el ataque.	A blast on the trumpet will be the signal to begin the attack.
Iban con la cabeza inclinada como **signo** de perpetua esclavitud.	They walked with their heads bowed like a mark of their perpetual slavery.
El cazador siguió las **huellas** del oso hasta la cueva.	The hunter followed the tracks of the bear to the cave.
Dio al chófer la **dirección** del hotel.	He gave the driver the address of the hotel.
El guía **señaló** con la mano la casa de Cervantes.	The guide pointed out with his hand the house of Cervantes.
Me hizo **señas** para que no dijese nada.	He made a sign to me not to say anything.

10. es forzoso, es preciso, es menester—it is necessary
    hay que + infinitive—one must; it is necessary

11. indomable—untamable, indomitable
    domar—to tame or break (an animal)
    amansar—to tame or break (an animal); to soothe, calm
    dominar—to dominate; to master (a skill, knowledge); to overlook
    dominarse—to control oneself

El caballo sigue sin **domar**.	The horse is still unbroken.
Tal vez la música le **amansará**.	Perhaps the music will calm him.
En poco tiempo **dominó** las matemáticas.	In a short time he mastered mathematics.
Mi alcoba **domina** el jardín.	My bedroom overlooks the garden.

12. quienes—literary usage for que or los que, the normal relative pronouns

13. llevar—to take (a person or thing to some place); to carry something somewhere
    tomar—to take (an object or a person in one's hands or arms); to take a vehicle

Me **llevaron** al aeropuerto donde **tomé** el avión para Nueva York.	They took me to the airport where I took the plane to New York.
Tomó al niño en brazos.	He took the child in his arms.

14. el vocablo—synonym for palabra
    el voquible—word (purely literary use indicating ironic intent)
    la palabrota—vulgar word

el taco—swear word
soltar tacos—to swear, curse
cumplir la palabra—to keep one's word

En un momento de ira soltó una serie de **palabrotas**.	In a moment of anger he let loose a series of vulgar words.
Que conocía el significado del **vocablo** «canícula» se infiere de sus mismas palabras. (JM)	That he knew the meaning of the word "dog days" may be inferred from his very words.

15. la fatiga—fatigue
las fatigas—nausea
el cansancio—tiredness, weariness, fatigue
rendido, molido—worn out, exhausted, tired
cansarse, fatigarse—to become tired

La pobre padecía de **fatigas**.	The poor woman was suffering from nausea.
Rendido por el trabajo, dedicaba sus pocos momentos de ocio a leer novelas.	Exhausted from his work, he dedicated his few leisure moments to reading novels.
Pero tendrás que sustituirme, porque estoy **molida**. (TV)	You'll have to replace me, because I'm exhausted.

16. suscitar—to provoke; to stir up
resucitar—to resuscitate; to resurrect

La reseña **suscitó** gran interés en la novela.	The review stirred up great interest in the novel.
Todos creyeron que el soldado **había resucitado** de entre los muertos.	Everyone believed that the soldier had risen from the dead.

17. acosar—to harass; to pursue unremittingly
perseguir—to pursue
hostigar—to lash; to pursue

Ahab **persiguió** a la ballena blanca hasta la muerte.	Ahab pursued the white whale until his death.
Su curiosidad por saber lo que querían le **acosaba** día y noche.	His curiosity to find out what they wanted pursued him night and day.

18. cercar—to fence in; to encircle, surround; to lay siege to
la cerca—fence
rodear—to surround
sitiar—to surround; to lay siege
asediar—to blockade; to besiege

Una tapia de ladrillos **cerca** (**rodea**) el jardín.	A brick wall encloses (surrounds) the garden.

Los griegos **asediaron** a Troya diez años antes de tomarla.	The Greeks besieged (laid siege to) Troy for ten years before taking it.

19. suspender—to suspend; to stop temporarily; to hang; to fail or not to pass
dar calabazas a—to turn down; jilt; to flunk

La huelga les obligó a **suspender** el trabajo.	The strike forced them to suspend work.
La muchacha le **ha dado calabazas**.	The girl has turned him down.

20. retirarse—to retire; to withdraw
retirar—to retire (something); to withdraw; to take away (synonymous with quitar)
jubilarse—to retire (on pension)
recogerse—to retire; to go to bed (literary or rustic usage)

El incendio hizo que la gente **se retirase** a las calles inmediatas.	The fire made people withdraw to the adjacent streets.
Después de **jubilarse**, el profesor fue a vivir a España.	After retiring, the professor went to live in Spain.
Ya es hora de **recogernos**.	It's time for us to retire.

21. ensimismarse—to turn (withdraw) within oneself
el ensimismamiento—introspection, withdrawal within oneself

These words are closely associated with Ortega and have no completely satisfactory translation equivalents in English.

EXERCISES ON NOTES

1. I am of the opinion that he is very thick-headed. 2. In order not to lose time, it will be necessary (*three ways*) to have the exact address. 3. His success has stirred up some incredible jealousies (*use* **envidias**) around here. 4. Everyone had a thick cane in his hand. 5. It requires years of studying to master a foreign language. 6. It wouldn't be amiss to congratulate them. 7. The hot chocolate is thicker than usual. 8. He doesn't look like his father, but his mother. 9. He is intelligent, but very quiet. 10. The Nobel prize is a sign of international distinction. 11. The child-actor was so cute that he stole (*add reflexive pronoun*) the scene. 12. They surrounded the enemy platoon during the night. 13. In the winter my family always retires early. 14. They returned exhausted from the long trip. 15. The railroad suspended service during the strike. 16. The trade fair stirred up a great deal of interest in Spanish furniture. 17. You shouldn't withdraw within yourself so much. 18. In Andalusia thick walls keep the houses cool during the summer. 19. We must teach children to wait for the walk signal before crossing the street. 20. My father bought half a dozen

boards one inch thick. 21. He is never quiet when I have to concentrate. 22. I didn't wait because there were too many people in line. 23. He had three years left before he could retire [go on pension]. 24. The Spanish people harassed the armies of Napoleon. 25. The maid withdrew all the dishes before serving the dessert. 26. The Civil Guard pursued the murderer [relentlessly] before catching up with him in the pine grove. 27. I don't think it's too late to change your mind. 28. His vulgar words revealed that he was a coarse person. 29. He is much taller than (**de lo que**) he seemed from a distance. 30. The children jumped over the fence with the agility of monkeys. 31. Some animals are more difficult to (*use* **de**) tame than others. 32. He's too young to know what we are referring to. 33. His comments have stirred up much criticism among the students. 34. He kept his word and took his children to the park. 35. From sheer exhaustion the traveler was unable to take another step. 36. The yellow lemons stood out against the green foliage. 37. Misfortune has pursued her all her life. 38. This soil is so fertile that it produces (*use* **dar**) three crops a year. 39. They decided to blockade the port. 40. He made a sign for me to close the door.

CUESTIONARIO

a. contenido

1. ¿Por qué se advierte mejor el atributo esencial del hombre en el Jardín Zoológico?
2. ¿Qué rasgo simiesco nos llama la atención en seguida?
3. ¿Hasta qué grado es sensible el mono a todo lo que pasa a su alrededor?
4. ¿Por qué dice Ortega y Gasset que el mono no vive desde sí mismo?
5. ¿Cuál es la diferencia más substancial entre el hombre y el animal?
6. ¿Cómo explica el concepto de ensimismamiento la diferencia entre el hombre y el mono?

b. estilo

1. Describa y comente Vd. una característica estructural compartida por casi todas las frases.
2. Señale cuatro o cinco imágenes (no necesariamente visuales) que contribuyan al espíritu de inquietud, tensión, y movimiento que prevalece en el segundo párrafo.
3. ¿Por qué habrá tantos infinitivos en la última frase del tercer párrafo? ¿Qué efecto produce?
4. Escoja y explique Vd. una frase que exemplifique la técnica orteguiana de establecer y ampliar un concepto o una idea dentro de la misma oración.
5. ¿Cómo organiza Ortega este pasaje para llevar al lector de lo concreto a lo conceptual?

TEMA—TRADUCCION

Crustaceans, birds, and other forms of animal life differ so much from human beings that rarely do they stimulate us to think about our relationship with the rest of creation. However, the features that tie (**ligar**) us to the other members of the animal kingdom are immediately apparent when (**al**) we contemplate the monkeys at the zoo.

Observing these animals from any point of view, one can't help but notice that they are constantly alert, and that they live in perpetual restlessness. The little beasts never seem to be still, for they are always watching and listening to everything that happens around them. It is as if they feared danger were always stalking them. Yet, at the same time, the monkeys live with an uncontrollable appetite for (**de**) many things in the world that surrounds them. These little animals do not control their destiny from within, for their existence is determined by the objects and events of their surroundings, which govern them like puppets. In brief, the monkey does not live from within, but is tyrannized by what happens outside of him.

The mere fact that man is aware of the constant restlessness of the monkey's existence underlines the basic difference between him and this animal. But, is man not also a prisoner of the world that surrounds him? The answer is, doubtless, yes. However, there is a fundamental difference, for man can do what is for other animals zoologically impossible. He can disassociate himself completely from the world and withdraw within himself. It is this capacity for abstraction, this capacity to live from within oneself, that is expressed in Spanish by the verb *ensimismarse*.

TEMAS A ESCOGER

Escríbanse unas 200 palabras sobre uno de los temas siguientes usando a lo menos 20 de las palabras y expresiones estudiadas en este capítulo.

1. El hombre en el mundo de los animales
2. La unicidad del hombre
3. Factores que distinguen al hombre de los demás animales

chapter 12

ADJECTIVE POSITION

57. LIMITING ADJECTIVES

Limiting adjectives tell *which* or *how many*, but do not describe. In Spanish they almost always precede the noun they modify.

una subasta—an (one) auction
tu colega—your colleague
muchos (**algunos**) baúles—many (some) trunks
este andén—this platform
la **primera** lección—the first lesson

Some limiting adjectives (possessives, demonstratives, ordinals) may also follow the word they modify for purposes of sharper discrimination or stress. When so used, these adjectives are normally employed in conjunction with a preceding article. The possessive adjective has a different form when its position is inverted.

el tipo **ese**—that guy (pejorative, derogatory implication)
la lección **primera**—the (very) first lesson (in a series)
un colega **tuyo**—a colleague of yours (perhaps as opposed to my colleague)

58. DESCRIPTIVE ADJECTIVES

A. GENERAL STATEMENT

A descriptive adjective indicates something about the nature of the noun it qualifies, such as shape, size, color, condition, or affiliation with some group or class. Whereas in Spanish limiting adjectives regularly precede the noun they modify, descriptive adjectives are very flexible as to position. When a descriptive adjective follows a noun, it differentiates the noun in some way from others of its class. If, however, an adjective indicates a quality we expect a given noun to have or one we know is characteristic of a given noun because it has been mentioned or stressed earlier, the adjective functions as an enhancer or epithet and precedes the noun. This pre-position is frequently used for poetic effect.

las **doradas** naranjas de California	the golden oranges of California
las **verdes** palmeras de Jamaica	the green palms of Jamaica

The differentiating or post-position of the Spanish adjective often corresponds to heavy stress or pause (or both) in English.

el equipo **bueno** de Boston	the *good* team from Boston
el **buen** equipo de Boston	the good team from Boston

The first example implies the existence of another (and less accomplished) team. Post-position carefully avoids the possibility of confusion by making the referent clear. Pre-position in the second example reflects either that there is only one team, hence no differentiation is possible, or that the speaker prefers to ignore the existence of the other team and not use it as background for purposes of differentiation. Thus pre-position serves to enhance the well-known quality conveyed by the adjective.

59. DESCRIPTIVE ADJECTIVES WITH UNIQUE NOUNS

An adjective following a noun indicates some degree (however slight) of contrast or comparison; but if a noun is the only one of its kind, no differentiation is possible, so descriptive adjectives precede unique nouns.

| la **hermosa** mujer del general | the general's beautiful wife |
| el **amigable** rector de nuestra universidad | our university's friendly president |

Post-position of the adjective in the first example could make a bigamist of the general, and in the second might suggest that our university has two or more presidents.

60. MODIFICATION OF MEANING ACCORDING TO POSITION

Certain descriptive adjectives that retain their literal meaning when they follow the noun (i.e., when they are in normal position) often have a more figurative meaning when they precede it.

Adjective	Following	Preceding
antiguo	(very) old, ancient	old, former, ex-
bajo	short; low	low, common, vile
gran(de)	large, big	great
mismo	(one)self, itself	same; very (emphatic)
nuevo	(brand) new	new (different, another)
pobre	poor (without money)	poor (unfortunate, wretched)
único	unique	only
viejo	old (age in years)	old (relatively, affectionately)

61. POETIC EFFECT AND RELATIVE IMPORTANCE OF NOUN AND ADJECTIVE

The position of a descriptive adjective is often determined by one (or more) of several factors. The adjective is in a stronger position when it follows the noun, for then it does more work. Its appeal is mainly to the intellect, since it differentiates in some degree by setting the noun apart from others of its class. When the adjective precedes the noun, however, there is a greater appeal to our poetic or emotional sense, and any differentiating force is greatly diminished. Consequently, a descriptive adjective may be used to enhance a known characteristic more or less in isolation.

Position, then, depends largely on whether the speaker wishes emotion or intellect to predominate. When a quality is to be taken for granted or a noun is to be regarded in its usual meaning, the adjective precedes the noun. But if the noun is not to be taken in its usual sense, or if some degree of distinction is to be indicated or emphasized, the adjective follows the noun.

The adjective in **la blanca nieve**, for example, merely enhances a quality that is part of the normal concept of snow: **blanca** is used as an epithet and is largely ornamental. It does little more than highlight a well-known characteristic. Within a given context we may refer to an old judge or an old building in a similar way, although the words *judge* and *building* obviously do not suggest age in the same way as *snow* suggests whiteness. Nevertheless, a context in which readers or listeners were familiar with the age of the judge or the building in question would justify pre-position. Thus it is possible to begin a description or discussion with an adjective in post-position and to shift to pre-position when the reader or listener is deemed to be sufficiently well informed regarding a given characteristic.

Since pre-position of an adjective highlights a quality and implies that it is inherent, typical, or characteristic of the noun in question, the affective force of adjectival pre-position explains its heavy use in rhetorical, propagandistic, and poetic writing. Nevertheless, no rule can indicate where an adjective should be placed in every circumstance. Position is often influenced by some ineffable rhythmical consideration on the part of the writer or speaker. The alternation of the position of adjectives used in almost identical environments reveals that the distinction between poetic and differentiating intent is at times a very personal and subtle one, indeed.

Vestido de luto, con mi barba **nazarena** y mi **breve** sombrero **negro,** debo cobrar un **extraño** aspecto cabalgando en la blandura **gris** de Platero. (PY)

Dressed in mourning, [and] with my Nazarene beard and my small black hat, I must make a strange impression riding along on the gray softness of Platero.

Yo la veo en una **inmensa** sala de uno de **estos** caserones **yeclanos,** sentada en un **ancho** sillón, con la cabeza pensativamente apoyada en la **blanca** y **suave** mano. (CPF)

I [can] see her in the immense living room of one of these large run-down Yecla houses, sitting in a broad easy chair with her head pensively resting on her soft white hand.

Es un paisaje **verde** y **suave;** la **fresca** y **clara** alfombra se extiende hasta las **ligeras** colinas de los cerros **rojizos** que cierran el horizonte. (CPF)

It is a green and soft countryside; the fresh, bright carpet [of grass] extends as far as the gentle slopes of the reddish hills that mark the horizon.

EXERCISES

Some of the sentences can take either the pre- or postposition of the adjective.

1. Have you heard about the lamentable event that occurred in Los Angeles?
2. According to others, Fernando was a former teacher. 3. He returned to his village to live among those he considered his old and intimate friends.
4. The actress was wearing (*use* **lucir**) a magnificent pearl necklace. 5. Among the tender words of farewell we noticed an occasional ironic phrase.
6. The poor criminal was going to be hanged on (**al**) the following day.
7. Happiness is not found in this mortal life, but in another, more lasting one. 8. The new Italian film has won important awards. (*Use* **premio**.)
9. We need a house that has five large and cheerful bedrooms. 10. I met his charming wife when I was in Naples. 11. Don't send me the green book, but the thick red one. 12. Tell my dear cousin that I received her interesting letter yesterday. 13. The poor man lost his entire family in the automobile accident. 14. His very own brother avoids him since he began telling off-color jokes. 15. In spite of her bad reputation, she is a good woman. 16. I don't trust that guy. 17. Your utopian desire to improve society will lead you to unhappiness. 18. His apparent purpose was to help us, but his real aim was to make us look ridiculous. 19. I prefer this white sand to that which we found on the other beach. 20. The immense cataracts of Iguassú produce a deafening noise. 21. What you are saying is pure myth. 22. His only daughter married a high official in the government. 23. It was a cold winter night, and the full moon resembled a giant globe in the black sky. 24. With brilliant brush strokes the artist captured the vibrant beauty of the landscape. 25. He made extensive notes about the numerous novels we read in class. 26. A painful event disturbed our peace. 27. She forgave him when she read the loving words of his last letter. 28. The high peaks of the Rockies are reflected in the silent waters of the lake. 29. The courageous general risked his life by visiting the front during the battle. 30. We return to the green hills of Vermont every summer.

62. SELECCION LITERARIA

Una tarde

Gabriel Miró

Nadie ha captado con mayor intensidad lírica que Gabriel Miró (1879–1930) la belleza sensorial de tierra y mar. Su poética prosa, casi siempre teñida de una vaga melancolía, revela su amor y compasión por toda la creación, hasta por lo no vivo. Leerle es muchas veces embriagarse de luz, de colores, y de fragancias. En el estilo de Miró, cuidadoso, lento, acertado en la selección del término más revelador, se percibe al observador penetrante de las acciones humanas. «Una tarde», escrita en 1909, es de la sección

titulada «Muelles y mar», que forma parte de El libro de Sigüenza
*(1917). El libro es una serie de relatos e impresiones autobiográficos
y Sigüenza es el joven Gabriel Miró, cuya ciudad natal, el luminoso Alicante, aparece en el fondo. Es frecuente en los escritos de
este gran poeta que la hermosura de la naturaleza invite a los hombres
a quererse y sentirse unidos como parte íntegra de la creación
universal. Pero la triste realidad es que pocas veces se realiza este
amor anhelado por Sigüenza.*

Nunca tuvo nuestro mar[1] la pureza, la alegría y quietud de esa tarde.
Sigüenza vio algunas gentes asomarse[2] a los balcones. Todas le parecieron
comunicadas de la gracia infantil, de la inocencia antigua del Mediterráneo.
Si pasaba algún barco de vela se veía todo su dibujo primorosamente[3] calado
5   sobre el cielo y las aguas. La isla de Tabarca, que siempre tiene un misterio
azul de distancia, como hecha de humo, mostrábase cercana,[4] clara, desnuda
y virginal.
      Las gaviotas parecía que volasen en un recinto guardado entre dos cris-
tales: el del cielo y el del mar; porque el mar estaba tan liso, tan inmóvil
10   como si se hubiera cuajado[5] en una delgada lámina[6] y bajo de ella no hubiese
más agua, sino el fondo enjuto, alumbrado de sol.
      No pudo contenerse Sigüenza en su ventana. Ansiaba y necesitaba ir a
la ribera, gozar del Mediterráneo, hasta tocándolo. Seguramente asistiría
a algún raro prodigio; se le ofrecerían todos los encantos de las entrañas[7]
15   del mar.
      . . . Halló un amigo, y juntos se fueron a los muelles,[8] prefiriendo el de
Levante, porque se entra, se aleja mucho encima de las aguas, y desde
el cabo alcanza la mirada toda la ciudad reflejada, y a sus espaldas se asoman
unas montañas remotas y azules, un delicado relieve del cielo. El menos
20   imaginativo cree que va viajando. Todo ofrece una belleza nueva, desconocida.
      . . . Pasaban los dos camaradas al lado de otros hombres, y se miraban
con más dulzura que nunca. Es que debían sentirse hermanos por eficacia
de la belleza y de la paz que les rodeaban . . . ¡Así se hubieran mirado los
25   hombres en el Paraíso—pensó cristianamente Sigüenza—si Dios hubiese
creado muchos primeros padres al mismo tiempo![9] . . . ¿No fue una lástima?
. . . ¿Y no serían estos momentos de triunfo, de exaltación de la hermosura
y del arte? ¡Seguramente, todos pensarían entonces[10] en los artistas como
en hermanos predilectos,[11] dotados de especiales gracias! . . . En estas
30   tardes, los artistas, por humildes que fueran, tenían sus frentes coronadas
de resplandores de elegidos, y recibían un dulce y gustoso rendimiento
aun de los más desaforados,[12] de los rudos, de los más vanos,[13] hasta de
los políticos y de los banqueros, y de todos los fenicios de la vida.
      Un marinero[14] enorme, macizo, con un gorro[15] doblado y encendido como

una llama, le estaba comprando a una recovera[16] del puerto. Seis huevos mercó,[17] y holgadamente se los puso en el cuenco de su manaza. Y como Sigüenza le preguntase si su barco—un viejo falucho, negro, bravo, de velas remendadas,[18] nave homérica—había llegado de tierras muy remotas, él, para indicarle que de Orán, alzó con gallardía su cargada mano y tendió el brazo lo mismo que una estatua de don Cristóbal Colón, y los huevos se estuvieron muy quietos en el seno de su diestra,[19] que parecía un nidal de gaviotas. 5

En justa alabanza de la recovera y de la grandeza de la mano del marinero, nos atrevemos a jurar que aquellos huevos eran de los más hermosos y cabales[20] concebidos por madrecilla de gallina. 10

Y así se lo dijo Sigüenza a la buena mujer, que no hacía más que mirarle menudamente. Era ancha, blanda, enlutada, de cara rugosa, torrada de sol, las manos ásperas de cortezas de salvado, como las patas de las aves de su corral, y el vientre de una cansada robustez. 15

Sigüenza también la miró mucho. Hallábala de grata[21] presencia; le era hasta familiar su gesto y su habla. ¿No les acercaría sus voluntades la dulce emoción de la tarde honda, clara, purísima?...

63. NOTES

1. el mar—sea
   la mar de—a great deal of, lots of

   Seafaring people regularly use **la mar**, and the feminine form is also employed in artistic or poetic usage. Most idioms are also rendered with **la mar**. **El mar** is the standard form, however, and must be used when a specific body of water is named or understood: **el mar Amarillo**, **el mar Caribe**, etc. In this selection Miró, with few exceptions, takes the sea to be **el Mediterráneo**.

El viento había amainado y **el mar** estaba sereno y negro.	The wind had died down, and the sea was calm and dark.
Viven mirando a **la mar**. (LE)	They live looking at the sea.
Sí, hoy vendrán; hoy tiene que venir **la mar de** gente, a bañarse en el río. (EJ)	They'll come today; lots of people have to come to swim in the river today.

2. asomarse (a)—to appear (at); to show (up)

   Asomar(se) has two basic uses. It is first a synonym of **aparecer**, *to appear*. English has no exact translation for the other common use of **asomar(se) a** or **estar asomado a**, which means *to appear* or *to be at some opening* (door, window, etc.) *for the purpose of looking out*. Although **mirar por** may translate *to look through* or *to look out*, it is little used. Forms of **asomarse** usually suffice to convey the basic idea of appearing or being at some type of aperture and looking through it. **Asomar** has another meaning that presents no difficulty: it is a synonym of **sacar** and means *to put* or *to stick something out* through an opening.

A ver si **se asoma** pronto.	Let's see if he shows up (appears) soon.
En nombrando al ruin de Roma, luego **asoma**.	Speak of the devil (and he will appear).
Una nube blanca, redonda, **ha asomado** por allá lejos. (BA)	A round, white cloud has appeared there in the distance.
Saltó de la dura cama, abrió una ventana y **se asomó a** ella. (CP)	He jumped out of the hard bed, opened a window, and looked out of it.
Cuando **se asome** el carcelero, podrá creer que sigo durmiendo. (ZA)	When the jailer appears (to look in), he may think that I am still sleeping.
Dingo contemplaba la escena **asomando** la cabeza por el ventanuco . . . (FN)	Dingo observed the scene by sticking his head out the window . . .

3. primoroso—exquisite; careful; skillful
    diestro, hábil—skillful
    la destreza, la habilidad—skill

Pepita Jiménez cuidaba **primorosamente** sus hermosas manos.	Pepita Jiménez took exquisite care of her beautiful hands.
La **hábil** colocación de los muebles revelaba su buen gusto.	The skillful arrangement of the furniture revealed her good taste.

4. cercano—near
    próximo—near

Cercano and **próximo** both mean *near* in spatial and temporal contexts. **Próximo**, however, is more common than **cercano** when referring to time.

La **proximidad** del mar se hacía sensible por un rumor sordo. (F)	The nearness of the sea was perceptible in a soft murmur.

5. cuajar(se)—to curd(le), to thicken (milk products); to set
    espesar(se)—to make (become) thick, thicken
    complicarse—to become involved; to thicken (figurative)

Ponga la leche en la nevera para que no **se cuaje**.	Put the milk in the refrigerator so it won't curdle.
Debiste **espesar** un poco más la sopa antes de servirla.	You should have thickened the soup a little more before serving it.

| El argumento de la novela **se complica** muy temprano. | The plot of the novel thickens very early. |

6. la lámina—(very thin) sheet, layer
   la sábana—(bed) sheet
   la hoja—sheet (or leaf) of paper; razor blade
   hojear—to leaf (page) through
   la plancha—metal sheet or plate
   hacer una plancha—to put one's foot in it

| Hay quinientas **hojas** de papel en una resma. | There are five hundred sheets of paper in a ream. |
| Esta vez sí que **hiciste una plancha**. | This time you really put your foot in it. |

7. las entrañas—here, depths
   entrañable—deep-felt, heartfelt, intimate

   Entrañas, *entrails, guts,* etc., is also very common in expressions of affection, where it conveys an idea akin to the English *heart, feeling, love,* etc. The very colloquial **no tener agallas**, literally *to have no gills* or *to have no tonsils,* renders *to have no guts* or *to lack intestinal fortitude.*

Los de la policía secreta son gente **de malas entrañas**.	The men of the secret police have no heart (are heartless).
Y si se resistían, la emprendería a bofetadas, pues le sobraban **agallas** para ello. (FM)	And if they resisted, she would go settle it with a few slaps, for she had more than enough courage (guts) to do it.
Siempre nos ha profesado un cariño **entrañable**.	He has always professed a very deep-felt affection for us.

8. el muelle—dock, pier; (metal) spring
   el resorte—(metal) spring
   muelle (adjective)—soft (especially for what requires little effort or is sensually gratifying)
   mullido—soft (fluffy)

Yo llevé su equipaje hasta el **muelle**. (LE)	I carried her baggage to the pier.
Una vida **muelle** es lo que quiere.	What he wants is a soft life.
Las mujeres iban en busca de los **mullidos** asientos de la sala. (AT)	The women sought out the soft chairs in the living room.

9. al mismo tiempo, a la vez—at the same time
   a un tiempo—at the same time (mainly literary)

10. entonces—then (at that moment, in that case)
    luego—then (soon afterward, in a sequence of time or events)
    después—then (later, afterward)

11. predilecto—favorite, preferred

    Predilecto has two main uses: first as a somewhat learned synonym
    for **favorito**; also to convey a note of special favoritism, affection,
    or love not present in **favorito** alone. It is close in meaning to *very
    favorite* and is used especially to refer to people.

De todos sus hijos, **el predilecto** era el primogénito.	Of all his children, his favorite was the first-born.
Este es mi plato **favorito** (**predilecto**).	This is my favorite dish.

12. desaforado—lawless, outrageous
    el ultraje—outrage, insult
    la injuria, el insulto—insult, offense
    el denuesto—insult
    ultrajar, injuriar, insultar, denostar—to insult, offend

    Ultraje indicates the most serious degree of offense or insult. All
    except **denuesto** may refer to injury or insult by word or deed, but
    denuesto, a literary term, refers exclusively to verbal insult or abuse.
    Moreover, **injuriar** rarely indicates a physical injury.

Nunca olvidaré **los ultrajes** que he recibido.	I shall never forget the insults I have received.

13. vano—(here) vain, conceited

    The use of **vano** for *vain* or *conceited* is purely literary, since the
    standard word for *vain* or *conceited* in both everyday speech and
    literature is **vanidoso**. **Vano** normally means *empty, hollow, without
    substance*. **En vano** and **en balde** both mean *in vain*, and **engreído**,
    conceited, is a synonym for **vanidoso**.

No creía que fuera tan **vanidoso** para leer sus versos en público.	I didn't believe he was so vain as to read his poetry in public.
Los años no pasan **en balde**.	The years don't pass in vain.
Sus promesas siempre resultan **vanas**.	His promises always turn out to be empty promises.

14. el marinero, el marino—sailor, seaman
    la marina (mercante)—merchant marine
    la marina (de guerra)—navy

    Marinero, though common for a member of either organization, is
    used most often to indicate a member of the navy.

15. el gorro—cap, bonnet
    la gorra—cap (usually with a visor)

This is another example of pairs of words ending in -a and -o with little change in meaning. In most cases -a indicates larger size or a mass noun as opposed to a single unit. There are, nevertheless, many exceptions:

el cuenco—earthenware bowl; hollow, depression
la cuenca—wooden bowl; valley, large depression enclosed by cliffs
el leño—log
la leña—firewood
el gimnasio—gymnasium (building)
la gimnasia—gymnastics
el charco—puddle
la charca—pool

But **cruzar el charco** is the colloquial, humorous expression for *to cross the ocean*.

16. la recovera—poultry dealer
    la recova—poultry business

17. mercar—to buy (rural in flavor)
    comprar—to buy, purchase
    acaparar—to buy up; to corner the market (implies speculation)

Acaparando la cosecha entera, la compañía pudo vender su producto a un precio especial.	By buying up the entire crop, the company was able to sell its product at a special price.

18. remendar—to patch, mend
    reparar, componer—to repair; to fix (up)
    arreglar—to repair; to put in order

El zapatero **remendón** tenía su taller en el sótano.	The shoemaker (cobbler) had his shop in the basement.
El automóvil se halla ya **reparado** . . . (BA)	The automobile is now repaired (fixed) . . . .
El fontanero vendrá mañana a **arreglar** los tubos.	The plumber will come tomorrow to fix the pipes.

19. la diestra—right hand

In **la diestra**, **la mano** is understood. This is a common literary synonym for **la mano derecha**.

Dio su **diestra** al joven, y éste la llevó a sus labios.	She gave her right hand to the young man, and he put it to his lips.

20. cabal—perfect, finished; trustworthy
no estar en sus cabales—to be not all there

The two main uses of **cabal** overlap somewhat: it is used for **perfecto** to indicate that something or someone is a perfect or finished model of its kind, and it is also used in the sense of reliable, trustworthy, moral, etc. Something is thus perfect and can be relied on for this reason. In our example, **huevos cabales** are perfect eggs and, at the same time, eggs in which one may have full confidence. **Cabal** is mostly confined to certain patterned expressions.

Su hijo es ya un hombre **cabal**.	Their son is a complete (real) man now.
Han seleccionado los hechos para dar una idea **cabal** de este período.	They have selected the facts to give a complete (perfect) idea of this period.
En esta novela los personajes son **cabales** en todo detalle.	In this novel the characters are perfect (complete) in every detail.

21. grato—pleasing, pleasant
agradable—pleasant, agreeable
ameno—pleasant, agreeable
agradar, gustar, complacer—to please

These words are often interchanged without distinction. **Ameno**, however, has two common uses: to refer to the world of nature, and to human activities that are light and pleasant (conversation, style, manner, etc.). **Complacer** often connotes an attempt to accommodate someone or to do something that is useful, satisfying, or pleasing to another person.

Acabo de recibir su **grata** carta.	I have just received your pleasant letter.
Nuestro hotel daba a un valle muy **ameno**.	Our hotel faced a very pleasant valley.
Para **complacer** a su madre, Galdós fue a Madrid a estudiar leyes.	To please his mother, Galdós went to Madrid to study law.
Lo que más me **gusta** (**agrada**) de Madrid es la vida nocturna.	What I like most about Madrid is the night life.

EXERCISES ON NOTES

1. She took the food out of an enormous basket.   2. It pleases me that you have finally decided to accept our offer.   3. It will cost $25 to repair the television set.   4. A deep-felt love united the two brothers.   5. The man's outrageous conduct scandalized his partners.   6. The moment of her death seemed very near.   7. I find that he is a very pleasant person.   8. By buying up 25 per cent of the stock, the banker was able to control the

company. 9. They had lots of (*use idiom*) fun at the beach. 10. The plot doesn't thicken until the last act. 11. A sheet of steel one inch thick protects the soldier. 12. We spent two weeks at a spa on the Black Sea. 13. Because she put fresh pineapple in the gelatine, it didn't set. 14. He shows up from time to time. 15. My favorite Spanish painter is El Greco. 16. Next time don't thicken the gravy so much. 17. He has led a very soft life since he received the inheritance. 18. They found a pleasant spot in the meadow and sat down to eat lunch. 19. Gazpacho is one of my favorite soups. 20. She bought the baby a bonnet and then discovered it was too large. 21. He became very vain after he received the national prize for poetry. 22. When they returned, they tied (*use* **amarrar**) the rowboat to the dock. 23. The poet never forgot that his rival had insulted him in public. 24. He wound the music box so much that the spring broke. 25. We had a very pleasant chat with her on the terrace of the cafe. 26. He frequently appeared at the balcony [window] to observe what was happening in the street. 27. He is a perfect lawyer. 28. A group of investors purchased the fields for a housing development. 29. The bus driver warned the child not to stick his head out of the window. 30. The teacher's thoughtless words offended the sensitive student. 31. Everything he says seems like an empty (*not* **vacío**) formula taken from some book. 32. His recent actions demonstrate that he is not all there. 33. The mother was very frugal and always mended her children's clothes. 34. He avoids talking of things that are not pleasant. 35. If he had guts, he wouldn't permit them to insult him like that. 36. The fisherman said that in the afternoon a cool breeze would blow [in] from the sea. 37. Whenever I passed their house, I saw the grandmother standing at the window. 38. The sailor was sitting on the pier skillfully patching the sail. 39. The old servant deeply loved the children of the house. 40. Who is the favorite son of this state?

CUESTIONARIO

a. contenido

1. ¿Cómo veía Sigüenza al mar aquella tarde?
2. ¿Cómo creía que el mar afectaba a las gentes?
3. ¿Por qué no pudo contenerse en su ventana?
4. ¿Por qué prefirieron Sigüenza y su amigo el muelle de Levante?
5. ¿Por qué se sentían hermanos?
6. ¿Cómo era el marinero? ¿Qué hacía?
7. ¿Por qué compara al marinero con Cristóbal Colón?
8. Describa Vd. el aspecto físico de la recovera.

b. estilo

1. Explique Vd. las colocaciones del adjetivo en: **delgada lámina, raro prodigio, delicado relieve.**
2. ¿Qué efecto produce el amontonamiento de adjetivos en la oración que comienza: «La isla de Tabarca . . . »?
3. Explique Vd. la estructura de la oración que empieza: «Halló un amigo . . . ».

4. ¿Cómo se relaciona la alusión al Paraíso con la descripción de la tarde?
5. ¿Cómo consigue el autor ampliar las dimensiones de su retrato del marinero? ¿En qué imágenes específicas basa Vd. su respuesta?
6. ¿En qué rasgos de la cara y de las manos de la recovera concentra el autor su atención? ¿Qué acertada imagen le ayuda a lograr su propósito?

TEMA—TRADUCCION

Sigüenza recalled no day when the sea was more brilliant and calm than on that afternoon. Looking out his balcony window, he watched the white sails of the boats that floated on the blue waters near the island of Tabarca, which today appeared closer and brighter than ever.

The surface of the sea was so smooth that it resembled a thin sheet of glass under which the bottom of the sea reflected the blinding brilliance of the sun. Sigüenza yearned to go down to the shore, for he was certain he would witness something extraordinary. Sigüenza found a friend, and together they set out for the pier of Levante, where the marvelous view encompassed the city and the blue mountains in the distance.

The ineffable beauty and peace of the afternoon made Sigüenza think of Paradise. As they walked [along], he realized how the beauty of nature could fill man with love for his fellow man. Then they stopped to watch a sailor buying eggs from an old poultry dealer. Sigüenza went up to the tall seaman and asked him if his old *felucca* had just arrived from some remote and exotic port. The sailor answered by extending his arm in the direction of Oran. For the imaginative Sigüenza, the enormous hand, holding the recently purchased eggs, seemed like a seagull's nest. He and the poultry dealer observed each other carefully. What most attracted his attention were her wrinkled and sunburnt face and her very rough hands. He found her speech and her gestures pleasing, and wondered if his liking for her were not also a result of the contagious beauty of the afternoon.

TEMAS A ESCOGER

Escríbanse unas 200 palabras sobre uno de los temas siguientes usando a lo menos 20 de las palabras y expresiones estudiadas en este capítulo.

1. Descripción poética de una costa del mar
2. Geografía y clima como factores que influyen sobre el hombre
3. Retrato de una persona inolvidable

chapter 13

64. SELECCION LITERARIA

Una tarde

Gabriel Miró

Y parece que no fue eso, porque conversando vinieron a recordarse en otro lugar: en los pasillos de la Excelentísima Diputación, de cuyo Hospicio y Hospital era esta mujer proveedora[1] de huevos y averío.[2] Allí se encontraron muchas mañanas.

5 —¿Acaso sería él alguno de los señores diputados?—preguntó la gallinera, ofreciéndole una sonrisa de acatamiento.

Y Sigüenza le correspondió con otra más humilde. Nunca había sido diputado; nada más era cronista.

—¡Cronista, cronista!—murmuraba pasmadamente[3] la vendedora, no 10 entendiéndolo.

Entonces el amigo de Sigüenza le explicó que aquello era oficio[4] de escribir libros de historia y de fantasía, y que de este modo se ganaba la vida . . .

—¡Historias . . . , libros!—gritó riéndose la buena mujer, y se enjugaba[5] 15 con sus dedos recios y morenos la saliva de su risa—. ¿A así se ganaba la vida? ¡María Santísima!

Y midiendo con la mirada a Sigüenza, le volvió la espalda y le dijo:
—¡Fantasías? ¿Cronista? ¡Más me estimo yo mis huevos!

Del homérico falucho salía un gustoso olor de guiso picante de pescados[6] 20 y un blando ruido de batir de yemas.[7]

Y Sigüenza murmuró:
—¿No serán un símbolo estos huevos que tanto estima la recovera? ¿Y no habremos de estimar o preferir el símbolo a los libros?

—Todavía sí—le repuso[8] su amigo.

25 Y silenciosos prosiguieron su camino, subiendo por el muro de las escolleras.

Desde allí veían el mar libre, limpio, inocente, no como el del puerto, cuya transparencia muestra vilezas de las ciudades. Aquella agua ancha, pálida, tenía pureza y misterio de verdadero mar. Agarrados[9] a las piedras 30 se veían los moluscos-erizos[10] esponjándose silenciosamente bajo la luz de la tierra, que penetraba encantada hasta lo hondo; allí, acostados, muy quietos, relucientes de plata, estaban esos peces anchos, gordos y ladinos, cebados por los buenos pescadores, las *doradas*, cuyas escamas de fastuosos tornasoles recuerdan los recamados coseletes de las bailarinas, 35 y tendidas al amor de una peña o encima de las algas, roen con exquisitez de dama los anzuelos, hasta dejarlos mondos[11] y brillantes.

Mirando estaban Sigüenza y su amigo este retazo de vida submarina, cuando pasaron unos chicos que traían un perrito blanco, jovial, ganoso de bullicio y de fiestas, según brincaba[12] para lamer las manos de los muchachos. Ellos se reían, acariciándole[13] y untándole el hocico[14] con el companage de sus meriendas, para verle torcer golosamente la roja lancilla de la lengua.[15]

Sigüenza estuvo contemplando aquel grupo, que participaba de la inocencia y de la buena alegría de la tarde. Olvidado de las palabras de la recovera, se afirmaba que la paz y la belleza del ambiente eran como un perfume que regalaba y purificaba todos los corazones, todas las criaturas del mundo.

Pero los rapaces, ya lejos, bajaron a las piedras; sus manos descogían, alargaban una soga; el perrito gañía lastimeramente. Sigüenza y su amigo corrieron a ver su travesura. Los mozos, tendidos en las rocas, miraban el fondo, que allí estaba somero, del todo transparente.

—¿Qué hiciste del perro? ¿Se escapó de vosotros?

—¡No, siñor; no siñor; aún puede verlo!

Acercóse Sigüenza. El perrito se retorcía ahogándose[16] con los ojos abiertos, mirando a sus amigos, que le habían atado el cuello y los brazuelos[17] a una piedra muy gorda para que no se levantase. Y los ojos del animal tenían una angustia y una esperanza humana. ¡Veía tan cerca las manos que había lamido; hacía tan poco que le habían agasajado! ¡Hasta le dieron de merendar, como si fuera un chico pequeño de la misma escuela! ¡Cómo habían de dejarlo morir! ¡Eso no era más que por divertirse asustándole!

Y sí que lo dejaron que se ahogase. Cuando Sigüenza se asomó, ya estaba resignada la víctima; había doblado la cabeza.

Y murió.

Sigüenza les injurió enfurecidamente. Y ellos, entre pesarosos y risueños, le dijeron con sencillez:

—¡Si ha sido sin querer! Le queríamos[18] mucho; pero estaba la mar tan quieta y tan clara, que, sin pensarlo, pues... lo atamos, para ver cómo se ahogaba un perro y todo lo que hacía!...

Y se quedaron mirando la paz y hermosura de la tarde, que eran como un perfume que llegaba a todos los corazones...

65. NOTES

1. proveedor(a)—supplier, purveyor (of food)
    proveer—to supply; to provide
    suministrar—to supply
    surtir—to stock; to supply
    el surtido—supply, stock, line, assortment

    Either **proveer** or **suministrar** is appropriate in most situations that require *to supply*. **Proveer**, however, may also be used with more abstract ideas, whereas **suministrar** generally refers to supplies or provisions, often on a large scale.

Ahora estamos **provistos** del apoyo moral que nos hacía falta.	Now we have (are provided with) the moral support that we needed.
En esta papelería los alumnos pueden **proveerse** de todo lo necesario para sus clases.	In this stationery store the pupils can supply themselves with everything necessary for their classes.
El comisario está encargado de **suministrar** (**proveer**) uniformes a los reclutas.	The quartermaster is in charge of supplying the recruits with uniforms.

2. el averío—poultry; flock of poultry
   la avería—aviary; mechanical breakdown
   la bandada—flock (of birds)
   el ave (feminine), el pájaro—bird

   Ave is the generic term for the class of feathered vertebrates. It is also the standard word to refer to most large birds, birds of prey, fowl, and game birds. **Pájaro** in standard usage refers to smaller birds and songbirds. Since the category **ave** includes the category **pájaro**, the former often replaces the latter to avoid repetition. **Pájaro** is not usual, however, for a bird which, like the eagle, is specifically **ave**.

El pavo es un **ave** americana.	The turkey is an American bird.
En nuestra **avería** sólo hay **aves** de rapiña.	In our aviary there are only birds of prey.
Los **pajaritos** (las **avecillas**) están cantando en sus jaulas.	The little birds are singing in their cages.
Llegaron tarde porque tuvieron una pequeña **avería** en el camino.	They arrived late because they had a small breakdown on the way.

3. pasmar—to astound, amaze
   asombrar—to astonish, amaze; to frighten
   maravillar—to amaze; to fill with wonder

   The three verbs convey the general idea of *to astonish* or *to amaze* and are frequently used reflexively with **de** or another preposition to render *to be amazed at* or *to be astonished by*. **Pasmar** indicates the most intense state of amazement; it implies being left stunned, speechless, or unable to react. **Asombrar** usually has a somewhat less intense meaning and can thus render *to amaze* in almost all cases. Although **asombrar** and **pasmar** may refer to fortunate or unfortunate circumstances, **maravillar** almost always indicates something pleasant.

El **se quedó pasmado** al saber que el banco había quebrado.	He was astounded (shocked, stunned) when he learned that the bank had failed.

A mí no me **asombra** nada.	Nothing astonishes (amazes) me.
El turista **se maravilló de** los rascacielos de Nueva York.	The tourist was amazed by (marveled at, was awed by) the skyscrapers of New York.

4. el oficio—occupation, trade
   la profesión—profession, occupation
   la ocupación—occupation (what one is occupied or working with at a
             particular time)
   el empleo—job, employment
   el trabajo—work, job (most general term)

The line between **oficio** and **profesión** is becoming less clearly defined: **oficio** ordinarily implies manual or mechanical work, whereas **profesión** refers to occupations requiring more education. There are, however, categories that are technically **oficios** (**sastre**, **relojero**, etc.), but are now sometimes rendered as **profesiones**, a euphemistic upgrading of occupational categories.

Dos **oficios** muy remunerativos son el de mecánico y el de fontanero.	Two well-paying trades (occupations) are those of mechanic and plumber.

5. enjugar—to dry, wipe dry

Enjugar, etymologically *to extract the juice from*, means *to wipe dry* or *to dry*. It is primarily a literary expression, but it is sometimes used in spoken Spanish as a synonym for **secar** in referring to tears, sweat, saliva, etc. The adjective **enjuto**, *thin* or *dry*, has broader uses.

Se enjugaba las lágrimas de sus ojos.	She wiped the tears from her eyes.
Me sequé con una toalla.	I dried myself with a towel.
Era alto, **enjuto**, desgarbadote y algo cargado de espaldas. (AT)	He was tall, thin, ungainly, and rather stoop-shouldered.
Con mucha calma **se enjugó** las manos en un papel de periódico que se sacó del bolsillo. (EA)	He very calmly wiped his hands in a piece of newspaper that he took out of his pocket.

6. el pescado, el pez—fish

Pescado refers to **lo pescado**, *that which has been caught and is dead*. **Pescado** generally suggests something that is to be eaten, as well as fish removed from the water. **Pez** is used in other contexts.

Con viejas y mohosas navajas iban abriendo el plateado vientre de **los pescados**. (FM)	With rusty old knives, they were cutting open the silvery stomachs of the fish.
Los espectadores ríen también, en tanto que **el pez** brinca en la cesta. (LP)	The onlookers, too, are laughing while the fish jumps about in the basket.

7. la yema—yolk of an egg; (fleshy) tip of the finger
la clara—white of an egg
la punta del dedo—the tip of the finger

Le enseñaba las **yemas** arrugadas por el baño tan largo. (EJ)	She showed him the tips of her fingers, wrinkled by her long swim.

8. reponer—to reply (especially to some statement or challenge)
responder—to respond; to answer
contestar—to answer
replicar—to respond; to answer back, argue
responder (contestar) a una carta, pregunta—to respond to (answer) a letter, question

Reponer is common in literary and journalistic Spanish, not in the spoken language. It is almost always used in the preterit (**repuse**) to report a past event. **Replicar** means *to answer* and *to talk back to* or *answer back*. **Contestar** and **responder** are close in meaning, though the first is more common. In usage the preposition **a** in *to answer a letter, question*, etc., is often omitted.

Cuando te doy una orden, no me **repliques**.	When I give you an order, don't answer (talk) back.
No **han contestado** (a) mi carta.	They haven't answered my letter.

9. agarrar—to grasp; to grab
las garras—talons, claws
asir—to seize; to grasp (mainly literary)
arrebatar—to grab; to take; to snatch (away from)
embargar—to seize (take legal possession of)

Agarrar is used as a synonym of **coger** and **tomar**, *to take*, in many Spanish-speaking countries. It must be used in regions where **coger** has acquired meanings that cause it to be avoided in normal conversation.

El viento **arrebató** las últimas hojas al roble.	The wind snatched (carried, took) away the last leaves from the oak tree.
Le **asió** y empezó a sacudirle.	He seized (took hold of) him and began to shake him.
Entonces, uno de los guardias **agarrándome** del brazo, sin más explicaciones me metió en el carro, junto a su comandante. (MP)	Then, one of the guards, grabbing me by the arm, without further explanation, put me into the car, next to his commander.
Le **embargaron** el automóvil porque no lo pagó.	They seized his automobile because he didn't pay for it.

10. el molusco—mollusk
    el marisco—shellfish
    los mariscos—seafood, shellfish
    la almeja—clam
    la ostra—oyster

    Las gaviotas que vimos por la costa se alimentaban de **mariscos**.

    The gulls we saw along the coast were feeding on shellfish.

11. mondo (adjective)—clean (especially of what is extraneous or useless)
    mondar—to pare; to peel
    pelar—to peel
    la piel—skin, peel
    la mondadura—peel (often plural)
    la cáscara—shell (by extension, rind, thick skin, or peel)

    Although **mondar** usually implies the use of a sharp-edged implement and **pelar** the use of the hands, **pelar** is standard for certain fruits and vegetables (such as apples and potatoes) that are pared or peeled with a sharp utensil. However, the distinction has several common exceptions, and with certain fruits both verbs are frequently used. Also, **cáscara**, *the shell of a nut or an egg*, is often used for fruit having a relatively thick outer covering.

    Pelaron las patatas antes de cocerlas.

    They peeled the potatoes before cooking them.

    ¿**Has mondado** la fruta para el postre?

    Have you pared (peeled) the fruit for the dessert?

12. brincar—to jump, leap
    saltar—to jump, leap
    saltar a la vista—to be self-evident

    Saltar is used more often since it may indicate jumping up and down, over, or across. **Brincar** always suggests a springlike up-and-down motion. In literature, often, no distinction is made. Neither verb requires a preposition to render the English *over*.

    Los muchachos **saltaron** (**brincaron**) la tapia.

    The boys jumped over the wall. (**Brincar** is possible since it implies up and thus over.)

    Carlos **saltó** la zanja sin dificultad.

    Charles jumped over (across) the ditch without trouble.

    ¿**Saltará, brincará** para que los niños rían? (SH)

    Will he skip and jump so the children will laugh?

    Vamos a **saltar** este pasaje.

    We are going to skip this passage.

    Los delfines **saltaron** fuera del agua para agarrar el pescado.

    The dolphins leaped out of the water to get the fish.

| Mirábamos a las cabras **brincando** por la ladera del monte. | We watched the goats jumping (bounding) along the mountain slope. |

13. **Acariciar**, *to caress*, means *to stroke* or *to pet* when referring to an animal. **Mimar**, *to spoil* an animal or person, is often *to pet* a lap dog.

14. el hocico—nose (of an animal); muzzle, snout
    la jeta—snout (of a pig, boar); pigface
    caer de hocicos—to fall flat on one's face

Whenever possible, Spanish avoids using the same anatomical term for people and animals. Notice also that **hocico** may refer to an animal's nose or to a much larger part of its face. **Hocico**, like **nariz** and other words that indicate what may be viewed as a unit or as composed of two (or more) parts (**bigote[s]**, *mustache*; **espalda[s]**, *back*), is common in the plural, especially in idiomatic expressions. When animal terms are applied to human beings, they are used pejoratively or humorously.

| . . . y él sólo asomaba el **hocico** de tarde en tarde como huésped condescendiente . . . (MP) | . . . he would only stick his nose in from time to time like some condescending guest . . . |

15. la lengua—tongue; language
    el lenguaje—language
    el idioma—language
    el modismo—idiom (i.e., expression with a particular or nonliteral meaning)
    hacerse lenguas de—to speak enthusiastically about; to rave about

Lengua is the oral means by which members of a political entity or racially related group communicate. **Lenguaje** may share this meaning, especially when a synonym is required for **lengua**; ordinarily it refers to a more personal or professional use of a given language. **Idioma** refers to both a national language and the speech or language of a particular group.

Cuida la **lengua**.	Watch your tongue.
He procurado entenderle, pero no hablamos el mismo **lenguaje**.	I have tried to understand him, but we do not speak the same language.
La **lengua** inglesa no es fácil.	The English language isn't easy.
Ten cuidado del **lenguaje** cuando estés con María.	Be careful of your language when you are with Mary.
Las mujeres **se hacían lenguas de** la piedad del nuevo párraco.	The women were raving about the piety of their new parish priest.

16. ahogar(se)—to drown; to suffocate (notice that the context serves to distinguish *to drown* from *to suffocate*)
    morir ahogado—to choke to death; to drown
    desahogarse—to unburden oneself
    sofocar—to choke someone
    atragantarse con—to choke on (i.e., to get something caught in one's throat)

He visto **ahogados**, y este hombre no **se ha ahogado**.	I have seen drowned persons, and this man didn't drown.
Yo aparté la cabeza porque me **sofocaba** el olor a cebolla. (LE)	I turned my head away, for the smell of onion was choking (stifling) me.

17. **Brazuelos**, diminutive of **brazo**, does not contradict the statement in Note 14, for **brazuelo** is a synonym for the front leg, **pata delantera**, of four-legged animals; however, its use instead of the more common **patas** doubtless increases the affective force of the incident.

18. querer—to love; to want; to be fond of
    amar—to love
    enamorarse de—to fall in love with
    estar enamorado de—to be in love with

There is no absolute difference between **querer** and **amar**. **Querer** is the standard term, whereas **amar**, which is more literary and elevated in tone, is used for that which is abstract. To avoid confusion with the other common meaning of **querer**, *to want*, **amar** is ordinarily used with things. **Amar** also means *to love* when physical passion is involved.

No sabes cuánto te **quiero**.	You don't know how much I love you.
Yo no la **quiero** a usted sólo como amigo; yo la **amo** . . . (AT)	I'm not only fond of you as a friend; I love you . . .
No, no **estaba** de veras **enamorado de** Liduvina, y tal vez no lo había estado nunca. (HA)	No, he wasn't really in love with Liduvina, and perhaps he never really had been.
Hay muchas maneras de **amar** a la patria.	There are many ways of loving one's native land.

EXERCISES ON NOTES

1. He has been so nervous lately that he jumps at the least (**menor**) noise. 2. This store has an excellent stock of records. 3. When I saw him, I was amazed by his youthful appearance. 4. The breakdown of the air conditioner occurred on the hottest day of the year. 5. The fish they serve here is always fresh. 6. He jumped out of bed as soon as the phone rang. 7. The mother snatched the knife from the child's hand. 8. Don't put (**meter**) your [big] nose in my affairs! 9. Fried clams and

raw oysters are my favorite seafoods. 10. He choked to death before they could take him to the hospital. 11. I don't want you to love any other woman. 12. I would like to polish the language of my essay before handing it in. 13. Law has always been a popular profession. 14. The canary is a bird with (**de**) brilliant plumage. 15. I was astonished by his command of English. 16. When he failed to pay his taxes, the government seized his property. 17. Don Quixote often became annoyed when Sancho answered him back. 18. She grasped me by (**de**) the arm before inoculating me. 19. The maid dried her hands in her apron. 20. The mother peeled the banana before giving it to the child. 21. The guests raved about how delicious the paella was. 22. He said he would never fall in love, but it's self-evident that he is in love with Tina. 23. The news of his death stunned (*use* **dejar**) us. 24. The hummingbird is one of the world's smallest birds. 25. Everyone was amazed at the parrot's large vocabulary. 26. The aviary of the Rio de Janeiro zoo has a marvelous collection of tropical birds. 27. The travel agent has promised to provide us with the information for our trip. 28. The printer's trade has always fascinated me. 29. She prepared the carrots with lemon peel to improve the flavor. 30. Since the dog's nose was cold, we knew he was not sick. 31. The eagle seized the rabbit in its claws and flew off with it to his nest. 32. The man wiped his sweaty forehead with a large white handkerchief. 33. Idioms are probably the most difficult thing to master in a foreign language. 34. He loves the city in which he was born. 35. Don't pet the dog so much or you will spoil him. 36. To prepare some kinds of omelette it is necessary to separate the whites from the yolks. 37. Those red trucks supply milk to the entire city. 38. I am amazed that they answered our letter so quickly. 39. They love nature and spend every summer observing wild birds in the mountains. 40. She wiped the tears from her eyes when they told her she had not lost her job.

CUESTIONARIO

a. contenido

1. ¿Dónde se habían encontrado antes Sigüenza y la gallinera?
2. ¿Por qué habían ido ellos allí?
3. ¿Cómo compara la recovera su oficio con la profesión de Sigüenza?
4. ¿En qué consiste el retazo de vida submarina visto por los dos amigos desde la escollera?
5. ¿De qué imágenes del mundo femenino se vale Miró para describir los peces que ve?
6. ¿A qué conclusión prematura le lleva a Sigüenza la belleza de la tarde?
7. ¿Qué hicieron los chicos poco después con el perro?
8. ¿Cómo tratan de justificar ante Sigüenza el haber ahogado al perro?

b. estilo

1. Explíquese el uso del pronombre **me** en «¡Más me estimo yo mis huevos!»

2. Contraste la posición del adjetivo en «homérico falucho» con la de «nave homérica» en la primera parte del cuento.
3. ¿Qué imágenes evoca el uso de la palabra *inocente* para contrastar el agua del mar libre con el del puerto?
4. ¿Cómo logra el autor crear un ambiente de luz en la escena de los peces?
5. ¿Cuál es el tono de la primera descripción del perro? ¿Cómo consigue Miró establecer este tono?
6. ¿Qué recursos usa el autor para hacernos compadecer del perro?
7. ¿Es convincente la ambigüedad de los motivos de los chicos al terminar el cuento? ¿Por qué?

TEMA—TRADUCCION

Since the poultry dealer recalled having seen Sigüenza many mornings at the House of Deputies, whose hospital she supplied with eggs and poultry, she asked him if he were by chance a deputy. He answered her question humbly, explaining that he was only a chronicler. But since the woman was amazed to hear such a strange word, Sigüenza's friend had to explain to her that he wrote books. It seemed unbelievable to the good woman that anyone could earn a living by writing books. Sizing up Sigüenza and skeptical about his occupation, she said: "I'll take my eggs any time."

As they left the poultry dealer behind and resumed their walk, Sigüenza was still wondering if the eggs were not really a symbol. From the breakwater they saw the open sea, whose waters were still pure and innocent, unlike those of the port. The transparent water revealed sea urchins, fastened to the rocks and swelling and contracting slowly like sponges. Farther down the rays of the sun were reflected on the brilliant scales of the *doradas*. Sigüenza knew that these beautiful fish nibble delicately on the fishermen's hooks until they leave them bare. While they were looking at these fish, some boys passed [by] with a small white dog. The dog was jumping and licking the boy's hands. They were petting him and smearing his nose with the remains of their lunch, in order to see him twist his little tongue (*use diminutive*) greedily. Sigüenza knew that this happy group shared in the innocence of the afternoon, and that the peace and beauty of the surroundings were like a perfume that reached the heart of every human being, purifying it.

But a little later, on hearing the dog's pitiful yelps, Sigüenza and his friend ran to find out what mischief the boys had gotten into (**meterse**). They found them stretched out on the rocks with their eyes fixed on the drowning (*use clause*) animal. They had tied a large rock around the dog's neck and had thrown him into the water. There was an almost human expression of hope and anguish in the poor animal's eyes, as if he did not believe that those who had been so good to him would let him die. But when Sigüenza appeared, the animal was already resigned to its fate. And it died.

Sigüenza berated the boys furiously, and they, regretful and smiling at the same time, replied that it was unintentional. They loved their dog, but the sea was so calm that, without thinking about it, they had thrown him into the water to see how a dog drowns. They remained looking at the beauty of the sea, which was like a perfume that reached every heart.

TEMAS A ESCOGER

Escríbanse unas 200 palabras sobre uno de los temas siguientes usando a lo menos 20 de las palabras y expresiones estudiadas en este capítulo.

1. La amistad entre el hombre y el animal
2. Un retazo de vida submarina
3. La crueldad de los niños

chapter 14

PRONOUNS

66. PERSONAL AND REFLEXIVE PRONOUNS

SINGULAR

Person	Subject	Indirect Object	Direct Object	Prepositional	Reflexive
1.	yo	me	me	mí	me
2.	tú	te	te	ti	te
3.	él	le	le, lo	él	se
	ella	le	la	ella } sí	se
	usted	le	le, lo, la	usted	se
				ello	

PLURAL

Person	Subject	Indirect Object	Direct Object	Prepositional	Reflexive
1.	nosotros(as)	nos	nos	nosotros(as)	nos
2.	vosotros(as)	os	os	vosotros(as)	os
3.	ellos	les	les, los	ellos	se
	ellas	les	las	ellas } sí	se
	ustedes	les	les, los, las	ustedes	se

67. SUBJECT PRONOUNS

Since the endings of first- and second-person verbs indicate the pronoun subject, these personal pronouns are normally omitted. They may be added, however, for emphasis. Since the third-person verbal endings may refer to one of six possible subjects—él, ella, usted, ellos, ellas, ustedes—the personal pronoun may be included for clarity or emphasis. **Usted(es)**, the formal pronoun for *you*, usually appears at least once in every sentence for reasons of courtesy.

Yo pago el taxi si **tú** sacas las entradas.	I'll pay for the taxi if you'll get the tickets.
¿Dónde está el libro que encontraste?	Where is the book you found?
Usted tiene derecho a quejarse.	You have a right to complain.

68. INDIRECT OBJECT PRONOUNS

When an action results in some advantage or disadvantage for a person who is not the direct object, an indirect object pronoun is used. Indirect object pronouns precede all verbal forms except infinitives, gerunds, and affirmative commands, which they follow and to which they are attached. When an infinitive or gerund is used with a conjugated verb, the indirect object pronoun may either precede the conjugated verb or be attached to the gerund or infinitive.

Le leía su cuento favorito.	I was reading his favorite story to him.
Estaba leyéndo**le** su cuento favorito.	I was reading his favorite story to him.
Le estaba leyendo su cuento favorito.	I was reading his favorite story to him.
Cómpre**me** media docena de huevos.	Buy me half a dozen eggs.
No **me** compre media docena de huevos.	Don't buy me half a dozen eggs.

Since **le** and **les** each has three possible antecedents, a pronoun qualifier with **a** may be used to avoid ambiguity. This qualifier normally follows the verb, but it may precede it for greater emphasis. It is always good form to include the corresponding indirect object pronoun before the verb, although this pronoun is often omitted in conversational Spanish.

A. **Le** hablé (**a ella**) ayer.	I spoke to her yesterday.
B. **A ella** le hablé ayer.	I spoke to *her* yesterday.
C. Hablé **a ella** ayer.	I spoke to her yesterday.

In (A) the qualifier **a ella** is redundant and therefore omitted if the context makes it clear that **le** referred to *her*, and not to *him* or to *you*. The initial position of the qualifier in (B) stresses that it is used for emphasis or clarity or both. (C) exemplifies a common colloquial usage in which the indirect object pronoun itself is eliminated and the prepositional qualifier of that pronoun retained.

69. DIRECT OBJECT PRONOUNS

A direct object pronoun indicates the person or thing that receives the action of a transitive verb, whereas the indirect object is the person or thing to or for whom or which something is said, given, or done. In

Spanish the rules governing the position of the indirect object pronoun also apply to that of the direct object pronoun. When an indirect object pronoun and a direct object pronoun are both used in connection with the same verb, they appear together and the indirect comes first. Furthermore, if both are in the third person (i.e., both begin with *l*), the first (the indirect) is changed to **se**. (This is etymologically a form of the indirect object pronoun and is not to be confused with the reflexive pronoun **se**.) Finally, verbs of telling regularly take both a direct and an indirect object pronoun in Spanish, though English often omits the direct.

Nos los mandaron.	They sent them to us.
Se lo pedí (a él).	I asked him for it.
Mañana **te lo** digo.	I'll tell you tomorrow.
Ha prometido contár**selo**.	He has promised to tell him.

70. LOISMO, LEISMO, LAISMO

A.   In most of Spanish America and in some parts of Spain, the third-person forms of the indirect and direct object pronouns are always clearly differentiated. **Le** (**les**) is always indirect, and **lo**, **la** (**los, las**) is always direct and therefore used both for people and for things. This use is known as **loísmo** because the pronoun for things (**lo** or **los**) is also used for persons. From a practical point of view, this usage has obvious advantages. Both **loísmo** and **leísmo** are considered correct by the Spanish Academy.

Lo encontré en el café.	I found it (him, you) in the café.
Los vimos entrar en el cine.	We saw them (you) go into the theater.

B.   While **loísmo** distinguishes direct and indirect object pronouns only, **leísmo** reflects an understandable desire to differentiate people from things in the accusative by using a different direct object pronoun for each. Thus **leísmo** is the use of **le** (**les**) as the direct object pronoun for masculine people (him, you, them) and of **lo** (**los**) for things. **Leísmo** is standard in most parts of Spain, although some peninsular authors are **loístas**.

C.   **Laísmo** is the use of **la**, the direct object pronoun, for the indirect object pronoun **le** when referring to women. Although many condemn this usage (**leísmo** and **loísmo** are both accepted by the Spanish Academy; **laísmo** is not), **laísmo** is standard in Madrid and other parts of Spain. It is found in both spoken and written Spanish, and probably arose from a desire to distinguish between the masculine and feminine forms of the indirect object pronoun.

Sí, la he visto y **la** he hablado. (ZA)	Yes, I have seen her and I have spoken to her.
A Juani **la** dije que cada martes me mandaban un ramo de flores. (LN)	I told Juani that each Thursday they used to send me a bouquet of flowers.
. . . ¡y ahora su madre!, ¿qué **la** decimos a su madre, Daniel? (EJ)	. . . And now her mother! What are we going to say to her mother, Daniel?

71. REFLEXIVE PRONOUNS

A. POSITION

Several uses of reflexive verbs are discussed in Chapter 11. Notice that the reflexive pronoun **se** precedes all other object pronouns with which it is used.

| **Se** me acercó cuando salía del hotel. | He came up to me as I was leaving the hotel. |

B. AS INTENSIFIERS

The reflexive pronoun is often used to increase the subject's emotional concern with, or his degree of participation in, an action. Obviously not a true reflexive meaning, this use is very common in colloquial speech. In English the distinction between a verb used with or without this reflexive pronoun is not always apparent.

Oye, **tómate** un café con nosotros.	Listen, have a cup of coffee with us.
El chico **se comió** todo lo que teníamos en la nevera.	The boy ate up everything we had in the refrigerator.
No **me** lo **creo**.	I don't believe it.
Pero **me** lo **sé** de memoria.	But I know it by heart.

C. TO RENDER POSSESSIVE ADJECTIVES

Just as the indirect object pronoun is used in Spanish with the definite article to render the English possessive adjective, the reflexive pronoun is used for the possessive adjective when a person does something for himself or in his own interest. This is the standard construction in Spanish to render the English possessive with reference to clothing or the body.

| **Le** tapé **la** boca para que no hablara durante la misa. | I covered his mouth (for him) so that he wouldn't speak during mass. |
| **Me** tapé **los** oídos para no oír el ruido del tren. | I covered my ears in order not to hear the noise of the train. |

Le vacié **los** zapatos de arena.	I emptied the sand out of his shoes (for him).
Ella **se** vaciaba **los** zapatos de arena.	She was emptying the sand out of her shoes.

72. PREPOSITIONAL PRONOUNS

These pronouns follow prepositions and are most frequently used (1) in the redundant construction after the preposition **a**, (2) with verbs that require prepositions, or (3) to replace the indirect object pronoun when the verb is omitted.

1. A **ti** ya te expliqué lo que queríamos.	I already explained to you what we wanted.
2. No se queja de **mí**, sino de **Vds.**	He doesn't complain about me, but about you.
3. ¿A quién mirabas? ¿A **él** o a **ella**?	Whom were you looking at? At him or at her?

Although **entre** is a preposition, it takes a subject pronoun. The preposition **con** has the special forms **conmigo, contigo, consigo.** The reflexive form **consigo**, however, is frequently replaced by **con él**, etc., in actual usage.

Es un secreto entre mi hermano y yo.	It is a secret between my brother and me.
Antonio dijo para **sí** que no volvería.	Anthony said to himself that he would not return.
Salieron **con él** hace un rato.	They went out with him a while ago.
No creo que lo tenga **consigo**.	I don't believe he has it with him.
Le suplicó que le llevase **con él**, pero Marco no le hizo caso. (PT)	He begged that he take him with him, but Marco paid no attention.

73. OTHER PRONOUNS

A. DEMONSTRATIVES

Only the written accent distinguishes the demonstrative pronouns from the demonstrative adjectives. The Spanish Academy recommends that this accent be retained only in the few cases where the pronoun might be mistakenly interpreted as an adjective. This new "norm," however, has so far won little acceptance. The neuter demonstrative pronouns **esto, eso,** and **aquello** correspond to no adjective forms and bear no accent. They refer to concepts or ideas, but not to specific words that have a definite gender and number.

Esta mesa y **aquélla**.	This table and that one.
Sí, **éstos** son los libros a que me refiero.	Yes, these are the books to which I am referring.
Todo **eso** me parece poco convincente.	All that seems unconvincing to me.

When a noun is understood, its definite article is often retained and followed by an adjective or a prepositional modifier to render the pronoun *one*.

Me quedo con este traje y **el** [traje] **gris**.	I'll take this suit and the gray one.
Esta silla y **la** [silla] **de mimbre** son baratas.	This chair and the wicker one are cheap.

B. POSSESSIVES

The possessive pronouns are the long forms of the possessive adjectives, generally used with the article: **el, la, los, las, lo**. Like adjectives, possessive pronouns agree in number and gender with the things possessed.

el mío, la mía, los míos, las mías—mine
el tuyo, la tuya, los tuyos, las tuyas—yours
el suyo, la suya, los suyos, las suyas—his, hers, yours
el nuestro, la nuestra, los nuestros, las nuestras—ours
el vuestro, la vuestra, los vuestros, las vuestras—yours
el suyo, la suya, los suyos, las suyas—theirs, yours

The article is regularly omitted after **ser**, but it may be included to distinguish between objects rather than between possessors. Clearly, the dividing line between possessive adjective and possessive pronoun is hard to draw in this context. Notice that only the third-person forms (**el suyo**, etc.) can be ambiguous; they may be replaced when necessary by **el (la, los, las) de él (ella, Vd., ellos [ellas], Vds.)**, etc.

Tengo mi libro y **el de ella** (or **el suyo** if context is clear).	I have my book and hers.
Este **es** (**el**) **tuyo**.	This one is yours.
Tenemos **las nuestras**, pero ¿dónde está **la de Vd.**?	We have ours, but where is yours?

C. INTERROGATIVES

The interrogative pronouns are:

1. quién, quiénes—who? (identity of persons)
2. qué—what? (identity of things or persons)
3. cuál, cuáles—which? what? (selection from a group or class)
4. cuánto (–a, –os, –as)—how much? how many?

Although it is considered better form to use **cuál** or **cuáles** (grammatically a pronoun) exclusively as a pronoun, both are commonly used as interrogative adjectives for **qué**.

¿**Cuál** de los libros prefiere Vd.?	Which of the books do you prefer?
¿**Cuál** es el libro que prefiere Vd.?	Which one is the book you prefer?
¿**Qué** libro prefiere Vd.?	What (which) book do you prefer?
¿**Cuál** libro prefiere Vd.? (common use of interrogative pronoun as an interrogative adjective)	Which book do you prefer?
Martín le explica **cuáles** comercios son clientes y cuáles no. (VA) (indirect question using pronoun as adjective)	Martin explains to him which businesses are his customers and which are not.

D. INDEFINITES

Indefinite pronouns are used for persons or things that the speaker prefers not to, or is unable to, identify more specifically: **alguien, nadie, algo, nada, quienquiera**. They also include the following words when they are used as pronouns: **uno(–a, –os, –as), alguno(s), ninguno(s), mucho(s), poco(s), bastante(s), demasiado(s), varios**, etc.

Algunos vinieron a la reunión.	Some came to the meeting.
Compré **varios** en la tienda.	I bought several at the store.

EXERCISES

1. Paco, be (*use* **tener**) patient and wait (*use reflexive pronoun*) a moment. 2. We were unable to determine which were the soldier's boots. 3. If you are ready to go, Mrs. García, I'm willing to take you. 4. Robert removes his glasses and puts them in their case. 5. "I've turned as red as a crab," she said, on looking at her sunburnt shoulders. 6. He felt within himself a need that he was unable to satisfy. 7. I have never given (*use* **concedir**) it too much importance. 8. She bit her lip in order not to cry. 9. I tried to catch him, but he slipped away from me. 10. The prisoner didn't know what was the cause of his arrest. 11. I don't deserve (*use reflexive pronoun*) this treatment, for I have always done my duty faithfully. 12. Her fiancé is coming to pick her up at four o'clock (*pronoun in two positions*). 13. He got all wet when they threw him into the pool. 14. The teacher will let us leave early, but not them. 15. The mother insisted that the children wash their hands before having breakfast. 16. It's polite to cover your mouth when you yawn. 17. What are your ideas on this subject? 18. What you told me yesterday was so interesting that I am still thinking

about it. 19. It took them a long time to recognize each other. 20. I don't want the roast to burn. 21. His eyes don't look like yours. 22. Shivering from cold, the child snuggled up to his mother seeking warmth. 23. If you bring the potato salad, we will bring the dessert. 24. They saw the highway and then noticed a group of boys moving away from it. 25. I found the blue pencil, but I still don't know where the red one is. 26. When John and Mary come this evening, we will tell them. 27. She refused to live alone because she feared loneliness (*use redundant pronoun*). 28. The doctor took her pulse. 29. The fisherman took off his cap and scratched his head. 30. You will pass that exam and those that you have next year. 31. I approached them to ask what time it was. 32. The stranger sensed hostility around him. 33. I have studied my speech so much that I know (*reflexive*) it by heart. 34. It was so bright that the man covered his eyes with his hat. 35. If he wants something for himself, he will have to earn (*reflexive*) it. 36. You are afraid that I will open their eyes to the truth. 37. The man spoke to her without looking at her. 38. How many of these oranges are ours, and how many are yours? 39. He knew that if he saw Doña Clara, he was not to go near her. 40. We asked the girls what was the capital of the state.

74. SELECCION LITERARIA

Al cabo de los años

José María Castillo-Navarro

*José María Castillo-Navarro nació en Lorca, provincia de Murcia, en 1930. Desde la publicación de su primera novela en 1957, La sal viste luto, ha escrito muchos cuentos y varias novelas. Una de las mayores preocupaciones del autor es, sin duda, la individualidad del hombre, tema que predomina en su obra. En «Al cabo de los años», Castillo-Navarro, al relatar la triste situación de una vida resignada, revela su considerable don de penetración psicológica.**

Todo por la maldita[1] carne.[2] Por la asquerosa y repugnante obesidad que de un tiempo a esta parte[3] ha ido desarrollándose alrededor del hueso.[4] Diez años. Diez sin pisar la calle por no ser capaz de subir los ciento y pico[5] escalones sin diñarla.[6] Diez años sin caminar. Diez sin tener que limpiar el polvo o el barro[7] de sus zapatos. Diez sin descalzarse[8] y acariciar sus pies como hacía antes al acostarse . . . . Diez sin ver un corro, un atropello, una disputa o un racimo[9] de gente, desgajándose del estribo de cual-

---

* Pay particular attention to the use of both indirect object and reflexive pronouns in the following selection.

quier tranvía. Diez sin hacer cola ante el autobús, sin llegar a casa calado
o jadeante . . . . Diez años supeditado a los demás, amarrado a ellos, es-
clavizado; pendiente de cuanto quieran contarle espaciada y condescen-
dientemente como si él no fuera alma de este mundo y no tuviese que
importarle nada de cuanto de paredes afuera[10] ocurre sin su concurso.
Diez años sin poder valerse. Diez . . . .

—¡Cuánta impertinencia!

—¡Qué vida!

—¡Qué vida la de una, Señor!

Quejas y más quejas, lamentaciones: por tener que calzarle los zapatos,
por abrocharle los botones, por arrascarle[11] el cogote, la espalda o la cabeza;
por limpiarle los pies, por agacharse cada vez que se le cae algo de entre las
manos. Mil tropiezos: en el pasillo,[12] en las puertas, en el lavabo,[13] en la
cocina, en el recibidor, a la hora de comer, así se levantan o cuando vuelven
del trabajo. En cualquier parte . . .

—¡Tú no te preocupes por nada!

—¡Lo haces a propósito y no aciertas![14]

—¡Naturalmente que estorbas![15]

Siempre lo mismo . . . Voces y más voces, gritos, imprecaciones al cielo
y al infierno . . . El girando y girando. Dando vueltas como una peonza[16]
loca, o titubeando.[17] Sin poder asomarse a los balcones, por no haberlos,
y acechando el momento de quedar a solas para sentarse frente a la ventana
y contemplar el cielo. Lo ve en franja, por ser estrecha, y la línea es como
un resquicio[18] a lo imposible. Cada pájaro tiene un nombre diferente. Cada
nube representa un barrio que él imagina cubre con su manto. Cada gota
de lluvia, un sitio, una esquina, o un trozo[19] de piedra. Más que imaginar,
crea, arregla. Se ve en las bocas del metro, en las plazas, en los tumultos,
voceando el periódico o billetes de lotería . . . .

—¡Naturalmente que entorpeces!

—¡Ocupas demasiado sitio!

—¡A tu cuarto!

La pared de encima, la del lado derecho y la del izquierdo, la de enfrente
y la de la espalda: blanco, blanco, blanco, blanco . . . . Un día y otro.
Una noche y la siguiente. Uno y tres meses. Años. Siempre igual, sin varia-
ción posible. Idénticas voces, idéntico desprecio, idéntico paisaje, idénticos
sueños . . . .

—¡Adiós!

—¡No, no sé a qué hora volveremos!

—¡Al cine!

—¡Lee!

—¡Qué quieres que te diga, entonces!

—Si no hay remedio, ¡muérete!

Cada día un poco, cada momento, cada instante de momento: cuando se sabe observado de soslayo,[20] cuando no cuenta para nada en aquella familia a pesar de haber ido formándola a costa de tanta privación y sacrificio, lleno de amor, y lleno de esperanza; cuando prescinden de[21] él, lo esconden ante la curiosidad de los extraños o se avergüenzan .... Y cavila y decide que lo mejor es acabar, arrimar la silla a la ventana, empinarse   5 como le dé Dios a entender y echarse abajo. Y según piensa, hace. Y según hace, se alegra. Y según se alegra, apalanca el respaldo contra la pared, se encarama, intenta una vez y otra y, como no pasa a través de la abertura,[22] desiste, baja de nuevo y se sienta donde siempre.

75. NOTES

1. maldito—damned, accursed
   bendito—blessed, happy

   These two adjectives are the irregular past participles of **bendecir** and **maldecir**. The regular past participles, **bendecido** and **maldecido** are used to form compound tenses.

Mi **bendito** yerno siempre acude cuando necesitamos su ayuda.	My blessed (*ironic*) son-in-law always comes when we need his help.

2. **La carne** means both *meat* and *flesh* in Spanish. Unlike English, which usually has a different term for the animal and the meat of that animal, Spanish uses **la carne** modified by the name of the animal.

   la carne de cordero—lamb
   la carne de ternera—veal
   la carne de cerdo—pork
   la carne de vaca—beef
   la carne de res—beef

Esta receta requiere **carne de vaca** picada y muchas especias.	This recipe calls for ground beef and many spices.

3. De un tiempo a esta parte—recientemente, últimamente

4. el hueso—bone; stone, pit (of fruit)
   la espina—(fish) bone; spine; thorn
   ser de carne y hueso—to be of flesh and blood; to be only human
   no poder con sus huesos—to be exhausted; to be all in (colloquial)
   estar en los huesos—to be (nothing but) skin and bones

No quiero pescado si tiene muchas **espinas**.	I don't want fish if it has a lot of bones.
Han producido un melocotón, cuyo fruto se separa fácilmente del **hueso**.	They have produced a peach whose fruit separates easily from its stone.

El novelista ha creado un personaje **de carne y hueso** que nos convence con su gran realismo.

The novelist has created a flesh-and-blood character who convinces us through his great realism.

5.   y pico—a little bit more than, a little bit over; after; odd

This expression is used only with numerical concepts.

¿Por qué no vienes a las ocho **y pico**?

Why don't you come at a little after eight?

Tengo veinte dólares **y pico**.

I have a little over twenty dollars.

6.   diñarla—to kill oneself; to die (colloquial)

7.   el barro—mud, clay
      el lodo—mud
      el fango—mud, mire
      el cieno—mud, slime
      la mugre—dirt, filth
      el guardabarros, el guardafango—fender

The first four words above are frequently used without distinction. In general **barro** has the widest range of meaning and is used to indicate *earth* fashioned into earthenware objects. It thus renders *clay* (though **arcilla** is the more technical term). **Cieno** is *mud* found in swamps and on the bottom of lakes or other bodies of water. **Fango** suggests *mud* in which something is stuck; **lodo** and **barro** indicate *mud* formed after a rain, in which a person steps, or by which he is splashed.

Se compró un gran tiesto de **barro** para plantar el geranio.

She bought a large clay flowerpot to plant the geranium in.

El chico volvió salpicado de **lodo**.

The boy came back all splashed with mud.

...ése fue el **barro** santo de donde sacó Cervantes la creación literaria más original de todos los tiempos. (JM)

That was the holy clay from which Cervantes took the most original literary creation of all time.

8.   descalzarse—to take off one's shoes (or other footwear)
      calzarse—to put on one's shoes
      el calzado—footwear
      descalzo—barefoot (adjective)
      desnudarse, desvestirse—to undress

(Des)calzarse is less common than **(quitarse) ponerse los zapatos**. There is no basic difference between **desnudarse** and **desvestirse**, although the former is much more common, especially in spoken Spanish.

| En verano muchos niños andan descalzos. | In the summer many children go around barefoot. |

9. el racimo—bunch (something whose separate parts grow naturally in a cluster) of grapes, bananas, etc.

la ristra—bunch (things usually tied together by their stems) of carrots, garlic, onions, etc.

el manojo—bunch (handful) of violets, parsley, keys, etc.

el ramillete—bunch (larger than manojo and usually gathered or picked), bouquet of flowers

10. paredes afuera—outside

In Spanish the adverbs **arriba**, *up*, **abajo**, *down*, **adentro**, *within*, **afuera**, *outside*, combine with nouns to form expressions indicating direction.

río arriba (abajo)—up(down)stream; up (down) the river
mar adentro—out to sea
tierra adentro—inland
calle arriba (abajo)—up (down) the street
tejas arriba (abajo)—in the other world (in this world)

11. arrascar—to scratch
rascar—to scratch
arañar—to scratch
rasguñar—to scratch
raspar—to scratch; to scrape
el arañazo, la rascadura, el rasguño, la raspadura—nouns of preceding verbs

Rascar normally indicates *to scratch in order to relieve an itch.* **Arrascar** is used in the same way as **rascar**, but is much less common. **Arañar** usually indicates *to scratch in an offensive way*, or, when referring to inanimate objects, *to leave the surface badly marred.* **Rasguñar** means *to scratch with something especially sharp*; it is also a synonym of **arañar**, though it indicates scratches that are deeper or acquired accidentally.

Ráscame la espalda, por favor.	Please scratch my back for me.
Le **arañó** la cara.	She scratched his face.
Arañando la puerta y ladrando, el perro logró despertar a su amo.	By scratching at the door and by barking, the dog managed to wake its master.

12. el pasillo—hall(way), passage (standard word for hall in a home or other building)

el corredor—hall, corridor

el hall—hallway (now used as a synonym of pasillo)

el vestíbulo—vestibule, hall; lobby (in a theater)

Claudette nos acompañó hasta el **hall**. (TV)	Claudette accompanied us as far as the hall (in a home).
Dejó la nota en la mesilla del **pasillo**.	He left the note on the hall table.

13. el lavabo—washbasin, sink; bathroom
    el baño—bathroom
    el water—toilet
    el retrete—bathroom
    el excusado—bathroom

El lavabo, *washbasin* or *sink*, also means *bathroom*. **El baño** is another very common euphemistic synonym for *bathroom*. **El water** is standard for *toilet* in public buildings and on trains. **El retrete** and **el excusado**, though commonly used in some places, are often avoided by most people, the first because it sometimes has rural connotations, the second because it is a euphemism that in certain social circumstances might be considered too obvious an attempt to be refined.

14. lo haces a propósito y no aciertas—if you had done it on purpose, you could not have done it better (an ironic statement)

15. estorbar—to be in the way; to hinder; to annoy
    incomodar—to inconvenience; to be in the way
    el estorbo—obstruction, obstacle, hindrance

No seré yo quien **estorbe** sus planes de divorciarse.	I shall not be the one to obstruct (stand in the way of) your plans to get a divorce.

16. la peonza, el peón—(toy) top
    la trompa—musical top
    la copa—top (of a tree)
    la tapa—top (of a box, container, cooking vessel, etc.)
    la capota—top, hood (of an automobile)
    destapar—to take the top off

...levanté los ojos hacia las **copas** de los árboles. (N)	...I raised my eyes toward the treetops.

17. titubear—to waver; to hesitate; to stagger
    vacilar (en) + infinitive—to hesitate + infinitive or present participle
    oscilar—to oscillate, fluctuate; to hesitate

18. el resquicio—opening (by extension, opportunity)
    el quicio—pivot hole of a hinge
    sacar de quicio a—to exasperate, drive crazy; to unhinge, upset
    desquiciar—to upset, turn upside down

Esta palabra le **saca de quicio** al profesor.	This word completely upsets the professor.
Oye, **no saques** las cosas **de quicio**.	Listen, don't upset things (turn things upside down).

19. el trozo—piece, literary selection (trozo often has a slightly more technical connotation than pedazo)
el pedazo—piece
la porción—piece, portion, serving
la ración—portion, serving

Vamos a examinar un **trozo** de su novela.	We are going to examine a fragment (selection) of his novel.
¿Le sirvo otra **ración**?	May I serve you another portion?

20. mirar de soslayo—to glance at; to look askance; to watch out of the corner of one's eye
mirar con el rabo (rabillo) del ojo—to watch (look) out of the corner of one's eye

. . . Claudette me **miró de soslayo**, con una sonrisa burlona. (TV)	. . . Claudette looked at me out of the corner of her eye, with a mocking smile.

21. prescindir de—to dispense with; to do without
pasar sin—to get by without, do without

Prefiero **prescindir de** la compañía de una persona tan asquerosa.	I prefer to dispense with the company of such a disgusting person.
Para él era un sacrificio **pasarse sin** la bebida por una semana.	It was a sacrifice for him to do (to get by) without drinking for a week.

22. la abertura—opening (hole or aperture)
la apertura—opening (commencement or ceremonial opening, as with a store, a will, etc.)
el cierre—(physical) closing of store, etc.
la clausura—(ceremonial) closing

Han anunciado la **apertura** de negociaciones para resolver la huelga.	They have announced the opening of negotiations to settle the strike.
Se ha celebrado la **clausura** de la sesión de verano.	The closing of the summer session has been held.

EXERCISES ON NOTES

1. I'll meet you in the cafe at a little after three. 2. He continued scratching his thin (**rala**) beard. 3. Next week they are coming to carpet our hallway. (*Do not use the possessive adjective.*) 4. The child picked up a bunch of grapes and began to eat them one by one. 5. He had gotten soaked to the bone (*plural*). 6. Some stews require pork and veal. 7. The child's endless questions exasperated his mother. 8. His request inconvenienced us very much. 9. You can't make cherry preserves without removing the pits. 10. We bought several hand-painted clay vases from the Indians. 11. The price of meat has gone up again. 12. They cursed the man who was responsible for (**de**) the death of their child. 13. There are a little over 500 students in this school. 14. When he grabbed the cat, it scratched him. 15. The procession was slowly going down the street. 16. All this paperwork only hinders us in our efforts to finish on time. 17. During the war we did without many things which we now consider necessary. 18. It was difficult for the child to remove the top from the jar. 19. Between night and day the temperature in the desert fluctuates a great deal. 20. The governor was ill, and they had to do without his presence at the opening of the new museum. 21. It grieved us to see that a man who had once been so healthy was now nothing but skin and bones. 22. The villagers watched the priest bless the new fishing boat. 23. Every time the boy went out to play with his friends, he came back covered with mud. 24. I scraped off the varnish before painting the table. 25. He went through (**recorrer**) the whole train looking for an unoccupied lavatory. 26. This boat goes up river as far as Manaus. 27. When I arrived, she still hadn't finished dressing for the party. 28. Because it had fleas, the dog never stopped scratching itself. 29. As I floated in the swimming pool, I was able to see the tops of the cypress trees. 30. Be careful not to scratch the table. 31. The tragedy that occurred recently proved to everyone that the principal was only human. 32. The opening of the will was a very important event. 33. The cook sent the boy to buy one bunch of parsley and two bunches of carrots. 34. The prince knew that only Cinderella would be able to put on the glass slipper. 35. The explorers went inland in search of gold. 36. He scratched his head, trying to recall the name of the actor. 37. It was difficult to make the mother-in-law believe that she was not in the way. 38. He sent her a bouquet of daisies on her anniversary. 39. The children scratched their legs when they walked through the brambles. 40. Of all his toys, the child preferred the musical top.

CUESTIONARIO

a. contenido

1. ¿Por qué lleva el personaje diez años sin salir a la calle?
2. ¿Cuáles son algunas de las cosas que no ha podido hacer durante este tiempo?

3. ¿Por qué se quejan los miembros de la familia?
4. ¿Le parecen a Vd. justificadas las quejas? ¿Por qué?
5. ¿Creen los de la familia que él no aprecia lo que hacen por él?
6. ¿Por qué anhela él estar a solas?
7. ¿Qué nos indican los reproches de la familia?
8. ¿Cómo se logra evitar el suicidio del protagonista al final del cuento?

b. estilo

1. ¿Desde qué punto de vista se narra este cuento?
2. ¿Qué efecto produce la repetición de la palabra *diez*?
3. Comente la división del cuento entre la narración y las series de exclamaciones de los familiares.
4. ¿Cómo crea el autor una atmósfera de tedio en el párrafo que comienza con «La pared de encima . . . »?
5. ¿Cómo identifica el autor a las personas que figuran en el cuento? ¿Por qué de esta manera?
6. ¿Cómo logra el autor matizar el tono de resignación que prevalece al final del cuento?

TEMA—TRADUCCION

His accursed flesh was to blame for his wretched life. For ten years he had not gone down to the street. He would not have been able to climb the more than one hundred steps without killing himself. Ten years without being able to take off his own shoes. Ten [years] without running into a friend on the sidewalk. Ten years without waiting in line for a bus.

"How impertinent!"

"Anyone would say . . . !"

"It's impossible!"

Such were the complaints he endured whenever they put on his shoes, washed or dried his feet, or did anything else for him. He bumped into them everywhere: in the hallway, in the kitchen, and even in the bathroom.

"You don't have to worry about anything!"

"Of course, you are in the way!"

"Are you in there, too!"

Each day equal to the next . . . the same voices, the same faces, the same walls. He liked it when they left him alone so that he could sit down opposite the window and contemplate the sky. In his imagination he would see himself doing all the things he would like to do.

"Again!"

"You take up too much room!"

"Go to your room!"

"If there is nothing else you can do, drop dead!"

He knew that someone was always observing him out of the corner of his eye, and that the family he had formed at the expense of privation and sacrifice now preferred to do without him. Then one day he decided that perhaps the best thing was to end it all, and he pushed the back of the chair up to the window. He climbed up on top of it, but since he couldn't fit through the opening, he gave up and sat down, resigned.

TEMAS A ESCOGER

Escríbanse unas 200 palabras sobre uno de los temas siguientes usando a lo menos 20 de las palabras y expresiones estudiadas en este capítulo.

1. La tragedia de vivir dependiente de otros
2. La dieta en la vida de la mujer moderna o del hombre moderno
3. Factores que producen la desesperación en el hombre

chapter 15

RELATIVE PRONOUNS

76. GENERAL STATEMENT

A relative pronoun introduces a subordinate clause and joins it to the preceding noun or pronoun that is its antecedent.

I see a tall man. He is talking with a student.
I see a tall man *who* is talking with a student.

The forms of the relatives *that*, *who(m)*, *whose*, *which*, *that which* vary in Spanish according to person, gender, number, and environment.

77. FORMS

que—that, who, which
quien, quienes—who, whom
cuyo(–a, –os, –as)—whose
el cual, la cual, los cuales, las cuales ⎫
el que, la que, los que, las que ⎭ which, who, whom

78. RELATIVE PRONOUNS AFTER PREPOSITIONS

A. To refer to *people* after short prepositions (**con, de, en, a**), **quien** (**quienes**) is regularly used.

El amigo de **quien** te hablé viene hoy.	The friend of whom I spoke to you is coming today.
Los hermanos con **quienes** fuimos a Guatemala son simpáticos.	The brothers with whom we went to Guatemala are very nice.

B. To refer to *things* after short prepositions, **que** is generally used.

El juguete con **que** juega es peligroso.	The toy he's playing with is dangerous.

C. To refer to *people* or *things* after long (and especially after compound) prepositions, a longer form of the relative pronoun is required. Forms of **el cual** are somewhat more common to refer to *people*, whereas forms of both **el cual** and **el que** are widely used for *things*.

La muchacha detrás de **la cual** estaba sentado acaba de invitarme a su casa.	The girl behind whom I was sitting has just invited me to her house.
La casa dentro de **la cual** (**que**) se celebraba la fiesta pertenece a Joaquín.	The house in which they were holding the party belongs to Joaquín.

Notice that although **sin**, **por**, and **tras** are short (monosyllabic) prepositions, long forms (normally **el cual**) and not **que** alone are used with them to refer to *things*. This usage avoids possible confusion with the conjunctions **sin que** and **porque**.

Los consejos, sin **los cuales** . . .	The advice, without which . . .
La razón por **la cual** rechacé la oferta . . .	The reason for which I rejected the offer . . .
Las rocas tras **las cuales** desapareció son las a la derecha.	The rocks behind which he disappeared are those at the right.

D. Notice also that even after short prepositions some form of **el cual** or **el que** often replaces **que** or **quien**. The general circumstances that favor this replacement are examined briefly in subsequent sections. The choice between forms of **el que** and **el cual** after the long prepositions seems to be largely a matter of individual preference.

79. QUE

Que, the most frequently used relative pronoun, is invariable. It refers to *persons* or *things* in either gender and in both the singular and the plural.

El libro **que** has traído no sirve.	The book that you brought is no good.
Las muchachas **que** están con Carlos son gemelas.	The girls who are with Charles are twins.

80. QUIEN

Quien (**quienes**) in present-day Spanish refers only to *people* and is used mainly in nonrestrictive clauses. These clauses, set off by commas in English and Spanish, add accessory information but do not give information essential to the basic identification. In nonrestrictive clauses **quien** tends to replace **que** when the speaker wishes a greater pause to diminish somewhat the smooth connection normally made by **que**. At times either **que** or **quien** is correct in a nonrestrictive clause.

RESTRICTIVE

Muchos soldados **que** murieron en la batalla fueron enterrados aquí.	Many soldiers who died in the battle were buried here.

NONRESTRICTIVE

Domingo, **quien** (**que**) fue alumno mío, ha ganado un premio literario.	Dominick, who was a student of mine, has won a literary prize.

81. EL CUAL, EL QUE

El cual, la cual, los cuales, las cuales, have close equivalents in **el que, la que, los que, las que.** Although no rule can always indicate when a long form (**el cual** or **el que**) is preferable to **quien** or **que** alone, the long forms are used most often:

A.   to avoid ambiguity when there are two (or more) possible antecedents of different gender. Since **que** may refer to any antecedent (though generally it is assumed to refer to the one closest to it), substitution by a form with an article prevents confusion where the context does not clearly establish the referent.

La prima de mi amigo, **que** está aquí . . .	The cousin of my
La prima de mi amigo, **el cual** está aquí . . .	friend, who is here
La prima de mi amigo, **la cual** está aquí . . .	. . .

El cual refers to the friend, **la cual** to the cousin. When both antecedents are of the same gender, the long form does not suffice to avoid ambiguity, and some circumlocution must be employed for this purpose.

B.   when there is a significant pause before the relative pronoun, or when the connection between the relative and its antecedent is interrupted by a considerable amount of intervening material.

El otro era un viejo a **quien** llamaban Paco, **el cual** ayudaba a la criada con sus quehaceres.	The other one was an old man whom they called Paco, [and] who helped the maid with her chores.

82. COMPARISON OF RELATIVE PRONOUNS

In general, forms of **el cual** are the strongest relative pronouns. Those of **el que** are only slightly weaker.* **Quien** is weaker than both long forms, but still much stronger than **que.** Thus when the connection or relationship conveyed by a relative pronoun is strong (i.e., is obvious or clear), the weak pronoun **que** suffices. When the connection is weaker, either because of a greater than normal pause or because of the amount of intervening material, a stronger relative is required. The choice of relatives in such cases depends largely on the speaker's intent. In fact, the usual relative pronoun **que**

---

* This distinction between the forms of **el cual** and those of **el que** derives in part from the feeling of many that the former is somewhat literary, which results in a tendency to use **el que** in place of **el cual** in many situations in which the latter would be more appropriate.

after short prepositions is often replaced by forms of **el que** or **el cual** when the speaker believes his identification or reference may not be immediately clear or obvious.

Recibe enseñanzas del cura Juan Casado, **quien** es gran amante de la Naturaleza, pero **el cual** es al mismo tiempo profundo conocedor del corazón humano. (SRNPG)	He receives instruction from the priest Juan Casado, who is a great lover of Nature, but who is at the same time a profound judge of the human heart. (**el cual** is used instead of **quien** after **pero** because of the intervention of the first relative clause)
Pienso fundar un colegio, **del cual** Vd. será el director.	I intend to found a school, of which you will be the director. (new information; relationship not obvious)
Mi padre, **que** no estaba muy fuerte en historia . . . sólo sabía de vinos y caballos. (CA)	My father, who was not very good in history . . . only knew about wines and horses. (assumption is that the connection will be obvious)

83. CUYO

Cuyo (**cuya**, **cuyos**, **cuyas**), *whose*, is a relative possessive pronoun used mainly to refer to *people*. It is not used in questions, for which **de quién** is employed. Because it is a possessive pronoun, it must agree in number and gender with the word it modifies.

Es un señor **cuyos** conocimientos de España son enormes.	He's a man whose knowledge of Spain is enormous.
¿**De quién** son estos libros?	Whose books are these?

84. OTHER FORMS AND USES

A.   **Quien**, an equivalent of **el que**, may be used as the subject of a clause, in which case it is a relative pronoun containing its own antecedent.

Quien no trabaja no come.	He (anyone) who doesn't work doesn't eat.

B.   **Cuanto**, a neuter pronoun form, is used as an equivalent of **todo lo que** and is often written **todo cuanto**.

Cuanto dijo esta noche fue una tontería.	All (everything) that he said tonight was (a lot of) nonsense.

C. **Lo que,** *what, that which,* may be the subject of a clause, the object of a preposition, or a relative pronoun referring to a previous clause or phrase. **Lo cual** may replace it except when it is used as a subject.

Hablamos con ellos, después de **lo cual** nos dirigimos a casa.	We spoke with them, after which we went home.

EXERCISES

1. The island, whose strategic importance was great, was poorly defended. 2. You can't write a letter to Pierre, who is a Frenchman, in English. 3. He is already informed about everything that (*one word*) you have done. 4. He's an intelligent man who understands the situation but who nevertheless refuses to do his part of the work. 5. The hand in (**con**) which he held the telephone was trembling. 6. She's a woman whose true character was revealed at the time of the crisis. 7. They finished the task on time, which surprised us very much. 8. It had a small door, through which, at the moment I am referring to, two officers were entering. 9. If you find a modest and hard-working girl, which isn't easy, you should get married immediately. 10. The professor gave a lecture which more than 200 persons attended. 11. The man about whom you were inquiring (**preguntar por**) has just moved. 12. It seems to be the theme around which every conversation turns. 13. He mentioned the elections through (**a través de**) which the workers will designate their representative. 14. We hope to increase our foreign trade, for which we shall need our government's assistance. 15. The servant in whom I have the most confidence is Maria. 16. The scientist found that the cell from which life is born has a strange similarity to the microbe that produces the disease. 17. The new highway, along which they will plant trees, connects the two largest cities in the province. 18. A woman suddenly appeared with a child, whom she was accompanying to school. 19. What you want isn't impossible, but it is difficult. 20. The children ran to get the basket, in which their grandmother was bringing toys and candy. 21. The books that are necessary for this class are now in the bookstore. 22. I am talking about the mountain from whose summit the view embraces the entire coast. 23. He who lives by the sword (**a hierro**) dies by the sword. 24. The economists say that we are entering a period in which the national income will double in twelve years. 25. The coins turned black because the hands through which they passed were so dirty. 26. He's a man whose books we have read, but about whom no one knows very much. 27. It was an infinite hour, at the end of which he came to tell us his decision. 28. He is a talented artist who has many friends, but who refuses to work. 29. It was pure chance that the pirates seized (**apoderarse de**) the young man, who was then walking alone along the coast. 30. I went into the casino that's on the corner and saw that the table I liked to sit at was occupied by a man whose face I didn't know.

El «Lazarillo de Tormes»

Américo Castro

*Américo Castro, nacido en Rio de Janeiro de padres españoles
en 1885, es uno de los más grandes expositores de la historia y
la literatura de España. Después de haber sido profesor en impor-
tantes universidades europeas y americanas, obtuvo la cátedra de
español de Princeton University en 1940. En su obra monumental,*
La realidad histórica de España, *Américo Castro nos ha dado una
brillante y original interpretación de la estructura vital de España.
En el pasaje siguiente, tomado de uno de los ensayos de* Hacia
Cervantes, *Américo Castro nos explica con su acostumbrado vigor
el origen, la novedad, y la importancia del personaje de Lazarillo.*

El hecho[1]—ilusorio o imaginativo, en tanto que artístico—de que un
personaje[2] de la clase ínfima apareciera en la España de 1554 narrando su
propia vida no fue una novedad[3] caprichosa y desarticulada de la historia.
Los grandes y valiosos acontecimientos realizados por personas de carne
y hueso o imaginarias (los Reyes Católicos o Amadís) justificaban por sí   5
mismos el esfuerzo narrativo de cualquier biógrafo. Pero un ser de la
insignificancia de Lázaro de Tormes no podía atraer la atención[4] de nadie
que no fuese él mismo. Ahora bien, desde fines del[5] siglo xv (por ejemplo,
en *La Celestina*, en el teatro de Sánchez de Badajoz y en otras obras), venían
usándose los personajes de las clases más bajas como una especie de pro-   10
yectil para ser lanzado[6] contra los señores o los eclesiásticos y los valores
encarnados por ellos secularmente. Quienes carecían de[7] dignidad social
comenzaron a adquirir entonces una posible significación[8] literaria merced,
además, a circunstancias históricas, de índole[9] política y religiosa. Sorprende
así menos que al final de prólogo escriba el autor-personaje[10] que se ha   15
decidido a narrar su propia vida a fin de que «consideren los que heredaron
nobles estados *cuán poco se les debe*, pues Fortuna fue con ellos parcial;
y *cuánto más hicieron* los que siéndoles contraria, con fuerza y maña remando,
salieron a buen puerto.» Se ve, por consiguiente,[11] como una nueva manera
de narración aparece en la historia a favor de un estado de ánimo rebelde   20
y agresivo. Los temas de amor y de esfuerzo caballeresco fueron reem-
plazados por el tema del hambre, expresado por quien la padecía.[12]

Olvidando la España magnífica y conquistadora de tiempos de Carlos V,
el interés se concentra ahora sobre una figurilla humilde, vacía de cualidades

estimables para aquel mundo, aunque llena de la conciencia de su desnuda
persona y de la voluntad de sostenerla frente a los más duros contratiempos.[13]
Pero como una biografía de tan minúsculo[14] ser habría carecido de toda
justificación (estaba muy lejos del Romanticismo del siglo XIX), el autor
5 hubo de inhibirse y ceder la palabra a la criatura[15] concebida en su imaginación. El estilo autobiográfico resulta[16] así inseparable del mismo
intento de sacar a la luz[17] del arte un tema hasta entonces inexistente o
desdeñado.[18] La persona del autor (un cristiano nuevo) se retrajo tanto,
que ni siguiera quiso revelar[19] su nombre. El autobiografismo del *Lazarillo*
10 es solidario de su anonimato.

El éxito de la obra fue instantáneo, pues aparecieron tres ediciones[20] ya
en 1554. La impresión de vitalidad producida por el personaje llevó a dar
su nombre a la persona que guía a un ciego, aunque el autor lo llamó así
por ser Lázaro—el pobre leproso mencionado en los Evangelios—un pro-
15 totipo para cualquier existencia miserable y doliente.

El tono de la obra es irónico y sarcástico, más bien que didáctico y moralizante. Críticas de este último tipo venían haciéndose desde la Edad Media,
y abundan a comienzos del siglo XVI; mas ninguna de ellas posee un interés
perdurable.[21] En el *Lazarillo* lo de menos es la crítica y la doctrina; su valor
20 decisivo reside en la vida de sus figuras, hechas visibles y oíbles. No es
fácil olvidar al ciego rezador: «Ciento y tantas oraciones sabía de coro.
Un tono bajo, reposado, y muy sonable, que hacía resonar la iglesia donde
rezaba;[22] un rostro humilde y devoto, que con muy buen continente ponía
cuando rezaba, sin hacer gestos ni visajes, como otros suelen[23] hacer.»
25 Este tipo del fingido devoto cruzará toda la novela picaresca, y a través
de Cervantes y del teatro del siglo XVII llegará hasta el *Tartuffe* de
Molière.

86. NOTES

1. el hecho—fact, deed (usually something done)
    el dato—fact (information from which an inference can be drawn)
    los datos—facts, data
    de hecho—in fact

El **hecho** de que su hijo le mintiera le desilusionó.	The fact that his son lied to him disillusioned him.
Todos los **datos** comprueban lo que he venido diciendo.	All the facts verify what I have been saying.

2. el personaje—character (especially in a literary work); figure
    el carácter—character (the sum of distinguishing qualities, consisting
        of an individual's personality, moral principles, etc.)
    el genio—temperament, character, disposition

el natural—character, temperament (commonly used, but mainly colloquial)

hacer el papel de—to play the role (character, part) of

Genio and **carácter** are synonymous, but **carácter** is preferred for moral or ethical distinctions and **genio** for emotional traits.

El profesor preguntó: «¿Cuáles son los **personajes** principales de *La vida es sueño?* »	The professor asked: "Which are the main characters of *Life Is a Dream?*"
El hijo tenía el buen **carácter** de su padre.	The son had the good character of his father.
Tiene muy buen **genio**.	He is very good-natured.
¿Quién **hará el papel del** rey Lear?	Who will play the part of King Lear?

3. la novedad—novelty; news; something new
    la noticia—news (one item of new information)
    las noticias—news
    la(s) nueva(s)—news (in spoken Spanish nueva[s] is colloquial or rustic; in literature it is synonymous with noticia[s], but used much less frequently)

—¿Cómo te encuentras?	How do you feel?
—Sin **novedad**.	The same (unchanged).
Si hay **novedades**, me avisará. (CBA)	If there is news (anything new happens), he will let me know.
La **noticia** me la dieron en el colegio donde estaba estudiando. (LH)	I was given the news (piece of news) in the school where I was studying.

4. atraer la atención—to attract attention
    llamarle la atención a uno—to attract one's attention; to draw one's attention
    prestar (poner) atención—to pay attention
    hacer caso de—to heed; to pay attention to

Atraer la atención is much less common than **llamarle la atención a uno**.

Nunca voy en su coche porque no **presta atención** al volante.	I never go in his car because he doesn't pay attention to the wheel.
No te pongas así porque vas a **llamar la atención**.	Don't act that way, for you are going to attract attention.
El conferenciante le **llamó la atención** sobre un episodio significativo del *Quijote*.	The lecturer called his attention to a significant episode of the *Quixote*.

No le hagas caso. Está hablando por hablar.	Don't pay any attention to him. He is talking just for the sake of talking.
Me encontraba muy cansado, y la verdad, **he hecho poco caso.** (IC)	I was very tired and, to tell the truth, I didn't pay much attention.

5. desde (a, hacia) fines de—since (toward) the end of
   a mediados de—toward the middle of
   a principios (comienzos) de—toward the beginning of

Las uvas maduraron **a mediados de** septiembre. (LM)	The grapes ripened toward the middle of September.

6. lanzar—to throw, hurl
   tirar—to throw; to throw away; to throw out
   echar—to throw, toss, put
   arrojar—to hurl, throw, toss
   botar—to hurl, throw with force (used mainly on a colloquial level)
   ir tirando—to get by

The first five verbs above all translate *to throw,* and often (especially in written Spanish) there is no careful distinction made between or among them. **Tirar** is *to throw away* or *to dispose of* something no longer useful. It sometimes indicates throwing with the intent of injuring a person. **Echar** has a wide range of meanings and frequently suggests not throwing, but a much gentler putting or lightly tossing. (**Echarse a la cama**, for example, renders *to lie down.*) **Echar** also means *to throw out* in the sense of to evict. **Arrojar** indicates a more intensive type of action and is usually accompanied by some sign of violence, effort, emotion, or impulsiveness. In Spanish America **botar** often means *to fire* or *to evict* someone.

Cogió el plato y se lo **tiró** a la cabeza. (N)	She took the dish and threw it at his head.
Mi mujer siempre **tira** el diario antes de que yo termine de leerlo.	My wife always throws out the paper before I finish reading it.
Aún **vamos tirando,** pero los tiempos no están tan buenos como antes.	We are still getting by, but times aren't so good as before.
Se suicidó **tirándose (arrojándose)** del puente.	He committed suicide by throwing himself from the bridge.
Hoy me **echaron** a patadas de otro café. (LC)	Today they kicked me out of another café.
Elisa **se echó** un jersey sobre los hombros y abrió la ventana de par en par. (EC)	Elisa put (tossed) a sweater over her shoulders and opened the window wide.

Con un suspiro, el chófer **arrojó** el cigarrillo a la acera, y puso el motor en marcha. (N)	With a sigh, the driver threw (tossed) the cigarette to the sidewalk and started the motor.
Arroja al horno rabiosamente unas paletadas de carbón. (NOC)	He angrily throws a few shovelfuls of coal into the fire.

7. carecer de—to lack (especially something desirable or essential)
   faltarle a uno—to lack (something desirable, or simply not to have)
   falto de + noun—lacking in

It is not possible to distinguish between the above two verbs. Both may be used when the subject is a person or thing, but **carecer** is much more common in the second case.

Aunque no era atractiva, no **carecía de** (**le faltaban**) encantos.	Although she wasn't attractive, she didn't lack (certain) charms.
Este asunto **carece de** (**no tiene**) importancia.	This affair is unimportant.
Faltos de aliciente, abandonaron el proyecto.	Lacking incentive, they abandoned the project.

8. la significación—significance; meaning
   el significado—meaning (to refer to words, sentences, questions, etc.)
   la acepción—meaning (usually a dictionary meaning or definition)
   el sentido—sense, meaning
   significar—to mean; to signify
   querer decir—to mean (to have in mind, imply)
   digo—I mean (said to correct oneself)

Había en aquella iglesia, **digo** catedral, un hermoso retrato de Murillo.	There was in that church, I mean cathedral, a beautiful portrait by Murillo.
«Pero no sé lo que **quiere usted decir**», repitió el alcalde.	"But I don't know what you mean," repeated the mayor.
¿Cuál es la primera **acepción** de esta palabra?	What is the first meaning of this word?
El **sentido** y la forma del *Quijote* han sido estudiados por muchos críticos.	The meaning and the form of the *Quixote* have been studied by many critics.
El autor y el crítico no estaban de acuerdo sobre lo que **significaba** el cuento.	The author and the critic did not agree about what the story meant.

9. la índole—nature, class, kind (more literary than the synonyms listed below)
   la clase—class, kind
   la especie—species, kind
   el tipo—type

Aquí venden toda **clase** de coches.	Here they sell all kinds of cars.
Todavía no hemos determinado la **especie** de fiebre que padece su hijo.	We still haven't determined the kind of fever that his child is suffering from.
Es un **tipo** de trabajo que no me gusta.	It's a type of work that I don't like.

10. el autor-personaje—the author-character

Spanish at times juxtaposes two nouns, using the second as an adjective to modify the first: **un hombre-rana**, **los países-miembros**, **los pantalones-vaqueros**, **el rey-poeta**, etc.

11. por consiguiente—therefore, consequently
por eso—therefore, for that reason
por lo tanto—therefore, consequently

| Nuestra familia ha crecido y **por eso** buscamos una casa más grande. | Our family has grown, and therefore we are looking for a larger house. |

12. padecer—to suffer
sufrir—to suffer
pasar—to suffer
el padecimiento, el sufrimiento—suffering

Sufrir and **padecer** are synonyms, and both refer to physical or mental suffering. When longer periods of time are involved, **sufrir** is more common. Both may be used with or without the preposition **de** to mean *to suffer from*. **Padecimiento** often means *illness*. **Pasar** is used to mean *to suffer* mainly with words like hunger, thirst, etc.

| No sabes cuánto **ha padecido** la infeliz señora con sus hijos. | You don't know how much the poor woman has suffered with her children. |
| Durante la guerra los habitantes de este pueblo **pasaron** mucha hambre. | During the war the inhabitants of this town suffered great hunger. |

13. el contratiempo—mishap, misfortune
el percance—(unexpected or sudden) misfortune
la desgracia—misfortune
la deshonra—disgrace

| Hasta de las **desgracias** se saca algún partido. (EJ) | You can gain some advantage even from misfortunes. |
| El viaje resultó ser una serie de **contratiempos**. | The trip turned out to be a series of mishaps. |

El descubrimiento de la estafa del hijo le trajo **deshonra** a toda la familia.	The discovery of the son's swindle disgraced the entire family.

14. minúsculo—small
letras minúsculas—small letters
mayúsculo—large; important
letras mayúsculas—capital letters
menudo—tiny, insignificant (may also be used ironically)

Gay era **menudo** y desgreñado. (SH)	Gay was small and disheveled.
En alemán todo sustantivo comienza con **letra mayúscula**.	In German every noun begins with a capital letter.
Menudo calor hace hoy.	It's nice and cool today.

15. la criatura—(very young) child; creature
la creación—creation
el crío—child; kid (familiar)
criar—to rear; to raise a child; to raise (animals)
educar—to rear, bring up; (sometimes) to educate
instruir—to educate (in an academic sense)

Le **educaron** como español.	They brought him up as a Spaniard.
Está muy bien **instruido**.	He is very well educated.
Los críos están contentísimos . . . (TV)	The kids are just delighted . . .
Acaba de nacer una **criatura**; no sé dónde, por ahí. (NOC)	A child has just been born; I don't know where, over there.

16. resultar ser, salir ser—to turn out, to come out (salir is often followed by an adjective or a noun, and frequently omits the verb ser)

Resultaba imposible calmar a los críos, después de lo que habían visto.	It (was) turned out to be impossible to calm the children after what they had seen.
A ver si el próximo cuadro me **sale** mejor.	Let's see if my next picture comes out better.
Resultó (**ser**) un hombre muy terco.	He turned out to be a very stubborn man.
Salieron ilesos del accidente.	They came out of the accident unhurt.

17. sacar a la luz—to bring to light
dar a luz—to give birth to; to have a child
parir—to give birth to
el parto—childbirth

Although **parir** is used for human beings as well as animals, it is almost always replaced by the more euphemistic **dar a luz** when one is referring to people.

La perra **parió** seis cachorros.	The dog gave birth to six puppies.
Dio a luz un hijo que pesaba ocho libras.	She gave birth to a son who weighed eight pounds.
Cuando el periodista **sacó a la luz** los verdaderos hechos, se produjo un escándalo.	When the journalist brought to light the true facts, there was a scandal.

18. desdeñar, despreciar—to scorn, disdain

Ahora **desdeñaba** al que había sido su mejor amigo.	Now he scorned the one who had been his best friend.
Despreciaba al hombre que había acusado falsamente a su padre.	He disdained the man who had falsely accused his father.

19. revelar—to reveal; to develop (film)
desarrollar—to develop

Prometió nunca **revelar** el secreto.	He promised never to reveal the secret.
Quieren **desarrollar** la industria química más rápidamente.	They want to develop the chemical industry more rapidly.

20. la edición—printing

Notice that the English *edition* is often translated not simply by **edición**, but by **edición revisada (y aumentada)** or **edición** similarly modified. **La primera edición** is, of course, both the first edition *and* the first printing.

Van a publicar una **edición revisada** de sus obras completas.	They are going to publish a new edition of his complete works.
. . . una novela, llegando a **ediciones** de cientos de miles de ejemplares, alborota a la opinión.	. . . a novel, when it reaches printings of hundreds of thousands of copies, arouses public opinion.

21. perdurable—everlasting
sempiterno—everlasting (rather serious or solemn in tone)
duradero—(long) lasting
perpetuo—perpetual, everlasting
eterno—eternal

Los economistas están luchando por crear una prosperidad **duradera**.	The economists are struggling to create a lasting prosperity.

| Los románticos creían que el amor era **perdurable**. | The Romantics believed love was everlasting. |

22. rezar—to pray
     orar—to pray; to orate
     la oración—prayer
     la plegaria—prayer
     hacer (rezar) una oración—to say a prayer
     como reza el refrán—as the saying goes

Rezar is the standard word for *to pray*. Colloquially, it often means *to say* or *to read*: (¿Cómo **reza** ese renglón, otra vez? What does that line say again?) **Orar**, which also means *to orate*, is used much less than **rezar** for *to pray*. Nevertheless, **oración** is standard for *a prayer*. **La plegaria** is a prayer in which a special request is made.

Cumplí la promesa y no he dejado de **rezar** ni un solo día por ella.	I kept my promise and have not failed a single day to pray for her.
Mi tía **rezaba** todos los días **una oración** muy larga.	My aunt said a very long prayer every day.
Dirigía su **plegaria** a la Virgen, pidiéndole que salvara a su hijo.	She directed her prayer to the Virgin, asking that she save her son.

23. soler + infinitive—to be accustomed to; to be wont to (present and
       imperfect only; in the imperfect tense, this construction performs
       almost the same function as the imperfect of the verb in the infinitive)
     acostumbrar (a) + infinitive—to be accustomed (used) to + gerund
     acostumbrarse a + infinitive—to become accustomed (used) to +
       gerund

Los domingos **solíamos** merendar en el campo.	On Sundays we used to (would) have a light lunch in the country.
Habla como quien **acostumbra** mandar a otros.	He talks like a person who is used to giving orders to others.
No puedo **acostumbrarme** a ciertas cosas que otros aceptan con indiferencia.	I can't become used to certain things that others accept indifferently.

EXERCISES ON NOTES

1. The waves tossed the shipwrecked man's body onto the beach. 2. She prays two hours a day and never fails to hear mass. 3. This word has many meanings in English. 4. The Third Army played an important role in that victory. 5. Around the beginning of March, the almond trees are in bloom in the province of Alicante. 6. My sister has just given birth to twins. 7. He is 62 and therefore has a right to receive Social Security

benefits. 8. The apple trees were covered with tiny blossoms. 9. The effects of that illness are long lasting. 10. They threw out the tenant for not paying his rent. 11. He has endured his physical suffering with great courage. 12. I despise him for his weak character. 13. Anthropology has brought to light several previously unknown reasons for the fall of the Roman Empire. 14. I don't understand what you mean. 15. It turns out that we cannot accept your generous offer. 16. His son has a very violent temperament. 17. When you finish that magazine, don't throw it away. 18. You can't deny the fact that you were there. 19. At the end of the nineteenth century, Spain lost Cuba, Puerto Rico, and the Philippines. 20. Pirandello wrote a play titled *Six Characters in Search of an Author.* 21. He will soon be accustomed to our way of doing things. 22. What kind of book does he intend to write? 23. The bankruptcy was a misfortune from which the family never recovered. 24. The photographs came out better than we had expected. 25. There were more than 50 printings in English of *The Four Horsemen of the Apocalypse.* 26. You haven't developed your ideas very clearly. 27. He was 55, I mean 45, when he retired from the Air Force. 28. He threw more wood on the fire. 29. The children said their prayers before going to bed. 30. The goal of the United Nations is to establish a lasting peace. 31. The biography contains many new facts about the author's life. 32. This morning they gave her the terrible news that her son had died. 33. Do you mean that finally we shall be able to go on a vacation? 34. The teacher asked the student to explain the meaning of the word. 35. Children should learn to read capital letters before small letters. 36. She threw a shawl over her shoulders and ran out the door. 37. He had such a weak character that he was afraid to reveal his opinion. 38. A few facts will suffice to familiarize them with the plot of the novel. 39. As a child, the pianist had already revealed his artistic temperament. 40. The lack of data obliges us to formulate an hypothesis.

CUESTIONARIO

a. contenido

1. ¿Que justificaba por sí el esfuerzo narrativo de cualquier biógrafo?
2. ¿Con qué fin se preocupan los autores de esta época con personajes de la clase ínfima como Lázaro?
3. ¿Por qué indica el autor-personaje que los que heredaron nobles estados no deben enorgullecerse?
4. ¿Por qué surge ahora con tanta importancia el tema del hambre?
5. ¿Cómo es la figurilla en que se concentra el interés ahora?
6. ¿Por qué llamó el autor al personaje Lázaro? ¿Qué significa el nombre «Lazarillo» hoy día?
7. ¿En qué se diferencia esta obra de las didácticas y moralizantes?
8. ¿Qué tipo de persona era el ciego a quién servía Lazarillo?

b. estilo

1. ¿De qué manera emplea Américo Castro los adjetivos en este pasaje?

2. ¿Qué efectos produce este uso de los adjetivos?
3. ¿Qué contribuyen las dos citas a las ideas expuestas por Américo Castro?
4. ¿De qué recursos estilísticos se sirve el autor para exponer con tanta lucidez las características del *Lazarillo de Tormes*? Ténganse en cuenta (1) organización de ideas, (2) vocabulario, (3) estructura de las frases, (4) tono.

TEMA—TRADUCCION

It is understandable that the great deeds accomplished by the Catholic sovereigns or the paladin Amadís should justify in themselves the attention of any narrator. But one would not have expected that an insignificant being like Lázaro would have interested any biographer. Nevertheless, lower-class characters had been appearing (**venían** + *gerund*) since the end of the fifteenth century in works like *La Celestina*. These characters, used to criticize the values of the privileged, began to acquire a certain literary meaning in their own right. (*Use* **en sí**.) This same criticism is evident in the *Lazarillo*, where the autobiographical point of view is that of the lower class, and where the theme of hunger replaces love and chivalry. Interest is now focused on a humble figure, who lacks the values esteemed by society, but who has a strong will to survive in the face of all kinds of adversity.

The fact that three printings of the *Lazarillo* appeared in 1554 proves the immense popularity of the work. So alive was this character that his name became the term for a blind man's guide. Unlike many works of its period, the *Lazarillo* is not didactic and moralizing, but rather ironic and sarcastic. While the purpose of all these works is to criticize, this book's enduring value resides in the visual and audible presentation of its characters. Who can forget the blind man praying? This old man knew more than a hundred prayers. And whenever he recited one of them, he would assume a humble expression and his voice would resound throughout the church. This falsely pious type will appear later in other picaresque novels, in Cervantes and in Molière.

TEMAS A ESCOGER

Escríbanse unas 200 palabras sobre uno de los temas siguientes usando a lo menos 20 de las palabras y expresiones estudiadas en este capítulo.

1. La hipocresía en la sociedad
2. La novela como crítica social
3. Descripción de un personaje de novela

chapter 16

Hijo de hombre

Augusto Roa Bastos

Con Augusto Roa Bastos (nacido en 1917) el Paraguay hace su primera contribución importante a la literatura hispanoamericana. Su novela Hijo de hombre *ganó el primer premio del Congreso Internacional Losada de 1959 e hizo famoso a su autor. Los sucesos de los nueve capítulos de esta obra abarcan el período de 1910 a 1935, y presentan el trágico drama del Paraguay desde una perspectiva histórica, artística, y sociológica. En algunas páginas Roa crea un verdadero sentido épico al describir la valentía de los paraguayos en la lucha contra sus enemigos. En el trozo que sigue, el viejo Macario, ya casi centenario, evoca para los chicos la figura sombría de José Gaspar Rodríguez de Francia, dictador del Paraguay desde 1816 hasta 1840. Lo hace con tanta maestría que somos trasladados casi sin darnos cuenta a la época de Francia, donde presenciamos el perfil sugestivo de El Supremo, cuyo recuerdo vive indeleble en la memoria de Macario.*

El que mejor conocía la historia era el viejo Macario. Esa y muchas otras. Por aquel tiempo no todos los chiquilines[1] nos burlábamos de él. Algunos lo seguíamos no para tirarle tierra sino para oír sus relatos y sucedidos, que tenían el olor[2] y el sabor de lo vivido.[3] Era un maravilloso contador
5 de cuentos. Sobre todo, un poco antes de que se pusiera tan chocho[4] para morir. Era la memoria viviente del pueblo. Y sabía cosas de más allá de[5] sus linderos.[6] El mismo no había nacido allí. Se murmuraba que era un hijo mostrenco de Francia. En el libro de Crismas[7] estaba registrado[8] con ese apellido.[9]
10 Macario habría nacido algunos años después de haberse establecido la Dictadura Perpetua. Su padre, el liberto Pilar, era ayuda de cámara de El Supremo. Llevaba su apellido. Muchos de los esclavos que él manumitió —mientras esclavizaba en las cárceles[10] a los patricios—, habían tomado este nombre, que más se parecía al color sombrío de una época. Estaban
15 teñidos[11] de su signo indeleble como por la pigmentación de la motosa[12] piel.
Macario también. Lo escuchábamos con escalofríos. Y sus silencios hablaban tanto como sus palabras. El aire de aquella época inescrutable nos salpicaba la cara a través de la boca del anciano. Siempre hablaba en

guaraní.[13] El dejo[14] suave de la lengua india tornaba apacible el horror, lo metía en la sangre. Ecos de otros ecos. Sombras[15] de sombras. Reflejos de reflejos. No la verdad tal vez de los hechos, pero sí su encantamiento.

—El hombre, mis hijos—nos decía—, es como un río. Tiene barranca[16] y orilla. Nace y desemboca[17] en otros ríos. Alguna utilidad debe prestar. Mal río es el que muere en el estero . . .

El fluctuaba estancado en el pasado.

—El Karaí Guasú[18] mandó tumbar las casas de los ricos y voltear los árboles—contaba—. Quería verlo todo. A toda hora. Los movimientos y hasta el pensamiento de sus contrarios, vendidos a los mamelucos y porteños.[19] Conspiraban día y noche para destruirlo a él. Formaban el estero que se quería tragar a nuestra nación. Por eso él los perseguía y destruía. Tapaba[20] con tierra el estero . . .

No le entendíamos muy bien. Pero la figura de El Supremo se recortaba imponente ante nosotros contra un fondo de cielos y noches, vigilando[21] el país con el rigor implacable de su voluntad y un poder omnímodo como el destino.

—Dormía con un ojo abierto. Nadie lo podía engañar . . .

Veíamos los sótanos oscuros llenos de enterrados vivos que se agitaban en sueños bajo el ojo insomne y tenaz. Y nosotros también nos agitábamos en una pesadilla que no podía, sin embargo, hacernos odiar la sombra del Karaí Guasú.

Lo veíamos cabalgar en su paseo vespertino por las calles desiertas, entre dos piquetes armados de sables y carabinas. Montado en el cebruno sobre la silla[22] de terciopelo carmesí con pistoleras y fustes de plata, alta la cabeza, los puños engarfiados sobre las riendas, pasaba al tranco venteando el silencio del crepúsculo bajo la sombra del enorme tricornio, todo él envuelto en la capa negra de forro colorado,[23] de la que sólo emergían las medias blancas y los zapatos de charol con hebillas de oro, trabados[24] en los estribos de plata. El filudo perfil de pájaro giraba[25] de pronto hacia las puertas y ventanas atrancadas como tumbas, y entonces aun nosotros, después de un siglo, bajo las palabras del viejo, todavía nos echábamos hacia atrás para escapar de esos carbones encendidos que nos espiaban desde lo alto del caballo, entre el rumor de las armas y los herrajes.

88. NOTES

1. el chiquilín (American)—youngster
   el chicuelo—little boy
   el chiquillo—child, youngster
   chiquitín—tiny, small

   The above diminutives may be used as nouns or adjectives.

En una de las travesías, estuvo a punto de derribar a un **chiquillo** . . . (F)

At one of the crossings, he was about to knock over a child . . .

Un **chicuelo** de ocho años jugaba con el perro.

A child of eight was playing with the dog.

El libro es tan **chiquitín** que cabe en la palma de la mano.

The book is so tiny that it fits in the palm of the hand.

2. el olor—smell
   el hedor—stench, smell
   el tufo—(unpleasant or foul) smell, odor
   la peste—stink
   oler—to smell
   heder—to smell bad; to stink
   apestar—to stink
   oler a—to smell of (like)

La habitación **hedía** a desinfectante.

The room smelled of disinfectant.

Del asfalto vino un **olor** a polvo mojado. (N)

From the asphalt there came the smell of wet dust.

El baúl despedía un **tufo** de alcanfor.

The trunk gave off a smell of camphor.

La cocina **huele a** cebolla.

The kitchen smells of onion.

El tendero era un hombre chato que **apestaba** a aguardiente. (NB)

The storekeeper was a flat-nosed man who stank of liquor.

3. lo vivido—life, that which has been lived

Lo has several important uses in Spanish. With (a) the masculine singular past participle, it renders *that which has been* + *participle,* or a close noun equivalent; with (b) adjectives, it is used as a substitute for **qué,** *how,* and (c) also translates *part* or *thing*; when followed by (d) **de** + noun or adverb, **lo** renders *the affair (matter, situation) of (concerning, regarding),* or an equivalent like *what happened to.*

A. Yo, en cambio, soy capaz de revivir siempre **lo vivido** y raramente **lo sentido.** (THI)

I, on the other hand, am capable of always reliving what has been lived and rarely what has been felt.

B. Entonces . . . me di cuenta de **lo vacía** que estaba aquella casa . . . (NB)

Then . . . I realized how empty that house was . . .

C. El gato iba por **lo alto** de la tapia.

The cat was going along the top (part) of the wall.

Está Vd. en **lo mejor** de la vida.

You are in the best part of your life.

Lo más importante es terminar a tiempo.	The most important thing is to finish on time.
D. No tomes a pecho **lo de Carlos** (de ayer).	Don't take to heart what happened to Charles (yesterday).

4. chocho—doting
senil—senile
la chochez—dotage
la senilidad—senility
chochear—to dote; to become childish

Creo que el anciano **chochea**. (NB)	I think the old gentleman is becoming childish.

5. más allá de—beyond
el más allá—the other world, the great beyond
allende—beyond; besides (literary, poetic)

Más allá de estas montañas, hay un hermoso valle.	Beyond these mountains there is a beautiful valley.
Tarde o temprano, todos los hombres piensan en **el más allá**.	Sooner or later, every man thinks about the great beyond.

6. el lindero—limits, boundary
el límite—limit, boundary
lindar—to adjoin, border (mainly for property)
limitar—to limit; to border (especially for geography)

Sa propiedad **lindaba** con la nuestra.	His property adjoined ours.
Suiza **limita** con varios países.	Switzerland borders on several countries.
Me llevó hasta el **lindero** del camino que atravesaba las tierras de mi abuelo. (NB)	He took me as far as the boundary of the road that cut across my grandfather's lands.

7. el libro de Crismas—book in which baptisms are recorded (crisma is holy oil for certain sacraments, including baptism)

8. registrar—to register; to examine; to search; to inspect
matricular(se), inscribir(se)—to enroll, register
la matrícula—registration or license fee; roster
examinar—to examine
reconocer—to examine (especially in a medical context)

Se **registró** los bolsillos para saber si tenía dinero.	He searched his pockets to see if he had any money.
Hace tres años **se matriculó** en la Facultad de Medicina. (LN)	Three years ago he enrolled in the School of Medicine.

| El médico vendrá pronto a **reconocer** la herida. | The doctor will come soon to examine the wound. |

9.   el apellido—family name, last name
     el nombre—name (general term)
     el nombre de pila—first name (pila—baptismal font)
     el apodo, el mote—nickname
     poner nombre (apodo) a—to give a (nick)name to; to name
     nombrar—to appoint, nominate, name

Ignoraba por completo su **nombre** y **apellido**. (F)	I was completely ignorant of his full name.
Sé a quien te refieres, pero se me escapa su **apodo**.	I know whom you are referring to, but his nickname escapes me.
Le pusieron el nombre de Mónica.	They named her Monica.
El gobernador **nombró** juez a su cuñado.	The governor appointed his brother-in-law judge.

10.   la cárcel—jail
     la prisión—prison
     el penal—penitentiary
     el presidio—penitentiary (fortress)
     la mazmorra—dungeon
     el calabozo—(underground) dungeon; cell (for solitary confinement)

Le guardaron encerrado dos años en una **mazmorra** oscura y húmeda.	They kept him locked up for two years in a dark, humid dungeon.
Estuvo en el **penal** diez años antes de que se descubriera su inocencia.	He was in the penitentiary ten years before his innocence was discovered.
La humedad del **calabozo** le hizo contraer una pulmonía.	The dampness of the cell caused him to catch pneumonia.

11.   teñir(se)—to dye, stain; to color
     desteñir(se)—to fade
     tintar—to color; to dye

Tintar is for artificial colors only; **teñir** may refer to the color something acquires by either a natural or an artificial process.

| La muchacha **se tiñó** el pelo de rubio. | The girl dyed her hair blond. |
| El horizonte empezaba a **teñirse** de púrpura con la puesta del sol. | The horizon began to turn purple (become stained with purple) from the sunset. |

12.   motoso—spotted, speckled
     la mota—speck, speckle

motear—to speckle
la mancha—spot, stain
manchar—to spot

En las paredes de la casa no se veía ni una **mota** de suciedad.

Not a speck of dirt could be seen on the walls of the house.

Las paredes del dormitorio estaban cubiertas de **manchas** negras de la lluvia.

The walls of the bedroom were covered with dark spots from the rain.

El niño **se manchó** la ropa con la pintura.

The child stained his clothes with the paint.

13. guaraní—Guarani (Even today Paraguay is largely a bilingual nation. Both the Indian language, Guarani, and Spanish are readily understood by most people there.)

14. el dejo—accent
el acento—accent

Dejo is much less common than **acento** and is used principally to refer to a regional or personal inflection or accent. **Acento** may also be used in this sense.

Tiene un **dejo** (**acento**) extranjero cuando habla inglés.

He has a foreign accent when he speaks English.

15. la sombra—shadow, shade
a la sombra—in the shade
al sol—in the sun
hacer sombra a—to outshine
la pantalla—(lamp) shade
el transparente—(window) shade

Me paré, la **sombra** también paró. (FPD)

I stopped; the shadow stopped too.

Les hace sombra a los demás con su talento.

He outshines the others with his talent.

La **pantalla** de seda estaba tan manchada que tuvo que comprar otra.

The silk shade was so stained that she had to buy another.

16. la barranca—ravine, gorge
el cañón—ravine, canyon
el acantilado—cliff

El Gran **Cañón** es una de las maravillas naturales del mundo.

The Grand Canyon is one of the world's natural wonders.

17. desembocar—to empty into; to flow into
la desembocadura—mouth (of a river)
vaciar—to empty

vacío—empty
desocupado—empty, unoccupied (room, house, etc.)

Se veía en la cara del pescador que había regresado con las redes **vacías**.	One could see from the fisherman's face that he had returned with empty nets.
Pudiera haber ahí un rincón **desocupado** donde les permitan dejar los bultos. (NOC)	There could be an empty corner where they will allow them to leave the bundles.
La criada **vació** los ceniceros en cuanto salieron los invitados.	The maid emptied the ash trays as soon as the guests left.

18. el Karaí Guasú—big chief

In Guarani, **Karaí** means *chief* or *lord*, and **Guasú** means *big*.

19. el mameluco—Mameluke
el porteño—inhabitant of Buenos Aires

The **mamelucos** were Brazilian slaveholding pioneers—hence the use of the word in Paraguay to mean *pioneer*. **Porteño** (from **puerto**, *port*) is standard to refer to a person or thing from Buenos Aires.

20. tapar—to cover

Tapar means both **cubrir** and *to cover up, to plug up, to fill up*.

Se tapaba los oídos para no oír el tren.	He covered his ears in order not to hear the train.
Taparon el agujero con papel.	They plugged up the hole with paper.

21. vigilar—to watch over
velar—to watch (over); to keep guard
mirar—to watch; to look at

Vigila bien la maleta.	Keep a close eye on the suitcase.
El pobre nunca ha sabido **velar** por sus intereses.	The poor man has never known how to watch out for his own interests.

22. la silla—saddle; chair
el sillón—armchair, easy chair
la butaca—armchair; orchestra seat

La **silla** es de cerezo.	The chair is made of cherry (wood).
Estaban sentados en los mullidos **sillones** del salón.	They were sitting in the soft chairs in the lounge.

23. colorado—red
ponerse colorado—to blush
bermejo—brilliant red, vermillion
encarnado—red or flesh colored
rojizo—reddish
carmesí—crimson

El agua sabía a hierro y a veces salía **rojiza**. (MAH)

The water tasted of iron and at times came out reddish.

24. trabar—to fasten, join; to tie
trabarse—to become hooked, joined, fastened
el trabalenguas—tongue twister

Trabar is often used with nouns in the sense of *to begin, initiate, strike up*, etc.

Cuando llegué a Madrid, **trabé** relaciones con su familia.

When I reached Madrid, I established a relationship with his family.

Trabó conversación con el pasajero que estaba a su lado.

He struck up a conversation with the passenger at his side.

Si nos hablan demasiado de prisa . . ., las sílabas no **se traban** en palabras . . . (EI)

If they speak to us too rapidly . . ., the syllables don't join (mesh) into words . . .

Se nos trabaron los parachoques.

We locked bumpers.

25. girar—to spin; to turn; to gyrate
dar vueltas a—to turn (something); to cause to revolve
dar vueltas—to return; to keep going over the same thing
no hay que darle vueltas—you can't get around it
dar la vuelta a—to turn (something) over

En la esquina, un gitano **daba vueltas** a un organillo.

On the corner a Gypsy was turning a hurdy-gurdy.

Da la vuelta, para que se queme bien, **a** un grueso tronco de olivera. (LP)

He is turning over a thick olivewood log so that it' will burn better.

EXERCISES ON NOTES

1. They were convinced they would find wealth beyond the horizon. 2. I intend to enroll in the first summer session. 3. His name was Maximiliano, but we called him by his nickname, Maxi. 4. When he turned thirteen, his father gave him a leather saddle. 5. The mother watched over her son every night while he was sick. 6. You can't get around it; you will have to apologize. 7. While waiting to buy tickets, I struck up a conversation with the lady in front of me. 8. His latest play outshines everything he has done before. 9. Can't you see how (*not* **que**) tired the girls are? 10. He

turned over in bed for two hours before he fell asleep. 11. The farmer's shirt was faded from the sun. 12. Years ago prisoners often rotted away in dungeon cells. 13. After studying English for many years, he still had a heavy accent. 14. The worst thing about old age is dotage. 15. Ecuador borders on Peru and Colombia. 16. The stench of the dead animal was unbearable. 17. He searched the closet looking for the gloves. 18. Be careful when you turn the omelette over. 19. When the doctor finished examining him, he recommended that he consult a specialist. 20. The Mississippi River empties into the Gulf of Mexico. 21. The house on the cliff overlooked a magnificent beach. 22. After the rain the air smelled of earth and grass. 23. The railroad tracks and the freeway are the boundaries of the industrial district. 24. Our cars locked bumpers as I was pushing him to the service station. 25. That is the only important thing (*not* **cosa**) that he has done for us. 26. They had to empty the pool completely before cleaning it. 27. The president appointed the professor ambassador to Belgium. 28. I noticed a slight regional accent in his way of pronouncing that word. 29. The weather vane was spinning, and we knew a storm was approaching. 30. He wouldn't hesitate to change his name. 31. The little boy found a nest of speckled eggs while playing in the meadow. 32. The island of Alcatraz is no longer a penitentiary. 33. The situation involving Julio has been resolved in (**de**) the best possible way. 34. She smelled the violets that her husband had brought her. 35. The customs official examined our baggage before letting us pass. 36. He was more than one hundred years old and showed no sign of senility. 37. The chef went to the kitchen to keep an eye on the preparations for the banquet. 38. He spent the night in jail for having disturbed the peace. 39. They dragged his good name through the mud. 40. There were bright-red leather chairs in the living room.

CUESTIONARIO

a. contenido

1. ¿Qué le hacían al viejo Macario algunos chiquilines?
2. ¿Qué talento especial tenía?
3. ¿Cómo estaba registrado Macario en el libro de Crismas? ¿Por qué tenía ese nombre?
4. ¿Por qué sabía tanto de la dictadura de Francia?
5. ¿En qué lengua narraba los cuentos?
6. Según Macario, ¿qué querían hacer los contrarios del Karaí Guasú? ¿Qué medidas tomó el Karaí Guasú contra ellos?
7. ¿Cómo describía Macario a la figura de El Supremo?
8. ¿Cómo reaccionaron los chiquillos a la descripción del dictador en su paseo vespertino?

b. estilo

1. ¿Qué efecto producen las frases cortas al principio de la selección? ¿Y las de Macario al narrar. su cuento?

2. ¿Por qué se emplean tantos imperfectos en este pasaje?
3. ¿Cómo se logra crear una atmósfera de encantamiento para el cuento de Macario?
4. ¿Cómo consigue Macario crear una figura casi sobrehumana al describir Karaí Guasú?
5. ¿Por qué podemos decir que el último párrafo es un cuadro? ¿Cuáles son los elementos plásticos que dan valor a este cuadro?

TEMA—TRADUCCION

Until shortly before he began to dote, Macario was a wonderful teller of tales. Not all of us followed him to make fun of him, but to listen to his stories, which had the flavor of real experience.

It was rumored that he was an illegitimate son of Francia. But in fact, El Supremo had freed Macario's father, who, like many freed slaves, had taken the dictator's surname. The reason that Macario knew so much about Karaí Guasú was because his father had become the dictator's valet.

So great a storyteller was Macario that his pauses revealed as much as his words. In the soft accent of Guarani he would convey the atmosphere of that inscrutable period, and although perhaps sometimes he did not present the truth of the facts, he always enchanted us with his poetic magic. He related how Karaí Guasú was always vigilant and pursued the enemies who conspired to destroy him. They were the swamp that wanted to swallow our country, and Karaí Guasú covered it up with earth.

Although we did not understand all that he said, the imposing figure of El Supremo, watching over his country, always stood out vividly before us. No one could deceive him, for even while sleeping he kept one eye open. We visualized dark dungeons full of prisoners under the watchful eye of El Supremo. We saw him during his evening ride through the deserted streets, accompanied by two guards and seated on a saddle of crimson velvet. He would ride by with his head high and wearing a long black cape with a red lining. It covered him down to his white stockings and patent-leather shoes. Then suddenly his birdlike profile would turn toward the doors and barred windows. So great was Macario's magic in evoking this figure of one hundred years ago that, when El Supremo turned his head, we instinctively drew back to escape the burning coals of his glance.

TEMAS A ESCOGER

Escríbanse unas 200 palabras sobre uno de los temas siguientes usando a lo menos 20 de las palabras y expresiones estudiadas en este capítulo.

1. El cuento y la imaginación infantil
2. La creación del mito en torno a un dictador
3. Descripción de una persona en un momento dado

chapter 17

89. SELECCION LITERARIA

El forastero

Luis Romero

Luis Romero (nacido en Barcelona en 1916) ha sido militar, periodista y literato. Inició su carrera de novelista con La noria, *obra que le ganó el premio Nadal en 1951. De las novelas escritas desde aquella fecha, se destacan* Los otros *(1956) y* La nochebuena *(1960). Romero cultiva también el cuento, género en que revela el mismo don de análisis y observación que vemos en sus novelas. «El forastero», que reproducimos en los capítulos 17 y 18, es un cuento tomado de la colección* Esas sombras del trasmundo *(1957).*

Hacía muchos años que no se sentía tan feliz como se estaba sintiendo ahora. El médico le había prescrito[1] descanso y tranquilidad, y aquí realmente los hallaba. Alquilaron[2] este solitario chalet, junto al mar, y su salud era más salud que nunca. La esposa estaba con él. Tras muchos
5 años de convivencia superficial se habían encontrado[3] nuevamente en las veladas[4] largas, en los paseos por la orilla del mar, en las siestas felices bajo los pinos. Ni consejos de administración, ni partidas[5] de *poker* con los amigos, ni tertulia por la tarde en el lujoso club de los hombres ricos. Y ella tampoco echaba de menos el té de las señoras presumidas, ni aquellos
10 flirteos, más o menos inocentes, tras las conferencias de los caballeros calvos, ni el chismorrear[6] mientras le probaba la modista. Se habían encontrado, sencillamente, en esta reedición primaveral de su luna de miel, disfrutando de[7] los pequeños dones[8] de Dios: aire, pinos, acantilados, olas, césped, rosas, pan, campanas . . . , cosas todas ellas que hacía años habían olvidado[9]
15 o complicado de tal manera, que ni ellos mismos podían reconocerlas. Todo porque el médico había dicho: «Necesita usted unos meses de reposo.»[10] Y él, por primera vez en muchos años, había decidido escucharle. La recompensa fue tangible, inmediata, generosa. Aquí estaban los dos, amorosos, entusiastas, tiernos y agradecidos a Dios, que había creado tantas maravillas
20 y se las mostraba amablemente. Cada palabra tomaba un nuevo significado, y las cosas sabían,[11] olían, deleitaban. Después de muchos años habían vuelto a recordar cuán sencilla es la vida y como la felicidad está en disfrutar de todo lo que espontáneamente se nos ofrece.

Les gustaba tanto ver anochecer[12] desde las rocas, que casi todos los
25 atardeceres iban paseando hasta allí, y era como si tuvieran reservadas butacas en aquel cotidiano[13] espectáculo. (Butacas enteramente gratis,[14] por cierto.)

Hasta que vieron venir a aquel hombre no se habían dado cuenta de que existía otro sendero[15] un poco más arriba de donde acostumbraban a sentarse. No les gustó la intromisión de un forastero;[16] les parecía como si, al participar del espectáculo, les privara de alguna parte de él. Pero el forastero pasó de largo y ni siquiera los miró. Era un hombre alto, flaco, descuidado en su afeitado y en su atuendo. Aquella tarde, la puesta de sol fue tan maravillosamente perfecta como los demás días; pero el paso del forastero desaliñado y hosco les disminuyó la sensación de paz absoluta con que cada tarde se veían recompensados.

Por la mañana se trasladó al[17] pueblo a comprar el periódico, pues había decidido no romper[18] la vieja costumbre de leer su diario aunque tuviera que andar dos quilómetros[19] para conseguirlo. Al mismo tiempo, este paseo matutino era un saludable[20] ejercicio, y se sentía joven y ágil como no recordaba haberlo estado nunca, y eso sería porque los tiempos de su juventud quedaban lejos, más quizá por lo atareado de su vivir que por el número de años transcurridos. «Necesita usted una temporada de descanso.» ¡Hay que ver lo bien que le conocía su médico y como había acertado! No padecía ninguna enfermedad; cansancio, simplemente cansancio. Y en veinte días ya era un hombre nuevo. Veinte días sin firmar una carta, sin una junta, sin una conferencia telefónica. Veinte días sin emplear el coche más que para dar algún paseo por la carretera o ir a tomar un refresco a la ciudad vecina. Veinte días sin acordarse de sus negocios (¡allá que sus hijos se las compusieran!),[21] sin enterarse de las cotizaciones[22] más que por simple curiosidad; veinte días sin recibir otras cartas que las familiares; veinte días sin los ruidos del trabajo durante el día y sin los ruidos irritantes de la noche en la ciudad, en los clubs nocturnos o en los elegantes teatros. ¡Qué absurda aquella vida suya de siempre!

En una calleja apartada volvió a tropezarse con[23] el hombre flaco y desagradable. Le disgustó[24] el encuentro y la forma en que le miraba el forastero. Aquel hombre no era del pueblo; se notaba claramente en su forma de vestir y en esas inexplicables características que nunca inducen a error. Intentó leer el periódico mientras andaba, pero no conseguía fijar la atención. Aunque le contrariaba, retrocedió y fue a afeitarse[25] a la barbería, cosa que no había pensado hacer aquella mañana. Fue llevando la conversación al terreno propicio y acabó preguntando por el forastero. No le conocían ni el barbero, ni el mancebo, ni dos clientes que esperaban turno leyendo unas revistas atrasadas.[26]

90. NOTES

1. prescribir—to prescribe; to order
   recetar—to prescribe (almost always medicine)
   la receta—prescription; recipe

Los médicos le **prescribieron** un descanso completo después de la operación.	The doctors prescribed (ordered) a complete rest for him after the operation.
El médico se limitaba a **recetar** vitamina B.	The doctor limited himself to prescribing vitamin B.
El joven le pidió al farmacéutico que le despachara la **receta**.	The young man asked the pharmacist to fill the prescription.

2. alquilar—to rent; to let
   el alquiler—rent
   la renta—income
   rentar—to yield or produce (income)
   rendir—to yield or produce

Nos gustaba el piso, pero el **alquiler** era muy caro.	We liked the apartment, but the rent was very expensive.
La **renta** nacional ha aumentado un diez por ciento este año.	The national income has increased 10 per cent this year.
No sabía cuánto **rentaban** sus casas y pisos en Barcelona.	He didn't know how much income his houses and apartments in Barcelona produced.
Este naranjal **rinde** más fruta que el otro.	This orange grove yields more fruit than the other.

3. se habían encontrado nuevamente—they had rediscovered each other

4. la velada—gathering (at night)
   la tertulia—(habitual) gathering (late afternoon, evening, or night)

El dueño de la galería celebró una **velada** para presentar al nuevo pintor.	The owner of the gallery held a soirée to introduce the new painter.

5. la partida—game (of cards, chess, etc.)
   el partido—game, match, (athletic) contest
   el juego—game (the action or contest, especially a particular diversion as established and governed by rules)

Dos solitarios echan en un rincón una **partida** de ajedrez. (VA)	Two solitary men are having a game of chess in the corner.
Organizaron un **partido** de béisbol para la tarde.	They organized a baseball game for this afternoon.
El fútbol es el **juego** más popular de España.	Soccer is the most popular game in Spain.

6. chismorrear, chismear, cotillear—to gossip
   el chisme—(piece of) gossip; gadget, device
   la habladuría—gossip, rumor

No es una mujer mala pero le gusta contar **chismes**.	She isn't a bad woman, but she likes to gossip.
No sé por qué me he comprado este **chisme**.	I don't know why I bought this gadget.

7. disfrutar (de)—to enjoy
   gozar (de)—to enjoy

To enjoy in most cases may be rendered by either of these verbs. **Gozar** is preferred, however, when the subject experiences a real pleasure from something. **Disfrutar** is preferred when *to enjoy* merely indicates *to have the use of* or *to benefit from* something (privileges, advantages, comforts, etc.). **Disfrutar** is used more than **gozar**, and the above distinctions, often tenuous in normal conversation, tend to disappear in literature.

Disfruta (goza) de una salud estupenda.	He enjoys wonderful health.
Millones de franceses **disfrutaron** sus vacaciones bajo el sol español.	Millions of Frenchmen enjoyed their vacations under the Spanish sun.

8. el don—gift (of nature)
   tener don de gentes—to have a way with people
   el don de lenguas—gift for languages
   el regalo—gift, present (of any type)
   el presente—gift (often suggests something splendid or magnificent; used much less than regalo)
   la donación—donation; large gift
   la dádiva—gift (gratuitous, spontaneous, sudden, often in the sense of a tip, handout, bribe, etc.)

Gracias a su **don de gentes**, siempre se sale con la suya.	Thanks to his way with people, he always gets his own way.
El Museo de Arte fue una **donación** de los grandes industriales de la ciudad.	The Art Museum was a gift from the great industrialists of the city.
El tacaño esperaba una explosión de gratitud por **dádiva** tan espléndida.	The tightwad (miser) expected an explosion of gratitude for such a splendid gift.

9. olvidar—to forget
   olvidarse de—to forget
   olvidársele a uno—to forget
   dejar olvidado—to leave behind; to forget

Except for **dejar olvidado**, the meaning of which is clear, *to forget* may be rendered with any of the preceding verbal expressions. **Olvidársele a uno** is particularly common, for it fits a much used pattern employing a reflexive construction plus a dative of concern. This construction appears to place the responsibility for an unplanned (and often undesired) occurrence on an inanimate object rather than on the person concerned. It conveys a different idea in Spanish, however, and is regularly used in the pattern illustrated below.

Rompió el reloj.

He broke his watch. (little used, could imply deliberate action)

Se le rompió el reloj.

He broke his watch. (the watch broke itself on him—standard pattern)

Se me cayó la taza de las manos.

I dropped the cup.

Sus guantes, señor Marín...
Los **dejaba olvidados**. (FP)

Mr. Marín, your gloves. You have forgotten them.

Por más que quería **olvidarse de** la tragedia, no podía.

No matter how much he wanted to forget the tragedy, he couldn't.

Voy a apuntarla antes de que **se me olvide**. (CBA)

I am going to jot it down before I forget it.

Se nos olvidó decirte que Juan estaba preguntando por ti.

We forgot to tell you that John was asking about you.

No lo **olvides** esta vez.

Don't forget it this time.

10. el reposo—rest
    el descanso—rest
    reposar—to rest (usually suggests to lie down or to take a nap)
    sestear; dormir (echar) la (una) siesta—to take a nap; to rest
    apoyar—to rest; to lean on

Siempre **descanso** un rato después de mi primera clase.

I always rest awhile after my first class.

Mientras leía, **apoyaba** el brazo en la mesa.

While he was reading, he rested his arm on the table.

11. saber—to taste; to have a taste
    el sabor—taste, flavor
    saborear—to savor
    probar—to taste; to try
    el gusto—flavor, taste

Esta sopa me **sabe** igual.

This soup tastes the same to me.

El plato **sabe a** cebolla.

The dish tastes of (like) onion.

El gastrónomo **saboreaba** las primeras fresas de la primavera.

The gourmet savored the first strawberries of the spring.

Después de **probar** la sopa, el cocinero decidió que estaba sosa.

After tasting the soup, the cook decided that it needed salt.

Para el enfermo toda comida pierde el **sabor**.

For the sick person, all food loses its taste.

12. anochecer—to grow dark
amanecer—to dawn
atardecer—to draw toward evening
el anochecer—nightfall, dusk
el amanecer—dawn, daybreak
el atardecer—(late) afternoon

Whereas English uses verbs indicating natural phenomena in the third person singular, Spanish also employs a number of these verbs in a personal way. There are no exact English translations, but when they are used personally the above verbs convey the general idea of arriving at or being in a particular place or condition at approximately the same time the phenomenon in question occurs. At times context requires that another verb be supplied in the English translation. As is typical of many words in Spanish, the infinitives are also the standard nouns for these phenomena.

El reo **amaneció** ahorcado en su celda.	The prisoner was found hanged (literally, dawned hanged) in his cell.
Anochecimos pobres y **amanecimos** muy ricos.	We went to bed poor and woke up rich (literally, at dusk we were poor and at dawn, rich).
Mira, Platero: el canario de los niños **ha amanecido** hoy muerto en su jaula de plata. (PY)	Look, Platero: the children's canary was found (literally, woke up) dead this morning in his silver cage.
Estaba lloviendo cuando **atardecimos** en Málaga.	It was raining when we arrived in Malaga in the late afternoon.
Me acosté una noche escritor de folletos y **amanecí** periodista.	I went to bed one night a writer of pamphlets and got up a journalist.
El frescor del **anochecer** penetraba en el cuarto.	The coolness of evening (nightfall) came into the room.
Beatriz murió al **amanecer** del tercer día . . . (HM)	Beatrice died at dawn on the third day . . .

13. cotidiano—daily
diario—daily

Cotidiano has a somewhat more literary flavor than **diario**.

Lleva años asistiendo a una misa **diaria**.	For years he has been attending daily mass.

14. gratis—free, gratis
gratuito—free, gratis; gratuitous
libre—free (unrestricted)

Strictly speaking, **gratis** is an adverb and **gratuito** an adjective, but the former is also frequently used as an adjective and is much more common than **gratuito**.

El libro es **gratis**.	The book is free.
En diciembre el banco siempre da calendarios **gratis** a sus clientes.	In December the bank always gives calendars free to its clients.
La beca le garantiza una educación **gratuita**.	The scholarship guarantees her a free education.
Estás **libre** para hacer lo que quieras.	You are free to do what you want.

15. el sendero—(foot)path
    la senda—(foot)path; road
    el camino—road; path
    la vereda—path
    la vía—track; way

Sendero ordinarily indicates a specific or established path for walking. **Senda** may (but does not usually) have this meaning, but it generally indicates a more figurative type of path (**la senda de la vida**—*the path of life*) and is virtually synonymous with **camino**. It may mean **sendero**, but when it refers to a specific path, it often indicates a less well-established, a more obscure path or trail. **Vereda**, a narrow path most often found in the country, is formed by the continual passing of people or animals. Regional and literary usage tends not to differentiate among these three words in any systematic or regular fashion.

Durante las horas de clase, los **senderos** del campo universitario están desiertos.	During class hours, the campus paths are deserted.
El guía era el único que conocía la **senda** que atravesaba el bosque.	The guide was the only one who knew the path that went through the forest.
En el prado hay una **vereda** donde pasa el ganado al ir a beber al río.	In the meadow there is a path where the cattle pass on their way to drink at the river.

16. el forastero—stranger, outsider
    el extranjero—foreigner
    en el (al) extranjero—abroad

Había vivido tanto tiempo **en el extranjero** que se sentía como un **forastero** en su propia ciudad.	He had lived abroad such a long time that he felt like a stranger in his own city.

17. trasladarse a—to go (down) to

18. romper—to break; to tear
romper a + infinitive—to burst out; to start + gerund
romper con—to break with
quebrar—to break (into small pieces); to go bankrupt; to fail
quebradizo—fragile, breakable
quebrantar—to break (an agreement, a law, etc.); to smash
hablar un inglés chapurreado—to speak broken English

Romper now renders almost all nuances of *to break*, whether physical or figurative in nature. **Quebrar** may be used to emphasize the breaking of something into many pieces, and **quebrantar** to signify either a figurative breaking or the violence of a physical action. Even in these cases, however, **romper** is more common. Literary usage reveals greater variance than spoken Spanish.

Media docena de niñas **rompieron a** hablar al mismo tiempo. (F)	A half dozen girls began to talk at the same time.
Ha quebrado el Banco Español del Río de la Plata. (HM)	The Spanish Bank of the River Plate has failed.
Yo no hablaba nada, por temor a que algo precioso **se quebrase.** (LE)	I didn't talk at all, for fear that something precious might break.
Rompió la carta en mil pedazos.	He tore the letter into a thousand pieces.
Su salud está **quebrantada.**	His health is ruined (broken).
Tenía miedo de **romper** el silencio que reinaba en la casa.	He was afraid to break the silence that reigned in the house.
Después de ocho años en Nueva York, seguía **hablando un inglés chapurreado.**	After eight years in New York, he still spoke broken English.

19. quilómetro—variant spelling of kilómetro

20. saludable—healthful; wholesome
sano—healthy; healthful

At times **sano** is used to indicate *health-producing* or *enjoying good health*.

El clima de Arizona es muy **sano.**	The climate of Arizona is very healthful.
El clima de Arizona es **saludable** para los asmáticos.	The climate of Arizona is healthful for asthmatics.
Siempre ha estado muy **sano.**	He had always been very healthy.

21. ¡allá que sus hijos se las compusieran!—let his children take care of it!

22. las cotizaciones—the (stock) market (literally, the quotations)

23. tropezar con (contra, en)—to run or bump into; run across; to stumble
   against, upon
   topar con—to run into (across)
   encontrarse con—to meet; to encounter; to run into (across)

   Encontrarse con is the standard expression to indicate a chance meeting
   or encounter, and it thus renders *to run (bump) into* or *across*, as well
   as *to meet*. In addition to a chance meeting, it may also indicate a
   planned meeting or rendezvous. Both **topar(se) con** and **tropezar(se)**
   con are much less common than **encontrarse con**. **Topar** is used only
   for people, **tropezar** for people or things. Both stress the idea of
   actual physical contact more than **encontrarse**.

El ciego siempre **tropezaba con** los muebles en la sala.	The blind man was always bumping into the furniture in the living room.
En el zaguán, el viajero **se topa** con Martín . . . (VA)	In the entry, the traveler runs (bumps) into Martin . . .
Hoy **me he encontrado con** Pedro en la estación.	I ran into (met) Peter in the station today.

24. disgustar—to displease; to upset; to annoy
   el disgusto—unpleasantness; trouble
   disgustarse con—to fall out with; to become displeased (annoyed) with
   el asco—disgust
   asqueroso—disgusting
   dar asco—to disgust

Esta vida no trae más que **disgustos** . . . (LC)	This life brings nothing but troubles . . .
Estoy **disgustado** con él por lo de ayer.	I am annoyed with him because of what happened yesterday.
Lo que están comiendo me **da asco**.	What they are eating disgusts me.

25. fue a afeitarse—reflexive verb with causative meaning (see Chap. 11, 53)

26. atrasado—back (issue); backward (country, economy)
   retrasado—backward; retarded (child)
   atrasar, retrasar—to delay, retard
   con retraso—late, behind schedule
   adelantar—to be fast (said of a clock or watch); to gain

Anunciaron que el avión llevaba (llegaría **con**) media hora de **retraso**.	They announced that the plane was (would arrive) half an hour late.

Todos los días se me **atrasa** el reloj cinco minutos.	My watch loses five minutes every day.
El reloj de la torre **adelanta** diez minutos cada semana.	The tower clock gains ten minutes each week.

EXERCISES ON NOTES

1. Every morning she gets up (*not* **levantarse**) with a bad headache. 2. The student forgot to bring his textbook to class. 3. In Spain children receive their Christmas gifts on the sixth of January. 4. The new ice-cream parlor has twenty flavors of ice cream. 5. The World Bank is helping backward countries to develop new industries. 6. She broke off with her boy friend after the dance. 7. He waited for it to dawn before getting up. 8. The children were playing a game of checkers. 9. The doctor prescribed another potion and left. 10. What we heard yesterday turned out to be an idle rumor. 11. The Dutch have a gift for languages. 12. We have come to this place to enjoy the country. 13. These municipal bonds yield 5 per cent a year. 14. Milk is a wholesome drink. 15. A disgusting smell came from the factory. 16. We were in Los Angeles at dusk and in Madrid at dawn. 17. It was stupid for the friends to have a falling out over such an insignificant matter. 18. The child broke the only jar his mother had. 19. The sandy paths of the botanical garden were covered with fallen leaves. 20. He hasn't been healthy since before the war. 21. Every summer they rent a cabin in the mountains. 22. The child rested his head on his mother's shoulder. 23. On seeing me, they burst out laughing. 24. The train was delayed until the men finished working on the tracks. 25. This sherry has a very delicate taste. 26. We knew he was a stranger when he asked us to direct him to the city hall. 27. I ran into an old friend at the airport. 28. During the war a piece of stale bread tasted better to me than a lamb chop [does] today. 29. We would have missed the train if it hadn't arrived twenty minutes late. 30. On reaching the church, the woman discovered she had forgotten her rosary. 31. For years the writers have held their daily gathering in the same cafe. 32. The father wanted his son to enjoy many advantages that he had never had. 33. What is the gadget good for? (*Use* **servir**.) 34. When they irrigate these fields, they will yield three times as much. 35. What he just said disgusts me. 36. The price of coal went up, and the company went bankrupt. 37. One of the goals of every democracy should be a free education for all. 38. Although she followed the recipe carefully, the dish did not turn out well. 39. It is the best gift I have ever received. 40. Millions of Frenchmen enjoyed their vacations under the Spanish sun.

CUESTIONARIO

a. contenido

1. ¿Qué le había prescrito el médico?
2. ¿Cómo afectaba esta nueva vida al matrimonio?

3. ¿En qué consistía su nueva felicidad?
4. ¿A dónde solían ir al atardecer? ¿Por qué?
5. ¿Qué sintieron los dos esposos al ver al forastero?
6. ¿Qué vieja costumbre había decidido él no romper?
7. ¿Qué padecía? ¿Por qué se había convertido en un hombre nuevo en veinte días?
8. ¿Con quién volvió a tropezar en el pueblo? ¿Cómo sabía que no era del pueblo?

b. estilo

1. ¿Cómo nos indica el autor el estado económico del matrimonio?
2. ¿Cómo nos convence de la nueva felicidad del matrimonio?
3. ¿Cómo nos hace Romero compartir la nueva sensibilidad de los dos esposos a la naturaleza?
4. ¿Cómo se establece una nota de misterio en el cuento?
5. ¿De qué manera se subraya lo absurdo de la vida del marido?
6. ¿Cómo contribuye el último párrafo a revelarnos el efecto desquiciador del forastero sobre el esposo?

TEMA—TRADUCCION

Since the doctor had prescribed several months of rest for him, the couple rented a chalet by the sea. The doctor's orders proved wise, for he was soon enjoying better health than ever. After years of a superficial life together, the walks by the shore and the siestas under the pines had enabled husband and wife to rediscover each other.

He found that he did not miss the afternoon gatherings at the rich men's club, nor did his wife miss having tea with her conceited friends. It was like a new honeymoon in which they enjoyed together the little things of life: air, waves, roses, bread, bells. Everything had taken on a new meaning and a new delight, and they were grateful to God for having created so many marvelous things. In the late afternoon they would watch the sun set. But one day a tall, thin stranger passed [by] and ruined the feeling of perfect peace to which they had become accustomed.

Not wanting to break his habit of reading the daily paper, he did not mind walking two kilometers to get it. And besides, the morning walk was good exercise. The doctor had been right in ordering him to rest, for twenty days without a long-distance call, without a meeting, without worrying about the stock-market quotations had done wonders for him.

But then he ran across the unpleasant stranger on a side street, and the encounter upset him so much that he was unable to concentrate on his newspaper. Even though he had not planned to do it, he went to the barber shop for a shave, and at the opportune moment asked about the stranger. Neither the barber, nor his helper, nor the other customers knew him.

TEMAS A ESCOGER

Escríbanse unas 200 palabras sobre uno de los temas siguientes usando a lo menos 20 de las palabras y expresiones estudiadas en este capítulo.

1. Los verdaderos placeres de la vida
2. La artificialidad de la vida moderna
3. Las fuerzas recuperadoras de la naturaleza

chapter 18

91. SELECCION LITERARIA*

El forastero*

Luis Romero

No dijo nada a su mujer y disimuló cuanto pudo. Comieron, sestearon en las hamacas, bajo los pinos, y él fingió que dormía para no tener que charlar. Con gran esfuerzo se mostró cariñoso y ocurrente durante el largo paseo de la tarde, y otra vez en las rocas se deleitaron con los rojos encen-
5 didos, los azules vagos, los verdes malva y los blancos grisáceos con que el Creador les obsequiaba por haber regresado a su inocencia. Por la noche notó como su esposa se dormía feliz, agradecida, confiada;[1] sin modistas, sin tacones altos, sin vanos coqueteos, sin faja,[2] sin hablar mal de nadie.

El se sentía incómodo y desvelado. Notaba un pinchazo[3] terco en las
10 sienes, un pinchazo que había resistido, sin disminuir, las dos aspirinas que clandestinamente se había tomado. De su cuerpo se desprendía una humedad siniestra que no era sudor, sino algo viscoso, irremediable. A cada instante colocaba la yema del pulgar[4] sobre la muñeca[5] y contaba las pulsaciones: una, dos, tres . . . , cincuenta . . . , cien . . . . A veces le parecía que el ritmo
15 era aceleradísimo; otras, que la lentitud amenazaba con paralizar el curso de la sangre. Y todo esto, quieto, silencioso, con un enorme y sostenido esfuerzo para que su mujer, allí junto a él, no se enterara de lo que le estaba suce-diendo. En un momento determinado sintió la necesidad de asomarse a la ventana; comprendió que era inútil disimular, ignorar, engañarse; había
20 que dar la cara,[6] averiguar, ver. La luna se había ocultado tras unas nubes, pero su claridad iluminaba el paisaje. Junto a la verja del jardín pasaba el camino entre los árboles. Más allá, la playa; y al fondo, muy confusos, pero ciertos, empezaban los acantilados.

Antes que ver, oyó. Oyó unos pasos acompasados, no fuertes, pero sí
25 seguros, que se iban aproximando. A pesar de la oscuridad, le distinguió perfectamente. Era el forastero, desgarbado, triste, ausente, que venía por el camino. Aterrorizado, estuvo a punto de[7] gritar, de llamar a su esposa, de correr a buscar a los guardias,[8] a un médico, a un exorcista, a alguien que le ayudara en aquella cuita, en aquel peligro, en aquella angustia.
30 No hizo más que contemplarle tristemente y contener la respiración. El forastero pasó de largo y solamente miró de reojo; luego, su silueta y el ruido de sus pasos se perdieron en dirección a los acantilados.

---

*Continuation of the selection in Chap. 17.

Se volvió a la cama—¿qué otra cosa podía hacer?—y consultó el reloj. Eran las cinco de la mañana. Una luminosidad vaga empezaba a clarear en las nubes.

Fue a buscar[9] el periódico como el día anterior, como todos los días; saludó al lechero, que estaba a la puerta de su establecimiento, compró cerillas, y luego, lentamente, paseando, regresó a su casa. Fue con su mujer a la playa y hablaron, como siempre, de mil cosas tiernamente triviales. Hicieron proyectos de comprar el chalet que habían alquilado o construir otro en el mismo paraje;[10] hablaron de los hijos y de la novia de uno de ellos; recordaron cosas del pasado que habían estado enmohecidas muchos años en cualquier rincón de la indiferencia. Comieron con buen apetito y comentaron[11] lo sabroso de los alimentos, lo dulce de las frutas, lo exquisito del café. El se sentó, de sobremesa,[12] en el sillón de mimbre, a fumar el cigarro que constituía su cupo cotidiano de tabaco.

La mujer, aquella tarde, debía de ir al pueblo para que el peluquero la renovase el hermoso rubio del cabello. Al despedirse le besó en la frente, y él la contempló, mientras se dirigía[13] hacia el camino, esbelta, ágil, joven, como si no tuviera hijos de más de veinticinco años. Y vio, mientras una extraña ternura le acongojaba, que estaba hermosa con el color sano que el sol la regalaba. Por un momento deseó correr hacia ella, abrazarla y besarla, y decirle muchas cosas que hacía años y años no le decía; y decirle algo más, algo que ya no podría decirle nunca. Pero no se movió del sillón y siguió adormeciéndose voluptuosamente con el humo del habano.

Pensó que debía escribir, que convenía tomar medidas, dictar órdenes,[14] arreglar asuntos, prever situaciones. No hizo nada, y al terminar el cigarro entró en el vestíbulo y se sentó a esperar.

Vio como el forastero cruzaba el jardín y se detenía en el umbral; entonces se levantó y se acercó a él. Era inútil huir ni disimular. La voz del forastero era desagradable y ácida, y su amabilidad sonaba a falso: «¿Es usted Don Fulano . . . ?» Se saludaron cortésmente. Debajo de un cobertizo estaba el coche; él se puso una chaqueta de verano y la corbata. Por última vez tuvo la tentación de dejar unas letras,[15] por lo menos a su esposa, como recompensa por los veintiún días felices con que le había obsequiado. Estaba algo deprimido,[16] aunque conseguía disimularlo. «¿Por qué no conduce[17] usted mismo?» le dijo al forastero. Pero el hombre se negó. Hasta el final todo tenía que aparecer correcto, normal. Arrancó[18] el coche, y él contempló por última vez el chalet donde quedaba su efímera felicidad. Tras una corta vacilación, tomó el ramal de carretera que bordeaba los acantilados por su nivel más alto. El hombre iba sentado a su lado; había encendido un cigarrillo y ahora le ofrecía otro. «No, gracias; lo tengo prohibido por el médico. Hoy ya he fumado mi ración.» El forastero sacó del bolsillo un antiguo[19] reloj. Eran las cinco menos cinco minutos. Con su falsa voz amable, le dijo insinuante: «Tenemos un poco de prisa, caballero;

faltan cinco minutos solamente.» Apretó el acelerador y contempló el mar, tan brillante, tan azul, tan dilatado.

92. NOTES

1. confiado—trusting, unsuspecting
    confiar en—to trust (in), confide (in); to rely on
    fiarse de—to trust
    porfiar—to persist; to insist
    desafiar—to challenge; to defy

Confío en que no nos pondrá en ridículo.	I trust he won't make us look ridiculous.
No debemos **fiarnos de** sus notas, que muchas veces están equivocadas.	We shouldn't trust his notes, for they are often wrong.
No **me fío de** tus entusiasmos.	I don't trust your enthusiasm.
Porfió hasta conseguir el puesto.	He persisted until he obtained the position.
No debes **porfiar** tanto.	You shouldn't insist so much.
Le **desafío** a un partido de tenis.	I challenge you to a game of tennis.
El estudiante **desafió** al profesor.	The student defied the professor.

2. la faja—girdle, sash; strip (of land)

Han comprado la **faja** de tierra que se extiende hasta el parque.	They have bought the strip of land that stretches as far as the park.

3. el pinchazo—pain; puncture; flat tire
    pinchar—to puncture; to prick
    no pincha ni corta—he carries no weight, has no influence
    pellizcar, dar un pellizco—to pinch (with the fingers)
    apretar—to pinch (said of shoes)
    en un aprieto—in a pinch, in a tight spot
    pizcar—colloquial form of pellizcar
    una pizca de sal—a pinch of salt

El niño **pinchó** el globo con un alfiler.	The child punctured (burst) the balloon with a pin.
Se **pellizcó** para ver si estaba soñando.	He pinched himself to see if he were dreaming.
Los zapatos le **apretaban**, pero los compró de todos modos.	The shoes pinched, but she bought them anyway.

4. el (dedo) pulgar—thumb
   el (dedo) meñique—little finger
   el (dedo) índice—index finger
   la uña—fingernail
   el dedo del pie—toe

Al hablar, se metió la **uña** del **pulgar** entre los dientes.	As he spoke, he stuck his thumbnail between his teeth.
Lucía una sortija de oro en el **meñique**.	She was wearing a gold ring on her little finger.
Padecía un dolor agudísimo en el **dedo** gordo **del pie**.	He suffered a very sharp pain in his big toe.

5. la muñeca—wrist; doll
   el muñeco—manikin; puppet

La niña pasaba la mañana vistiendo y desnudando su nueva **muñeca**.	The little girl spent the morning dressing and undressing her new doll.

6. dar la cara—to face (take) the consequences
   arrostrar (con)—to resist; to face
   afrontar—to confront; to face
   encararse con—to stand up to; to face

   The above verbal expressions all convey the basic idea of *to face*: **cara**, **rostro**, **frente**, etc., is patent in each of them.

Hay que **arrostrar** la muerte para acabar con la tiranía.	We must face death in order to put an end to tyranny.
—Ande, compóngase, muchacho. Son desgracias. Hay que **arrostrar** con ellas. (EJ)	"Come on, take hold of yourself. They are misfortunes. You have to face them."
Carecía de la firmeza que necesitaba para **afrontar** la adversidad.	He lacked the firmness he needed to face adversity.

7. estar a punto de + infinitive—to be about + infinitive (more common than estar para + infinitive)
   estar para + infinitive—to be about + infinitive
   estar por + infinitive—to be in favor of + gerund

El senador **está a punto de** comenzar su discurso.	The senator is about to begin his speech.
Estaba para salir.	I was about to leave.

8. los guardias (el guardia)—the guards (here, members of the Civil Guard)
   la guardia—the guard (body of armed men)
   el guarda—guard (ordinarily not armed), custodian, guide
   el ángel de la guarda—guardian angel

el guardián—guardian
guardar—to guard; to keep
guardarse de + infinitive—to guard against + present participle

Tan pronto como ocurrió el accidente, aparecieron dos **guardias** civiles.	As soon as the accident occurred, two members of the Civil Guard appeared.
El **guarda** le dijo al chico que no tocara el cuadro.	The guard told the child not to touch the painting.
Todos los días el **guardián** del monasterio daba de comer a los pobres.	Every day the guardian of the monastery would feed the poor.

9. ir a buscar—to go get
ir por—to go get; to go for (colloquial)
ir a recoger—to go get; to go pick up

Fue a buscar el traje a la tintorería.	He went to get the suit at the dry cleaner's.
Fueron por (a buscar, comprar) el diario.	They went for (to get, to buy) the paper.
Vendrá por (a recogernos) nosotros a las cinco.	He will come for us (to pick us up) at five o'clock.

10. el paraje—place, spot
el local—place
el lugar, el sitio—place

Sitio and **lugar** are appropriate for *place* used in almost any context. **Paraje** (often used in the plural with a singular meaning) very often connotes a *secluded*, *deserted*, or *remote location*. **Local** usually indicates someplace indoors, most often the premises of a business establishment.

La gente acudía los sábados a los **parajes** hermosos. (SH)	The people would go to the lovely places on Saturdays.
El sastre ha tenido mucho éxito en su nuevo **local**.	The tailor has been very successful in his new place.
Lo mismo da un **sitio** que otro.	One place is as good as another.
Es muy ordenado y quiere poner cada cosa en su **lugar**.	He is very orderly and wants to put everything in its (proper) place.

11. comentar—to comment (on)

Comentar is one of a group of Spanish verbs which often take a preposition when rendered in English, but which have no preposition in Spanish, except for the personal **a** in appropriate cases:

llorar—to cry (over)
buscar—to look for

mirar—to look (at)
solicitar—to apply (for)
agradecer—to be grateful (for)
pagar—to pay (for)
compensar—to compensate (for)
pisar—to step on

Nadie **comentó** la idea. (SH)	No one commented on his idea.
Agradezco su hospitalidad.	I am grateful for your hospitality.
Solicitó la beca.	He applied for the scholarship.
Miraba a la muchacha que iba calle abajo.	He was looking at the girl who was going down the street.
. . . **lloraron** en común la muerte de la ilusión. (HA)	. . . together they wept over the death of their illusion.

12. de sobremesa—after the meal, after lunch

De sobremesa refers to the custom of remaining (often at the table) to talk after the completion of a meal.

Estaban **de sobremesa** hablando con su invitado.	They remained at the table talking with their guest.

13. dirigirse hacia (a)—to go, make one's way (toward)
dirigirse a—to address oneself to
dirigir—to direct

Al llegar a Madrid, **me dirigí a** casa de mi primo.	On arriving in Madrid, I headed straight for my cousin's house.
Si tiene alguna pregunta, **diríjase** al gerente.	If you have a question, address yourself to the manager.
Después del partido, varios policías **dirigían** el tráfico cerca del estadio.	After the game, several policemen were directing traffic near the stadium.

14. **Orden** is both masculine and feminine in Spanish. When it means *arrangement*, it is masculine. The feminine form refers to a *command* or an *established religious community*.

Estudiamos los autores en **orden** cronológico.	We are studying the authors in chronological order.
Ha cambiado algo el **orden** de los acontecimientos.	He has changed somewhat the order of the events.
—Al menos tenemos paz, **orden** público—repuso don Paco. (F)	"At least we have peace and public order," replied Don Paco.
Daba una **orden** tras otra.	He gave one order after another.
¿A qué **orden** pertenece?	To which order does he belong?

15. unas letras—a few lines
la letra—letter (of the alphabet); lyrics, words (of a song); handwriting
las primeras letras—elementary education, the three R's
al pie de la letra—literally

Esta **letra** es ilegible.	This (hand)writing is illegible.
La música de la zarzuela es superior a la **letra**.	The music of the zarzuela is better than the words.
Aprendió **las primeras letras** en este colegio.	He learned his three R's in this school.

16. deprimido—depressed
abatido—downcast, depressed
desanimado—discouraged

Estoy muy **deprimido** desde que tuve la carta.	I have been very depressed since I received the letter.
La enfermedad le dejó **abatido**.	The illness left him dejected.

17. conducir, guiar—to drive (a vehicle)
manejar—to handle (used instead of conducir in most of Spanish America)
dar un paseo (en coche)—to take a drive
llevar—to take, drive someone (somewhere)

No aprendió a **conducir** hasta los cincuenta años.	He didn't learn to drive until he was fifty.
Los domingos solemos **dar un paseo** en coche al campo.	On Sundays we are accustomed to taking a drive to the country.
Ofreció **llevarme** al aeropuerto.	He offered to drive (take) me to the airport.

18. arrancar—to start (up)
poner(se) en marcha—to start

A ver si **arranca** el coche esta vez.	Let's see if the car starts this time.
Llamó al mecánico porque no podía **poner en marcha** el motor.	He called the mechanic because he couldn't start the motor.

19. antiguo—old, ancient; former (when it precedes the noun)
la tienda de antigüedades—antique shop
anciano—old
viejo—old
vetusto—(very) old
rancio—rancid; old

Viejo may be applied to any situation requiring *old*. **Antiguo** is most common for *old* in the sense of *ancient* or *storied*. **Anciano** is used only for people and connotes *venerable,* thus indicating special respect on the part of the speaker. **Vetusto** is literary and suggests *decaying* or *crumbling.* **Rancio** with reference to wine may be a term of great praise. It is commonly employed as *old* to indicate things related to tradition, customs, ancestry, etc.

Visitamos las **antiguas** ciudades de la Tierra Santa.	We visited the ancient cities of the Holy Land.
El juez es un hombre **anciano** que tiene una barba blanca.	The judge is a venerable old man who has a white beard.
Santiago de Compostela tiene algunos edificios **vetustos**.	Santiago de Compostela has some old (crumbling) buildings.
Es una familia de **rancia** estirpe.	It is a family from an old line.
Quiere suprimir ciertas **rancias** costumbres que datan del siglo xv.	He wants to abolish certain old customs dating from the fifteenth century.
Este tocino está **rancio**.	This bacon is rancid.

EXERCISES ON NOTES

1. She pricked her finger while picking roses. 2. I won't confide the family secrets to a woman who likes to gossip. 3. Everyone was surprised when he stood up to the boss. 4. This sauce needs a pinch of pepper. 5. I don't know why, but I have been very depressed lately. 6. They had to renovate the place before opening the store. 7. The letter was (**iba**) addressed to the ambassador. 8. He took everything I said literally. 9. When it's cold, it's hard (*use* **costar**) for me to start the station wagon. 10. Few composers write the lyrics for their own music. 11. I don't trust what he says. 12. The boy yelled when his brother pinched him. 13. Our situation is difficult, but we are going to face it with dignity. 14. He always went around with his thumbs in his vest pockets. 15. He stepped on a piece of glass and cut his big toe. 16. Don Quixote challenged the Knight of the Forest to battle. 17. She sprained her wrist when she fell. 18. The bell is about to ring. 19. With his index finger, he pointed out on the map the road we were to take. 20. Guard yourself against false friends. 21. To prepare the index, put the cards in alphabetical order. 22. The teacher helped the child to improve his handwriting. 23. He was so discouraged that he gave up his studies. 24. Can you direct me to the Administration Building? 25. No one disobeyed the sergeant's orders. 26. The mother asked her son to go get bread. 27. My cousin is afraid to drive in heavy traffic. 28. No one knew which was the last place the student visited before he disappeared. 29. It was so hot that they decided to take a drive to the beach. 30. Drop me a few lines when you get to Lima. 31. Every two hours they change the guard in front of the Presidential Palace. 32. The child was crying over the loss of his bicycle. 33. One should have experience before driving on the freeway. 34. They always camped in some place in the mountains. 35. It was about to rain when we left the house. 36. The crew defied the

captain. 37. Despite many obstacles, the owner persisted until he was successful with his restaurant. 38. There was no one to whom she could confide her personal problems. 39. If you are in a tight spot, John will lend you fifty dollars. 40. They went to get more paint for the kitchen.

CUESTIONARIO

a. contenido

1. ¿Cómo se sentía aquella noche? ¿Qué síntomas notaba?
2. ¿Qué temía en cuanto a su mujer?
3. ¿Qué vio el hombre desde la ventana?
4. ¿Qué oyó que le aterrorizó?
5. ¿Cómo pasó el hombre el día siguiente?
6. ¿Por qué quiso correr tras su esposa?
7. ¿Por qué quería dejar unas letras para ella?
8. ¿A qué hora partió con el forastero?
9. ¿Por qué no aceptó el cigarrillo que le ofreció el forastero?
10. ¿A dónde se dirigieron? ¿Quién era el forastero?

b. estilo

1. ¿Qué efecto produce el uso de tantos colores en el primer párrafo?
2. ¿Cómo emplea el autor los adjetivos para captar la felicidad de la esposa mientras duerme?
3. ¿Qué sentido(s) subraya Romero en las dos frases: «A cada instante ... » y «A veces le parecía ... »? ¿Qué efecto le producen a Vd. estas frases?
4. Comente Vd. la estructura de la frase «comprendió que era inútil .... »
5. ¿Cómo consigue el autor crear un ambiente apropiado para la aparición del forastero?
6. Comente Vd. el retrato físico del forastero comparado con las impresiones que produce en el hombre.
7. El autor menciona **las cinco** dos veces. ¿Cómo emplea esta hora para lograr ciertos efectos estructurales y temáticos?

TEMA—TRADUCCION

In order not to worry his wife, he concealed from her what (*use* **lo de**) had happened in town. During their walk that afternoon he was affectionate and witty, and they took delight in the marvelous colors of the sunset with which the Creator regaled them.

That night, while his wife slept peacefully, he felt a constant pain in his temples. One moment the rhythm of his pulse was very fast, the next so slow it almost seemed to stop. Something was happening. He had to face it; it was impossible to pretend any longer. Quietly, and without waking his wife, he went to the window and looked out. The light of the moon revealed the countryside. And in the background, barely perceptible, were the cliffs.

He heard steps approaching, and then he made out the stranger. He was about to call his wife, to go get the police, the doctor, or anyone who would help him. But all he could do was watch the stranger and hold his breath. The stranger passed by, and the noise of his steps soon disappeared in the direction of the cliffs. As he went back to bed, he noticed that it was five o'clock.

The next morning he went to town as usual for the paper. When he returned, he and his wife talked about their plans and their family. That afternoon she had to go to the hairdresser. He had wanted to run after her and tell her something she would now never know. But he had not moved from his chair. He realized he should put his affairs in order, yet did nothing. When the stranger appeared, he had a last temptation to leave his wife a few lines in return for the twenty-one wonderful days she had given him. But again he did nothing. The car started, and as they headed toward the highway that went along the cliffs, the stranger took an old watch from his pocket. "We must hurry," he said, "for there are only five minutes left." The driver depressed the accelerator and looked at the sea, so brilliant and so blue.

TEMAS A ESCOGER

Escríbanse unas 200 palabras sobre uno de los temas siguientes usando a lo menos 20 de las palabras y expresiones estudiadas en este capítulo.

1. La capacidad del hombre para presentir lo futuro
2. La figura de la muerte en una determinada obra literaria
3. Descripción de una puesta del sol o de una noche de luna

Annotated Prose Passages from American and British Authors
for Translation into Spanish

appendix

The Immense Journey*

Loren Eiseley

Darwin saw clearly that the succession of life on this planet was not a formal pattern imposed from without, or moving exclusively in one direction. Whatever else life might be,[1] it was adjustable and not fixed. It worked its way through[2] difficult environments. It modified and then, if necessary, it modified again,[3] along roads which would never be retraced. Every creature alive is the product of a unique history. The statistical probability of its precise reduplication on another planet is so small as to be meaningless. Life, even cellular life, may exist out yonder in the dark. But high or low in nature, it will not wear the shape of man. That shape is the evolutionary product of a strange, long wandering[4] through the attics of the forest roof, and so great are the chances of failure, that nothing precisely and identically human is likely[5] ever to come that way again.

*   *   *   *   *

In a universe whose size[6] is beyond human imagining, where our world floats like a dust mote in the void of night, men have grown[7] inconceivably lonely. We scan the time scale and the mechanism of life itself for[8] portents and signs of the invisible. As the only thinking mammals on the planet— perhaps the only thinking animals in the entire sidereal universe—the burden of consciousness has grown heavy upon us.[9] We watch the stars, but the signs are uncertain. We uncover the bones of the past and seek for our origins. There is a path there, but it appears to wander. The vagaries of the road may have a meaning, however; it is thus we torture ourselves.

Copyright 1953 by Loren Eiseley. Reprinted from *The Immense Journey* by Loren Eiseley, by permission of Random House, Inc.

---

* *El inmenso viaje.*
.[1] **whatever else life might be:** sea lo que fuere.
[2] **worked its way through:** conseguir con esfuerzo pasar por.
[3] **modified again:** volver a + *infinitive.*
[4] **wandering:** errar.
[5] **nothing precisely and identically human is likely:** *Translate this as if it were* "it is not likely that."
[6] **size:** dimensiones.
[7] **have grown:** quedarse.
[8] **for:** buscando.
[9] **has grown heavy upon us:** llegar a pesar sobre nosotros.

Lights come and go[10] in the night sky. Men, troubled at last by the things they build, may toss in their sleep and dream bad dreams, or lie awake while the meteors whisper[11] greenly overhead. But nowhere in all space or on a thousand worlds will there be men to share our loneliness. There may be wisdom; there may be power; somewhere across space great instruments, handled by strange manipulative organs, may stare[12] vainly at our floating cloud wrack, their owners yearning as we yearn. Nevertheless, in the nature of life and in the principles of evolution we have had[13] our answer. Of men elsewhere, and beyond, there will be none forever.

---

[10] **come and go:** aparecer y desaparecer.
[11] **whisper:** murmurar.
[12] **stare:** contemplar.
[13] **we have had:** *Translate this as if it were* "we have found."

For Whom the Bell Tolls*

Ernest Hemingway

Robert Jordan's luck held very good[1] because he saw, just then, the cavalry ride out of the timber and cross the road. He watched them coming riding up[2] the slope. He saw the trooper who stopped by the gray horse[3] and shouted to the officer who rode over to[4] him. He watched them both looking down at[5] the gray horse. They recognized him of course. He and the rider had been missing[6] since the early morning of the day before.

Robert Jordan saw them there on the slope, close to him now, and below he saw the road and the bridge and the long lines[7] of vehicles below it. He was completely integrated[8] now and he took a good long look at everything. Then he looked up at[9] the sky. There were big white clouds in it. He touched the palm of his hand against the pine needles where he lay and he touched the bark of the pine trunk that he lay behind.

Then he rested as easily as he could with his two elbows in the pine needles and the muzzle of the submachine gun[10] resting against the trunk of the pine tree.

As the officer came trotting[11] now on the trail[12] of the horses of the band he would pass twenty yards below where Robert Jordan lay. At that distance there would be no problem.[13] The officer was Lieutenant Berrendo. He had come up from La Granja where they had been ordered up after the first report[14] of the attack on the lower post. They had ridden hard[15]

Reprinted with the permission of Charles Scribner's Sons and by Jonathan Cape, Ltd., London, from *For Whom the Bell Tolls* by Ernest Hemingway. Copyright 1940 Ernest Hemingway.

* *Por quién doblan las campanas.*
[1] **held very good**: continuar a este respecto.
[2] **coming riding up**: ascender.
[3] **gray horse**: tordillo.
[4] **rode over to**: acercarse a.
[5] **looking down at**: examinar.
[6] **had been missing**: *Use the imperfect indicative.*
[7] **lines**: hileras.
[8] **integrated**: alerta.
[9] **looked up at**: alzar la mirada a.
[10] **submachine gun**: fusil automático.
[11] **came trotting**: aproximarse al trote.
[12] **on the trail**: siguiendo las huellas.
[13] **there would be no problem**: *Translate this as if it were* "it would be impossible to miss."
[14] **report**: aviso.
[15] **had ridden hard**: venir galopando.

and had then had to swing back,[16] because the bridge had been blown, to cross the gorge high above and come through the timber. Their horses were wet[17] and blown and they had to be urged into the trot.[18]

Lieutenant Berrendo, watching the trail, came riding up, his thin face serious and grave. His submachine gun lay across his saddle in the crook of[19] his left arm. Robert Jordan lay behind the tree, holding onto himself[20] very carefully and delicately to keep his hands steady.[21] He was waiting until the officer reached the sunlit place where the first trees of the pine forest[22] joined the green slope of the meadow. He could feel his heart beating against the pine needle floor of the forest.

---

[16] **to swing back:** volver sobre sus pasos.

[17] **wet:** *Translate this as if it were* "sweaty."

[18] **to be urged into the trot:** *Translate this as if it were* "they had to spur them to trot."

[19] **in the crook of:** recostado en.

[20] **holding onto himself:** mantener el dominio sobre sí.

[21] **keep . . . steady:** mantener firmes.

[22] **pine forest:** *Use one word.*

The Old Man and the Sea[*]

Ernest Hemingway

"Good luck old man."

"Good luck," the old man said. He fitted the rope lashings of the oars onto the thole pins and, leaning forward against the thrust of the blades in the water, he began to row out[1] of the harbour in the dark. There were other boats from other beaches going[2] out to sea and the old man heard the dip and push[3] of their oars even though he could not see them now the moon was below the hills.[4]

Sometimes someone would speak in a boat. But most of the boats were silent except for the dip of the oars. They spread apart[5] after they were out of the mouth of the harbour and each one headed for the part of the ocean where he hoped to find fish. The old man knew he was going far out[6] and he left the smell of the land behind and rowed out into the clean early morning smell of the ocean. He saw the phosphorescence of the Gulf weed in the water as he rowed over the part of the ocean that the fishermen called the great well because there was a sudden deep of seven hundred fathoms where all sorts of fish congregated because of the swirl the current made against the steep walls of the floor of the ocean. Here there were concentrations of[7] shrimp and bait fish and sometimes schools of squid in the deepest holes and these rose close to the surface at night where all the wandering fish fed on them.

In the dark the old man could feel the morning coming[8] and as he rowed he heard the trembling sound[9] as flying fish left the water and the hissing

---

Reprinted with the permission of Charles Scribner's Sons and by Jonathan Cape, Ltd., London, from *The Old Man and the Sea* by Ernest Hemingway. Copyright 1952 Ernest Hemingway.

---

[*] *El viejo y el mar.*
[1] **row out:** salir remando.
[2] **there were other boats from other beaches going:** *Translate this as if it were* "other boats were going."
[3] **dip and push:** *Use infinitives as nouns.*
[4] **now the moon was below the hills:** *Translate this as if it were* "now that the hills were hiding the moon."
[5] **they spread apart:** *Translate this as if it were* "they separated."
[6] **far out:** *Omit* "out."
[7] **here there were concentrations of:** aquí se concentraban *or* aquí se encontraban concentrados.
[8] **coming:** *Use the infinitive.*
[9] **trembling sound:** el temblar.

that their stiff set wings[10] made as they soared away[11] in the darkness. He was very fond of flying fish as they were his principal[12] friends on the ocean. He was sorry for the birds, especially the small delicate dark terns that were always flying and looking and almost never finding, and he thought, the birds have a harder life than we do except for the robber[13] birds and the heavy strong ones. Why did they made birds so delicate and fine as those sea swallows when the ocean can be so cruel? She is kind and very beautiful. But she can be so cruel and it comes so suddenly and such birds that fly, dipping and hunting, with their small sad voices are made too delicately for the sea.[14]

He always thought of the sea as *la mar* which is what people call her in Spanish when they love her. Sometimes those who love her say bad things of her but they are always said as though she were a woman. Some of the younger fishermen, those who used buoys as floats for their lines[15] and had motorboats, bought when the shark livers had brought much money, spoke of her as *el mar* which is masculine. They spoke of her as a contestant or a place or even an enemy. But the old man always thought of[16] her as feminine and as something that gave or withheld[17] great favours, and if she did wild or wicked things it was because she could not help them. The moon affects her as it does a woman, he thought.

He was rowing steadily and it was no effort for him since he kept well within his speed and the surface of the ocean was flat except for the occasional swirls of the current. He was letting the current do a third of the work and as it started to be light he saw he was already further out than[18] he had hoped to be at this hour.

---

[10] **stiff set wings**: *Omit "set."*
[11] **soared away**: volar.
[12] **principal**: *Translate this as if it were* "best."
[13] **robber**: robador.
[14] **are made too delicately for the sea**: ser muy delicados para el mar.
[15] **lines**: sedales.
[16] **thought of**: considerar.
[17] **withheld**: retener.
[18] **than**: de lo que.

The Grapes of Wrath*

John Steinbeck

This little orchard will be part of a great holding[1] next year, for the debt will have choked[2] the owner.

This vineyard will belong to the bank. Only the great owners can survive, for they own the canneries too. And four pears peeled and cut in half,[3] cooked and canned, still cost fifteen cents. And the canned pears do not spoil.[4] They will last for years.[5]

The decay[6] spreads over the State, and the sweet smell is a great sorrow on the land. Men who can graft the trees and make the seed[7] fertile and big can find no way[8] to let the hungry people eat their produce. Men who have created new fruits in the world cannot create a system whereby their fruits may be eaten. And the failure hangs over the State like a great sorrow.

The works[9] of the roots of the vines, of the trees, must be destroyed to keep up the price, and this is the saddest, bitterest thing[10] of all. Carloads of oranges dumped on[11] the ground. The people came for miles[12] to take the fruit, but this could not be. How would they buy oranges at twenty cents a dozen if they could drive out and pick them up? And men with hoses squirt[13] kerosene[14] on the oranges, and they are angry at the crime, angry at the people who have come to take the fruit. A million people hungry, needing the fruit—and kerosene sprayed over the golden mountains.

And the smell of rot fills the country.

Burn[15] coffee for[16] fuel in the ships. Burn corn to keep warm, it makes

From *The Grapes of Wrath* by John Steinbeck. Copyright 1939, © 1967 by John Steinbeck. Reprinted by permission of The Viking Press, Inc.

* *Las uvas de la ira.*
[1] **holding:** terreno.
[2] **will have choked:** ahogar.
[3] **in half:** por la mitad.
[4] **spoil:** echarse a perder.
[5] **they will last for years:** *Omit* "for."
[6] **decay:** ruina.
[7] **seed:** *Use the plural.*
[8] **no way:** ningún modo de que + *subjunctive.*
[9] **works:** *Use the singular.*
[10] **saddest, bitterest thing:** *Do not use* "cosa."
[11] **dumped on:** arrojadas a.
[12] **came for miles:** recorrer millas.
[13] **squirt:** *Translate this as if it were* "sprinkle."
[14] **kerosene:** petróleo.
[15] **burn:** *Use the infinitive.*
[16] **for:** como.

a hot fire. Dump potatoes in the rivers and place guards along the banks to keep the hungry people from[17] fishing them out. Slaughter the pigs and bury them, and let[18] the putrescence drip down[19] into the earth.

There is a crime here that goes beyond denunciation.[20] There is a sorrow here that weeping cannot symbolize. There is a failure here that topples[21] all our success. The fertile earth, the straight tree rows, the sturdy trunks, and the ripe fruit. And children dying of pellagra must die because a profit cannot be taken from an orange. And coroners[22] must fill in the certificates —died of[23] malnutrition—because the food must rot, must be forced to rot.

The people come with nets to fish for potatoes in the river, and the guards hold them back; they come in rattling[24] cars to get the dumped oranges, but the kerosene is sprayed. And they stand still and watch the potatoes float by,[25] listen to the screaming pigs being killed in a ditch and covered with quicklime, watch the mountains of oranges slop down to[26] a putrefying ooze; and in the eyes of the people there is the failure; and in the eyes of the hungry there is a growing wrath. In the souls of the people the grapes of wrath are filling and growing heavy, growing heavy[27] for the vintage.

---

[17] **keep . . . from:** para que . . . no.
[18] **let:** que + *subjunctive.*
[19] **drip down:** penetrar hondo.
[20] **that goes beyond denunciation:** que no tiene nombre.
[21] **topples:** anular.
[22] **coroners:** médicos forenses.
[23] **of:** por.
[24] **rattling:** desvencijado.
[25] **watch the potatoes float by:** *Omit* "by."
[26] **slop down to:** derramarse convirtiéndose en.
[27] **growing heavy, growing heavy:** *Omit the second* "growing heavy."

The Red Pony*

John Steinbeck

A red pony colt[1] was looking at him out of the stall. Its tense ears were forward[2] and a light[3] of disobedience was in its eyes. Its coat was rough and thick as an airedale's fur and its mane was long and tangled. Jody's throat collapsed in on itself[4] and cut his breath short.

"He needs a good currying," his father said, "and if I ever hear of[5] you not feeding him or leaving his stall dirty, I'll sell him off[6] in a minute."[7]

Jody couldn't bear[8] to look at the pony's eyes any more. He gazed down at his hands for a moment, and he asked very shyly, "Mine?"[9] No one answered him. He put his hand out toward the pony. Its grey nose came close,[10] sniffing loudly, and then the lips drew back[11] and the strong teeth closed on Jody's fingers. The pony shook its head up and down and seemed to laugh with amusement. Jody regarded his bruised fingers. "Well," he said with pride—"Well, I guess he can bite all right." The two men laughed, somewhat in relief.[12] Carl Tiflin went out of the barn and walked up a sidehill to be by himself,[13] for he was embarrassed, but Billy Buck stayed. It was easier to talk to Billy Buck. Jody asked again—"Mine?"

Billy became professional in tone.[14] "Sure! That is, if[15] you look out for him and break him right. I'll show you how. He's just a colt. You can't ride him for some time."

Jody put out his bruised hand again, and this time the red pony let his

From *The Red Pony* by John Steinbeck. Copyright 1933, 1961 by John Steinbeck. Reprinted by permission of The Viking Press, Inc.

* *El pony colorado.*
[1] **red pony colt:** *Omit* "pony."
[2] **forward:** echadas hacia delante.
[3] **light:** relámpago.
[4] **collapsed in on itself:** agolpársele la respiración en la garganta.
[5] **hear of:** enterarse de.
[6] **sell him off:** *Omit* "off."
[7] **in a minute:** *Translate this as if it were* "immediately."
[8] **couldn't bear:** *Omit* "bear."
[9] **Mine?:** *Translate this as if it were* "Is it mine?"
[10] **came close:** acercar. (*Use as transitive verb.*)
[11] **drew back:** fruncir.
[12] **somewhat in relief:** algo aliviados.
[13] **by himself:** a solas.
[14] **became professional in tone:** *Translate this as if it were* "assumed a professional tone."
[15] **if:** *Translate this as if it were* "provided that."

nose be rubbed. "I ought to have a carrot," Jody said. "Where'd we get him, Billy?"

"Bought him at a sheriff's auction," Billy explained. "A show[16] went broke in Salinas and had debts. The sheriff was selling off[17] their stuff."

The pony stretched out his nose and shook the forelock from his wild eyes. Jody stroked the nose a little. He said softly, "There isn't a—— saddle?"

Billy Buck laughed. "I'd forgot. Come along."

In the harness room he lifted down a little saddle of red morocco leather. "It's just a show[18] saddle," Billy Buck said disparagingly. "It isn't practical for the brush, but it was cheap at the sale."

Jody couldn't trust himself to look at the saddle either, and he couldn't speak at all. He brushed[19] the shining red leather with his fingertips, and after a long time he said, "It'll look pretty on him though." He thought of the grandest and prettiest things he knew. "If he hasn't a name already, I think I'll call him Gabilan Mountains," he said.

Billy Buck knew how he felt.[20] "It's a pretty long name. Why don't you just[21] call him Gabilan? That means hawk. That would be a fine name for him." Billy felt glad. "If you will collect tail hair, I might be able to make a hair rope for you sometime. You could use it for a hackamore."

Jody wanted to go back to the box stall. "Could I lead him to school, do you think—to show the kids?"

But Billy shook his head.[22] "He's not even halter-broke yet. We had a time[23] getting him here. Had to almost drag him. You better be starting for[24] school though."

"I'll bring the kids to see him here this afternoon," Jody said.

---

[16] **show**: circo.
[17] **selling off**: *Omit* "off."
[18] **show**: para lucimiento.
[19] **brushed**: acariciar.
[20] **knew how he felt**: *Translate this as if it were* "understood his feelings."
[21] **just**: a secas.
[22] **shook his head**: indicar que no con la cabeza.
[23] **had a time**: costar trabajo.
[24] **better be starting for**: ya deber irse a.

Pride and Prejudice*

Jane Austen

Two days after Mr. Bennet's return, as Jane and Elizabeth were walking together in[1] the shrubbery behind the house, they saw the housekeeper coming towards them, and[2] concluding that she came to call them to[3] their mother, went forward to meet her; but instead of the expected summons,[4] when they approached her, she said to Miss Bennet, "I beg your pardon, madam,[5] for interrupting you, but I was in hopes[6] you might have got some good news from town, so I took the liberty of coming to ask."[7]

"What do you mean, Hill? We have heard nothing from town."

"Dear Madam," cried Mrs. Hill, in[8] great astonishment, "don't you know there is an express[9] come for master[10] from Mr. Gardiner? He has been here this half hour,[11] and master has had a letter."

Away ran the girls, too eager to get in to have time for speech. They ran through the vestibule into the breakfast room, from thence to the library—their father was in neither,[12] and they were on the point of seeking him upstairs with their mother, when they were met by the butler, who said,

"If you are looking for my master, ma'am, he is walking towards the little copse."

Upon this information,[13] they instantly passed through the hall once more, and ran across the lawn after their father, who was deliberately pursuing his way towards a small wood on one side of the paddock.

Jane, who was not so light, nor so much in the habit of running as Elizabeth, soon lagged behind,[14] while her sister, panting for breath,[15] came up with[16] him, and eagerly cried out,

---

* *Orgullo y prejuicio.*
[1] **in:** por.
[2] **coming towards them, and:** *Omit* "and," *and start a new sentence with* "concluding . . . ."
[3] **to:** de parte de.
[4] **summons:** llamada.
[5] **madam:** *Here,* señorita.
[6] **in hopes:** *Translate this as if it were* "hoping."
[7] **ask:** *Supply pronouns as necessary to complete the thought in Spanish.*
[8] **in:** con.
[9] **express:** propio.
[10] **for master:** para el amo.
[11] **has been here this half hour:** *Omit* "this."
[12] **in neither:** *Translate this as if it were* "in neither place."
[13] **upon this information:** al saberlo.
[14] **lagged behind:** quedarse atrás.
[15] **panting for breath:** jadeante.
[16] **came up with:** alcanzar.

"Oh, Papa, what news? what news? have you heard from[17] my uncle?"

"Yes, I have had a letter from him by express."

"Well, and what news does it bring? good or bad?"

"What is there of good to be expected?" said he, taking the letter from his pocket; "but perhaps you would like to read it."

Elizabeth impatiently caught it from his hand. Jane now came up.[18]

"Read it aloud," said their father, "for I hardly know myself what it is about."[19]

---

[17] **have heard from**: saber algo de.
[18] **came up**: *Translate this as if it were* "approached."
[19] **it is about**: tratarse de.

Wuthering Heights*

Emily Brontë

That Friday made[1] the last of our fine days for[2] a month. In the evening, the weather broke:[3] the wind shifted from south to northeast, and brought rain first, and then sleet and snow. On the morrow one could hardly imagine that there had been[4] three weeks of summer: the primroses and crocuses were hidden under wintry drifts;[5] the larks were silent, the young leaves of the early trees smitten and blackened. And dreary, and chill, and dismal, that morrow did creep over![6] My master kept[7] his room; I took possession of the lonely parlour, converting it into a nursery; and there I was, sitting with the moaning[8] doll of a child laid on my knee;[9] rocking it to and fro,[10] and watching, meanwhile, the still driving flakes build up[11] the uncurtained window, when the door opened, and some person entered, out of breath and laughing! My anger was greater than my astonishment for a minute. I supposed it[12] one of the maids, and I cried—"Have done![13] How dare you show your giddiness[14] here? What would Mr. Linton say if he heard you?"

"Excuse me!" answered a familiar voice; "but I know Edgar is in bed, and I cannot stop myself."

With that the speaker[15] came forward to the fire, panting and holding[16] her hand to her side.

"I have run the whole way from Wuthering Heights!" she continued, after a pause; "except where[17] I've flown. I couldn't count the number of falls I've had. Oh, I'm aching all over![18] Don't be alarmed! There shall be

---

* *Cumbres borrascosas.*
[1] **made:** ser.
[2] **for:** *Translate this as if it were* "during."
[3] **broke:** estropearse.
[4] **there had been:** *Use the subjunctive.*
[5] **wintry drifts:** *Translate this as if it were* "snow."
[6] **did creep over:** amanecer *or* aparecer.
[7] **kept:** *Translate this as if it were* "didn't come out of."
[8] **moaning:** quejumbrosa.
[9] **of a child laid on my knee:** *Omit* "laid."
[10] **rocking it to and fro:** *Omit* "to and fro."
[11] **build up:** *Translate this as if it were* "accumulate."
[12] **I supposed it:** *Translate this as if it were* "I supposed it to be."
[13] **have done!:** ¡Basta!
[14] **show your giddiness:** mostrarse tan tonta.
[15] **the speaker:** la que hablaba *or* la interlocutora.
[16] **holding:** *Translate this as if it were* "with."
[17] **where:** *Translate this as if it were* "when."
[18] **I'm aching all over:** *Translate this as if it were* "my whole body aches me."

an explanation as soon as I can give it; only just have the goodness to step out and order the carriage to take me on to Gimmerton, and tell a servant to seek up a few clothes in my wardrobe."

The intruder was Mrs. Heathcliff. She certainly seemed in no laughing predicament:[19] her hair streamed on her shoulders, dripping with snow and water; she was dressed in the girlish dress she commonly wore, befitting[20] her age more than her position: a low[21] frock with short sleeves, and nothing on either head or neck. The frock was of light silk, and clung to her[22] with wet,[23] and feet were protected merely by thin[24] slippers; add to this a deep cut under one ear, which only the cold prevented from bleeding profusely, a white[25] face scratched and bruised, and a frame hardly able to support[26] itself, through fatigue;[27] and you may fancy my first fright was not much allayed when I had had leisure[28] to examine her.

---

[19] **she certainly seemed in no laughing predicament:** *Translate this as if it were* "her difficult situation was not to be laughed at."

[20] **befitting:** más adecuado para *or* conforme más a.

[21] **low:** escotado.

[22] **clung to her:** pegársele.

[23] **with wet:** *Translate this as if it were* "because of the dampness."

[24] **thin:** *Translate this as if it were* "light."

[25] **white:** *Translate this as if it were* "pale."

[26] **support:** sostener.

[27] **through fatigue:** de pura fatiga *or* de puro fatigada.

[28] **leisure:** *Translate this as if it were* "time."

A Tale of Two Cities*

Charles Dickens

Footsteps[1] in the stone passage outside the door.[2] He stopped.

The key was put in the lock, and turned. Before the door was opened, or as it opened, a man said in a low voice, in English: "He has never seen me here; I have kept out of his way.[3] Go you in alone; I wait near. Lose no time!"

The door was quickly opened and closed, and there stood before him face to face, quiet, intent upon him, with the light of a smile on his features,[4] and a cautionary finger on his lip, Sydney Carton.

There was something so bright and remarkable in his look, that, for the first moment, the prisoner misdoubted[5] him to be an apparition of his own imagining. But, he spoke, and it was his voice; he took the prisoner's hand, and it was his real grasp.

"Of all the people upon earth, you least expected to see me?" he said.

"I could not believe it to be you. I can scarcely believe it now. You are not" —the apprehension came suddenly into his mind— "a prisoner?"

"No. I am accidentally possessed of[6] a power over one of the keepers[7] here, and in virtue of it I stand before you. I come from[8] her—your wife, dear Darnay."

The prisoner wrung his hand.

"I bring you a request from her."

"What is it?"

"A most earnest, pressing, and emphatic entreaty,[9] addressed to you in the most pathetic tones of the voice so dear to you, that you well remember."

The prisoner turned his face partly aside.

"You have no time to ask me why I bring it, or what it means; I have no time to tell you. You must comply with it—take off those boots you wear, and draw on[10] these of mine."

---

* *Una historia de dos ciudades.*

[1] **footsteps:** *Translate this as if it were* "footsteps sounded."

[2] **stone passage outside the door:** pasadizo exterior.

[3] **have kept out of his way:** evitar su encuentro *or* alejarse de su paso.

[4] **with the light of a smile on his features:** con el rostro iluminado por una sonrisa.

[5] **misdoubted:** temer.

[6] **I am accidentally possessed of:** *Translate this as if it were* "chance has given me power over."

[7] **keepers:** *Translate this as if it were* "jailers."

[8] **from:** de parte de.

[9] **entreaty:** súplica.

[10] **draw on:** *Translate this as if it were* "put on."

There was a chair against the wall of the cell, behind the prisoner. Carton, pressing forward, had already, with the speed of lightning, got him down into[11] it, and stood over him, barefoot.

"Draw on those boots of mine. Put your hands to them; put your will to them. Quick!"[12]

"Carton, there is no escaping from this place; it never can be done. You will only die with me. It is madness."

"It would be madness if I asked you to escape; but do I? When I ask you to pass out[13] at that door, tell me it is madness and remain here. Change that cravat for this of mine, that coat for this of mine. While you do it, let me take this ribbon from your hair, and shake out[14] your hair like this of mine!"

With wonderful quickness, and with a strength both of will and action, that appeared quite supernatural, he forced all these changes upon him. The prisoner was like a young child in his hands.

"Carton!" Dear Carton! It is madness. It cannot be accomplished, it never can be done, it has been attempted, and has always failed. I implore you not to add your death to the bitterness of mine."

"Do I ask you, my dear Darnay, to pass the door? When I ask that, refuse. There are pen and ink and paper on this table. Is your hand steady[15] enough to write?"

"It was when you came in."

"Steady it again, and write what I shall dictate. Quick, friend, quick."

---

[11] **got him down into:** *Translate this as if it were* "sat him down in."
[12] **quick!:** *Translate this as if it were* "Hurry up! Don't waste a moment!"
[13] **pass out:** pasar por. (*Use the subjunctive.*)
[14] **shake out:** desarreglar *or* desordenar.
[15] **is your hand steady:** tener el pulso firme.

Aspects of the Novel*

E. M. Forster

The interesting and sensitive French critic who writes under[1] the name of Alain has[2] some helpful if[3] slightly fantastic remarks on this point.[4] He gets a little out of his depth, but not as much as I feel myself out of mine, and perhaps together we may move toward[5] the shore. Alain examines in turn the various forms of aesthetic activity, and coming in time to the novel (*le roman*) he asserts that each human being has two sides,[6] appropriate to history and fiction. All that[7] is observable in a man—that is to say his actions and such of his spiritual existence as can be deduced from his actions—falls into[8] the domain of history. But his romanceful[9] or romantic side (*sa partie romanesque ou romantique*) includes "the pure passions, that is to say the dreams, joys, sorrows, and self-communings[10] which politeness or shame prevents him from mentioning"; and to express this side of human nature is one of the chief functions of the novel. "What is fictitious[11] in a novel is not so much the story as the method by which thought develops into action, a method which never occurs in daily life .... History, with its emphasis on external causes, is dominated by the notion of fatality, whereas[12] there is no fatality in the novel; there, everything is founded on human nature, and the dominating feeling is of an existence where everything is intentional, even passions and crimes, even misery."

This is perhaps a roundabout[13] way of saying what every British[14] school-

---

From *Aspects of the Novel* by E. M. Forster, copyright, 1947, by Harcourt, Brace & World, Inc.; copyright, 1955, by E. M. Forster. Reprinted by permission of the publishers and by Edward Arnold (Publishers) Ltd., London.

---

* *Aspectos de la novela.*
[1] **under:** con.
[2] **has:** *Translate this as if it were* "has made."
[3] **if:** *Translate this as if it were* "although."
[4] **on this point:** sobre este punto.
[5] **may move toward:** avanzar hacia.
[6] **sides:** caras.
[7] **all that:** todo cuanto *or* todo lo que.
[8] **falls into:** quedar incluído en *or* quedar comprendido en.
[9] **romanceful:** novelesca.
[10] **self-communings:** intimidades.
[11] **what is fictitious:** lo ficticio.
[12] **whereas:** mientras que *or* en tanto que.
[13] **roundabout:** indirecto.
[14] **British:** *Translate this as if it were* "English."

boy knew, that the historian records[15] whereas the novelist must create. Still, it is a profitable roundabout, for it brings out the fundamental difference between people in daily life and people in books. In daily life we never understand each other, neither complete clairvoyance nor complete confessional exists. We know each other approximately, by external signs, and these serve well enough as a basis for society[16] and even for intimacy. But people in a novel can be understood completely by the reader, if the novelist wishes; their inner as well as their outer life can be exposed. And this is why they often seem more definite than characters in history, or even our own friends; we have been told all about them that can be told; even if they are imperfect or unreal they do not contain[17] any secrets, whereas our friends do and must, mutual secrecy[18] being one of the conditions of life upon this globe.[19]

---

[15] **records:** registrar.
[16] **basis for society:** *Translate this as if it were* "life in society."
[17] **do not contain:** no tener.
[18] **mutual secrecy:** reserva recíproca.
[19] **globe:** *Do not use* "globo."

The Problem of Style*

J. Middleton Murry

In literature there is no such thing as pure thought; in literature, thought is always the handmaid[1] of emotion. Even in comedy and satire, where the interposition[2] of thought is most constantly manifest, emotion is the driving[3] impulse, but in these kinds[4] the emotion is restricted, because it has a conventional basis. It is not the less real for that, of course, but it is of a peculiar kind, and needs to be mediated[5] in[6] a peculiar way. But the thought of which we are talking when we speak of it as predominant or subordinate in a work of literature has nothing to do with the pure thought of the logician, the scientist, or the mathematician. The essential quality[7] of pure thought (as far as I understand it at all) is that it should lend itself to complete expression by[8] symbols which have a constant and invariable value. Words, as we all know, are not symbols of this kind; they are inconstant and variable; and I believe that it is rapidly coming to be accepted that the metaphysician who uses ordinary words is merely a bad poet, or a good one. Plato and Spinoza were good poets; Hegel a rather poor one.

The thought that plays a part in literature is systematized emotion, emotion become habitual till it attains the dignity of conviction. The "fundamental brain-work"[9] of a great play or a great novel is not performed by the reason,[10] pure or practical; even the transcendental essayist is merely engaged in trying to get his emotions onto paper. The most austere psychological analyst, even one who,[11] like Stendhal, really imagined he was exercising *la lo-gique*, is only attempting to get[12] some order into his own instinctive reactions. In one way or another the whole of literature consists in this communication of emotions.

Reprinted with the permission of Oxford University Press, Inc., from *The Problem of Style* by J. Middleton Murry.

* *El problema del estilo.*
[1] **handmaid:** siervo.
[2] **interposition:** intervención.
[3] **driving:** principal.
[4] **kinds:** *Translate this as if it were* "literary kinds."
[5] **be mediated:** mediatizar.
[6] **in:** de.
[7] **quality:** calidad *or* cualidad?
[8] **by:** *Translate this as if it were* "by means of."
[9] **brain-work:** *Translate this as if it were* "intellectual work."
[10] **is not performed by reason:** *Translate this as if it were* "reason does not perform" *and use* "ejecutar."
[11] **one who:** el que.
[12] **to get:** *Translate this as if it were* "to put."

The Problem of Style*

J. Middleton Murry

We shall have[1] occasion to discuss the nature of metaphor more exactly; and perhaps it will suffice for[2] the moment to declare my conviction that true metaphor, so far from being[3] an ornament, has very little to do[4] even with an act of comparison. Logically, of course, it is based upon an act of comparison. We all remember the neat little proportion sums[5] in the *Poetics* of Aristotle. But creative literature of the highest kind is not amenable to[6] logical analysis, and in the development of a great master of metaphor like Shakespeare we can watch the gradual overriding[7] of the act of comparison. Metaphor becomes almost a mode of apprehension.

*   *   *   *   *

Metaphor is the unique expression of a writer's individual vision. The faculty of using it is in itself as simple and direct as the faculty of saying "Blue" is to the ordinary man[8] when he sees a midsummer sky.

Metaphor, in fact, gives no support to the superstition that style is a kind of ornament; but the superstition is as stubborn as nature itself. You may pitch it out with a fork,[9] but it returns again and again. And this is why in all the famous definitions of style by writers who knew what they were talking about, the emphasis infallibly falls on[10] what we may call the organic nature of style. The most famous of Buffon's definitions sweeps away[11] the whole mechanism of expression. Style is the man himself. Flaubert, who spent days and weeks in trying to perfect the rhythm of a paragraph, simply left the rhythmical element altogether out of his many definitions of style. It is the writer's individual way of seeing things: '*c'est une manière de voir.*' Occasionally, following Buffon, he will replace *voir*

Reprinted with the permission of Oxford University Press, Inc., from *The Problem of Style* by J. Middleton Murry.

* *El problema del estilo.*
[1] **shall have:** *Add* ya.
[2] **for:** por *or* para?
[3] **so far from being:** *Omit* "so."
[4] **has very little to do:** no tener mucho que ver.
[5] **little proportion sums:** formulitas proporcionales.
[6] **not amenable to:** indócil a.
[7] **overriding:** superación.
[8] **to the ordinary man:** para cualquiera.
[9] **may pitch it out with a fork:** lanzar con una horca.
[10] **the emphasis infallibly falls on:** *Translate this as if it were* "inevitably one insists on."
[11] **away:** con.

by *penser* or *sentir*, and say that style is the writer's own way of thinking or seeing. And in the same sense Tchekhov, the greatest of all writers of short stories,[12] said to Gorky: 'You are an artist ... You feel superbly, you are plastic; that is, when you describe a thing, you see and touch it with your hands. That is real writing.'

I am not upholding any of these definitions of style as in themselves acceptable, or in any sense final.[13] Criticism, at any rate, is bound to scrutinize the means by which the man himself, his manner of seeing, or his superb feeling, is expressed in language.[14] But these *obiter dicta* of the masters are significant in this respect. They all point the same way; they all lay stress solely on[15] the immediate nature of style; they all reduce the element of art or artifice to nothingness.

---

[12] **writers of short stories:** *Translate with one word.*
[13] **final:** definitiva.
[14] **lenguage:** lengua *or* lenguaje?
[15] **lay stress ... on:** subrayar *or* hacer hincapié en.

The Picture of Dorian Gray*

Oscar Wilde

After about a quarter of an hour Hallward stopped painting, looked for[1] a long time at Dorian Gray, and then for a long time at the picture, biting[2] the end of one of his huge[3] brushes, and frowning. "It is quite[4] finished," he cried at last, and stooping down he wrote his name in long vermilion letters on the left-hand corner of the canvas.

Lord Henry came over and examined the picture.[5] It was certainly a wonderful work of art, and a wonderful likeness as well.

"My dear fellow,[6] I congratulate you most warmly," he said. "It is the finest portrait of modern times. Mr. Gray, come over and[7] look at yourself."[8]

The lad started, as if awakened from some dream. "Is it really finished?" he murmured, stepping down from the platform.

"Quite finished," said the painter. "And you have sat[9] splendidly today. I am awfully obliged to you."

"That is entirely due to me," broke in Lord Henry. "Isn't it, Mr. Gray?"

Dorian made no answer, but passed listlessly in front of his picture and turned towards it. When he saw it he drew back,[10] and his cheeks flushed for a moment with pleasure. A look[11] of joy came into[12] his eyes, as if he had recognized himself for the first time. He stood there motionless and in wonder, dimly conscious[13] that Hallward was speaking to him, but not catching[14] the meaning of his words. The sense of his own beauty came on him like a revelation. He had never felt it before. Basil Hallward's compliments had seemed to him to be merely the charming exaggerations of friendship. He had listened to them, laughed at them, forgotten them. They had not influenced his nature.[15] Then had come Lord Henry Wotton with

---

* *El retrato de Dorian Gray.*
[1] **looked for:** *Omit* "for."
[2] **biting:** mordiscar.
[3] **huge:** *Translate this as if it were* "thick."
[4] **quite:** *Translate this as if it were* "completely."
[5] **picture:** cuadro.
[6] **dear fellow:** querido amigo.
[7] **come over and:** venir a + *infinitive.*
[8] **look at yourself:** contemplarse.
[9] **have sat:** posar.
[10] **drew back:** retroceder.
[11] **look:** *Translate this as if it were* "flash."
[12] **came into:** pasar por.
[13] **dimly conscious:** *Translate this as if it were* "barely realizing."
[14] **catching:** *Translate this as if it were* "understanding."
[15] **nature:** carácter.

his strange panegyric on youth, his terrible warning of its brevity. That had stirred him at the time, and now, as he stood gazing at the shadow of his own loveliness, the full reality of the description flashed across[16] him. Yes, there would be a day when his face would be wrinkled and wizen, his eyes dim and colourless, the grace of his figure broken and deformed. The scarlet would pass away[17] from his lips, and the gold steal from his hair. The life that was to make his soul would mar his body. He would become dreadful, hideous, and uncouth.

As he thought of it, a sharp pang of pain struck through him like a knife, and made each delicate fibre of his nature quiver. His eyes deepened[18] into amethyst, and across them came a mist of tears.[19] He felt as if a hand of ice had been laid upon his heart.

"Don't you like it?" cried Hallward at last, stung a little by the lad's silence, not understanding what it meant.

"Of course he likes it," said Lord Henry. "Who wouldn't like it? It is one of the greatest things in[20] modern art. I will give you anything you like to ask for it. I must have it."

"It is not my property, Harry."

"Whose property is it?"

"Dorian's, of course," answered the painter.

"He is a very lucky fellow."

"How sad it is!" murmured Dorian Gray, with his eyes still fixed upon his own portrait. "How sad it is! I shall grow old, and horrible, and dreadful. But this picture will remain always young. It will never be older than this particular day of June. . . . If it were only the other way![21] If it were I who was to be always young, and the picture that was to grow old! For that— for that—I would give everything! Yes, there is nothing in the whole world I would not give! I would give my soul for that!"

---

[16] **flashed across**: *Translate this as if it were* "seized him in a flash."

[17] **would pass away**: irse.

[18] **his eyes deepened**: *Translate this as if it were* "the color of his eyes darkened."

[19] **across them came a mist of tears**: *Translate this as if it were* "a mist of tears blurred them."

[20] **in**: *Do not use* en.

[21] **the other way**: al contrario *or* al revés.

bibliography

I. BILINGUAL DICTIONARIES

Cassell's Spanish Dictionary. New York: Funk & Wagnalls Co., 1959.

Dictionary of Spoken Spanish: Spanish-English, English-Spanish. New York: Dover Publications, Inc., 1959. This useful paperback, originally published by the U.S. War Department (1945) as TM 30-900, is rich in idioms and vocabulary distinctions illustrated in complete sentences.

Velázquez de la Cadena, Mariano, *New Revised Velázquez Spanish and English Dictionary.* Chicago and New York: Follett, 1959.

Williams, Edwin B., *Spanish and English Dictionary* (rev. ed.). New York: Holt, Rinehart & Winston, Inc., 1962. Probably the best and most widely used of the major bilingual dictionaries. There also exists a more expensive expanded or trade edition of this work; the standard edition, however, is highly satisfactory for normal needs.

II. SPANISH DICTIONARIES

Corominas, Joan, *Breve diccionario etimológico de la lengua castellana.* Madrid: Editorial Gredos, 1961. For those interested in etymologies, this is a useful one-volume work based on the author's four-volume *Diccionario crítico etimológico de la lengua castellana.*

Gili Gaya, Samuel, *Diccionario general ilustrado de la lengua española.* Barcelona: Editorial Spes, 1961. Generally referred to as the Vox Dictionary, this work, carefully edited by Samuel Gili Gaya, is probably the best one-volume Spanish dictionary now available for general use. It incorporates much of the material of the Academy *Dictionary* and expands the treatment of many items.

Malaret, Augusto, *Diccionario de americanismos* (3a ed.). Buenos Aires: Emecé Editores, 1946. This volume is the handiest dictionary of Americanisms.

Real Academia Española, *Diccionario de la lengua castellana de la Real Academia Española.* Madrid: 1956. Now in its 18th edition, this work is considered the standard lexical authority.

Santamaría, Francisco J., *Diccionario de mejicanismos.* Méjico: Editorial Porrúa, 1959. This one-volume work is the most popular guide to Mexicanisms.

———, *Diccionario general de americanismos.* Méjico: Editorial Pedro Robredo, 1942. These three large volumes contain a wealth of lexical and semantic information on American Spanish.

Seco, Manuel, *Diccionario de dudas y dificultades de la lengua española.* Madrid: Aguilar, 1964. The entries in this interesting "dictionary" cover a range of subjects such as vocabulary, correct usage, and controversial foreign words that have entered Spanish in recent years.

III. SEMANTICS AND THE LEXICON

Bolinger, Dwight L., "1464 Identical Cognates in English and Spanish," *Hispania* 31.271-279 (1948).

Kany, Charles E., *American-Spanish Euphemisms*. Berkeley and Los Angeles: University of California Press, 1960. This book, which lists and discusses taboo words used throughout Spanish America, contains much material not found elsewhere.

———, *American-Spanish Semantics*. Berkeley and Los Angeles: University of California Press, 1960. In this book Kany classifies and comments on many American-Spanish divergencies from general Spanish forms.

———, *American-Spanish Syntax* (2nd ed.). Chicago: University of Chicago Press, 1951. This contains topical treatment of major variations in peninsular-Spanish and American-Spanish usage.

Lyon, J. E., *Pitfalls of Spanish Vocabulary*. London: George G. Harrap & Company, Limited, 1961. This useful little book presents clearly documented explanations of lexical and semantic distinctions that are likely to trouble the English-speaking student of Spanish.

Reid, John T., "123 Deceptive Demons," *Hispania* 31.280-297 (1948).

Walsh, Donald D., "Spanish Diminutives," *Hispania* 27.11-20 (1944). American-Spanish diminutives have been gathered from readings and grouped here according to syntactical function and connotation.

IV. GRAMMAR AND SYNTAX

Most of the articles listed below are from the "Notes on Usage" section of *Hispania*, a journal published four times a year for persons interested in Spanish literature and language. This particular section contains many valuable reexaminations of troublesome aspects of syntax and grammar.

Allen, Martha E., "Notes on the Use of 'de' and 'que' with 'antes' and 'después'," *Hispania* 41.504-510 (1958).

Bolinger, Dwight L., "The Comparison of Inequality in Spanish," *Language* 26.28-62 (1950). This article is an important contribution to the study of Spanish equivalents of the English "than."

———, "The Future and Conditional of Probability," *Hispania* 29.363-375 (1946).

———, "On the -ra Form," *Hispania* 31.341-342 (1948).

———, "The Position of the Adjective in English—A Convenient Analogy to the Position of the Adjective in Spanish," *Hispania* 26.191-192 (1943).

———, "Subjunctive -ra and -se: 'Free Variation'?," *Hispania* 39.345-349 (1956).

Bull, William E., "New Principles for Some Spanish Equivalents of 'To Be'," *Hispania* 25.433-443 (1942).

———, "Spanish Adjective Position: Present Rules and Theories," *Hispania* 33.297-303 (1960).

———, *Spanish for Teachers: Applied Linguistics*. New York: The Ronald Press Company, 1965. This important book points out the areas of linguistic interference caused by the contrast in the ways the two languages reflect a different organization of reality. It contains many ingenious insights to help the English-speaking student recognize crucial distinctions in Spanish.

Bull, William E., and others, "Subject Position in Contemporary Spanish," *Hispania* 35.185-188 (1952).

Crespo, Luis A., "To Become," *Hispania* 32.210-212 (1949).

Crespo, " 'Ser' and 'Estar': The Solution of the Problem," *Hispania* 32.509-517 (1949). This article is both a refinement and amplification of Crespo's earlier examination of this question.

———, "Los verbos 'ser' and 'estar' explicados por un nativo," *Hispania* 29.45-55 (1946). This is a useful and lucid presentation of certain psychological distinctions that underlie the Spaniard's choice between these two verbs.

Davis, J. Cary., "Más sobre 'puede hacerlo', 'lo puede hacer'," *Hispania* 44.708-710 (1961).

Farley, Rodger A., "Sequence of Tenses: A Useful Principle?," *Hispania* 48.549-533 (1965).

Fernández, Salvador, *Gramática española: los sonidos, el nombre y el pronombre*, Vol. I. Madrid: Revista de Occidente, 1951. This first of several promised volumes treats the sounds, nouns, and pronouns in a nearly exhaustive fashion. It is abundantly documented with samples taken from the author's careful and extensive readings.

Fish, Gordon T., "El cual, el que, or quién?," *Hispania* 44.315-319 (1961).

———, "The position of subject and object in Spanish prose," *Hispania* 42.582-590 (1959).

Gili y Gaya, Samuel, *Curso superior de sintaxis española* (5a ed.). Barcelona: Editorial Spes, 1955. This is one of the soundest and most popular treatments of the major syntactical and grammatical topics in Spanish. Highly recommended.

González Muela, Joaquín, "Ser y estar: enfoque de la cuestión," *Bulletin of Hispanic Studies* 39.3-12 (1961).

Jackson, Robert, and Dwight Bolinger, "Trabajar para," *Hispania* 48.884-886 (1966).

Jones, Willis Knapp, "Spanish Relative Pronouns and Adjectives," *Hispania* 31.401-404 (1948).

Keniston, Hayward, *Spanish Syntax List*. New York: Holt, Rinehart & Winston, Inc., 1937. This is a frequency count of grammatical forms based on contemporary Spanish prose.

Levy, Bernard, " 'En' and 'sobre'," *Hispania* 32.206-208 (1949).

Mallo, Jerónimo, "El empleo de las formas del subjuntivo terminados en -ra con significación de tiempos del indicativo," *Hispania* 30.484-487 (1947).

———, "Las nuevas normas de prosodia y ortografía de la Academia Española," *Hispania* 36.278-283 (1953).

Pérez Soler, Vicente, "Construcciones con verbos de duda en español," *Hispania* 44.287-289 (1966).

Real Academia Española, *Gramática de la lengua española*. Madrid: Espasa-Calpe, 1931. This is the standard authority on normative grammar.

Ramsay, Marathon Montrose, *A Textbook of Modern Spanish*, rev. by Robert K. Spaulding. New York: Holt, Rinehart & Winston, Inc., 1956. This has been a long-time standard reference work for American students of Spanish and is useful mainly for the abundance of literary samples that illustrate its carefully graded grammatical classifications. A reference work only, it contains no exercises.

Sacks, Norman P., " 'Aquí', 'acá', 'allí', 'allá'," *Hispania* 37.263-266 (1954).

Seco, Rafael, *Manual de gramática española*, revisado y ampliado por Manuel

Seco. Madrid: Aguilar, 1960. A well-written little book dealing with parts of speech and problems of syntax, this volume is principally traditional in approach. It provides many psychological insights into Spanish usage.

Seelye, H. Ned, "The Spanish Passive: A Study in the Relation between Linguistic Form and World-view," *Hispania* 49.290-292 (1966).

Sondergard, Robert E., "The Spanish Preposition," *Hispania* 36.76-78 (1953).

Spaulding, Robert K., *Syntax of the Spanish Verb*. New York: Holt, Rinehart & Winston, Inc., 1931. This handy little reference book treats all noteworthy uses of the Spanish verb. It is clearly organized, illustrated with literary examples, and contains sets of exercises.

————, "Two Problems of Spanish Syntax," *Hispania* 24.311-315 (1941). This article is a discussion of "quizá" vs. "quizás" and the hortatory subjunctive.

Stockwell, Robert P., Donald J. Bowen, and John W. Martin, *The Grammatical Structures of English and Spanish*. Chicago: University of Chicago Press, 1965. This linguistic presentation analyzes and contrasts the principal structures of the two languages.

Wallis, Ethel, and William E. Bull, "Spanish Adjective Position: Phonetic Stress and Emphasis," *Hispania* 33.221-229 (1950).

THE SPANISH ACADEMY'S NEW NORMS FOR ACCENTUATION

In 1952 the *Real Academia Española* published a booklet of 134 pages entitled *Nuevas normas de prosodia y ortografía*. The work contains the collective judgments of a group of the Academy's members regarding certain troublesome and ambiguous points of Spanish accentuation and orthography, and provides an authoritative opinion on these questions. Because of the Academy's prestige, many of the norms are now widely accepted; others, however, are followed only irregularly.

Many of these norms are not really "new," but appeared earlier as entries or emendations in the Academy's own *Grammar* or *Dictionary*. With a few exceptions, the literary passages in this text have been made to conform to the new norms whenever they did not so conform in the original.

The following is a summary of the most important of these norms (the numbering does not correspond to that in the Academy's publication).

1. The one-syllable words **dio**, **fui**, **fue**, and **vio** are to be written without an accent. (This rule is widely followed.)

2. A small number of words may have two correct accentual patterns, such as:

    sánscrito—sanscrito
    dínamo—dinamo
    polígiota—poliglota
    período—periodo
    cántiga—cantiga

3. Words that begin with **ps** may be written with or without the **p**. The same principle applies to words beginning with **gn** and **mn**.

    psicología—sicología
    psicosis—sicosis
    gnomo—nomo

4. Words that normally have an orthographic accent (**río**, **décimo**, etc.) are written without that accent when they form the first part of a compound word.

    rioplatense
    decimoséptimo

    When, however, such words are compounded with the suffix **-mente** to form an adverb, they retain their written accent, for the new adverb has two prosodic accents.

    ágil—ágilmente
    cortés—cortésmente

5. Compounds of two or more adjectives will retain whatever written accent each adjective originally had.

    histórico-crítico-bibliográfico

6. The demonstrative pronouns (**este, ese, aquel**, etc.) no longer require a written accent to distinguish them from the demonstrative adjectives, provided that it is clear from context that their function is pronominal rather than adjectival. In cases where ambiguity is possible, however, the accent is used to mark the pronoun. (It should be pointed out that this norm has so far won little acceptance.)

7. The adverb **aún** will have an accent whenever it means "still," i.e., whenever it is a synonym of **todavía**. When it means "even," i.e., when it is a synonym of **hasta**, it will bear no accent.

Aún (todavía) viven allí.　　　　They still live there.
Aun (hasta) sus amigos no　　　Even his friends don't want to
quieren hablarle.　　　　　　　speak to him.

8. In compounds composed of two adjectives separated by a hyphen, only the second adjective will agree with the noun in number and gender.

un tratado teórico-práctico
una lección teórico-práctica

This vocabulary has been compiled for all exercises except the **Temas a escoger** and the selections in the Appendix. Gender is indicated only when it is not clear from the word itself.

vocabulary

A

able hábil, capaz
    to be — poder
absence ausencia
abstraction abstracción
abundant abundante
accelerator acelerador
accent acento, dejo
accept aceptar
accident accidente
accompany acompañar, escoltar
accomplice cómplice
accomplish realizar
according to según
account cuenta
    on — of debido a, por + *infinitive*
accursed maldito
accustomed acostumbrado
    be — to estar acostumbrado a
    become — to acostumbrarse a
ache dolor; doler (ue)
achieve lograr, conseguir, realizar
achievement realización
    highest — cumbre (*f.*)
acquire adquirir
act (theater) acto
action acción
actor actor
actress actriz
address dirección, señas; dirigir
administration administración
advance avanzar
advantage ventaja
adversity adversidad
advice consejo
advise aconsejar, asesorar, avisar
adviser consejero, asesor
affair asunto
affect afectar
affectionate cariñoso
affirm afirmar
afford permitirse el lujo de
afraid: be — of tener miedo de (a)
after después; despúes (de) que
afternoon tarde
    in the — por la tarde
again otra vez
    do something — volver a hacer algo
against contra, en contra de
age edad
agility agilidad
ago hace
aim fin, intento
air aire
air conditioner acondicionador del aire

airport aeropuerto
alcohol alcohol
alert alerta (*m. and f.*)
    to be on the — estar alerta
Alexander the Great Alejandro Magno
algae algas
alive vivo
all todo, entero
    not to be — there no estar en sus
    cabales
allegiance fidelidad, lealtad
almond tree almendro
almost casi
alone solo, a solas
along por, a lo largo de
    get — llevar (entender)se bien
alphabetical alfabético
already ya
although aunque
altitude altura
always siempre
A.M. de la mañana
amaze asombrar
ambassador embajador
ambition ambición
ambitious ambicioso
American americano, norteamericano
amiss de más
ammunition dump depósito de municiones
among entre, por entre
amuse divertir
    — oneself divertirse
analysis análisis (*m.*)
    in the last — en último término
anger ira, enojo
angry enojado, enfadado
    become — enfadarse, enojarse
anguish angustia
animal animal
anniversary aniversario
announce anunciar
annoy molestar
annoyed molestado
    become — molestarse
annoying molesto, latoso
another otro
answer respuesta; responder
    — back replicar
ant hormiga
antenna (of an insect) cuerno
anthropology antropología
antique antiguo
    — shop tienda de antigüedades
Antwerp Amberes
any cualquier (cualesquier)
anyway de todos modos
apartment piso

Apocalypse Apocalipsis (*m.*)
apologize disculparse
apparent aparente, evidente
appear aparecer
appearance apariencia, aspecto
appetite apetito
apple manzana
    — **tree** manzano
appliance aparato
appoint nombrar
approach acercarse a, aproximarse a
apron delantal (*m.*)
archives archivos
area área (*f.*)
arm brazo
armchair sillón
arms armas
army ejército
aromatic aromático
around por; alrededor de, en torno de
arrest detención; detener
arrival llegada
    new — recién llegado
arrive llegar
artificial artificial
artist artista (*m. and f.*)
as como
    — **far** — hasta
    — **if** como si
    — **usual** como de costumbre
ashamed avergonzado
    be — tener vergüenza
ask pedir; preguntar
asleep dormido
    fall — dormirse, quedarse dormido
asphalt asfalto
aspire to aspirar a
assassination asesinato
astonish asombrar
at en, a (*motion or direction*)
atmosphere atmósfera, ambiente
attempt procurar, intentar
attend asistir a
attention atención
attic ático, desván
attract atraer
    — **attention** llamar la atención
attractive atractivo
audible oíble
aunt tía
author autor
avenge vengar
aviary avería
avoid evitar
await esperar, aguardar
aware enterado
    be (fully)—of estar (bien) enterado de

B

back espalda, respaldo, dorso; trasero, de
    atrás (*adjectival*)
    go — **to** volver a
    turn one's — **on** volverle la espalda
    a
background fondo
backward atrasado
bad malo
baggage equipaje (*m.*)
balcony balcón
    — **window** balcón
bald calvo
baldness calvicie (*f.*)
banana plátano
banish desterrar, extrañar
bank banco, banca
    World Bank Banco Mundial
banker banquero
bankrupt quebrado, insolvente
    go — quebrar
bankruptcy bancarrota, quiebra
banquet banquete
barbershop barbería
barely apenas
bark corteza
barred atrancado
barrel barril
base base (*f.*)
baseball béisbol (*m.*)
basket cesto(-a), canasto(-a)
bathe bañar(se)
bather bañista (*m. and f.*)
bathroom cuarto de baño
battle batalla; batallar
be about to estar a punto de, estar para
beach playa
bearing porte (*m.*)
beast bestia
    little— bestezuela
beat pegar; batir, latir
beautiful hermoso
beauty hermosura, belleza
because porque;
    — **of** por, a causa de
become hacerse, ponerse, volverse, que-
    darse, llegar a ser
    — **of** ser de
bed cama, lecho, cauce (*river*)
    go to — acostarse
    stay in — guardar cama
bedroom alcoba, dormitorio
before antes, antes de, antes (de) que
begin comenzar, empezar
behalf: on — **of** en nombre de
behave portarse, comportarse

behind detrás de
being ser
      human — ser humano
believe creer, dar crédito a
bell campana, timbre (*m.*)
      — tower campanario
bench banco, banca
betray traicionar, delatar
better mejor
beyond más allá de, allende
bicycle bicicleta
bill billete; cuenta
biographer biógrafo
biography biografía
bird pájaro, ave (*f.*)
birdlike de pájaro
birth nacimiento
      give — dar a luz, parir
bite morder, picar (*insects*)
black negro
blame culpar
blanket manta
bleat balar
bless bendecir
blind ciego
      become — quedarse ciego
blinding cegador
block manzana
blood sangre
bloody sangriento
bloom florecer
blow soplar
      — one's nose sonarse (las narices)
      — up volar
blue azul
blush ponerse colorado, ruborizarse
board tabla
      checker— tablero
boast jactarse
boat barco, barca, bote
body cuerpo, cadáver (*m.*)
bolt (of a door) cerrojo
bombing bombardeo
bond bono
bone hueso (*fish*); espina
      be skin and —s estar en los huesos
bonnet gorra
book libro
bookstore librería
boot bota
border limitar, lindar
boring aburrido, pesado
born nacido
      be — nacer
boss jefe
botanical botánico
both los dos, ambos

bothersome molesto
bottle botella
bottom fondo
bougainvillaea buganvillas
boundary linde (*m. and f.*), límite, frontera
bouquet ramillete (*m.*)
bowl cuenco(–a)
      sugar — azucarero
box caja
boy muchacho, chico, niño
      — friend novio
boyhood mocedad (*f.*)
brakes frenos
      apply the — frenar
brambles zarzas
branch rama, ramo; sucursal (*f.*)
brand marca
brave valiente
bread pan
      a loaf of — un pan
break romper, quebrar, quebrantar
      — down descomponerse
      — down and cry deshacerse en lágrimas
      — out estallar
breakdown avería
breakfast desayuno
      have — desayunar, tomar el desayuno
breakwater escollera
breathe respirar
      — in aspirar
breeze brisa
bribe soborno, cohecho; sobornar
bridge puente (*m.*)
brief breve
      in — en resumen, en pocas palabras
bright brillante
brilliance brillantez (*f.*)
brilliant brillante
bring traer
      — back volver, devolver
brush stroke pincelada
bucket cubo
      kick the — estirar la pata
build construir, edificar
building edificio
bump chichón
      — into encontrarse con, tropezarse con, topar con
bunch racimo, ristra, manojo, ramillete (*m.*)
burden carga
burial entierro
buried enterrado
burn quemar (se), arder
      — out fundirse

burst reventar

    — **out** romper a

bury enterrar

bus autobús (*m.*)

bush arbusto

bust busto

busy ocupado, atareado

    — **oneself with** ocuparse con, entretenerse con

butt colilla

buy comprar

C

cabbage col

    a head of — una col

cabin cabaña; camarote

cafe café (*m.*)

call llamada; llamar

    — **at** hacer escala en

    — **up** llamar

calmly con calma

camp acampar

campus campo universitario

can bote (*m.*), lata

canary canario

    — **Islands** las (islas) Canarias

candy dulces (*m.*)

cane bastón

capacity capacidad

cape capa

capital capital (*f. city*; *m. money*)

    — **letter** letra mayúscula

captain capitán

capture capturar, prender, cautivar

car coche (*m.*), automóvil (*m.*)

card tarjeta, ficha (*index card*)

care cuidado

    take — **of** cuidar de

career carrera

careful cuidadoso

    be — tener cuidado

carefully con cuidado, cuidadosamente

caretaker conserje (*m.*)

Carioca Carioca (person from Rio)

carnival carnaval

carpet alfombra; alfombrar

carrot zanahoria

carry llevar

    — **away** llevarse

    — **no weight** no pinchar ni cortar

    — **out** realizar, llevar a cabo

carve grabar

case estuche (*m.*)

cataract catarata

catch coger, pillar, atrapar; pegársele a uno (*disease*)

    — **a cold** resfriarse

    — **up to (with)** alcanzar

cathedral catedral (*f.*)

Catholic católico

cause causa

cell celda; célula (*biology*)

cemetery cementerio, camposanto

censure censurar

Central America la América Central, Centro América

century siglo

certain cierto

    a — cierto

chair silla

chalet chalet (*m.*)

challenge desafiar

championship campeonato

chance casualidad, azar; ocasión

    by — por casualidad, por azar

character carácter (*m.*), personaje (*m.*)

charming encantador

chat charlar

cheap barato

check facturar (*baggage*)

checkerboard tablero (de damas)

checkers damas

cheerful alegre

chef jefe de cocina, cocinero

cherry cereza

    — **wood** cerezo

chestnut castaña

child niño

chivalry caballería

choice elección

    make a good — acertar, elegir bien

choke sofocar, ahogar, estrangular

    — **to death** morir ahogado

chop chuleta

Christian cristiano

chronicler cronista

church iglesia

cigar cigarro, puro

cigarette cigarrillo, pitillo

city ciudad

    — **hall** ayuntamiento

clam almeja

class clase

    lower — clase baja

classic(al) clásico

claw garra

clay barro, arcilla

clerk dependiente (*m.*)

cliff acantilado

climate clima (*m.*)

climb subir, trepar

    — **up on (top of)** encaramarse en (a)

clipping recorte (*m.*)

close cercano, próximo; íntimo
close cerrar
closely de cerca
closet armario
clothes ropa
cloud nube (*f.*)
coach diligencia, coche (*m.*)
coal carbón (*m.*)
coarse grosero
coast costa
coffee café (*m.*)
cold frío; resfriado, catarro
      become — enfriarse, ponerse frío, quedarse frío
      catch a — resfriarse, acatarrarse
colleague colega (*m.*)
collect cobrar, colectar
collection colección
colonist colono
color color (*m.*)
Columbus Colón
come venir
      — out salir, resultar
      — under acogerse a
comfort comodidad, confort (*m.*)
command dominio
comment comentario
common común
companion compañero
company compañía
compensate compensar
complain (**about**) quejarse (de)
complaint queja
complete completar
composer compositor, -a
conceal ocultar, esconder, encubrir
conceited engreído, orgulloso
conceive concebir
concentrate concentrar(se)
condition condición, estado
confide confiar
confidence confianza
congratulate felicitar, dar la enhorabuena
connect conectar
connection comunicación
consequence consecuencia
consider considerar
console consolar
conspire conspirar
constantly constantemente
consul cónsul
consult consultar
contact lenses lentillas, lentes de contacto
contagious contagioso
contain contener
contemplate contemplar
content contento

contents contenido
continually continuamente
continue seguir, continuar
continuously continuamente
contract contraer
control controlar, dominar
      — oneself dominarse
convent convento
conversation conversación
convertible convertible, descapotable
convince convencer
cook cocinero; cocer, cocinar
      be uncooked, not cooked enough estar crudo
cool refrescar
corner esquina, rincón, ángulo; comisura
      look out of the — of one's eye mirar con el rab(ill)o del ojo
corporation sociedad anónima
correctly correctamente
correspondence correspondencia
cost coste (*m.*), costo; costar
      — dearly salir (costar) caro
cottage casita
count on contar con
counter mostrador
country país (*m.*), campo
couple pareja, matrimonio
      a — of un par de
courage valor (*m.*)
courageous valiente
course curso
court corte (*f.*); tribunal (*m.*)
cousin primo
cover cubrir, tapar
coward cobarde (*m. and f.*)
crab cangrejo
crack grieta, rendija, resquicio
crane grúa (*f.*)
crazy loco
      go — enloquecer, volverse loco
creamy cremoso
create crear
creative creador
creator creador, -a
crew tripulación
crime crimen (*m.*)
criminal criminal; reo
crimson carmesí
crisis crisis (*f.*)
critical crítico
criticism crítica
criticize criticar
crop cosecha
cross cruzar, atravesar
cross-eyed bizco
crossing travesía

crossroads encrucijada, cruce (*m.*)
crowd multitud, muchedumbre (*f.*)
crowded atestado
crown coronar
crude grosero, tosco
cruel cruel
cruelty crueldad
crust corteza; costra
crustacean crustáceo
cry llorar; gritar
cunningly con sorna
cupboard alacena
cure cura (*f.*)
curl rizo; rizar
current corriente (*f.*)
curse maldecir
curtain cortina
      draw the —s correr las cortinas
custodian conserje (*m.*)
custom costumbre (*f.*)
customer cliente (*m. and f.*)
customs official aduanero
cut cortar
cute mono

D

daily diario, cotidiano
dairy lechería
daisy margarita
damp húmedo
dampness humedad
dance baile (*m.*); bailar
danger peligro
dangerous peligroso
dare atreverse (a)
dark oscuro
darkness oscuridad
date fecha; fechar
daughter hija
dawn alba, amanecer; amanecer
dead muerto
      be — estar muerto
      drop — morirse
deaf sordo
deafening ensordecedor
dean decano
dear querido
death muerte (*f.*)
decay pudrirse
deceive engañar
December diciembre
decently decentemente
decide decidir, decidirse (a)
decision decisión
      make a — tomar una decisión
deck cubierta

declare declarar
decoration decoración
dedicate dedicar
deed hecho
deep hondo, profundo
      deep-felt entrañable
defend defender
delay tardar, demorarse
delicate delicado
delicately con delicadeza
delicious rico, sabroso
delight deleite, delicia
      take — deleitarse
delightful delicioso, deleitoso
deliver entregar; pronunciar (un discurso)
demand reclamar, exigir
democracy democracia
demonstrate demostrar
demonstrator manifestante
deny negar
depart partir, salir
depend depender
      — on depender de, contar con
deposit depositar
depress apretar (*the accelerator*)
depressed deprimido
deprive privar
deputy diputado
      House of Deputies Diputación
derive derivar, deducir, extraer
desert desierto
deserted desierto
deserve merecer
deserving merecedor
designate designar, señalar
desire deseo; desear
      to be —d que desear
despise despreciar, desdeñar
despite a pesar de
dessert postre (*m.*)
destiny destino
destroy destruir
detail detalle, pormenor (*m.*)
determine determinar
develop desarrollar; revelar (*film*)
development desarrollo
dew rocío
dictator dictador (*m.*)
didactic didáctico
die morir(se)
      dying man moribundo
differ from diferenciarse de
difference diferencia
      tell the — distinguir
      What — does it make? ¿Qué importa?, ¿Qué más da?
difficult difícil

difficulty dificultad
dig cavar
dignity dignidad
dine cenar
dining room comedor
dinner cena
direct dirigir
direction dirección
dirty sucio
disappear desaparecer
disassociate disociar
discouraged desanimado
discover descubrir
discovery descubrimiento
discuss discutir
disease enfermedad
disembark desembarcar(se)
disguise disfrazar
disgust dar asco
disgusting asqueroso
dish plato
    small — platillo
disobey desobedecer
displeasure disgusto
disposal disposición
    have at one's — tener a su dis-
    posición
disregard pasar por alto
distance distancia
    in the — a lo lejos
distinction distinción
distinguish distinguir
distribute repartir
district barrio
    red-light — barrio chino
disturb turbar, perturbar
divorced divorciado
    get — from divorciarse de
dock muelle (m.)
doctor médico
document documento
dog perro
dollar dólar (m.)
door puerta, portezuela, portal (m.)
dotage chochera, chochez (f.)
dote chochear
doubt duda
    without a — sin duda
down abajo
    — the street calle abajo
downpour aguacero
drag arrastrar
draw dibujar
    — back retroceder, retirarse
dream sueño
    — of soñar con
dress vestido; vestir

drink bebida, trago
drive conducir
    take a — dar un paseo (en coche)
driver conductor, chófer (taxi)
drop gota; dejar caer
    — a few lines poner unas letras
drown ahogar(se)
drowning que se ahoga
druggist farmacéutico
drunk borracho
    become — emborracharse
dry seco; secar, enjugar
dull aburrido
dungeon mazmorra
during durante
dusk anochecer (m.)
Dutch holandés
duty deber
    do one's — cumplir con su deber
dying man moribundo

E

each cada
eager ansioso
    — for ansioso por
eagle águila (f.)
ear oído, oreja
earn ganar
    — one's living ganarse la vida
earth tierra
earthquake terremoto, temblor(es) (m.)
eat comer; tomar + name of meal
economist economista (m. and f.)
economy economía
edge borde (m.)
education educación, instrucción
effect efecto
effective eficaz
effort esfuerzo
egg huevo
elapse mediar, transcurrir
election elección(es)
elegant elegante
elevator ascensor (m.)
elm olmo
elsewhere en (a) otra parte
embrace abrazar; abarcar
emperor emperador (m.)
empire imperio
employee empleado
empty vacío, vano; vaciar
    — into desembocar en (river)
enable permitir, dejar
enchanting encantador
encompass abarcar
end acabar, terminar

endless sin fin
endure aguantar, tolerar
enemy enemigo
engineering ingeniería
England Inglaterra
English inglés
 —man inglés
enjoy disfrutar (de), gozar (de)
enormous enorme
enroll inscribir(se)
enter entrar (en)
enterprise empresa
entire entero
entrance entrada
envelope sobre (*m.*)
equal igual
escape escaparse
escort escoltar, acompañar
essay ensayo
essential esencial
estate finca, hacienda
esteem estimar
eulogy elogio
Europe Europa
even hasta
 — when aun cuando
evening tarde (*f.*); vespertino
event suceso, acontecimiento
ever jamás, alguna vez
 more than — más que nunca
every todo, cada uno
everyone todos, todo el mundo
everything todo
evident evidente
 be self- — saltar a la vista
evoke evocar
exact exacto
exam examen (*m.*)
examine examinar; reconocer
example ejemplo
 for — por ejemplo
exasperate exasperar, desquiciar, sacar de
 quicio
excel sobresalir
excitement agitación
exercise ejercicio; ejercer
exhausted rendido
existence existencia
exotic exótico
expense gasto
 at our — a costa nuestra
 at the — of a costas de
expensive caro
experience experiencia; experimentar
explain explicar
explorer explorador
expression expresión

assume a humble — poner una cara
 humilde
extend alargar
extensive extenso
extraordinary extraordinario
eye ojo
 keep an — on vigilar

F

face cara, rostro; arrostrar, afrontar, encararse con
 — the consequences dar la cara
 in the — of frente a
 make an unhappy — poner mal
 gesto
fact hecho, dato
 in — de hecho, en realidad
factory fábrica, factoría
fade desteñir(se)
fail faltar, suspender, quebrar, fracasar,
 fallar
 — to dejar de
faithfully lealmente
fall caída; caer
 — out with disgustarse con, reñirse
 con
false falso
falsify falsificar
family familia
famous famoso
far lejos
 go too — pasarse de rosca, ir
 demasiado lejos
farewell despedida
farmer labrador, -a
farsighted présbita
farther más lejos
 — on más adelante
fascinate fascinar
fascinating fascinador
fashionable de moda
fasten agarrarse
fate suerte (*f.*)
fault culpa
favorite favorito, predilecto
fear temor (*m.*), miedo; temer
feature(s) rasgo, característica; facciones
federal federal
feeble débil, enclenque, enteco
feed alimentar
feel sentir(se); palpar
 — like tener ganas de
feeling sentimiento
felucca falucho
fence cerca
fertile fértil, fecundo, feraz

fever fiebre (f.), calentura
few pocos
    a — unos cuantos
    a — lines unas letras
fiancé novio
field campo, sembrado
    wheat — trigal
fifteen quince
fifty cincuenta
fight luchar, pelear, reñir(se)
figure figura
fill llenar
film película
finally por fin
find encontrar, hallar
    — out averiguar, saber
finger dedo
    index — índice (m.)
finish terminar, acabar
    — off rematar
fire fuego, incendio; despedir, echar; disparar (weapon)
fireman bombero
first primero
fish pez (m.), pescado; pescar
fisherman pescador
fishing pescador (adjective)
fist puño
fit through pasar a través de
fix fijar; arreglar
fixed fijo
flat llano, plano
flavor gusto, sabor (m.)
flesh carne (f.)
flight vuelo
float flotar
flock manada, rebaño; bandada
flood inundación; inundar
Florida la Florida
flower flor (f.)
fluctuate fluctuar, oscilar
fly mosca; volar
    — by pasar volando
focus enfoque (m.); enfocar
fog niebla, neblina
fold doblar
foliage follaje (m.)
follow seguir
following siguiente
foot pie (m.)
    at the — of al pie de
    on — a pie
    put one's — in it meter la pata
for para, por; porque
forbid prohibir
force forzar
    — one's way abrirse paso

    — to obligar a
forehead frente (f.)
foreign extranjero
    — trade comercio exterior
foreman capataz (m.)
forest bosque (m.)
forewarning presentimiento
forget olvidar, olvidarse de, olvidársele a uno, dejar olvidado
forgive perdonar, disculpar
form forma; formar
former antiguo (precedes noun)
formula fórmula
formulate formular
fortress fortaleza
fragrance fragancia, olor
free libre; gratis, gratuito; librar, libertar, manumitir
freeway autopista
freeze helar(se), congelar(se)
French francés
    —man francés
frequent frecuente
frequently frecuentemente, con frecuencia
fresh fresco
fret apurarse
friend amigo
friendship amistad
frighten asustar, dar miedo a
frightened asustado
front frente (m., military)
    in — of frente a, delante de
frontier frontera
    the New — la Nueva Frontera
frown fruncir el ceño (entrecejo)
frugal ahorrativo
fruit fruta, fruto
frying pan sartén (f.)
fulfill cumplir
full lleno
fun diversión
    have lots of — divertirse la mar
    make — of burlarse de
fundamental fundamental
funeral funeral (m.), entierro
furious furioso
furnish amueblar
furniture muebles (m.)
    a piece of — un mueble
future futuro, porvenir (m.)

G

gadget chisme (m.)
game partido, partida, juego
garage garaje (m.)
garden jardín (m.), huerta

gardener jardinero
gate verja
gathering velada, tertulia
gaze mirada; mirar con fijeza
gelatine gelatina
generous generoso
genius genio
gentle manso, suave
gentleman caballero, señor
gesture gesto
get conseguir
    — **around it** darle vueltas
    — **up** levantarse
    you can't — **around it** no hay que darle vueltas
giant gigante (*m.*)
gift regalo, presente; don; aguinaldo; dádiva
    — **for languages** don de lenguas
    — **of gab** tener mucha labia
give dar
    — **up** abandonar; desistir; rendirse
    — **way to** ceder a
glad alegre
    be — (**of**) alegrarse (de)
glance mirada
glass vaso; cristal, vidrio
    a piece of — un cristal
glasses (**eyeglasses**) gafas, anteojos
globe globo
gloomy sombrío
glory gloria
glove guante (*m.*)
go ir
    — **around** andar
    — **down** bajar
    — **get** ir a buscar, ir por
    — **on** seguir, continuar
    — **out** salir
    — **too far** pasarse de rosca
    — **toward** acudir, ir hacia
    — **up** subir
    — **up to** acercarse a
goal fin (*m.*), meta
goat cabra
    wild — cabra montés
gold oro
Gordian gordiano
gossip chisme(s) (*m.*); chismear, chismorrear, contar chismes
govern gobernar, regir
government gobierno
governor gobernador
grab asir, agarrar
graduate graduarse
grain grano
grandmother abuela

grape uva
grasp asir
grass hierba
grate rallar
grateful agradecido
    be — **for** agradecer
grating reja
grave tumba, sepultura
gravestone lápida
gravy salsa
gray gris
    — **hair** canas
    a — **hair** una cana
greater mayor
Greece Grecia
greedily golosamente
Greek griego
green verde
grief pena, dolor (*m.*)
grieve afligirse
grow crecer
    — **up** crecer
guard guarda; guardia; guardar
guerrilla guerrillero
guess adivinar
    — **right** acertar
guest invitado; huésped
guide guía (*m. and f.*); guiar
gulf golfo
guts entrañas
    have no — no tener agallas
guy tipo

H

habit costumbre (*f.*), hábito
hail from ser oriundo de
hair pelo, cabello(s)
hairdresser peluquería
half medio
half-closed entornado
hallway corredor (*m.*), pasillo
hand mano
    shake —**s** dar (alargar, estrechar) la mano
    — **in** entregar
handkerchief pañuelo
handle mango, asa, puño
hand-painted pintado a mano
handwriting letra
hang ahorcar; colgar
happen ocurrir, pasar
    — **to be** acertar a ser
happiness felicidad
harass acosar
harbor puerto
hard duro

work — trabajar de firme
hardly apenas
hard-working trabajador
harshly ásperamente
hat sombrero
hatchway escotilla
hatred odio
have tener, contar con
    — a good time divertirse, pasarlo bien
    — it out with habérselas con
    — tea tomar té
    — to tener que
hazard azar (*f.*), peligro
head cabeza
    a — of lettuce una lechuga
    get something into one's — metérsele a uno en la cabeza una cosa
    — toward dirigirse hacia
health salud (*f.*)
healthy sano, saludable
hear oír
hearing oído
    hard of — duro de oído
heart corazón (*m.*), entrañas
    by — de memoria
heat calor (*m.*)
heavy pesado
    — accent acento marcado
heed hacer caso de (a)
heel talón (*m.*); tacón (*shoe*) (*m.*)
help ayuda, socorro; ayudar
    not be able to — no poder menos de
helper ayudante (*m.*)
here aquí
    around — por aquí
hermit ermitaño
hero héroe (*m.*)
hesitate vacilar, titubear
hide esconder, ocultar
high alto
    — part of lo alto de
highway carretera
hill colina
hinder impedir, estorbar
hit pegar; atropellar (*with a vehicle*)
    — upon dar con
hoarse ronco
hold tener; mantener
    — one's breath contener la respiración
hole hoyo; agujero
holiday día de fiesta
homemade casero
homework tarea
honest honrado; recto
honey miel (*m.*)

honeymoon luna de miel
honeysuckle madreselva
hook gancho; anzuelo (*fishing*)
hope esperanza
horizon horizonte (*m.*)
horseman jinete (*m.*)
hospital hospital (*m.*)
host anfitrión (*m.*)
hostility hostilidad
hot caliente
    be — estar caliente; hacer calor; tener calor
    become — calentarse, ponerse caliente
hotel hotel (*m.*)
housewife ama de casa
housing alojamiento
    — shortage crisis de vivienda
humble humilde
    assume a — expression poner una cara humilde
    become — volverse (ponerse) humilde
humid húmedo
hummingbird colibrí (*m.*), pájaro-mosca
hundreds centenares
    by the — a centenares
hunger hambre (*f.*)
hungry hambriento
    be — tener hambre
hurricane ciclón, huracán
hurry apresurar(se)
    be in a — tener prisa
hurt hacer daño, dañar, lastimar
husband marido, esposo
hypothesis hipótesis (*f.*)

I

ice cream helado
    — parlor heladería
idiom modismo
idle ocioso, de ocio
ill enfermo
    become — enfermar, ponerse enfermo
illegitimate ilegítimo
illness enfermedad
imagination imaginación
imagine figurarse, imaginarse
immense inmenso
immigrant inmigrante
impatience impaciencia
impatient impaciente
impertinent impertinente
importance importancia
important importante
imposing imponente

impossible imposible
improve mejorar
inauguration inaguración
inch pulgada
include incluir
    be —d under acogerse a
income renta
increase aumento; aumentar
index índice (*m.*)
indifference indiferencia
indignation indignación
indisposition malestar (*m.*)
inducement soborno
industrial industrial
industry industria
ineffable inefable
inevitable inevitable
infinite infinito
influence influencia, influjo
inform informar, enterar
    be — estar informado, enterado
information informes, información
inhabitant habitante (*m.*)
inheritance herencia
injured lisiado, lesionado
inland tierra adentro
innocent inocente
inoculate inocular
inscrutable inescrutable
insect insecto, bicho
insignificant insignificante
insist insistir (en), empeñarse (en)
inspection inspección
instinctively instintivamente
institute instituto
insulate aislar
insult insultar, injuriar, denostar
insurance seguro
insurrectionist insurrecto
intellectual intelectual
interest interés (*m.*); interesar
intermission entreacto, intermedio
international internacional
intimate íntimo
intolerable intolerable, insoportable
intoxicated borracho, embriagado
invade invadir
invent inventar
invest invertir
investor inversionista
invite invitar, convidar
involve enredar
    get —d in meterse en
invulnerable invulnerable
ironic irónico
irresponsible irresponsable
irrigate regar

island isla
isolate aislar
Italy Italia

J

jacket chaqueta
jail cárcel (*f.*)
jammed atestado
Japan Japón (*m.*)
jar tarro
joke chiste, broma
    play a — gastar (hacer) una broma
judge juzgar
jump saltar, brincar
June junio
jungle selva
just justo
    to have — acabar de
justify justificar

K

keep guardar, mantener
    — (something) cool mantener fresco
kerchief pañuelo
key llave (*f.*), clave (*f.*)
kill matar
    — oneself matarse, diñarla (*colloquial*)
kilometer kilómetro
kind clase (*f.*), especie (*f.*), índole (*f.*)
king rey
kingdom reino
kitchen cocina
knapsack mochila
knee rodilla
knife cuchillo
knight caballero
    —-errant caballero andante
knock llamar, tocar
    — at the door llamar (tocar) a la puerta
    — over tumbar
knot nudo
know saber; conocer
    — how to saber
    not — no saber, ignorar

L

label etiqueta
lack falta; faltarle a uno, carecer de
    —ing in carente de
lad mozo, muchacho
lake lago
lamb cordero

lame cojo
land tierra; aterrizar
landscape paisaje (*m.*)
language lengua, lenguaje (*m.*), idioma
(*m.*)
last último
lasting duradero
late tarde
lately últimamente, recientemente
later más tarde
Latin latín
latter éste
laugh reír(se)
laundress lavandera
lavatory water (*m.*), (*variant of* váter)
law ley (*f.*)
lawn césped (*m.*)
lawyer abogado
layer capa
lead llevar, conducir
leaf hoja
    — through hojear
learn aprender; saber, enterarse
least menor
    at — a lo menos, por lo menos
leather cuero, piel (*f.*)
leave dejar; salir; irse
    be left quedarle a uno
    — behind dejar atrás
    — for partir (salir para)
    take — of despedirse de
lecture conferencia
left izquierdo
leftovers sobras
leg pierna
    pull someone's — tomarle el pelo
    a uno
legible legible
legitimate legítimo
leisure ocio
lemon limón (*m.*)
lend prestar
less menos
let dejar, permitir
    — go of soltar
    — know avisar, dejar saber
letter carta; letra (*alphabet*)
lettuce lechuga
    a head of — una lechuga
liberty libertad
library biblioteca
lick lamer
lie mentira; mentir
lieutenant teniente
light luz (*f.*), señal (*f.*); ligero (*weight*), claro
(*color*); encender
    bring to — sacar a la luz

like como; querer, gustar
    be — ser como, parecerse a
    — that así
liking simpatía
line cola, fila, línea, renglón
    a few —s unas letras
    stand in — hacer cola
lining forro
lip labio
Lisbon Lisboa
list lista
listen escuchar
literally al pie de la letra, literalmente
literary literario
little pequeño
    a — un poco
    a — after (over) y pico
liver hígado
living room sala
lobby vestíbulo
local local
locate localizar
lock bucle (*m.*); esclusa (*water*)
    — bumpers trabar(se) parachoques
    — up encerrar
    under — and key bajo llave
lodge alojar
loneliness soledad
long largo
    as — as mientras
    — for anhelar
long-distance call conferencia
longing añoranza
look (at) mirar
    — for buscar
    — like parecerse a, parecer
    — out asomarse a, mirar por
    — up levantar la vista (los ojos)
loose flojo, suelto
loosen aflojar, soltar
lose perder
loss pérdida
lots of la mar de
love amor; amar, querer
    be in — with estar enamorado de
    fall in — with enamorarse de
loving cariñoso
low bajo
lower bajar
lukewarm tibio
lumber madera
    — dealer maderero
lunch almuerzo, comida
    eat — almorzar, tomar el almuer-
zo
lying echado
lyrics letra

M

magazine revista
magic magia; mágico
magnificent magnífico
mail correo
mailman cartero
main principal
maintain mantener
make hacer
    — clear poner de manifiesto
    — out distinguir, divisar
maneuver maniobra
manners maneras; modales
manuscript manuscrito
map mapa (m.)
march marchar
market mercado
    stock — bolsa
marry casar, casarse
    get married casarse
marvel at maravillarse de
marvelous maravilloso
mass misa
master amo; dominar
match cerilla
matter asunto
meadow prado
meal comida
mean significar, querer decir
    I — digo
meaning significado, acepción, sentido
measure medir
meat carne (f.)
medicine medicina
Mediterranean Mediterráneo
meet conocer, encontrarse con
meeting reunión, junta, mitin (m.)
member miembro, socio
mend remendar
mention mencionar
merge into convergir
microbe microbio
midday mediodía
middle medio
    about (in) the — of a mediados de
    (time expression)
    in the — of en medio de
midnight medianoche
military militar
milk leche (f.)
million millón
mind importar
    change one's — cambiar de parecer
miner minero
minute minuto
miracle milagro

mischief travesura
miser avaro, tacaño
misery miseria
misfortune desgracia, desventura
miss echar de menos; perder
missile proyectil (m.)
Mississippi Misisipí
mist neblina
mistake error (m.), falta
mix mezclar
    to — with mezclarse a
modest modesto
moisten mojar, humedecer
moment momento
money dinero
monkey mono
month mes (m.)
moon luna
moor amarrar
moralizing moralizante
more than más que, más de (with numbers)
    — enough de sobra
mortal mortal
most la mayor parte de
mother-in-law suegra
motionless inmóvil
mountain montaña; monte
    — pass puerto
mouse ratón
mouth boca
    from — to — de boca en boca
move mover; conmover; mudarse
    — away from alejar(se) de
    — closer to acercar(se) a
    — up arrimar
much mucho
    so — tanto
mud lodo, barro, fango
mule mula
multiple múltiple
municipal municipal
murder asesinato; asesinar
museum museo
music música
musician músico
must deber (de)
    — have been debía (de) ser (estar)
    sería (estaría)
mustache bigote(s) (m.)

N

naked desnudo
    stark — en cueros
name nombre, apellido
nap siesta
    take a — tomar (echar) una siesta

napkin servilleta
Naples Nápoles
narrator narrador (*m.*)
narrow estrecho
nation nación
native natal; indígena
nature naturaleza
near cerca; próximo, cercano
      go — to acercarse a
nearsighted miope
necessary necesario
      it is — es necesario (preciso, menester)
necessity necesidad
neck cuello, pescuezo
necklace collar (*m.*)
need necesidad; necesitar, hacer falta a
needy menesteroso
neighbor vecino
neighborhood vecindad, vecindario
nervous nervioso
nest nido
never nunca, jamás
nevertheless sin embargo
new nuevo
newcomer recién venido
news noticia(s); nueva, novedad
newspaper periódico, diario
      — office redacción
next próximo
      — door de al lado
      — time la próxima vez
nibble roer
nice simpático
nickname apodo, mote (*m.*)
night noche
      at — de noche, por la noche
      last — anoche
nobility nobleza
noble noble
noise ruido
no longer ya no
noon mediodía
no one nadie, ninguno
nose nariz (narices) (*f.*); hocico(s)
notice fijarse (en), reparar en, notar
nourish nutrir, alimentar
novel novela
now ahora
      right — ahora mismo
nuclear nuclear
numerous numeroso
nurse enfermera
nursery criadero
nylon nilón

O

oblige obligar
observe observar
obstacle obstáculo
obtain conseguir, obtener
occasional alguno que otro
occupy ocupar
occur ocurrir
ocean océano
off-color verde
offend ofender
offer oferta; ofrecimiento
office oficina, despacho, clínica, redacción, dirección
officer oficial
official funcionario
oil aceite (*m.*), petróleo
old viejo, antiguo, anciano, vetusto, rancio
      be . . . years — tener . . . años
      — age vejez, ancianidad
older mayor, más viejo
      grow —(er) envejecer
olive aceituna, oliva
      — grove olivar
      — tree olivo
omelette tortilla
once una vez
only sólo, solamente; único
ooze rezumar(se)
open abierto; abrir
opening abertura; apertura
opera ópera
opinion opinión, parecer
      be of the — ser del parecer
opportune oportuno
oppose oponerse a
opposite enfrente de, frente a
      directly — frente por, frente de
oppressive opresivo
orchard huerto, huerta
order orden (*m.* arrangement, *f.* command); mandar, ordenar
      follow —s cumplir órdenes
      out of — descompuesto, no funciona
ordinary vulgar, común
oriental oriental
orphan huérfano
orphanage orfanato
ostensible aparente
other people's ajeno
outline bosquejo
outrageous ultrajoso
outshine hacer sombra a
outside of fuera de
oven horno

over sobre
—look dominar
—take alcanzar
—whelm abrumar
own propio; poseer, tener
owner dueño, propietario
oyster ostra

P

pain dolor (*m.*)
painful doloroso
paint pintura; pintar
painter pintor; artista
palace palacio
paladin paladín (*m.*)
pale pálido
become — palidecer, ponerse pálido
Panama Panamá
paper work papeleo
paradise paraíso
pardon perdonar; indultar (*criminals*)
parents padres
park parque (*m.*)
parrot loro, papagayo
parsley perejil (*m.*)
party fiesta
political — partido político
pass paso; pasar
in —ing de paso
mountain — puerto
patch remendar
patent leather charol (*m.*)
path sendero, senda, vereda
patient enfermo; paciente
be — tener paciencia
pause pausa
pavement pavimento, empedrado
pay paga; pagar
— one's last respects despedir los
restos
pea guisante (*m.*)
peace paz (*f.*)
peak pico, cumbre (*f.*)
pearl perla
pebble china
peel piel (*f.*), mondadura; pelar, mondar
pencil lápiz (*m.*)
penicillin penicilina
penitentiary penal (*m.*)
people pueblo (*nation*); gente
pepper pimienta
perceive percibir
per cent por ciento
perceptible perceptible
perfect perfecto; cabal
perfume perfume (*m.*)

perhaps tal vez, quizá
period período
permit permitir
peroxide oxigenada
perpetual perpetuo
persist porfiar
person persona
persuasive persuasivo
pessimistic pesimista
pet acariciar
philosopher filósofo
photograph foto(grafía); sacar una foto
have one's — (portrait) taken retratarse
pianist pianista
pick up recoger
picture cuadro, imagen (*f.*)
piece pedazo
pier muelle (*m.*)
pig cerdo, puerco
pile montón
pillow almohada
pinch pellizcar, pizcar, apretar
a — of una pizca de
pine pino
pineapple piña
pine grove pinar (*m.*)
pious beato, piadoso
pirate pirata (*m.*)
pit hueso; fosa
pitiful lastimero
pity lástima
it's a — es lástima
placard letrero
place lugar (*m.*), sitio, paraje (*m*)., local
(*m.*); poner, colocar
set a — poner un cubierto
take — tener lugar
place-setting cubierto
plan plan (*m.*); plano; planear
plane avión
plant planta; plantar
platoon pelotón
play comedia, obra (pieza) teatral; jugar
(*game*), tocar (*instrument*)
— a part hacer un papel
pleasant agradable, ameno, simpático
please gustar, complacer
pleasure placer, gusto
plot argumento; trama (*f.*)
plug in enchufar
plumage plumaje (*m.*)
P.M. de la tarde
pneumonia pulmonía
pocket bolsillo
poem poema, poesía
poet poeta (*m.*)

poetic poético
poetry poesía, versos
point punto, punta (*sharp*); señalar
    — of view punto de vista
    — out indicar, señalar
poison envenenar
pole poste (*m.*)
police policía
    —man policía (*m.*)
policy política; póliza (*insurance*)
polish pulir
polite cortés
political político
politics política
polluted contaminado
pool (swimming) piscina
popularity popularidad
pork carne de cerdo
port puerto
portrait retrato
pose (a problem) plantear (un problema)
position puesto, colocación
possess poseer
possible posible
poster cartel (*m.*)
postman cartero
potato patata
potion poción
poultry aves
poultry dealer gallinero, -a, recovero, -a
power poder (*m.*), potencia
praise elogiar, alabar
pray rezar
prayer oración, plegaria
prefer preferir
preferable preferible
preparations preparaciones, preparativos
prepare preparar
    — to prepararse para
prescribe recetar, prescribir
present presente, actual
    at — actualmente, en la actualidad
    — with plantear
preserves conserva
presidency presidencia
president presidente (*m.*)
presidential presidencial
presume suponer
pretend fingir, aparentar
prevent impedir, evitar
price precio
prick pinchar
prince príncipe
princess princesa
principal director, -a
print estampa
    be out of — estar agotado

printer impresor
printing edición
prisoner prisionero
privation privación
privileged privilegiado
prize premio
problem problema (*m.*)
procession procesión
produce producir
profession profesión, carrera
professor profesor, catedrático
profile perfil (*m.*)
profound profundo
progress progresar
prolific prolífico
promise promesa; prometer
promising prometedor
promote ascender
pronounce pronunciar
prophetic profético
propose proponer
    —d propuesto
prostrated postrado
protect proteger
protest protestar
prove probar
    — to be resultar
provide (with) proporcionar, proveer
province provincia
prune podar
public público
publication publicación
pull tirar
    — someone's leg tomarle el pelo
    a uno
pulse pulso
punctual puntual
puppet títere (*m.*)
purchase comprar
purify purificar
purpose propósito, fin
pursue perseguir, acosar
push empujar
put poner
    — in meter
    — in order arreglar, poner en orden
    — into meter, introducir
    — out apagar

Q

quality cualidad; calidad
quantity cantidad
quarrel riña; reñirse
question pregunta; cuestión (*matter*)
quiet quieto, tranquilo
    —ly silenciosamente

quiver estremecimiento; estremecer(se)
quotations (stock) cotizaciones

R

rabbit conejo
race raza; carrera
radio radio (*f.*)
rage rabia, cólera
ragged harapiento
railroad ferrocarril
rain lluvia; llover
    — pitchforks llover a cántaros
raise cultivar, criar
rapidly rápidamente, rápido
rather bastante, algo; más bien
rave delirar
    — about hacerse lenguas de
raw crudo
razor navaja (de afeitar)
reach alcance; alcanzar, llegar a
    within — of al alcance de
read leer
reading lectura
ready listo
real verdadero, efectivo, real
reality realidad
realize darse cuenta
reap cosechar
    — rewards of recibir la recompensa
de
reason razón
rebellion rebelión
recall recordar
receipt recibo
receive recibir
receiver auricular (*m.*), receptor (*m.*)
recent reciente
recently recientemente, últimamente
recipe receta
recite recitar
recognize reconocer
recommend recomendar
recommendation recomendación
record (phonograph) disco
recourse: have — to recurrir a
recover recobrar; recuperar
re-create recrear
red-light district (in Barcelona) barrio
chino
reduce reducir
refer to referirse a
reflect reflejar
refugee refugiado
refuse rehusar
    — to do something negarse a hacer
algo

regale obsequiar
regard considerar
    with — to con respecto a, respecto a
regiment regimiento
regretful pesaroso
reject rechazar
rejoice alegrarse
relate contar, relatar, referir
relationship relación; parentesco
relax descansar; relajar
relive revivir
remain quedarse, permanecer
remains restos, sobras
remember recordar, acordarse de
remind recordar
remote remoto
remove quitar
    — one's hat descubrirse, quitarse
el sombrero
renovate renovar
rent alquiler (*m.*); alquilar
repair reparar
replace reponer; reemplazar
reply contestar, responder, replicar
report informe (*m.*)
representative representante (*m.*)
reputation reputación, fama
require requerir; exigir
resemble parecerse a
reserve reserva
reside residir
residential residencial
resigned resignado
resist resistir a
resolve resolver
resound resonar
respect respetar
resplendent resplandeciente
respond to responder a, acudir a
responsible responsable
responsibility responsabilidad
rest descansar, reposar; apoyar
    be —ed estar descansado
    the — of el resto de
restaurant restaurante (*m.*)
restlessness inquietud
result resultado
resume reanudar
retire retirarse, jubilarse; recogerse
return vuelta; volver, regresar, devolver
reveal revelar
revolutionary revolucionario
reward premio
rhetoric retórica
rhythm ritmo
rice arroz (*m.*)
rid: get — of librarse de, deshacerse de

ride paseo; montar a caballo
ridicule ridiculizar; poner en ridículo
ridiculous ridículo
right derecho
    be — tener razón
    — now ahora mismo
    to the — of a la derecha de
ring anillo, sortija; sonar, tocar
rings (under the eyes) ojeras
ripe maduro
ripen madurar
risk riesgo; arriesgar
rival rival (*m.*)
river río
road camino
roast asado; asar
rock roca; mecer
Rockies las (montañas) Rocosas
rocking chair la (silla) mecedora
role papel (*m.*)
    play a — hacer (desempeñar) un papel
roll rodar
Roman romano
Rome Roma
roof tejado
    tile — tejado
room cuarto, pieza, habitación
    waiting — sala de espera
rope cuerda, soga (*especially for hangmen*)
rosary rosario
rose rosa
    climbing —(bush) rosal trepador
rot pudrir(se)
rotten podrido
rough áspero
rowboat bote (de remos) (*m.*)
rub frotar, restregar, rozar
ruin arruinar
rumor rumor (*m.*); rumorear, murmurar
run correr
    — across cruzar corriendo; tropezarse con, encontrarse con
    — into tropezarse con, encontrarse con
    — through correr por
    — toward precipitarse hacia
Russian ruso

S

sacrifice sacrificio
sad triste
    become — ponerse triste, entristecerse
saddle silla
sadly tristemente
sadness tristeza

safe caja fuerte
sail vela; navegar
sailor marinero, marino
salad ensalada
same mismo
sample muestra
sand arena
sandpaper papel de lija
sandwich bocadillo
sandy arenoso
sap savia
sardine sardina
sash faja
satisfy satisfacer
sauce salsa
saucer platillo
save salvar, guardar
say decir
    — good-by despedirse, decir adiós
scab costra
scale escala, balanza; escama; escamar
    on a large — en grande escala
scandalize escandalizar
scar cicatriz (*f.*)
scare asustar; dar un susto
scarcely apenas
scene escena
school escuela; banco
    Medical — Facultad de Medicina
scientist científico
scrape raspar
scratch rascar; arañar, rasguñar
scream gritar
screech chillar
seafood mariscos
seagull gaviota
search registrar; buscar
    in — of en busca de
season estación, temporada
seated sentado
sea urchin erizo
secret secreto
secretary secretaria
security seguridad
    Security Council Consejo de Seguridad
    Social Security Seguridad Social
see ver
seek buscar
seem parecer
seep rezumar
seize agarrar; apoderarse de; embargar
sell vender
send mandar, enviar
senility senilidad
sense sentido; sentir
sensitive sensible, sensitivo

separate separar, apartar
sergeant sargento
serious serio, grave
servant criado
serve servir
service servicio
    — station gasolinera
session sesión
set cuajarse
    — out ponerse en camino
    — out for encaminarse a
several varios
shade sombra; transparente
shake sacudir
    — hands dar (estrechar, alargar) la mano
share parte, porción; compartir
    two —s of stock dos acciones
sharp agudo; en punto (*time*)
shave afeitado; afeitar(se)
shawl chal (*m.*), mantón
sheep oveja
sheer puro
    from — de puro + *adjective or noun*
sheet sábana; lámina; hoja
shelf estante (*m.*)
shepherd pastor
sherry jerez (*m.*)
shine brillar, lucir
    the moon was shining había luna
ship barco, buque (*m.*)
    —wrecked man náufrago
shirt camisa
    —sleeves mangas de camisa
shiver tiritar
shock sobresalto, susto
shoe zapato
    —maker zapatero
shoot disparar; tirar
    — oneself pegarse un tiro
shore orilla, costa
short corto, breve
shot disparo
shoulder hombro
shovel pala
show mostrar, enseñar
    — off lucirse
    — up asomarse
shriek chillido
shudder estremecerse
shuffle barajar
sick enfermo, malo
side apartado, lateral
    on all four —s por los cuatro costados
    split one's —s laughing desternillarse de risa

sidewalk acera
sight vista
sign letrero, señal (*f.*), rótulo
silent silencioso
silently silenciosamente
silk seda
simple sencillo; simple
sin pecado; pecar
since desde (que); como, ya que, puesto que
siren sirena
sister-in-law cuñada
sit sentar
    — down sentarse
    — up incorporarse
situation situación
    the — involving lo de
sixth sexto
    — of January el seis de enero
size tamaño
    — up medir con la mirada
skeptical escéptico
skid deslizar, patinar
skin piel (*f.*); cutis (*m.*); pellejo
    save one's — salvar el pellejo
sky cielo
slanted eyes ojos rasgados
slaughterhouse matadero
slave esclavo
sleep sueño; dormir
    be sleepy tener sueño
    fall asleep dormirse, quedarse dormido
slight ligero, leve
slip escurrir, resbalar, deslizar
    let — dejar escurrirse
    — away escurrirse
slippery resbaladizo, resbaloso
slow despacio
small letter letra minúscula
smear untar
smell olor (*m.*); oler (a)
smile sonreír
smiling sonriente
smoke humo; fumar
smooth liso
snack merienda
snatch arrebatar
sneeze estornudar
sniff (at) husmear
snow nevar
snuggle up to arrimarse a
so tan
    — much tanto
soak remojar, calar, empapar
    —ed to the skin calado hasta los huesos

social social
society sociedad
soft blando, muelle, suave
soil tierra
soldier soldado
sole suela; planta; único
sometimes a (algunas) veces
somewhat algo, un poco
son hijo
    ——in-law yerno
song canción
soon pronto
    as — as tan pronto como
sorrow dolor (*m*.), pena
sound sonido; sonar
soup sopa
sour agrio
sovereign soberano
    Catholic —s Reyes Católicos
spa balneario
Spain España
Spaniard español
speaker conferenciante (*m. and f*.); inter-
    locutor, -a
special especial
specialist especialista (*m. and f*.)
speckled motoso
speech discurso; habla (*f*.)
spend pasar; gastar
spin girar
spite rencor (*m*.)
    in — of a pesar de
splash salpicar
spoil mimar (*a person*)
spoiled pasado (*food*)
sponge esponja
spot mancha
    be in a tight — estar en un aprieto
sprain torcer
spree juerga
    go on a — ir de juerga
spring muelle (*m*.), resorte (*m*.); prima-
    vera; manantial (*m*.)
spy on acechar
square plaza; cuadro
squirrel ardilla
staff bastón
stage escenario
stale viejo; rancio
stalk acechar
stand aguantar, tolerar, resistir; estar de
    pie
    — out destacarse
    — up ponerse de pie
    — up to encararse con
stark naked en cueros
start poner(se) en marcha

    — up arrancar
state estado
station estación
    — wagon camioneta
steal robar
steamer vapor
steel acero
steep empinado
stench hedor (*m*.)
step paso; escalón, peldaño
    — on pisar
    —s escalinata
    take a— dar un paso
stew cocido
stick palo; pegar(se)
    — out sacar, asomar
still todavía, aún
stimulate estimular
stink peste (*f*.)
stir agitar
    — up suscitar
stock surtido; acciones
    share of — una acción
    — market bolsa
stocking media
stone piedra
stop detener(se), parar(se), cesar (de)
store tienda
    —keeper tendero
storm tormenta, tempestad, temporal (*m*.),
    aguacero, chubasco
story historia, cuento
    —teller narrador de cuentos
stranger forastero
strategic estratégico
straw paja
strawberry fresa
stray callejero, vagabundo
street calle
    down the — calle abajo
stretch extender
    —ed out tendido
strike huelga; pegar, dar con, golpear
    — up trabar
stroke acariciar
stroll dar un paseo; pasear(se)
strong fuerte
struggle (for) luchar (por)
stubborn terco, testarudo
student estudiante (*m*.)
study estudio
stumble tropezar con
stun dejar pasmado
stupid estúpido
    — thing estupidez (*f*.)
subject asunto, tema (*m*.)
substance substancia

subway metro
success éxito
    be —ful tener éxito
such tal
suddenly de pronto (repente, súbito)
suffer padecer, sufrir
suffering sufrimiento, padecimiento
suggest sugerir
suicide suicidio
    commit — suicidarse
suitcase maleta
    pack the — hacer la maleta
summer verano
summit cima
sun sol
    in the — al sol
    —-burnt quemado, torrado de sol
    —set puesta del sol
superficial superficial
superstitious supersticioso
supply surtido
support apoyo; apoyar, sostener, mantener
surface superficie (f.)
surname apellido
surprise sorpresa; sorprender
    be —d sorprenderse, asombrarse, maravillarse
surround rodear, cercar; asediar, sitiar
survive sobrevivir
suspect sospechar
suspend suspender
suspense suspenso
swallow golondrina; tragar;
    — up tragar
swamp pantano, marisma
swear jurar
sweat sudor (m.); sudar
sweaty sudoroso
sweep barrer
swell hinchar
sword espada
    by the — a hierro
symbol símbolo

T

table mesa
    set the — poner la mesa
    —cloth mantel (m.)
tact tacto
take tomar; tardar (time); llevar (somewhere)
    — off quitar(se)
    — out sacar
tale cuento
talented de talento
    be — tener talento

tall alto
tame manso; domar, amansar
tart agrio
task tarea
taste saber; probar
tavern taberna
taxes impuestos, contribuciones
teacher maestro, profesor
tear romper; rasgar
telephone teléfono; telefonear
    — book guía de teléfonos
    — directory directorio telefónico
television televisión
    — set televisor (m.)
tell decir
    — the difference distinguir
teller contador, narrador
temple sien (f.)
temptation tentación
tenant inquilino
tender tierno
    nice and — tiernecito
tennis tenis (m.)
term término
terrace terraza
textbook libro de texto
theme tema (m.)
therefore por eso (consiguiente, lo tanto)
thick espeso; grueso
    —headed torpe
thicken complicar(se), cuajar(se), espesar(se)
thin delgado
thing cosa
    the best — lo mejor
    the worst — lo peor
think pensar (en, de)
thirsty sediento
    be — tener sed
thought pensamiento
thoughtless inconsiderado
thousand mil
threaten amenazar
thrilled emocionado
throat garganta
through por, mediante; a través de
throw arrojar, tirar, echar
    —away tirar
thumb pulgar (m.)
Thursday jueves
    on — el jueves
ticket billete(m.); entrada
    — agent taquillero
tickle hacer cosquillas
tie corbata; amarrar, ligar
tile teja; azulejo
    — roof tejado

time tiempo
>**at the same —** a la vez, al mismo
>tiempo
>**from — to —** de vez en cuando
>**long —** mucho tiempo

timid tímido
tip punta; propina
tire llanta, neumático; cansar
>**grow —d of** cansarse de

title título
toast tostada
>**a piece of —** una tostada

tobacco tabaco
today hoy
toe dedo del pie
together junto(s)
tongue lengua
tonic tónico
too demasiado
>**— many** demasiados

top tapa, cima, capota (*car*); rematar
>**get up on —** of encaramarse
>**musical —** trompa
>**on — of** encima de

toss echar, arrojar
touch tocar
tourist turista (*m. and f.*)
tow remolcar
tower torre
>**bell —** campanario

town pueblo
toy juguete (*m.*)
track vía
trade oficio; comercio
>**foreign —** comercio exterior
>**— fair** feria mercantil

traffic tráfico, circulación
>**heavy —** tráfico denso
>**— light** luz (señal) de tráfico,
>semáforo

tragedy tragedia
tragic trágico
train tren (*m.*)
tranquility tranquilidad
transparent transparente
trap atrapar
trash basura
travel agent agente de viajes
traveler viajero
tray bandeja
treasure tesoro
treat tratar
treatment trato
tree árbol (*m.*)
tremble temblar
trick burla, truco
trip viaje

>**take a —** hacer un viaje

tropical tropical
trouble disgusto; dificultad; molestia;
molestar
>**take the — to** tomar(se) la molestia
>de

truck camión (*m.*)
true verdadero
trunk baúl (*m.*)
trust fiarse de, confiar en
truth verdad (*f.*)
try tratar (de), procurar
tube tubo
tugboat remolcador (*m.*)
turn doblar, girar, volver
>**— around** volverse
>**— on** poner
>**— one's back** volver la espalda
>**— out** salir, resultar
>**— over** dar la vuelta a
>**— thirteen** cumplir (los) trece años

twins gemelos, mellizos
twist torcer
two-tone de dos colores
type clase (*f.*)
tyrannize tiranizar
tyrant tirano

U

umbrella paraguas (*m.*)
unbalanced desequilibrado
unbearable inaguantable; intolerable
unbelievable increíble
>**it is —** parece mentira

uncertainty incertidumbre (*f.*)
uncle tío
uncontrollable indomable
under bajo, debajo de
underline subrayar
understand entender, comprender
understandable comprensible
>**it is —** se comprende

understanding comprensión
uneasy inquieto
unforgettable inolvidable
unfortunate desgraciado
unfortunately por desgracia, desgraciada-
mente
ungrateful desagradecido, ingrato
unhappiness infelicidad
unhappy infeliz, desdichado
unhurriedly sin prisa
unhurt ileso
uniform uniforme
unintentional sin querer
unitary unitario

unite unir
United States Estados Unidos
university universidad; universitario
unknown desconocido
unlike a diferencia de
unlikely difícil, poco probable
unload descargar
unoccupied desocupado
unpleasant desagradable, antipático
unsettled sin resolver
unstable inestable
untie desatar
until hasta (que)
untimely prematuro
untrustworthy indigno (poco digno) de
    confianza
unusual poco usual
up arriba
upset disgustar
upstairs arriba
usual de costumbre, usual
    as — como de costumbre
utopian utópico

V

vacation vacaciones
    go on a — ir de vacaciones
vain vanidoso; vano
    in — en vano, en balde
valet ayuda de cámara
valley valle (m.)
value valor (m.)
variety variedad
varnish barniz (m.)
vase vaso
veal carne de ternera
vegetable legumbre (f.)
vegetation vegetación
vein vena
velvet terciopelo
vendor vendedor, -a
Venetian blinds persianas
verify comprobar
very mismo
vest chaleco
vibrant vibrante
victim víctima (f.)
victory victoria
view vista
    point of — punto de vista
vigilant vigilante
    be — vigilar
vigorous vigoroso
village aldea, pueblo, lugar (m.)
villager aldeano
violent violento

violet violeta
visa visa
visit visita
visual visual
visualize visualizar
vital vital
vividly vívidamente
vocabulary vocabulario
voice voz (f.)
vulgar grosero

W

wait (for) esperar, aguardar
waiter camarero
wake despertar
    — up despertar(se)
walk paseo; pasear; andar, caminar, ir a
    pie
    — away alejarse
    — signal señal de paso
wall pared (f.), muro, tapia, muralla,
    tabique (m.), malecón (m.)
wander vagar
want querer, desear
war guerra
warm caliente; tibio
warmly calurosamente
warn advertir; avisar
wash lavar, limpiar
waste perder (time); malgastar (money)
watch mirar
    — over velar, vigilar
watchful vigilante
water agua
wave ola, onda, oleaje (m.); agitar la mano
    — good-by to decir adiós con la
    mano
wax encerar
way vía; modo, manera
    be in the — estorbar
    on the — to camino a
weakness debilidad
wealth riqueza
wealthy adinerado, rico
wear llevar
weather tiempo, clima (m.)
    — vane veleta
Wednesday miércoles
week semana
weekend fin de semana
weep llorar
weigh pesar
weight peso
welcome dar la bienvenida, acoger
well-being bienestar (m.)
well-intentioned bien intencionado

be — tener buenas intenciones
wet húmedo (*paint*); mojado
    get — mojarse
whatever lo que, cualquier cosa que
wheat trigo
    — field trigal (*m.*)
wheel rueda
    steering — volante (*m.*)
while rato; mientras
white blanco
    White House Casa Blanca
wholesome saludable
wicker mimbre (*m.*)
wide ancho
    be — open estar (abierto) de par
en par
widow viuda
    become a — enviudar, quedar viuda
wife mujer, esposa
wild beast fiera
wild goat cabra montés
will testamento; voluntad (*f.*)
willing dispuesto
    —ly de buena gana
win ganar
wind viento; dar cuerda a
window ventana; ventanilla
    shop — escaparate
wine vino
wing ala
winner ganador, -a
winter invierno
wipe limpiar
withdraw retirar
    — within oneself ensimismarse
within dentro de
without sin (que)
    do — prescindir de
witness testigo; presenciar

witty ocurrente
wolf lobo
woman mujer
wonder maravilla; preguntarse
wood madera; leña
    —en de madera
word palabra
    keep one's — cumplir la palabra
work obra, trabajo; trabajar
    —er obrero, trabajador
world mundo; mundial (*adjective*)
worry preocuparse
wretched miserable, desdichado
wrinkled arrugado
wrist muñeca
write escribir
writer escritor, -a
writing escrito

Y

yawn bostezo; bostezar
year año
yearn anhelar
yell gritar; dar voces
yellow amarillo
yelp gañido
yesterday ayer
    — afternoon ayer por la tarde
yield rendir; rentar
yolk yema
young joven (jóvenes)
youth juventud (*f.*)
youthful juvenil

Z

zoo jardín zoológico
zoologically zoológicamente

index

A

Abajo, 217
Abandonar, 81
Abatido, 274
Abertura, 219
Abrir, 156
Acaecer, 74
Acaecimiento, 74
Acantilado, 247
Acaparar, 189
Acariciar, 200
Acatarrarse, 64
Acechar, 27
Acento, 247
Acepción, 233
Acercar(se), 79
Acertado, 9
Acertar, 9
Achaque, 138
Achacoso, 138
Acierto, 9
Acoger, 129
Acogida, 129
Acompañar, 90
Aconsejar, 65
Acontecer, 74
Acontecimiento, 74
Acordarse, 127
Acosar, 175
Acostumbrar, 237
Actual, 23
Actualidad, 23
Actuar, 141
Acudir, 139
Adelantar, 262
Adentro, 217
Adiós, 109
Adjectives:
    descriptive, 180
      with unique nouns, 181
    limiting, 180
    position, 181
Administración, 65
Advertir, 65
Aeropuerto, 129
Afectado, 8
Afectar, 8
Afecto, 8
Aflojar, 66
Afrontar, 271
Afuera, 217
Agallas, 187
Agarrar, 198
Agradable, 190

Agradar, 190
Aguacero, 67
Aguantar, 27
Aguinaldo, 257
Ahogar(se), 201
Aislamiento, 24
Aislar, 24
Ajeno, 24
Alarido, 129
Alcance, 79
Alcanzar, 79
Alcoholizado, 139
Alegre, 75
Alejar, 79
Allá, 245
Allende, 245
Almeja, 199
Almorzar, 109
Almuerzo, 109
Alquilar, 256
Alquiler, 256
Amanecer, 259
Amansar, 174
Amar, 201
Ambiente, 63
Ameno, 190
Americano, 22
Amparar, 68
Amparo, 68
Anciano, 274
Andar, 89
Angel de la guarda, 271
Angulo, 93
Anilla, 143
Animo, 144
Anochecer, 259
Añoranza, 93
Añorar, 93
Ante, 81, 104
Antigüedades, 274
Antiguo, 274
Anudar, 138
Anuncio, 14
Aparecer, 185
Aparentar, 155
Aparición, 45
Apariencia, 45
Apartar, 130
Apellido, 246
Apertura, 219
Apestar, 244
Apodo, 246
Apoyar, 68, 258
Apoyo, 68
Apretar, 270